KIM HYUN SOOK   KO HYUNG-JU   RYAN ESTRADA

BANNED BOOK CLUB

IRON CIRCUS COMICS

strange and amazing

inquiry@ironcircus.com   www.ironcircus.com

writers
Kim Hyun Sook, Ryan Estrada

artist
Ko Hyung-Ju

publisher, editor
C. Spike Trotman

assistant editor
Andrea Purcell

book designer
Matt Sheridan

proofreader
Abby Lehrke

print technician
Beth Scorzato

published by
Iron Circus Comics
329 West 18th Street, Suite 604
Chicago, IL 60616
ironcircus.com

second edition: August 2021

print book ISBN: 978-1-945820-42-7

10 9 8 7 6 5 4 3

printed in China

BANNED BOOK CLUB

Publisher's Cataloging-In-Publication Data
(Prepared by The Donohue Group, Inc.)

Names: Kim, Hyun Sook, author. | Estrada, Ryan, author. | Ko, Hyung-Ju, illustrator. | Spike, 1978- editor, publisher. | Sheridan, Matt, 1978- designer.
Title: Banned book club / writers, Kim Hyun Sook, Ryan Estrada ; artist, Ko Hyung-Ju ; publisher, editor, C. Spike Trotman ; book designer, Matt Sheridan ; proofreader, Abby Lehrke ; print technician, Rhiannon Rasmussen-Silverstein.
Description: First edition. | Chicago, IL : Iron Circus Comics, 2019. | Interest age level: 012-015. | Summary: "The autobiography of a South Korean woman's student days under an authoritarian regime, and how she defied state censorship."--Provided by publisher.
Identifiers: ISBN 9781945820427
Subjects: LCSH: Kim, Hyun Sook--Comic books, strips, etc. | Women college students--Korea (South)--Biography--Comic books, strips, etc. | Student protesters--Korea (South)--Biography--Comic books, strips, etc. | Book clubs (Discussion groups)--Korea (South)--Comic books, strips, etc. | Prohibited books--Korea (South)--Comic books, strips, etc. | Korea (South)--History--1960-1988--Comic books, strips, etc. | CYAC: Kim, Hyun Sook--Cartoons and comics. | Women college students--Korea (South)--Biography--Cartoons and comics. | Student protesters--Korea (South)--Biography--Cartoons and comics. | Book clubs (Discussion groups)--Korea (South)--Cartoons and comics. | Prohibited books--Korea (South)--Cartoons and comics. | Korea (South)--History--1960-1988--Cartoons and comics. | LCGFT: Autobiographies. | Graphic novels.
Classification: LCC PZ7.7.K5562 Ba 2019 | DDC 741.5973 [Fic]--dc23

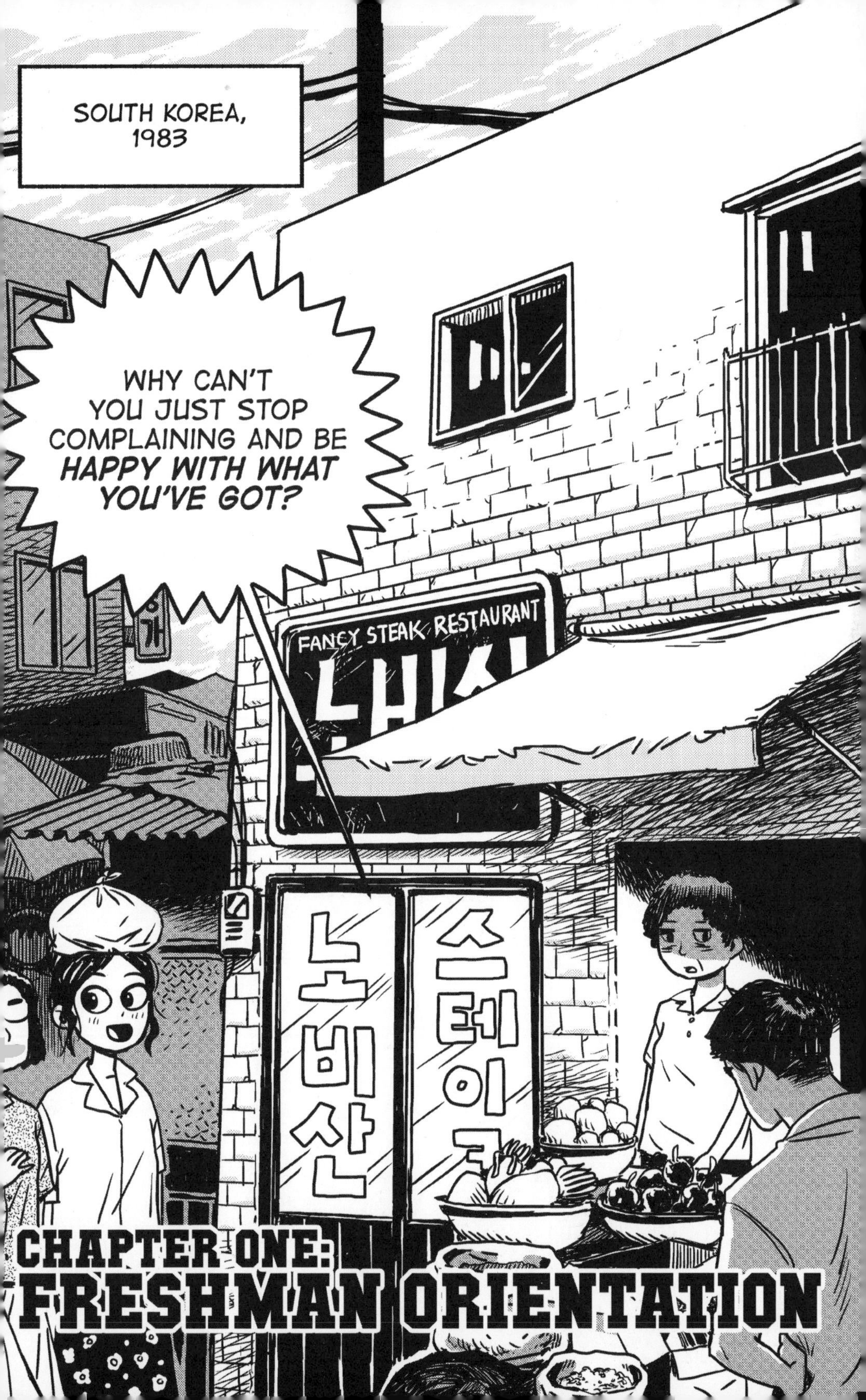
SOUTH KOREA, 1983
WHY CAN'T YOU JUST STOP COMPLAINING AND BE *HAPPY WITH WHAT YOU'VE GOT?*
FANCY STEAK RESTAURANT
노비산
스테이크

CHAPTER ONE: FRESHMAN ORIENTATION

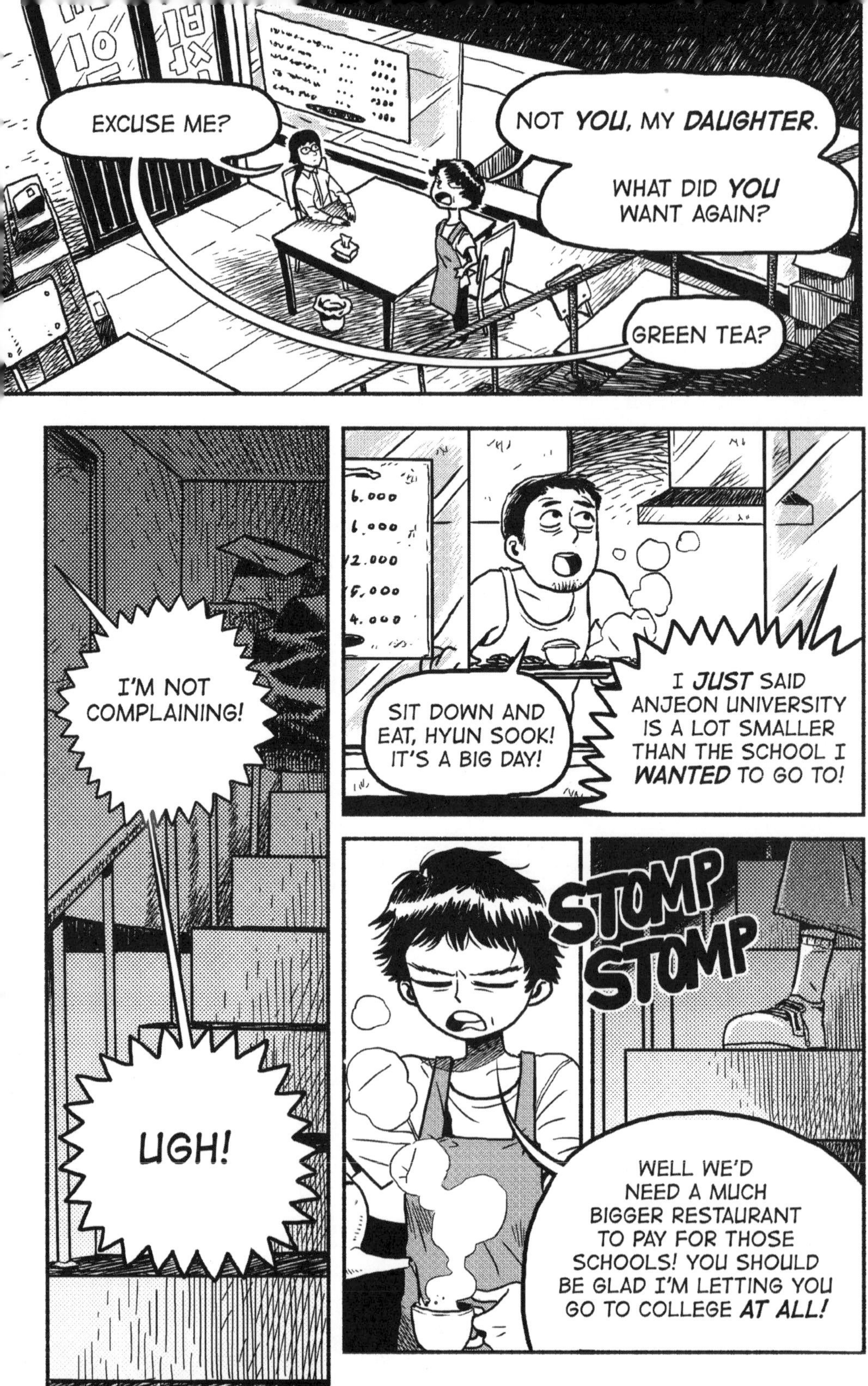
EXCUSE ME?
NOT YOU, MY DAUGHTER.
WHAT DID YOU WANT AGAIN?
GREEN TEA?
6.000
6.000
12.000
15.000
4.000
I JUST SAID ANJEON UNIVERSITY IS A LOT SMALLER THAN THE SCHOOL I WANTED TO GO TO!
SIT DOWN AND EAT, HYUN SOOK! IT'S A BIG DAY!
I'M NOT COMPLAINING!
UGH!
STOMP STOMP
WELL WE'D NEED A MUCH BIGGER RESTAURANT TO PAY FOR THOSE SCHOOLS! YOU SHOULD BE GLAD I'M LETTING YOU GO TO COLLEGE AT ALL!

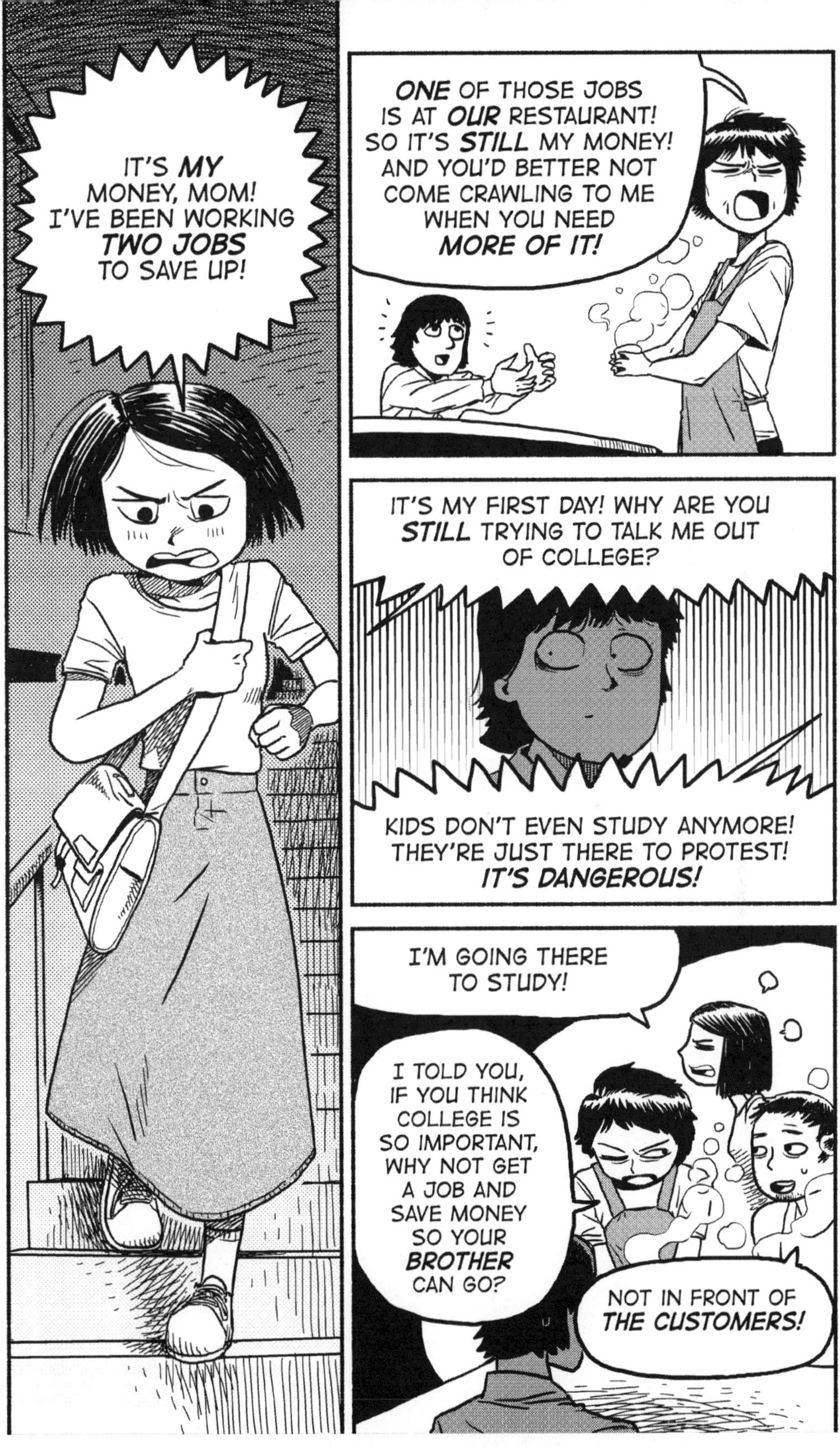
IT'S MY MONEY, MOM! I'VE BEEN WORKING TWO JOBS TO SAVE UP!
ONE OF THOSE JOBS IS AT OUR RESTAURANT! SO IT'S STILL MY MONEY! AND YOU'D BETTER NOT COME CRAWLING TO ME WHEN YOU NEED MORE OF IT!
IT'S MY FIRST DAY! WHY ARE YOU STILL TRYING TO TALK ME OUT OF COLLEGE?
KIDS DON'T EVEN STUDY ANYMORE! THEY'RE JUST THERE TO PROTEST! IT'S DANGEROUS!
I'M GOING THERE TO STUDY!
I TOLD YOU, IF YOU THINK COLLEGE IS SO IMPORTANT, WHY NOT GET A JOB AND SAVE MONEY SO YOUR BROTHER CAN GO?
NOT IN FRONT OF THE CUSTOMERS!

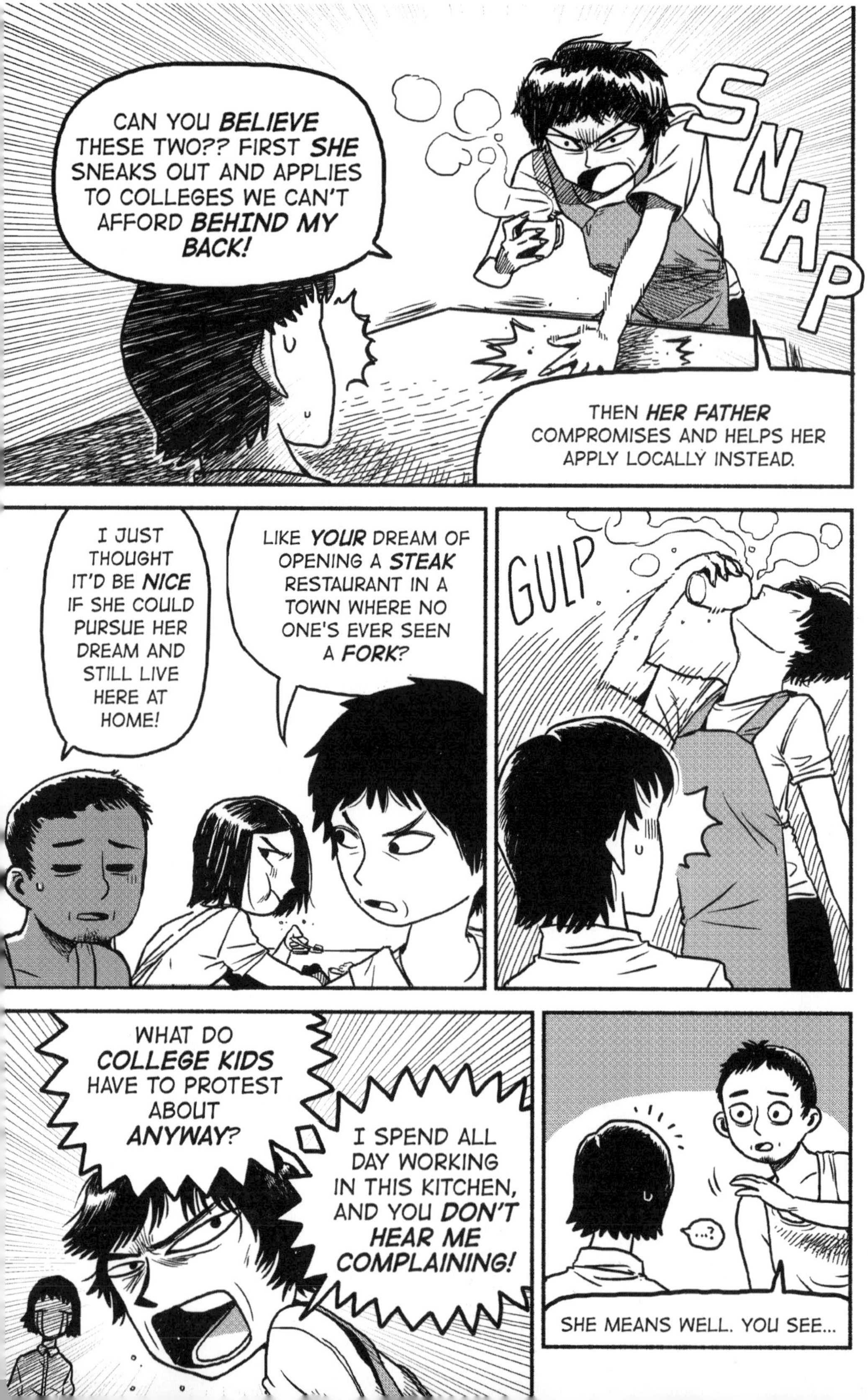
CAN YOU BELIEVE THESE TWO?? FIRST SHE SNEAKS OUT AND APPLIES TO COLLEGES WE CAN'T AFFORD BEHIND MY BACK!
SNAP
THEN HER FATHER COMPROMISES AND HELPS HER APPLY LOCALLY INSTEAD.
I JUST THOUGHT IT'D BE NICE IF SHE COULD PURSUE HER DREAM AND STILL LIVE HERE AT HOME!
LIKE YOUR DREAM OF OPENING A STEAK RESTAURANT IN A TOWN WHERE NO ONE'S EVER SEEN A FORK?
GULP
WHAT DO COLLEGE KIDS HAVE TO PROTEST ABOUT ANYWAY?
I SPEND ALL DAY WORKING IN THIS KITCHEN, AND YOU DON'T HEAR ME COMPLAINING!
...?
SHE MEANS WELL. YOU SEE...

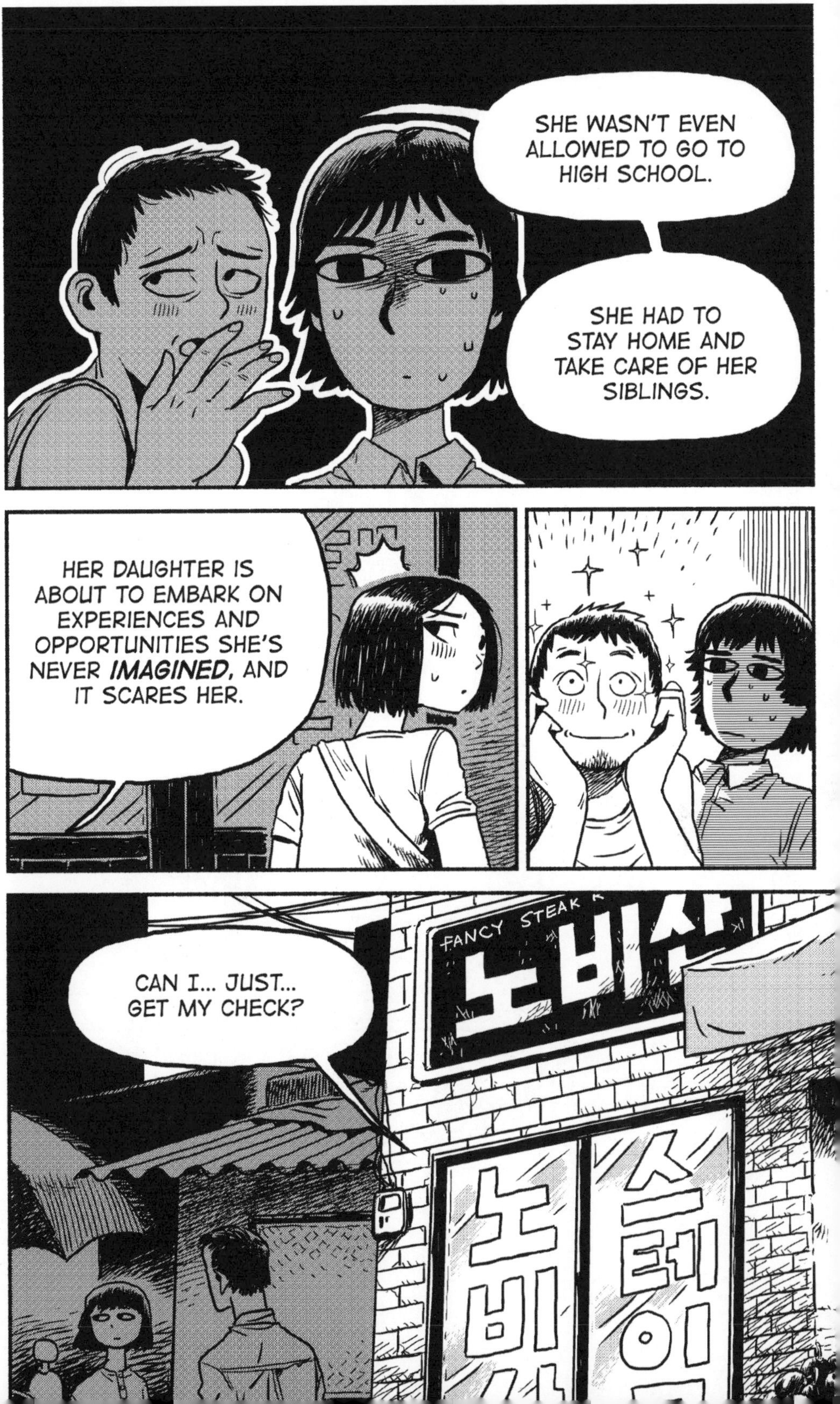
SHE WASN'T EVEN ALLOWED TO GO TO HIGH SCHOOL.
SHE HAD TO STAY HOME AND TAKE CARE OF HER SIBLINGS.
HER DAUGHTER IS ABOUT TO EMBARK ON EXPERIENCES AND OPPORTUNITIES SHE'S NEVER *IMAGINED,* AND IT SCARES HER.
FANCY STEAK
CAN I... JUST... GET MY CHECK?

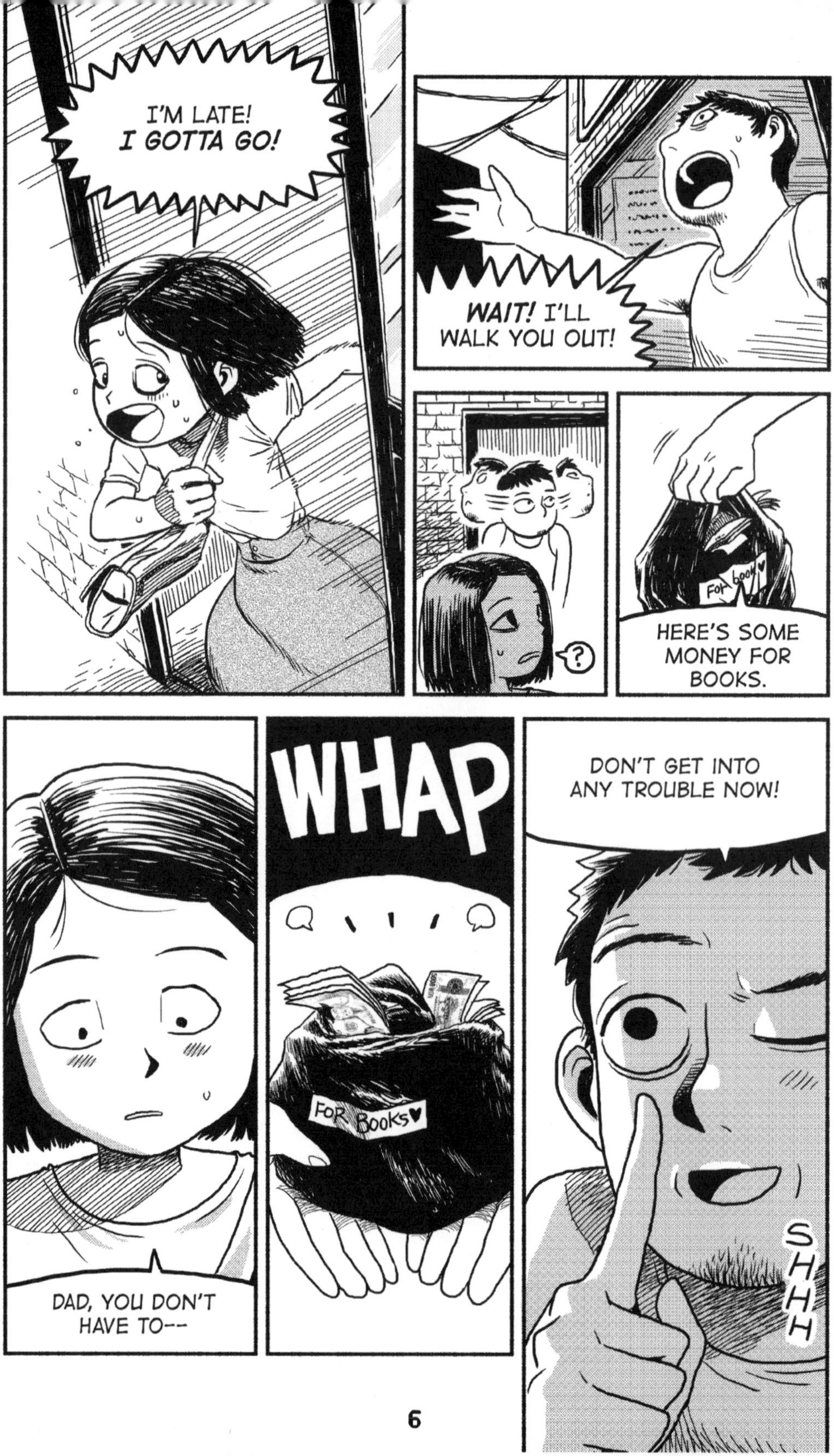
I'M LATE!
I GOTTA GO!
WAIT! I'LL WALK YOU OUT!
?
FOR book♥
HERE'S SOME MONEY FOR BOOKS.
DAD, YOU DON'T HAVE TO--
WHAP
FOR Books♥
DON'T GET INTO ANY TROUBLE NOW!
SHHH

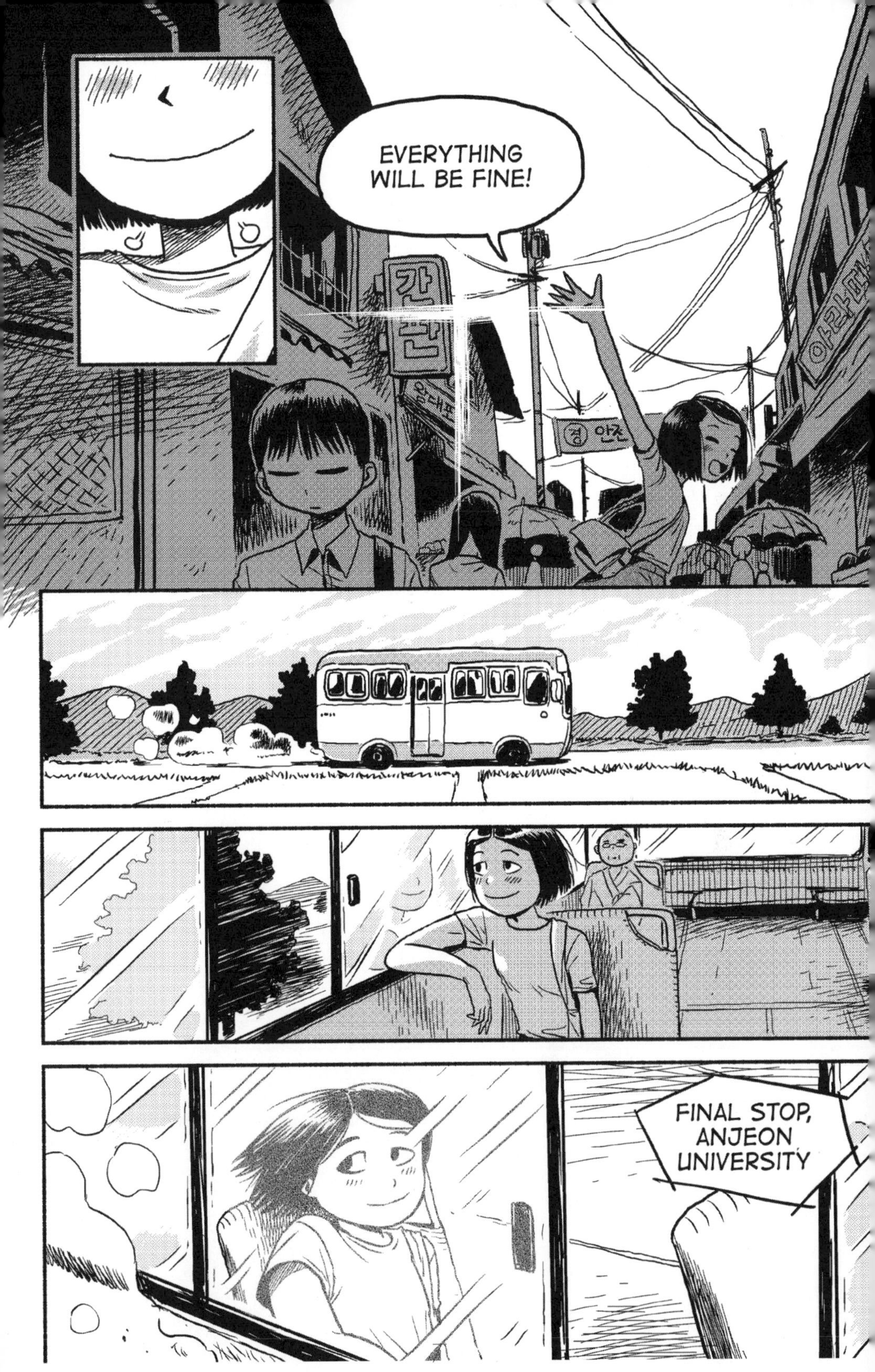
EVERYTHING WILL BE FINE!
FINAL STOP, ANJEON UNIVERSITY

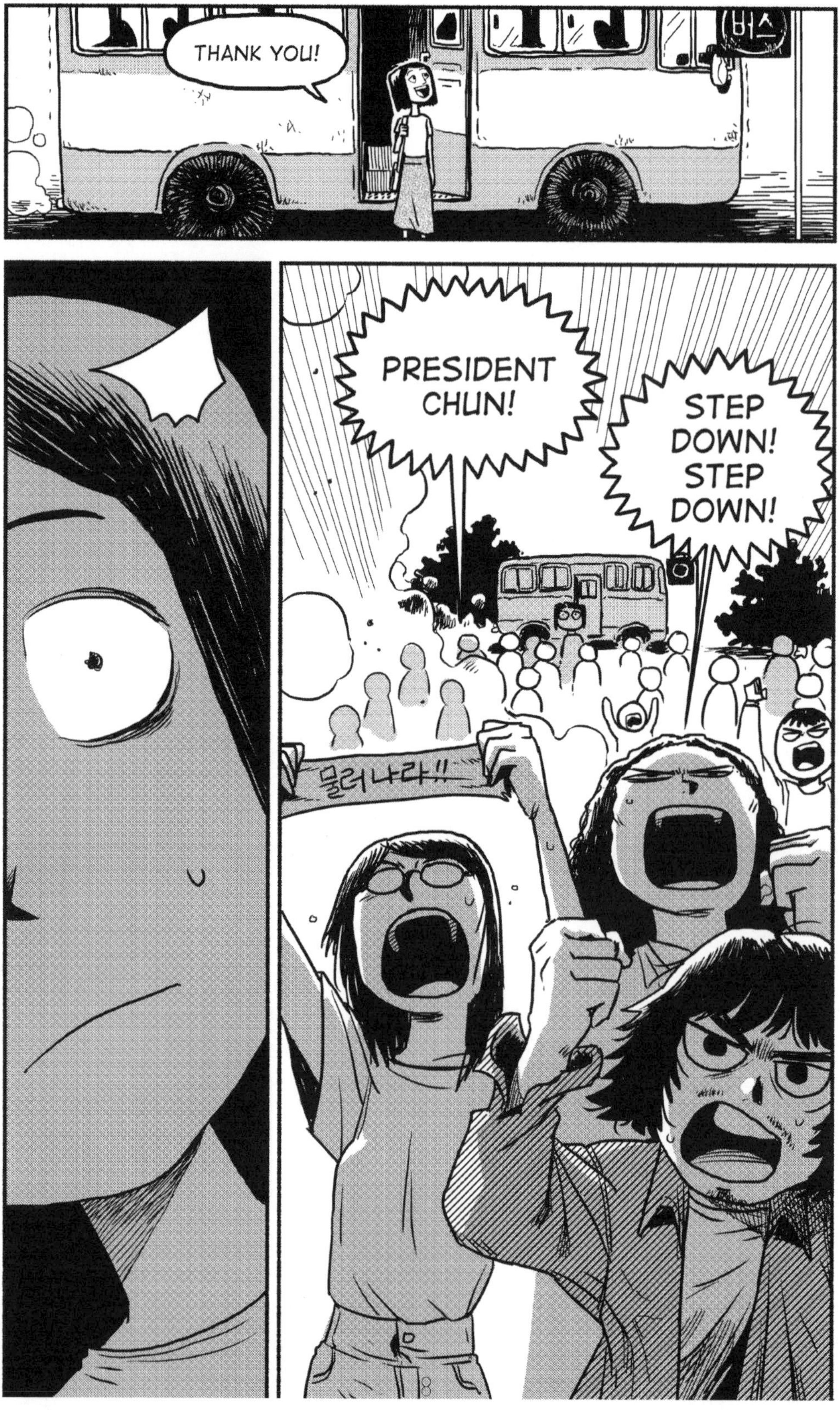
버스
THANK YOU!
PRESIDENT CHUN!
STEP DOWN! STEP DOWN!
물러나라!!

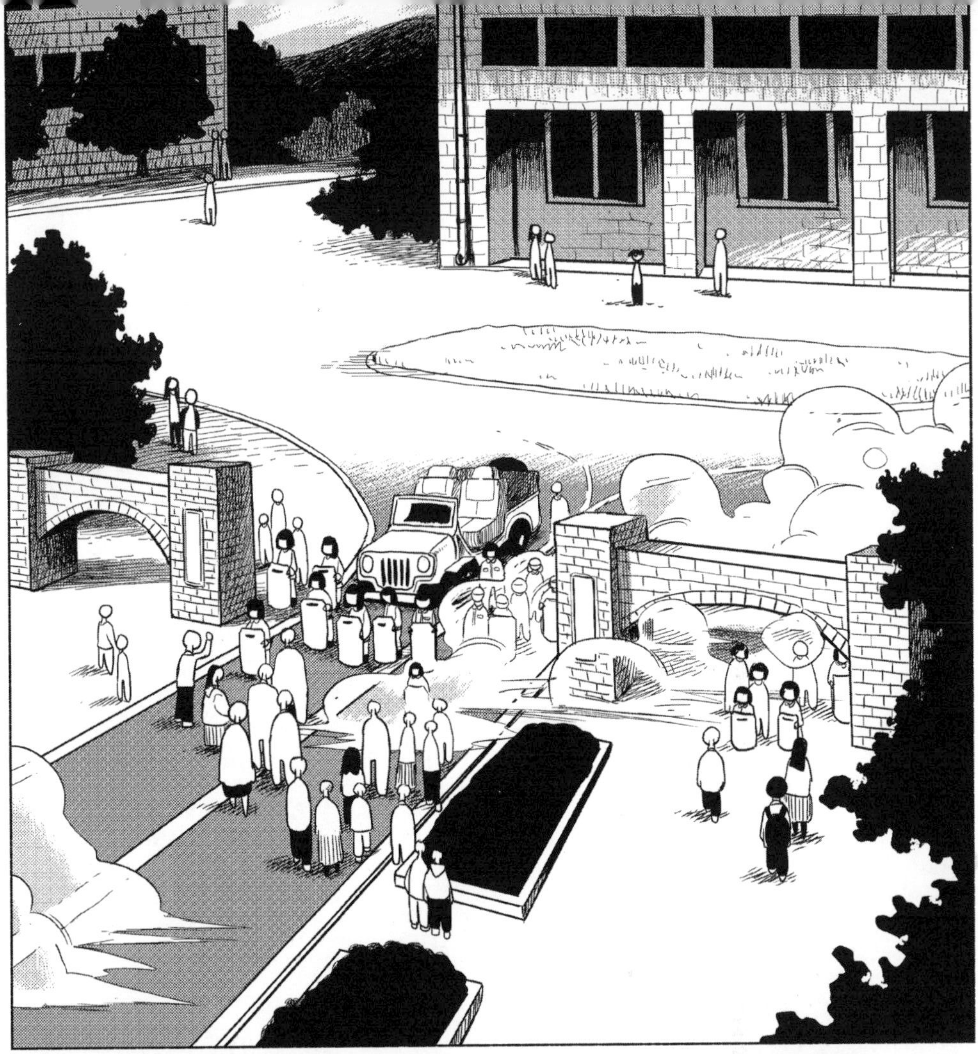

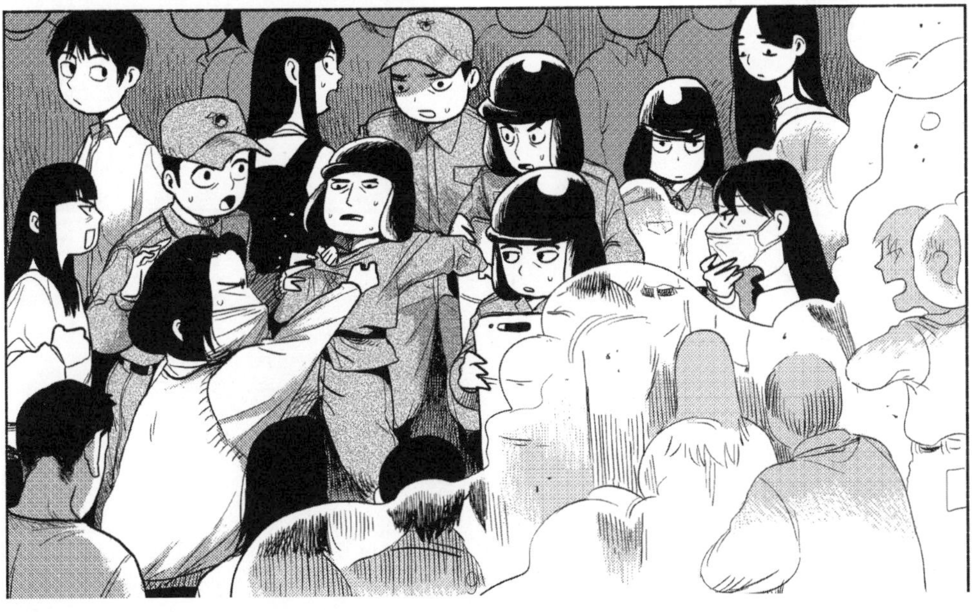

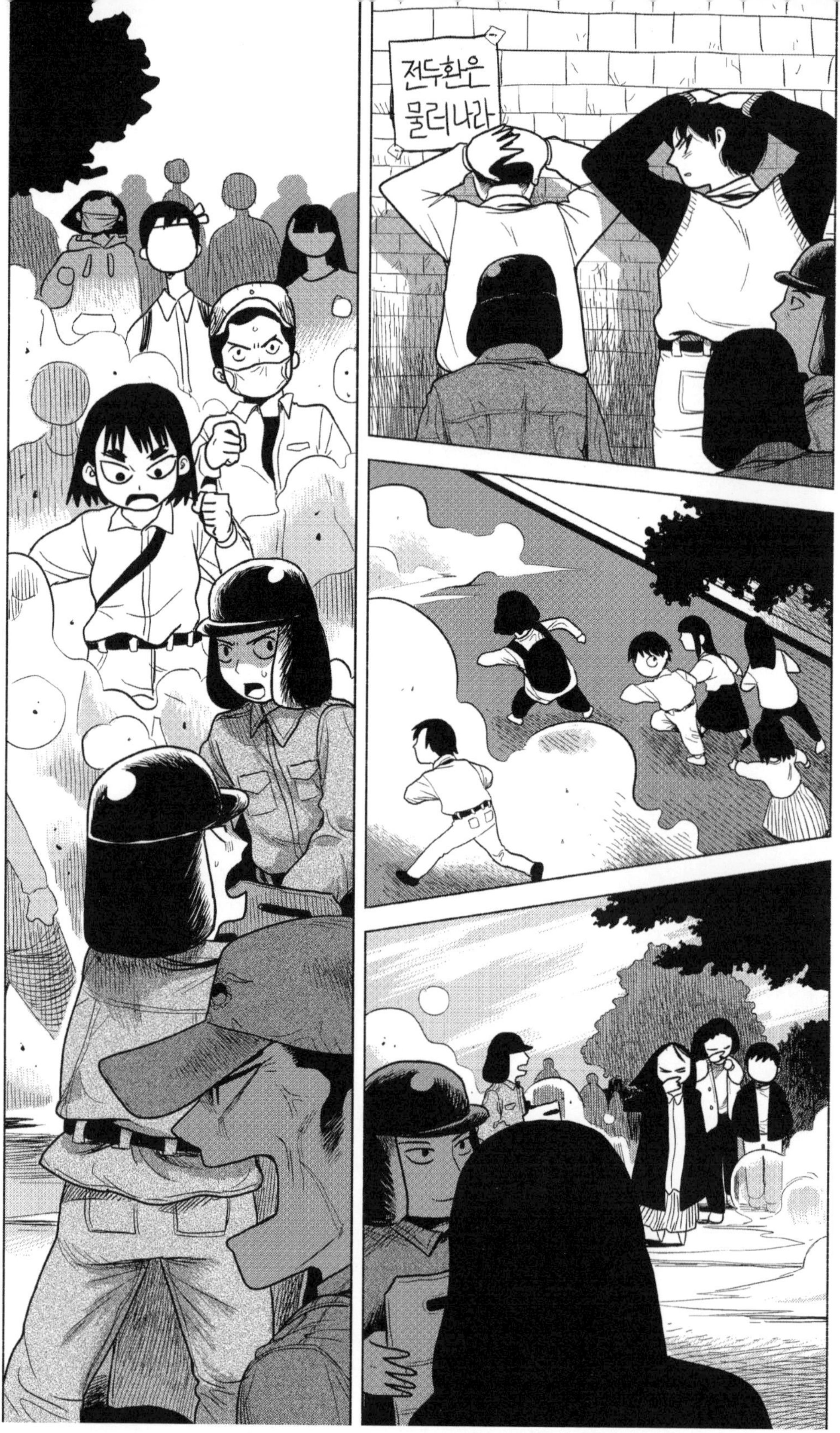
전두환은
물러나라

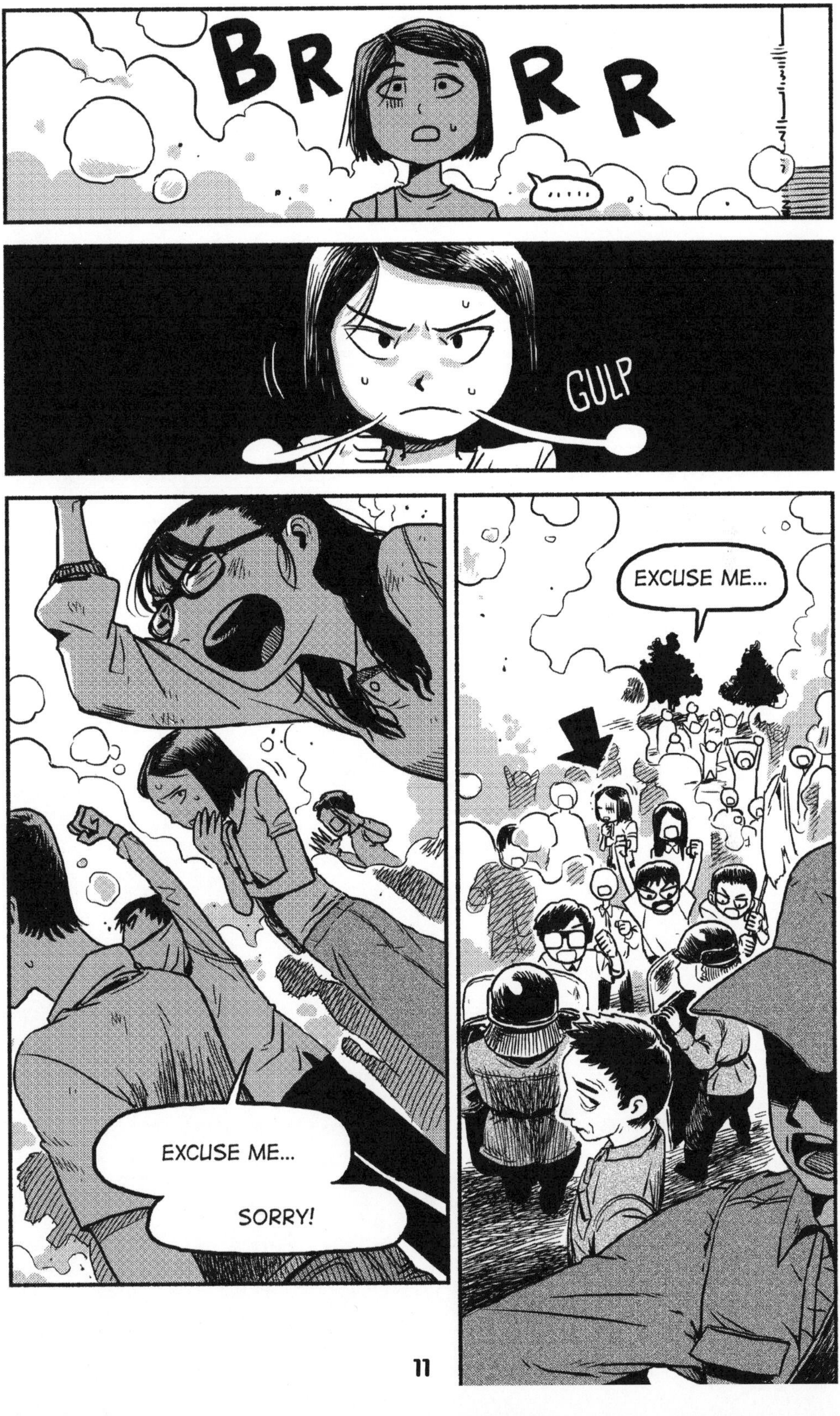
BRRRR
......
GULP
EXCUSE ME...
SORRY!
EXCUSE ME...

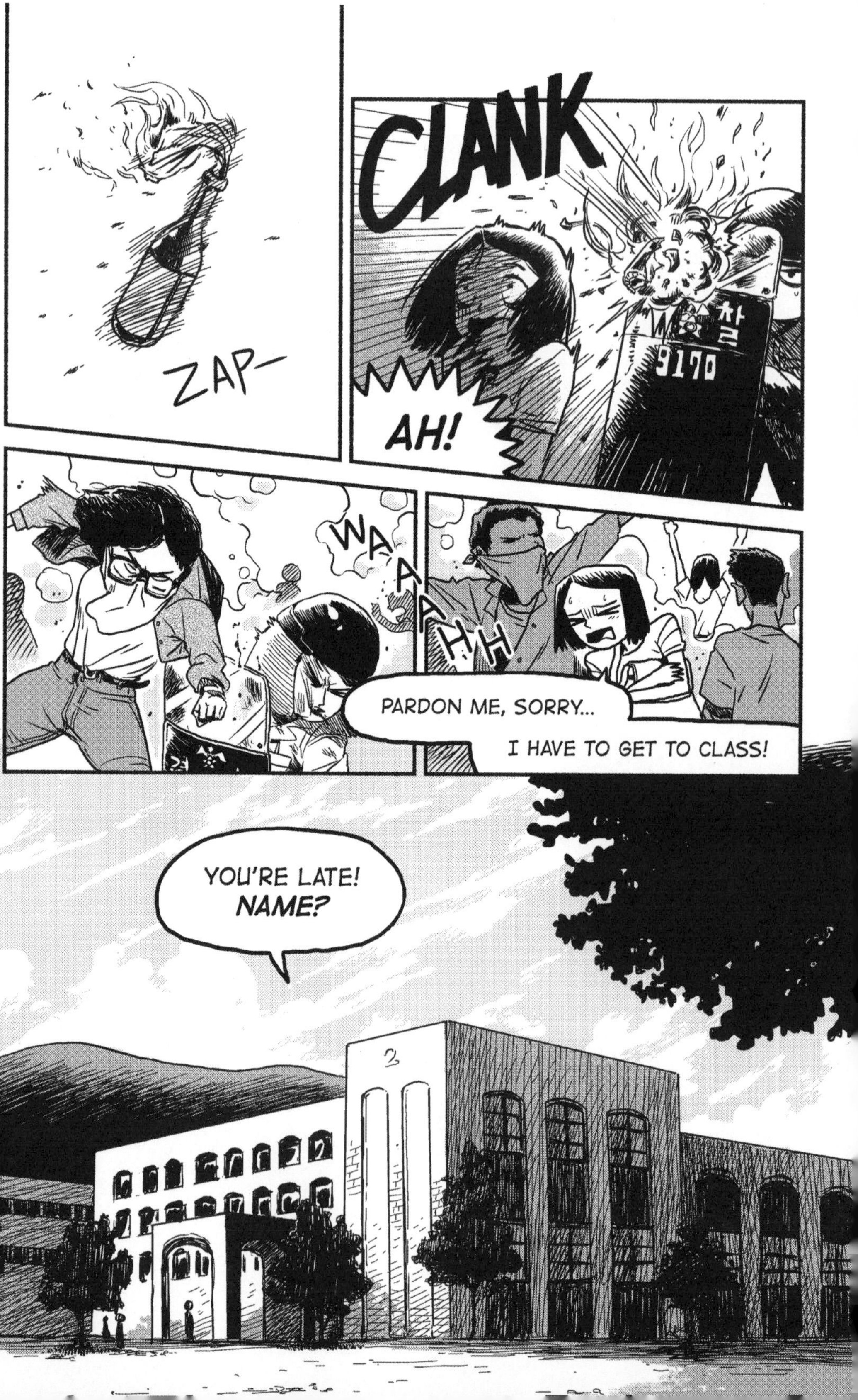
ZAP—
CLANK
찰
9170
AH!
WA-A-AHH
PARDON ME, SORRY...
I HAVE TO GET TO CLASS!
YOU'RE LATE!
NAME?

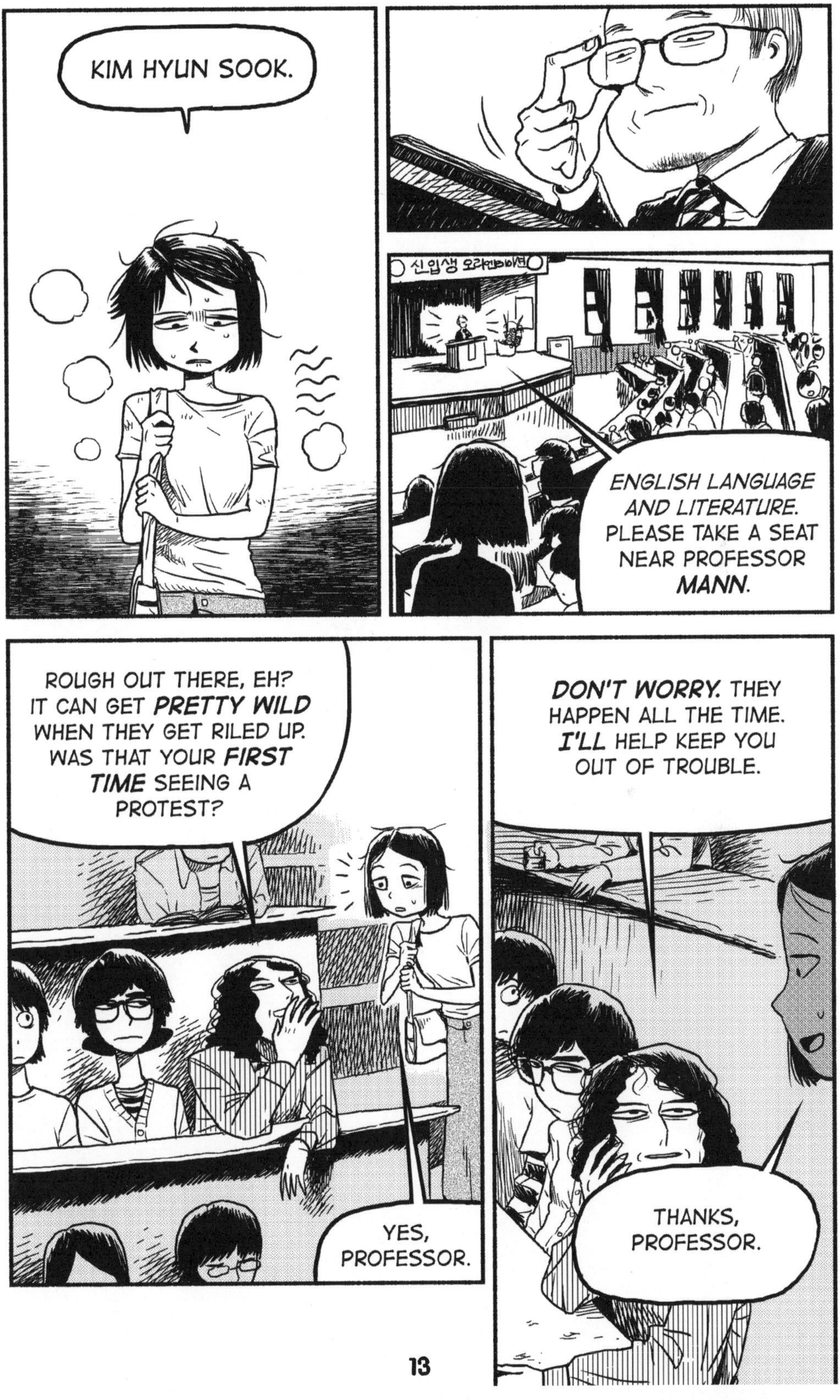
KIM HYUN SOOK.
신입생 오리엔테이션
ENGLISH LANGUAGE AND LITERATURE. PLEASE TAKE A SEAT NEAR PROFESSOR MANN.
ROUGH OUT THERE, EH? IT CAN GET PRETTY WILD WHEN THEY GET RILED UP. WAS THAT YOUR FIRST TIME SEEING A PROTEST?
YES, PROFESSOR.
DON'T WORRY. THEY HAPPEN ALL THE TIME. I'LL HELP KEEP YOU OUT OF TROUBLE.
THANKS, PROFESSOR.

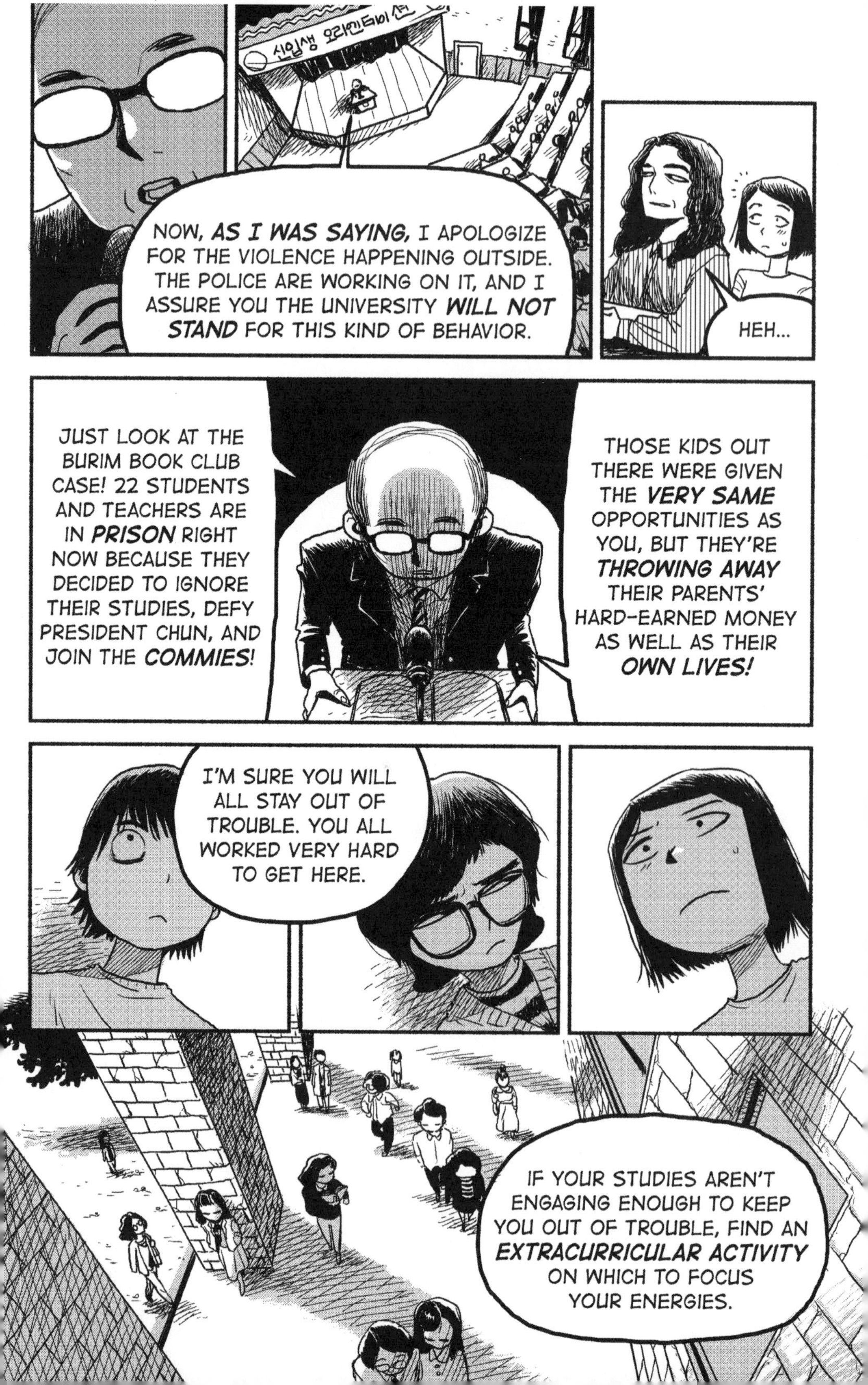
NOW, AS I WAS SAYING, I APOLOGIZE FOR THE VIOLENCE HAPPENING OUTSIDE. THE POLICE ARE WORKING ON IT, AND I ASSURE YOU THE UNIVERSITY WILL NOT STAND FOR THIS KIND OF BEHAVIOR.
HEH...
JUST LOOK AT THE BURIM BOOK CLUB CASE! 22 STUDENTS AND TEACHERS ARE IN PRISON RIGHT NOW BECAUSE THEY DECIDED TO IGNORE THEIR STUDIES, DEFY PRESIDENT CHUN, AND JOIN THE COMMIES!
THOSE KIDS OUT THERE WERE GIVEN THE VERY SAME OPPORTUNITIES AS YOU, BUT THEY'RE THROWING AWAY THEIR PARENTS' HARD-EARNED MONEY AS WELL AS THEIR OWN LIVES!
I'M SURE YOU WILL ALL STAY OUT OF TROUBLE. YOU ALL WORKED VERY HARD TO GET HERE.
IF YOUR STUDIES AREN'T ENGAGING ENOUGH TO KEEP YOU OUT OF TROUBLE, FIND AN EXTRACURRICULAR ACTIVITY ON WHICH TO FOCUS YOUR ENERGIES.

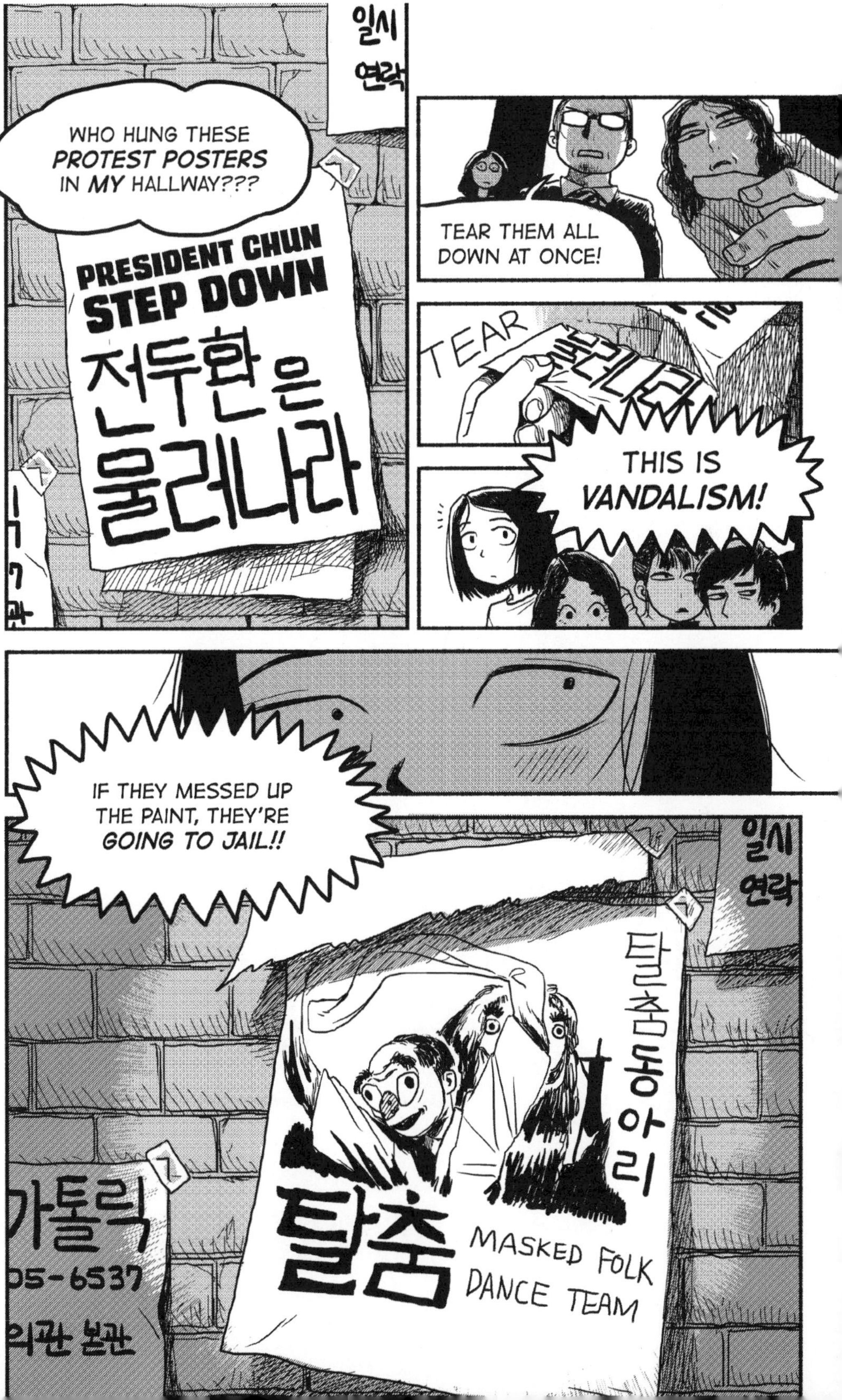

일시
연락
WHO HUNG THESE PROTEST POSTERS IN MY HALLWAY???
PRESIDENT CHUN STEP DOWN
전두환은 물러나라
TEAR THEM ALL DOWN AT ONCE!
TEAR
THIS IS VANDALISM!
IF THEY MESSED UP THE PAINT, THEY'RE GOING TO JAIL!!
일시
연락
탈춤동아리
탈춤
MASKED FOLK DANCE TEAM
가톨릭
05-6537
의관 본관

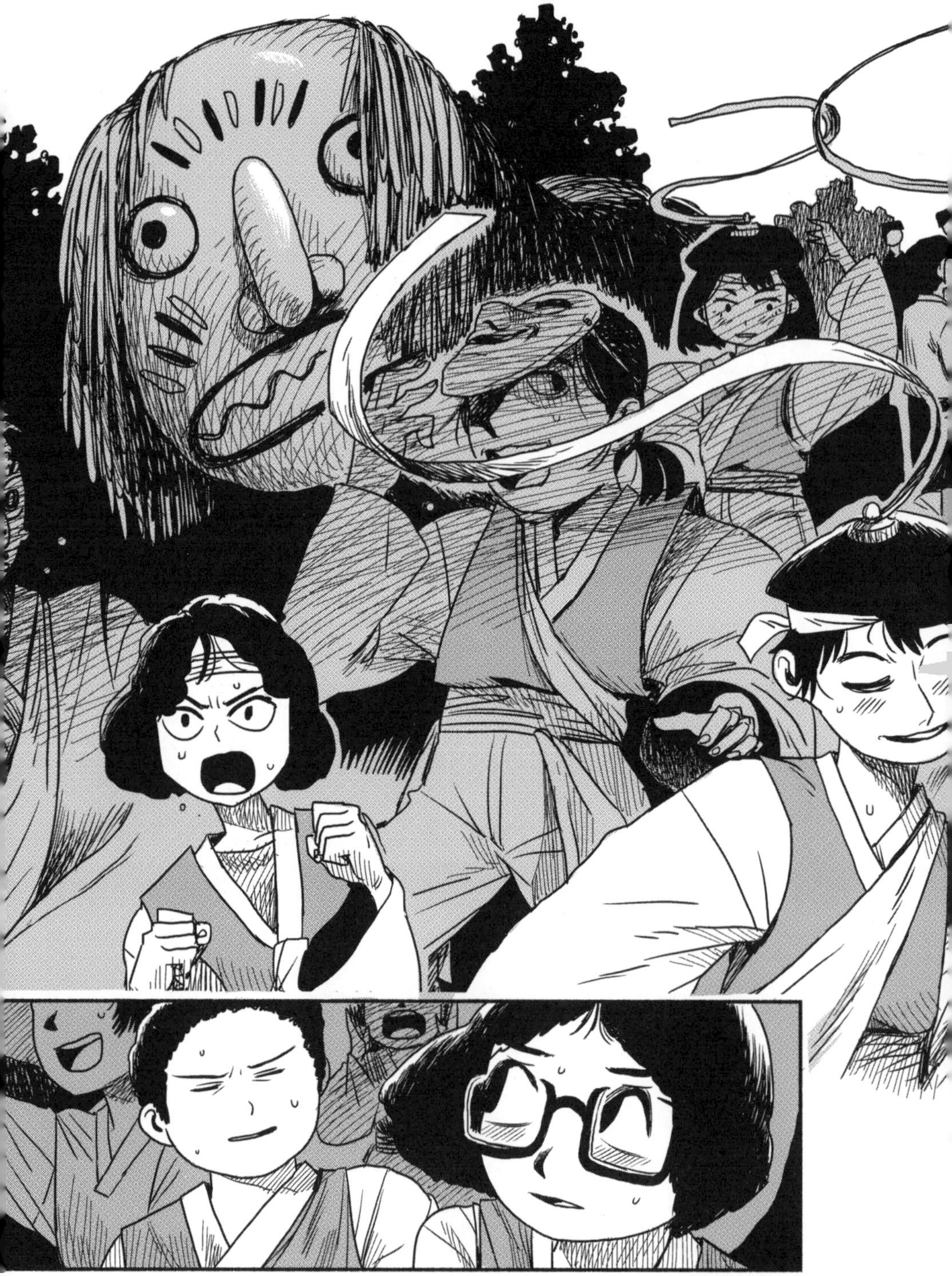

CHAPTER TWO:

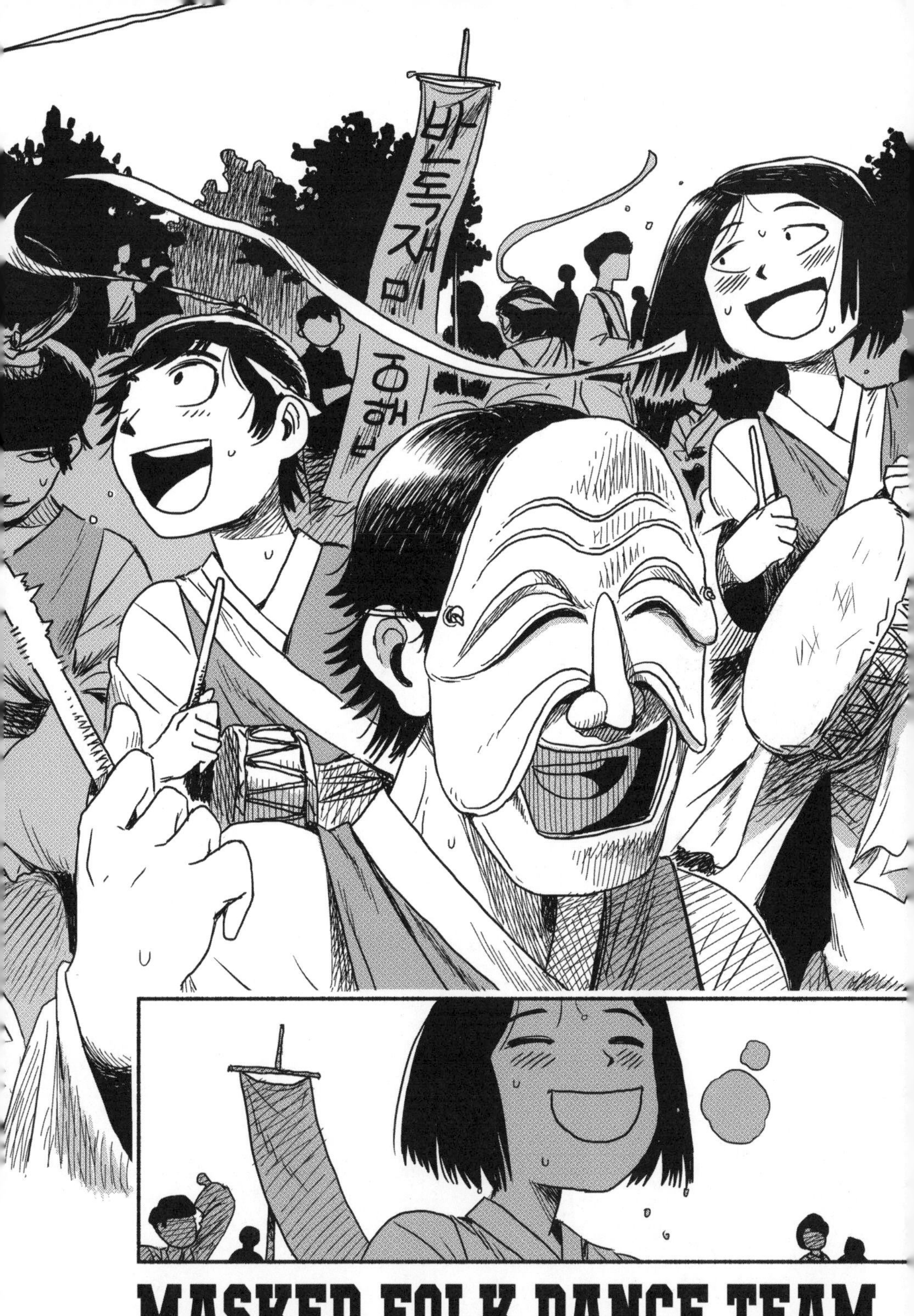

MASKED FOLK DANCE TEAM

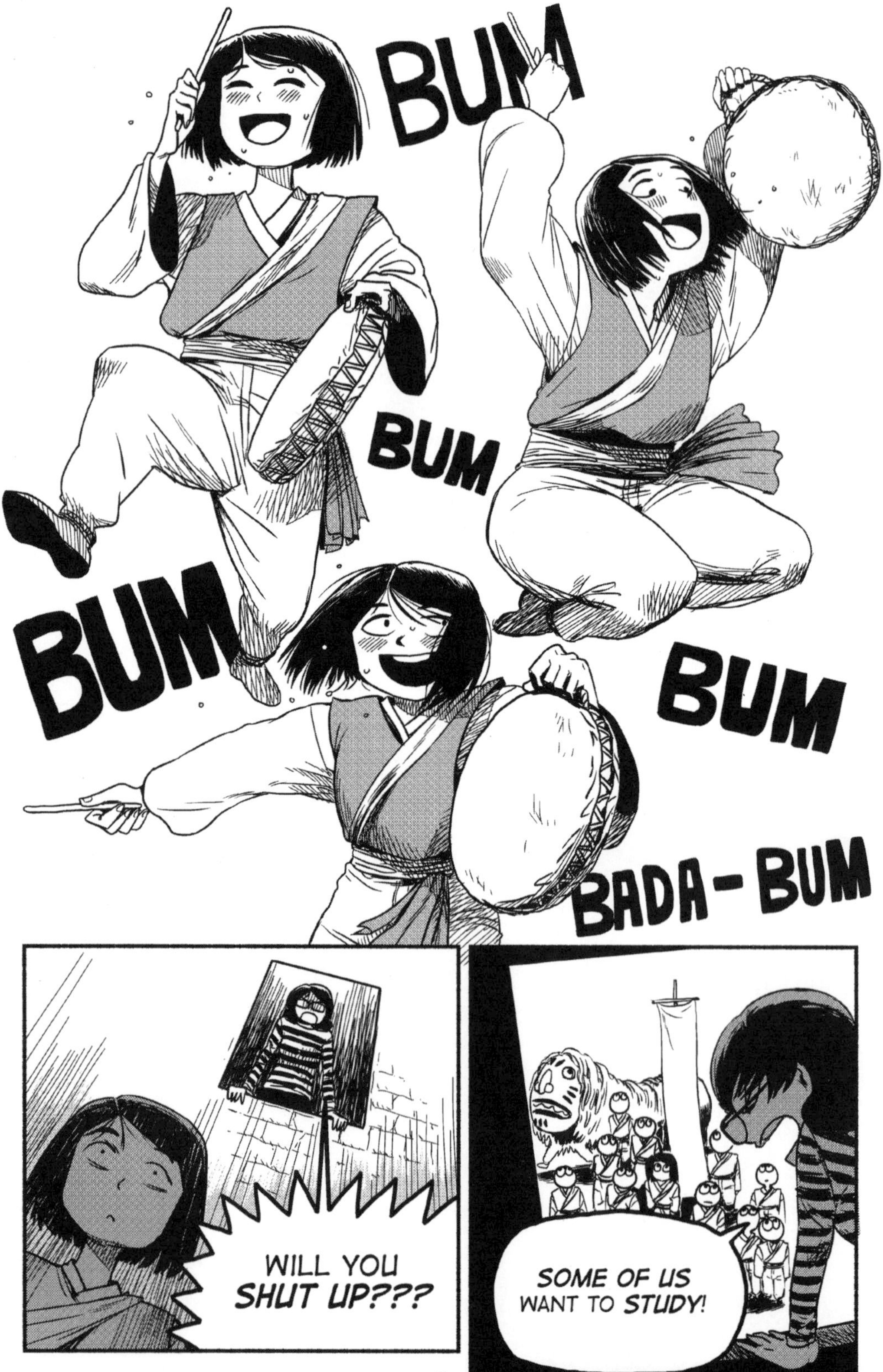
BUM
BUM
BUM
BUM
BADA-BUM
WILL YOU SHUT UP???
SOME OF US WANT TO STUDY!

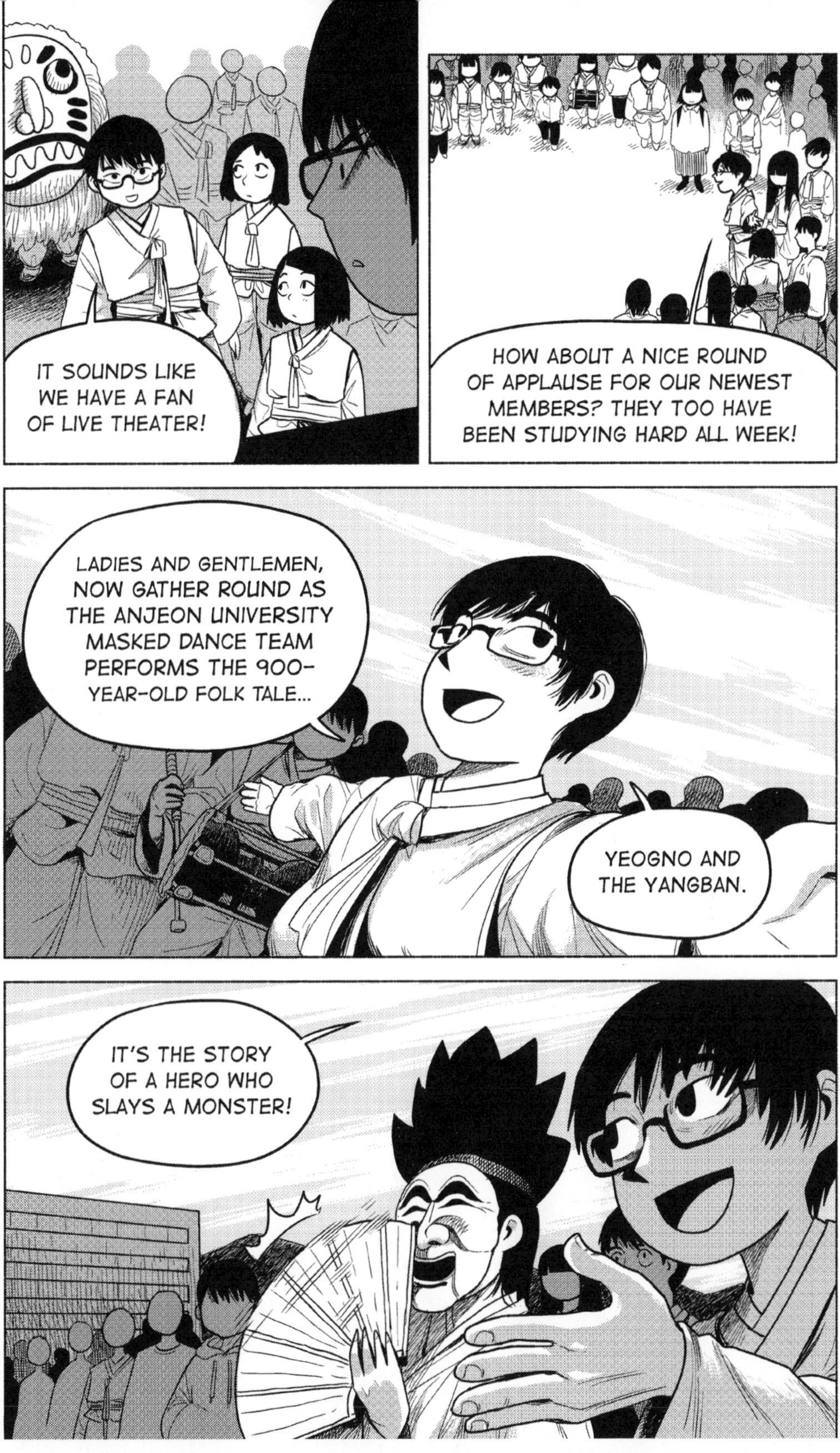
IT SOUNDS LIKE WE HAVE A FAN OF LIVE THEATER!
HOW ABOUT A NICE ROUND OF APPLAUSE FOR OUR NEWEST MEMBERS? THEY TOO HAVE BEEN STUDYING HARD ALL WEEK!
LADIES AND GENTLEMEN, NOW GATHER ROUND AS THE ANJEON UNIVERSITY MASKED DANCE TEAM PERFORMS THE 900-YEAR-OLD FOLK TALE...
YEOGNO AND THE YANGBAN.
IT'S THE STORY OF A HERO WHO SLAYS A MONSTER!

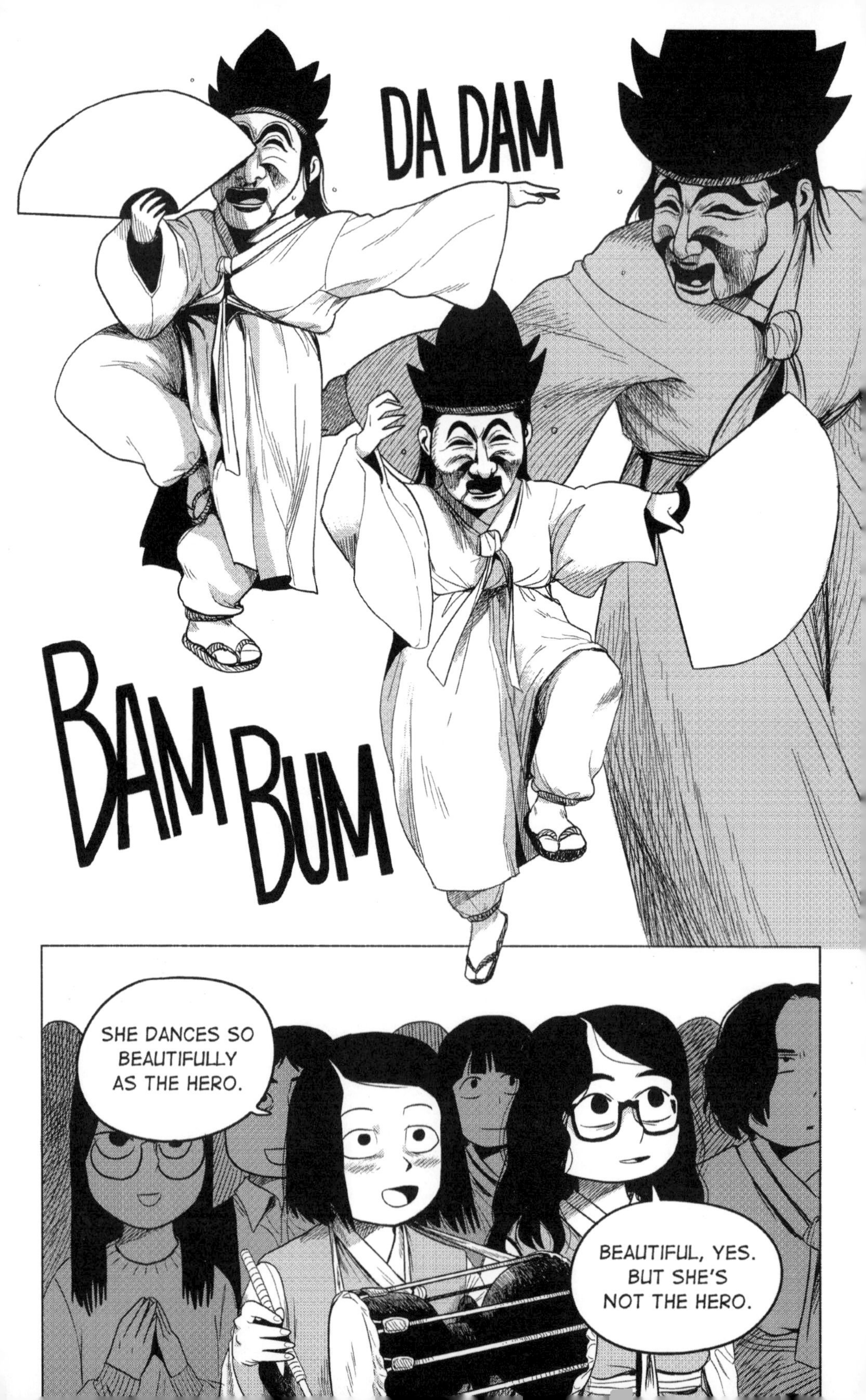
DA DAM
BAM BUM
SHE DANCES SO BEAUTIFULLY AS THE HERO.
BEAUTIFUL, YES. BUT SHE'S NOT THE HERO.

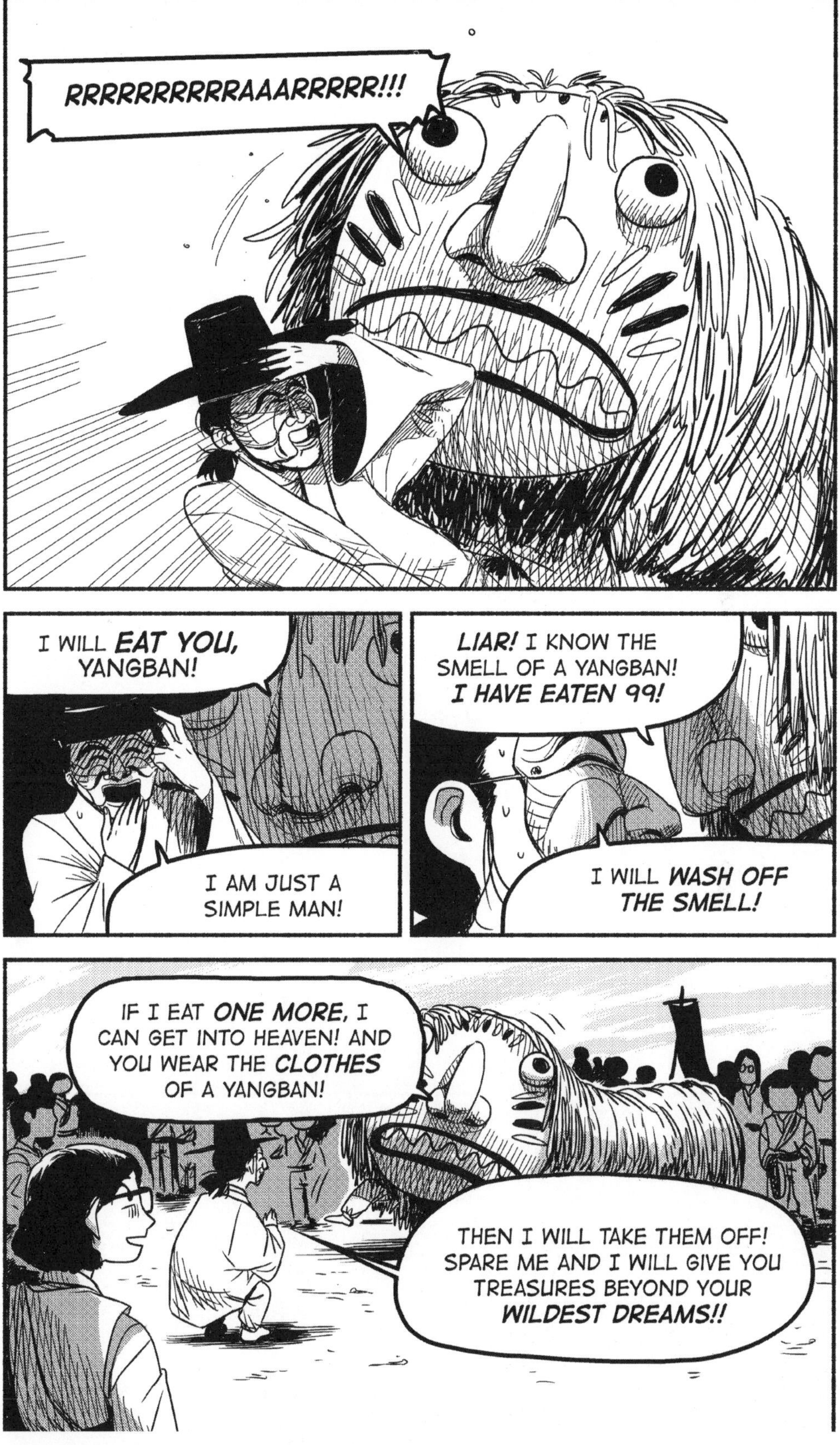
RRRRRRRRRRAAARRRRR!!!
I WILL EAT YOU, YANGBAN!
I AM JUST A SIMPLE MAN!
LIAR! I KNOW THE SMELL OF A YANGBAN! I HAVE EATEN 99!
I WILL WASH OFF THE SMELL!
IF I EAT ONE MORE, I CAN GET INTO HEAVEN! AND YOU WEAR THE CLOTHES OF A YANGBAN!
THEN I WILL TAKE THEM OFF! SPARE ME AND I WILL GIVE YOU TREASURES BEYOND YOUR WILDEST DREAMS!!

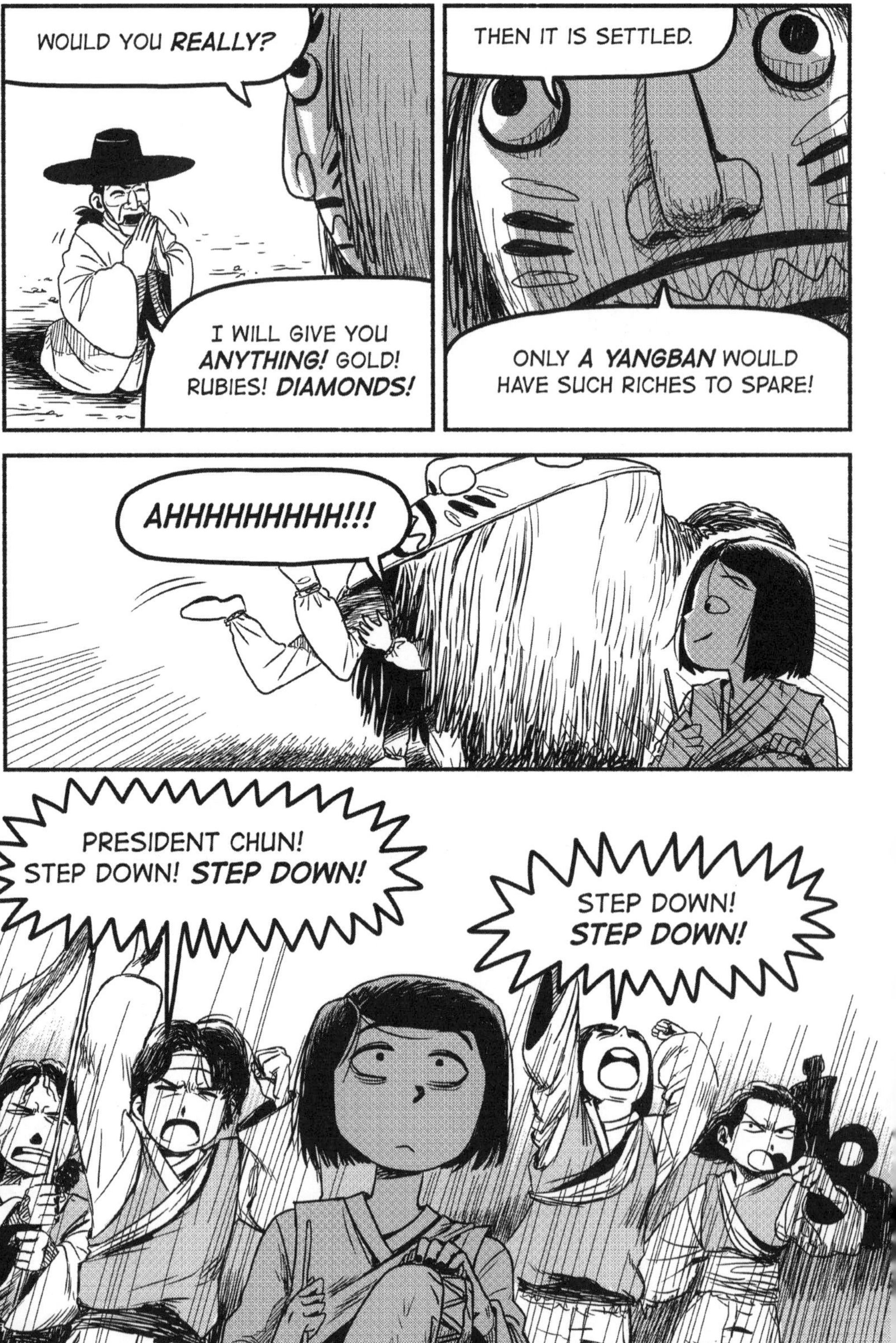
WOULD YOU REALLY?
I WILL GIVE YOU ANYTHING! GOLD! RUBIES! DIAMONDS!
THEN IT IS SETTLED.
ONLY A YANGBAN WOULD HAVE SUCH RICHES TO SPARE!
AHHHHHHHHHH!!!
PRESIDENT CHUN! STEP DOWN! STEP DOWN!
STEP DOWN! STEP DOWN!

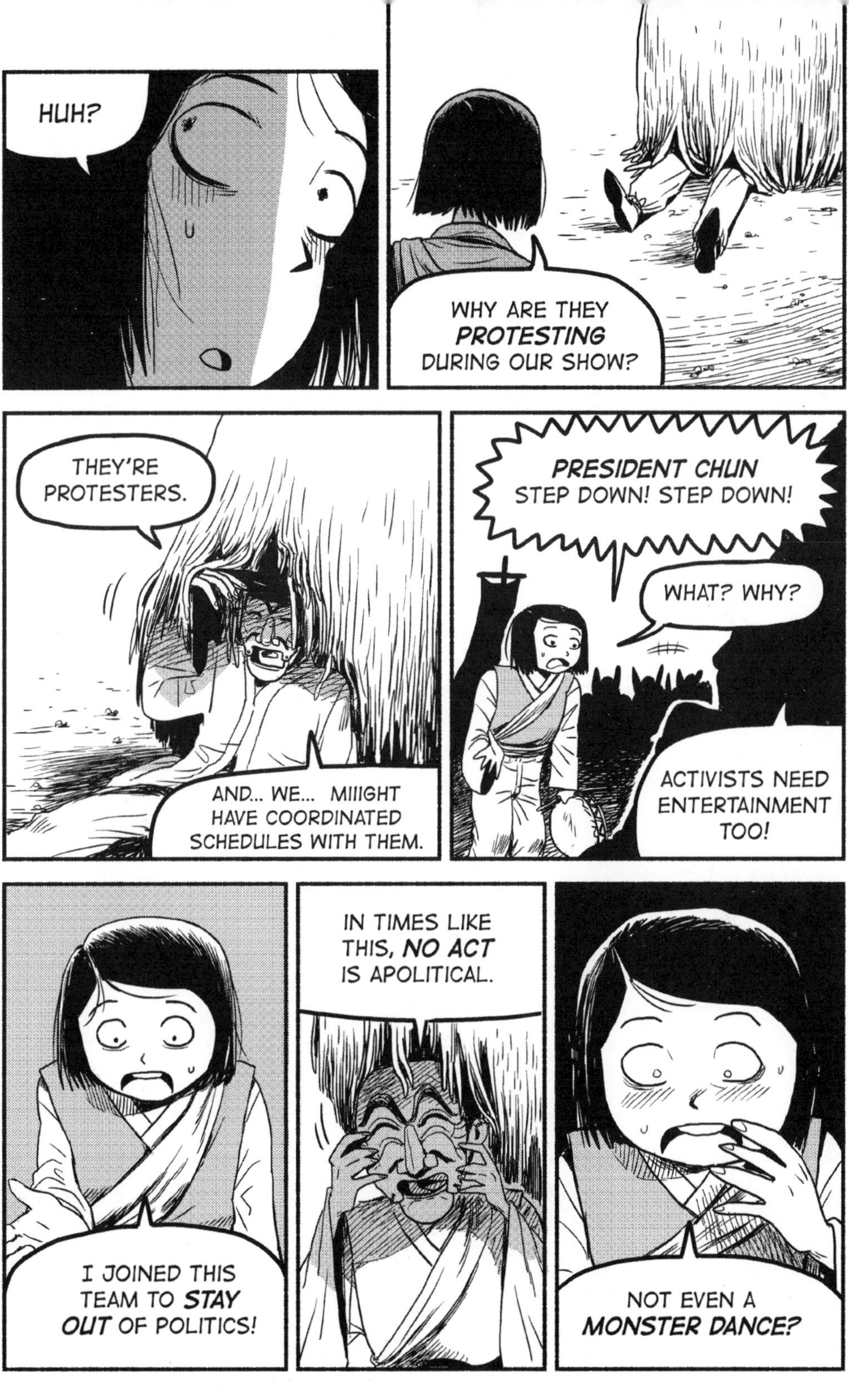
HUH?
WHY ARE THEY PROTESTING DURING OUR SHOW?
THEY'RE PROTESTERS.
AND... WE... MIIIGHT HAVE COORDINATED SCHEDULES WITH THEM.
PRESIDENT CHUN STEP DOWN! STEP DOWN!
WHAT? WHY?
ACTIVISTS NEED ENTERTAINMENT TOO!
I JOINED THIS TEAM TO STAY OUT OF POLITICS!
IN TIMES LIKE THIS, NO ACT IS APOLITICAL.
NOT EVEN A MONSTER DANCE?

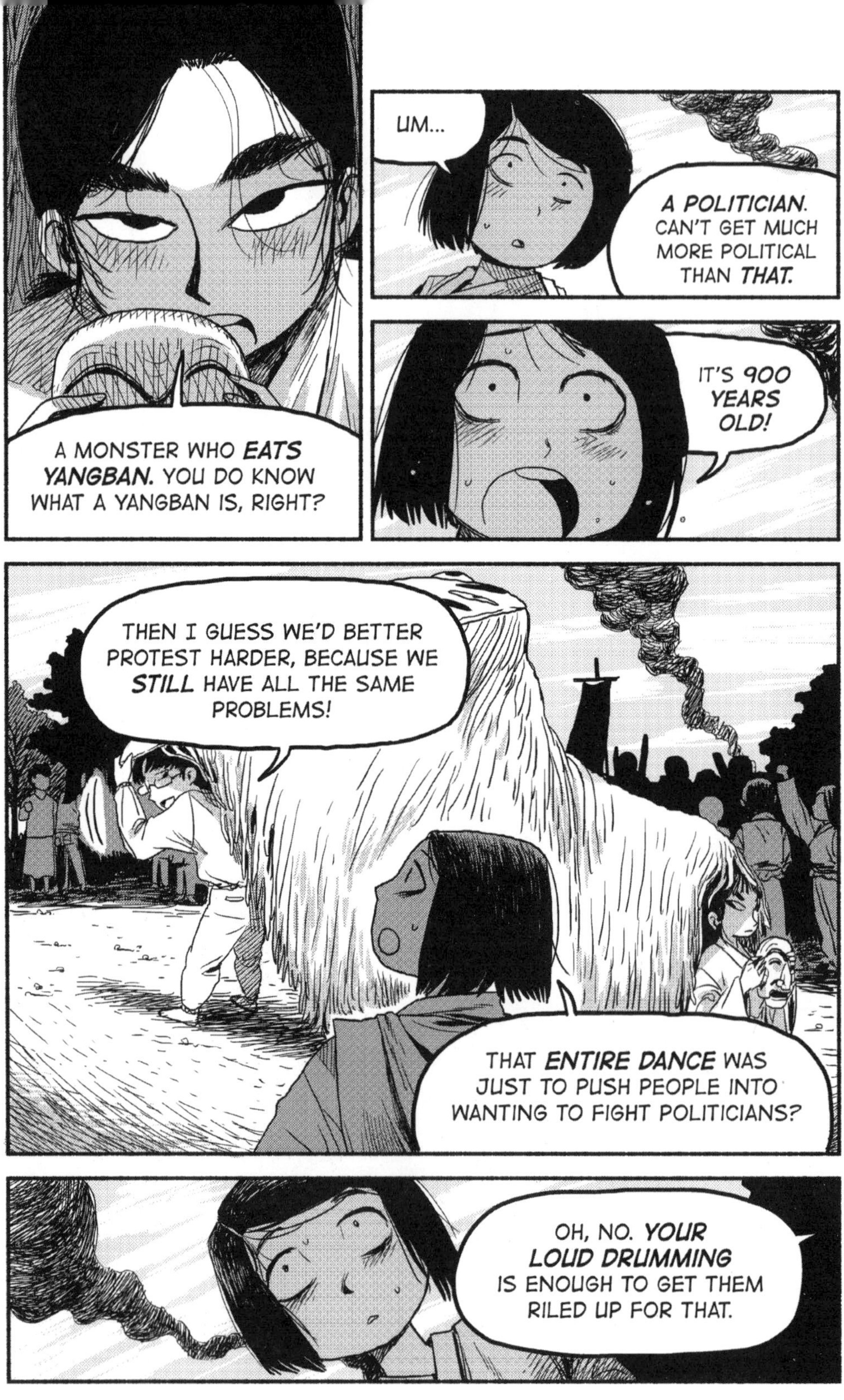
A MONSTER WHO EATS YANGBAN. YOU DO KNOW WHAT A YANGBAN IS, RIGHT?
UM...
A POLITICIAN. CAN'T GET MUCH MORE POLITICAL THAN THAT.
IT'S 900 YEARS OLD!
THEN I GUESS WE'D BETTER PROTEST HARDER, BECAUSE WE STILL HAVE ALL THE SAME PROBLEMS!
THAT ENTIRE DANCE WAS JUST TO PUSH PEOPLE INTO WANTING TO FIGHT POLITICIANS?
OH, NO. YOUR LOUD DRUMMING IS ENOUGH TO GET THEM RILED UP FOR THAT.

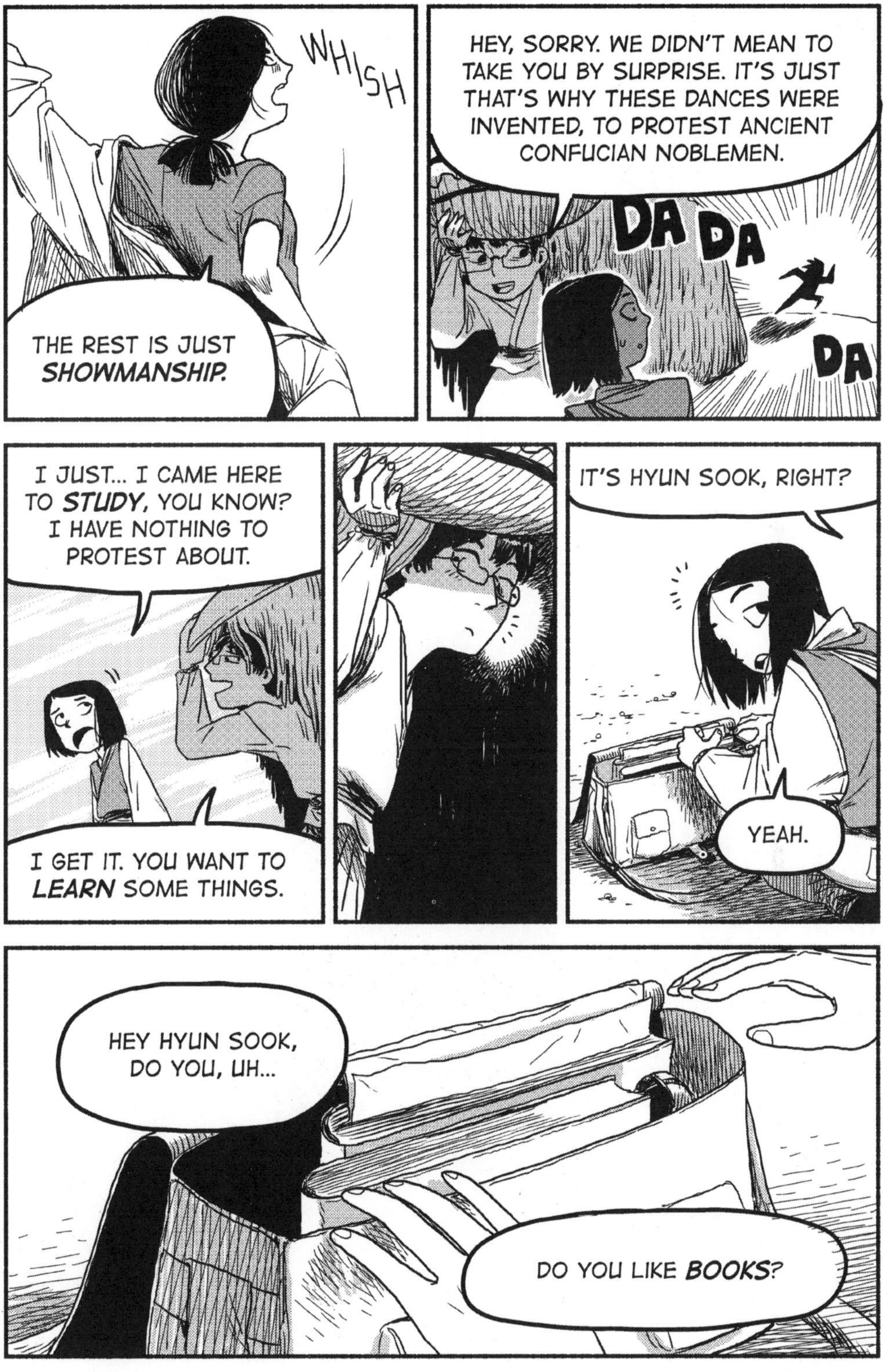
WHISH
THE REST IS JUST *SHOWMANSHIP.*
HEY, SORRY. WE DIDN'T MEAN TO TAKE YOU BY SURPRISE. IT'S JUST THAT'S WHY THESE DANCES WERE INVENTED, TO PROTEST ANCIENT CONFUCIAN NOBLEMEN.
DA DA
DA
I JUST... I CAME HERE TO *STUDY,* YOU KNOW? I HAVE NOTHING TO PROTEST ABOUT.
I GET IT. YOU WANT TO *LEARN* SOME THINGS.
IT'S HYUN SOOK, RIGHT?
YEAH.
HEY HYUN SOOK, DO YOU, UH...
DO YOU LIKE *BOOKS?*

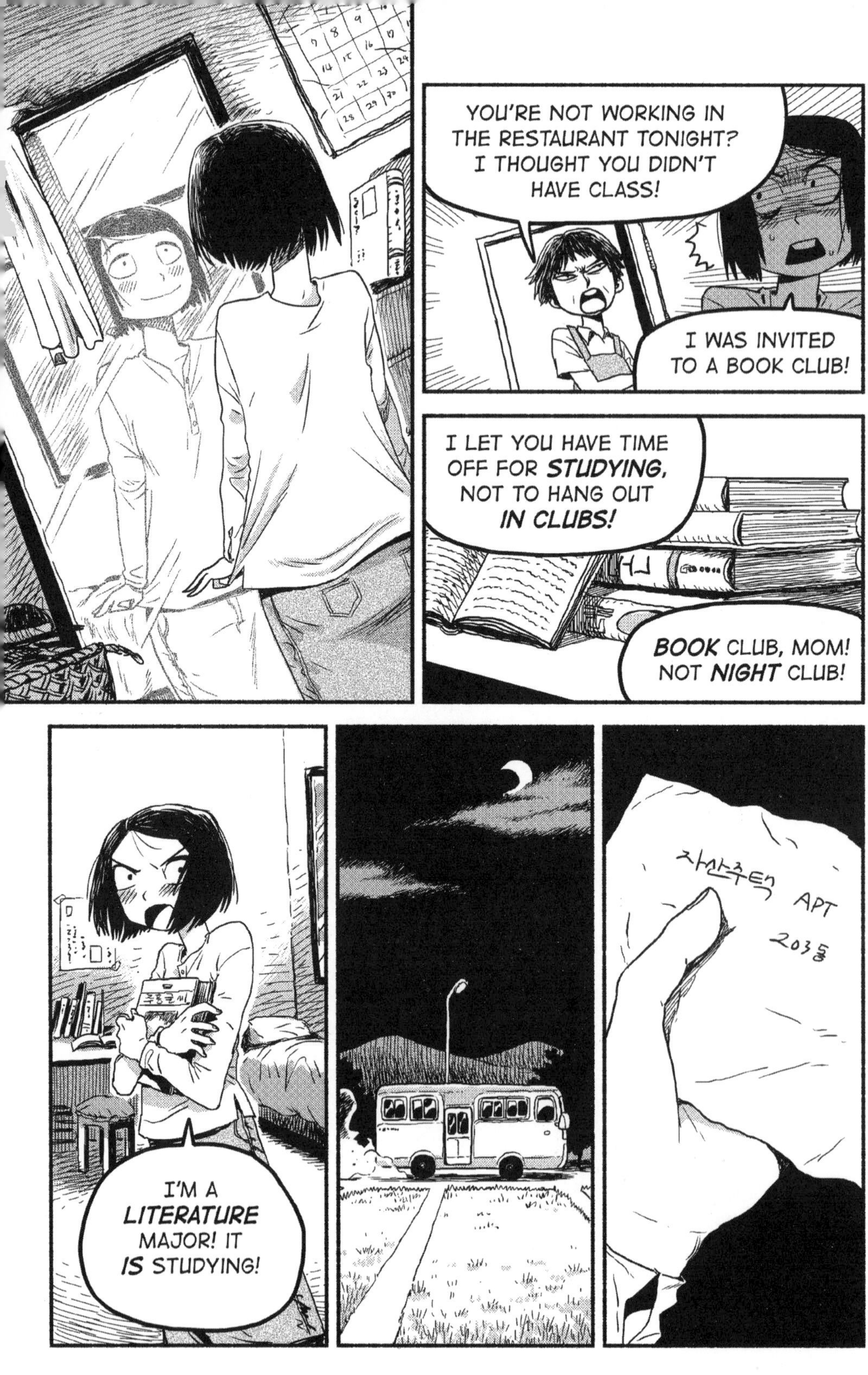

YOU'RE NOT WORKING IN THE RESTAURANT TONIGHT? I THOUGHT YOU DIDN'T HAVE CLASS!
I WAS INVITED TO A BOOK CLUB!
I LET YOU HAVE TIME OFF FOR STUDYING, NOT TO HANG OUT IN CLUBS!
BOOK CLUB, MOM! NOT NIGHT CLUB!
I'M A LITERATURE MAJOR! IT IS STUDYING!
APT

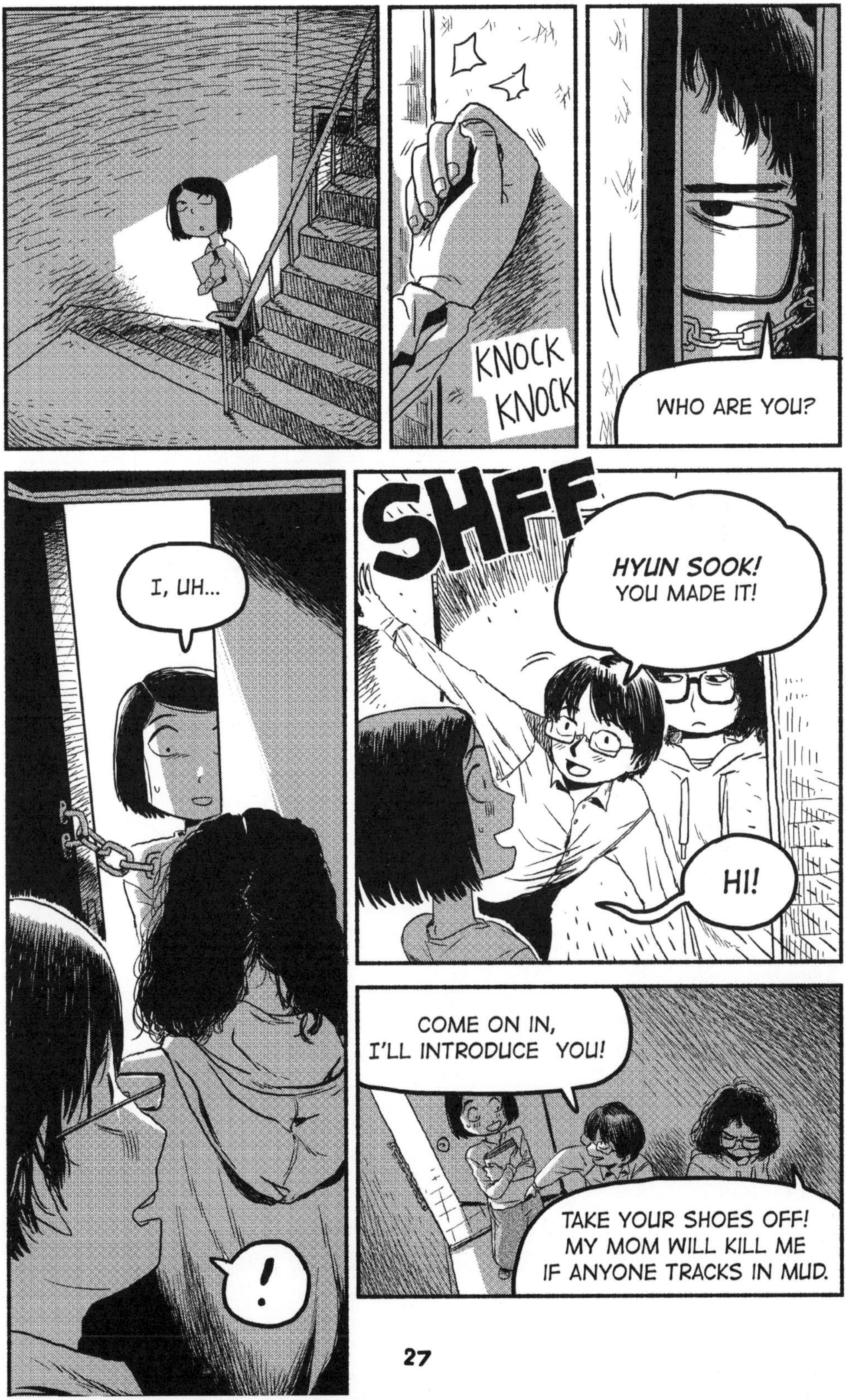
KNOCK
KNOCK
WHO ARE YOU?
I, UH...
!
SHFF
HYUN SOOK!
YOU MADE IT!
HI!
COME ON IN,
I'LL INTRODUCE YOU!
TAKE YOUR SHOES OFF!
MY MOM WILL KILL ME
IF ANYONE TRACKS IN MUD.

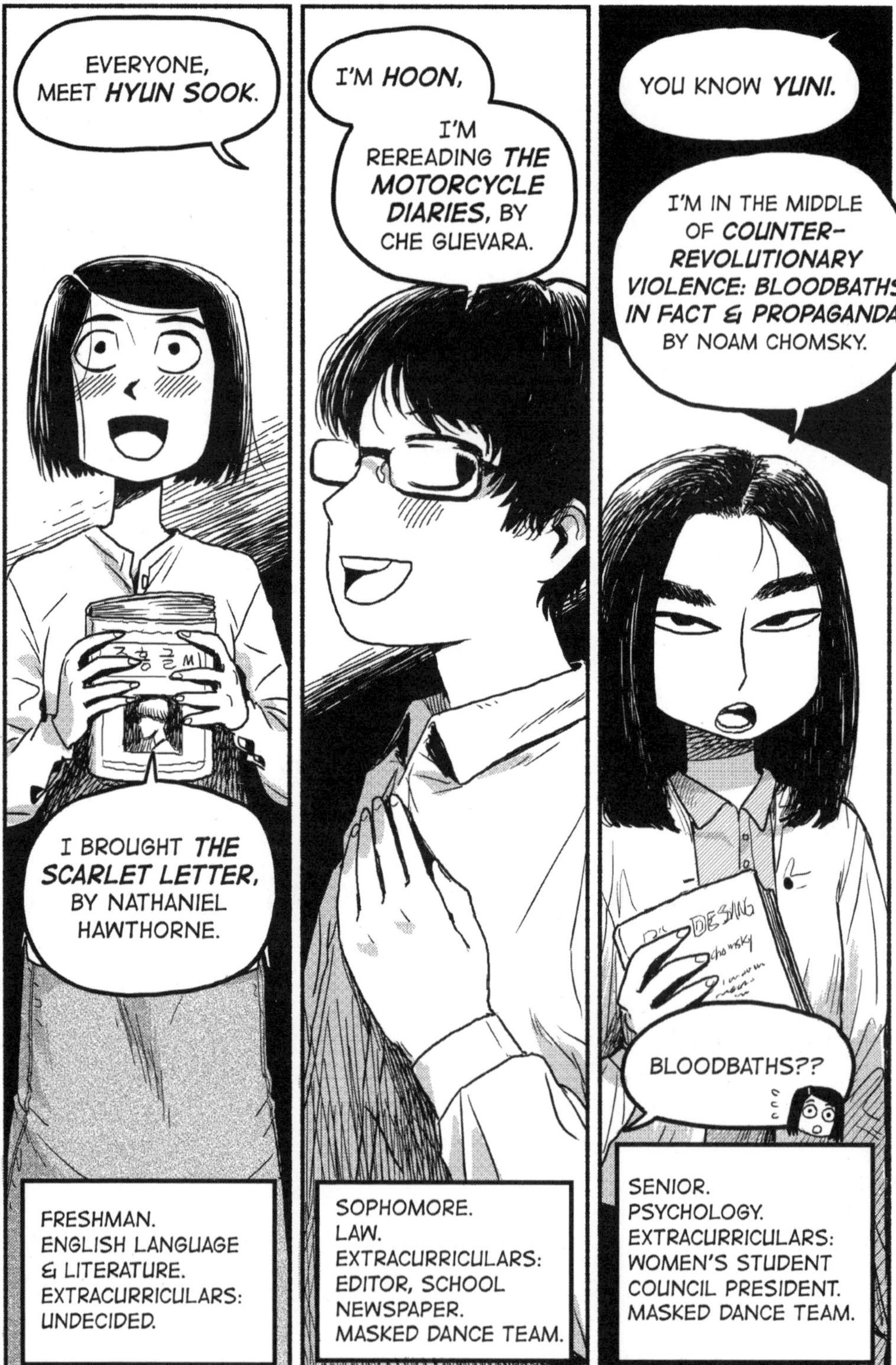

EVERYONE, MEET HYUN SOOK.
I BROUGHT THE SCARLET LETTER, BY NATHANIEL HAWTHORNE.
FRESHMAN.
ENGLISH LANGUAGE & LITERATURE.
EXTRACURRICULARS: UNDECIDED.
I'M HOON,
I'M REREADING THE MOTORCYCLE DIARIES, BY CHE GUEVARA.
SOPHOMORE.
LAW.
EXTRACURRICULARS: EDITOR, SCHOOL NEWSPAPER.
MASKED DANCE TEAM.
YOU KNOW YUNI.
I'M IN THE MIDDLE OF COUNTER-REVOLUTIONARY VIOLENCE: BLOODBATHS IN FACT & PROPAGANDA BY NOAM CHOMSKY.
BLOODBATHS??
SENIOR.
PSYCHOLOGY.
EXTRACURRICULARS: WOMEN'S STUDENT COUNCIL PRESIDENT.
MASKED DANCE TEAM.

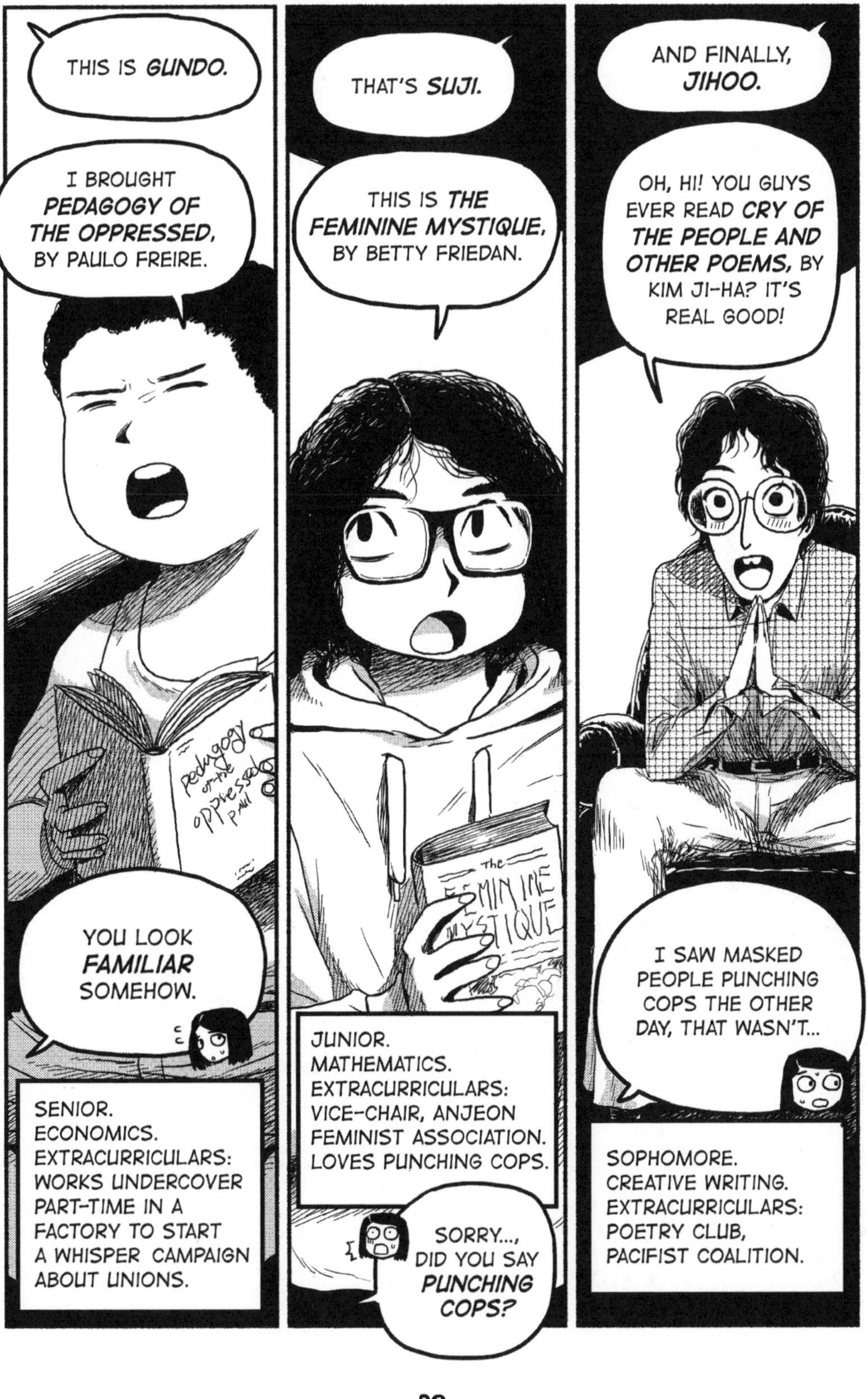
THIS IS GUNDO.
I BROUGHT PEDAGOGY OF THE OPPRESSED, BY PAULO FREIRE.
pedagogy of the oppressed Paul
YOU LOOK FAMILIAR SOMEHOW.
SENIOR. ECONOMICS. EXTRACURRICULARS: WORKS UNDERCOVER PART-TIME IN A FACTORY TO START A WHISPER CAMPAIGN ABOUT UNIONS.
THAT'S SUJI.
THIS IS THE FEMININE MYSTIQUE, BY BETTY FRIEDAN.
The FEMININE MYSTIQUE
JUNIOR. MATHEMATICS. EXTRACURRICULARS: VICE-CHAIR, ANJEON FEMINIST ASSOCIATION. LOVES PUNCHING COPS.
SORRY..., DID YOU SAY PUNCHING COPS?
AND FINALLY, JIHOO.
OH, HI! YOU GUYS EVER READ CRY OF THE PEOPLE AND OTHER POEMS, BY KIM JI-HA? IT'S REAL GOOD!
I SAW MASKED PEOPLE PUNCHING COPS THE OTHER DAY, THAT WASN'T...
SOPHOMORE. CREATIVE WRITING. EXTRACURRICULARS: POETRY CLUB, PACIFIST COALITION.

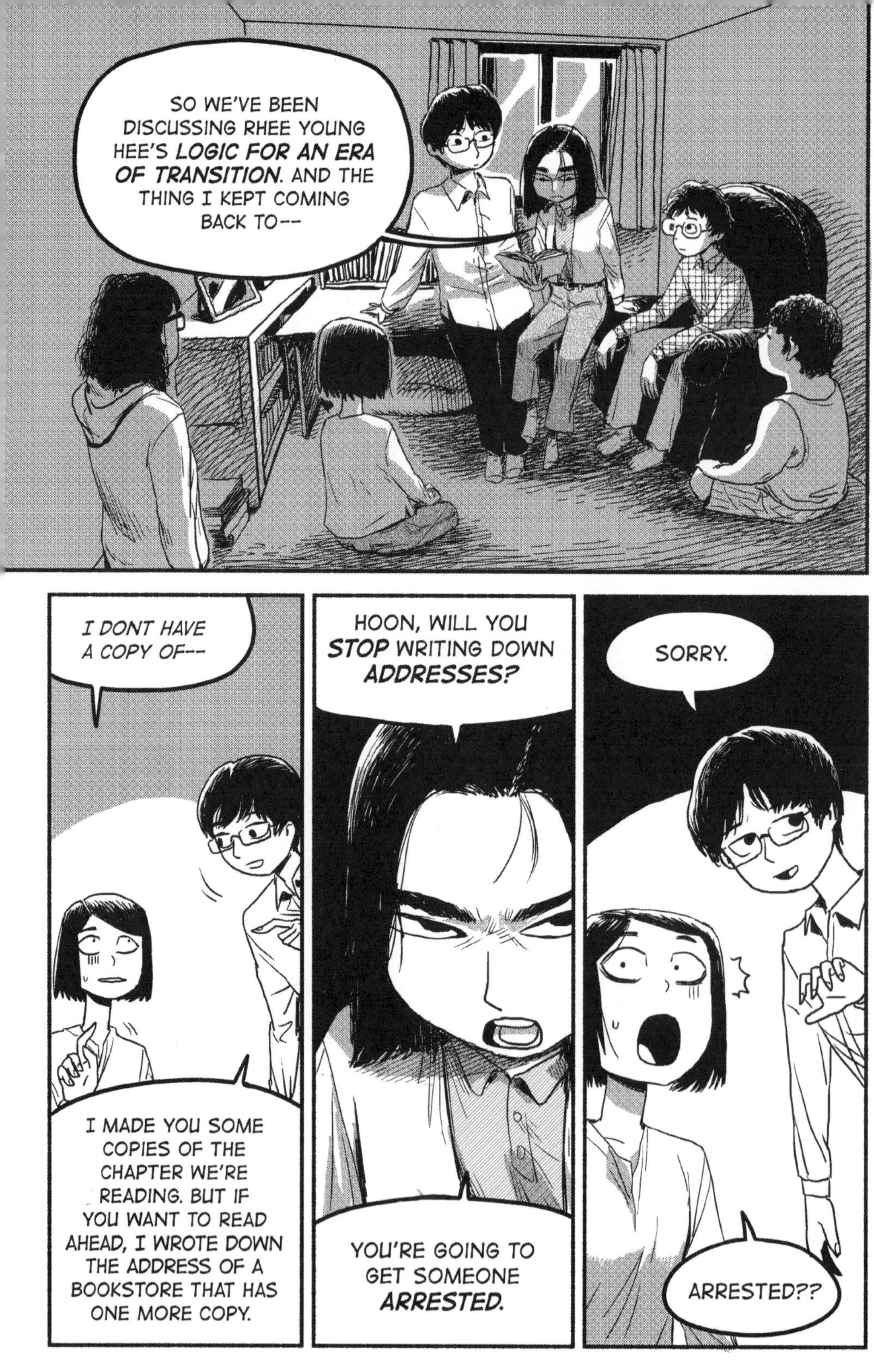
SO WE'VE BEEN DISCUSSING RHEE YOUNG HEE'S *LOGIC FOR AN ERA OF TRANSITION*. AND THE THING I KEPT COMING BACK TO--
I DONT HAVE A COPY OF--
I MADE YOU SOME COPIES OF THE CHAPTER WE'RE READING. BUT IF YOU WANT TO READ AHEAD, I WROTE DOWN THE ADDRESS OF A BOOKSTORE THAT HAS ONE MORE COPY.
HOON, WILL YOU ***STOP*** WRITING DOWN ***ADDRESSES?***
YOU'RE GOING TO GET SOMEONE ***ARRESTED.***
SORRY.
ARRESTED??

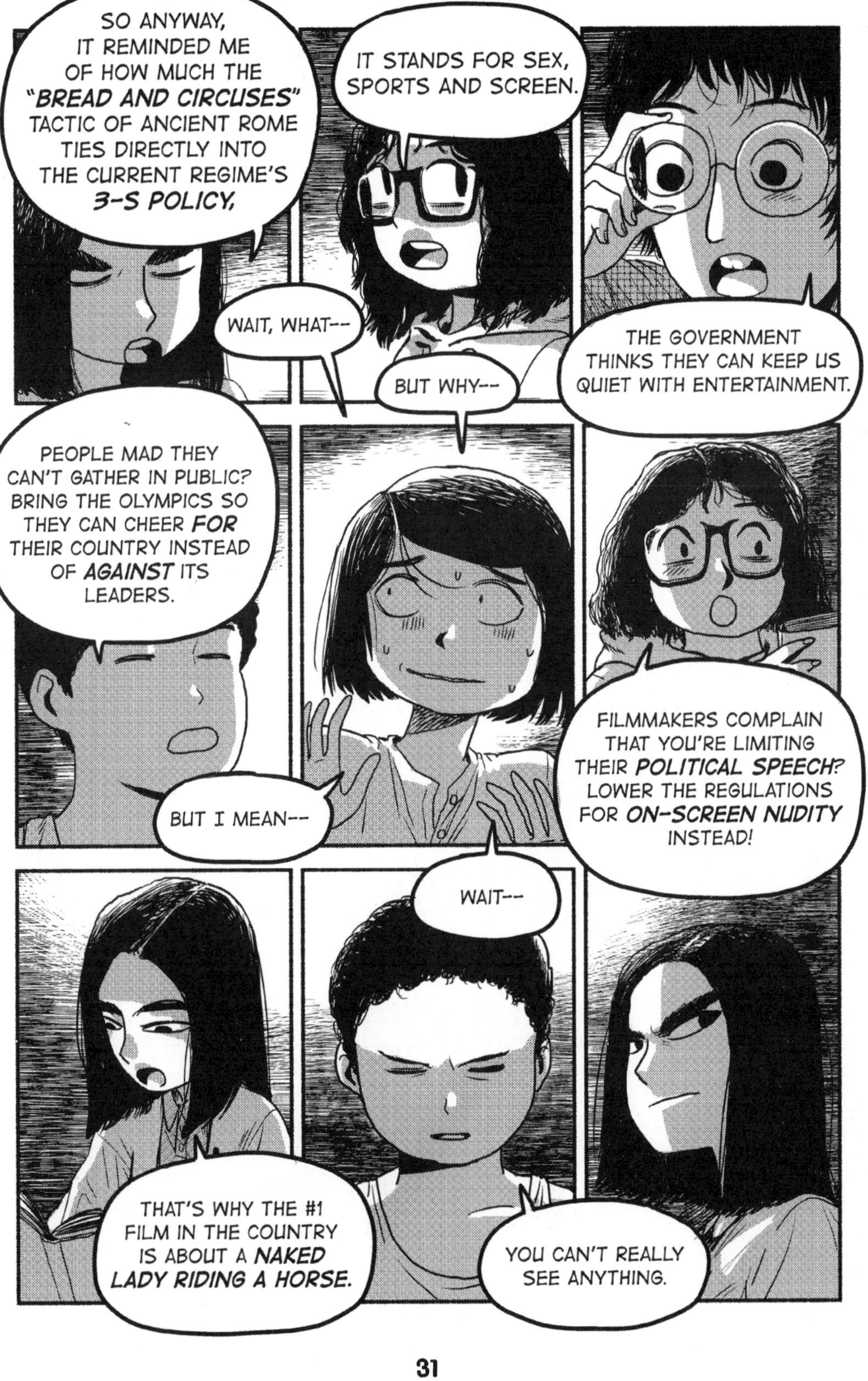
SO ANYWAY, IT REMINDED ME OF HOW MUCH THE "BREAD AND CIRCUSES" TACTIC OF ANCIENT ROME TIES DIRECTLY INTO THE CURRENT REGIME'S 3-S POLICY.
IT STANDS FOR SEX, SPORTS AND SCREEN.
WAIT, WHAT--
BUT WHY--
THE GOVERNMENT THINKS THEY CAN KEEP US QUIET WITH ENTERTAINMENT.
PEOPLE MAD THEY CAN'T GATHER IN PUBLIC? BRING THE OLYMPICS SO THEY CAN CHEER FOR THEIR COUNTRY INSTEAD OF AGAINST ITS LEADERS.
BUT I MEAN--
FILMMAKERS COMPLAIN THAT YOU'RE LIMITING THEIR POLITICAL SPEECH? LOWER THE REGULATIONS FOR ON-SCREEN NUDITY INSTEAD!
WAIT--
THAT'S WHY THE #1 FILM IN THE COUNTRY IS ABOUT A NAKED LADY RIDING A HORSE.
YOU CAN'T REALLY SEE ANYTHING.

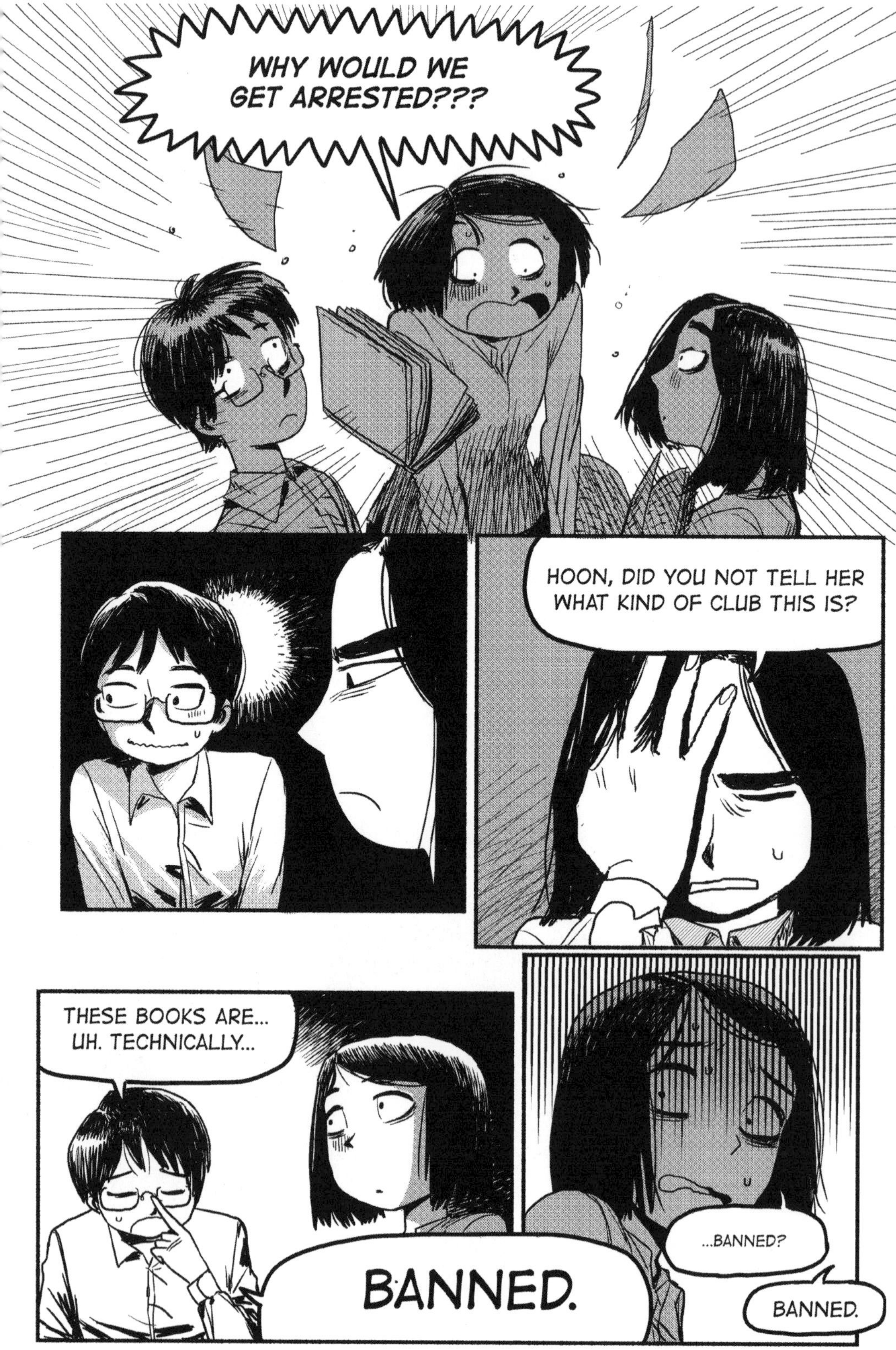
WHY WOULD WE GET ARRESTED???
HOON, DID YOU NOT TELL HER WHAT KIND OF CLUB THIS IS?
THESE BOOKS ARE... UH. TECHNICALLY...
BANNED.
...BANNED?
BANNED.

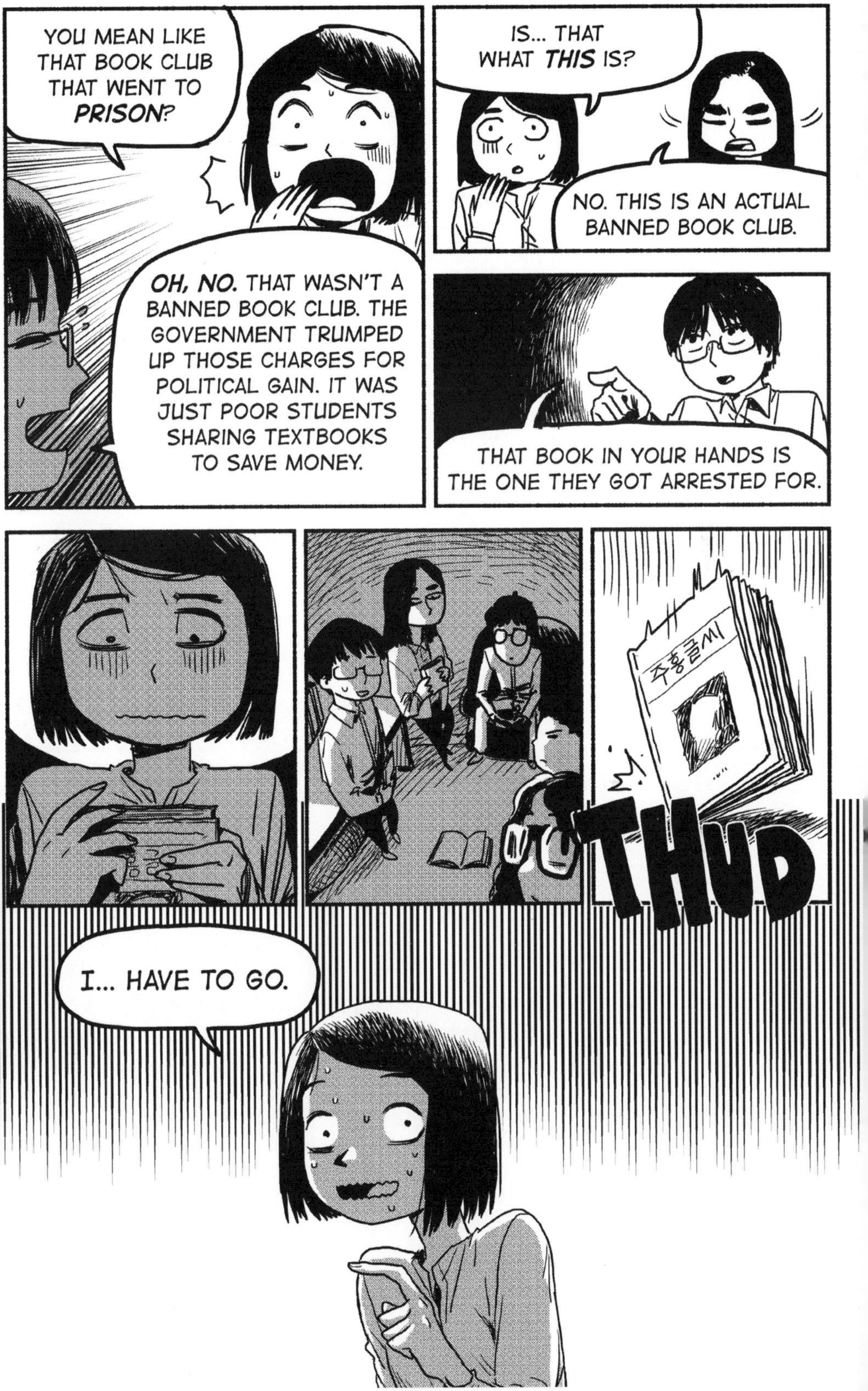
YOU MEAN LIKE THAT BOOK CLUB THAT WENT TO *PRISON*?
OH, NO. THAT WASN'T A BANNED BOOK CLUB. THE GOVERNMENT TRUMPED UP THOSE CHARGES FOR POLITICAL GAIN. IT WAS JUST POOR STUDENTS SHARING TEXTBOOKS TO SAVE MONEY.
IS... THAT WHAT *THIS* IS?
NO. THIS IS AN ACTUAL BANNED BOOK CLUB.
THAT BOOK IN YOUR HANDS IS THE ONE THEY GOT ARRESTED FOR.
주홍글씨
THUD
I... HAVE TO GO.

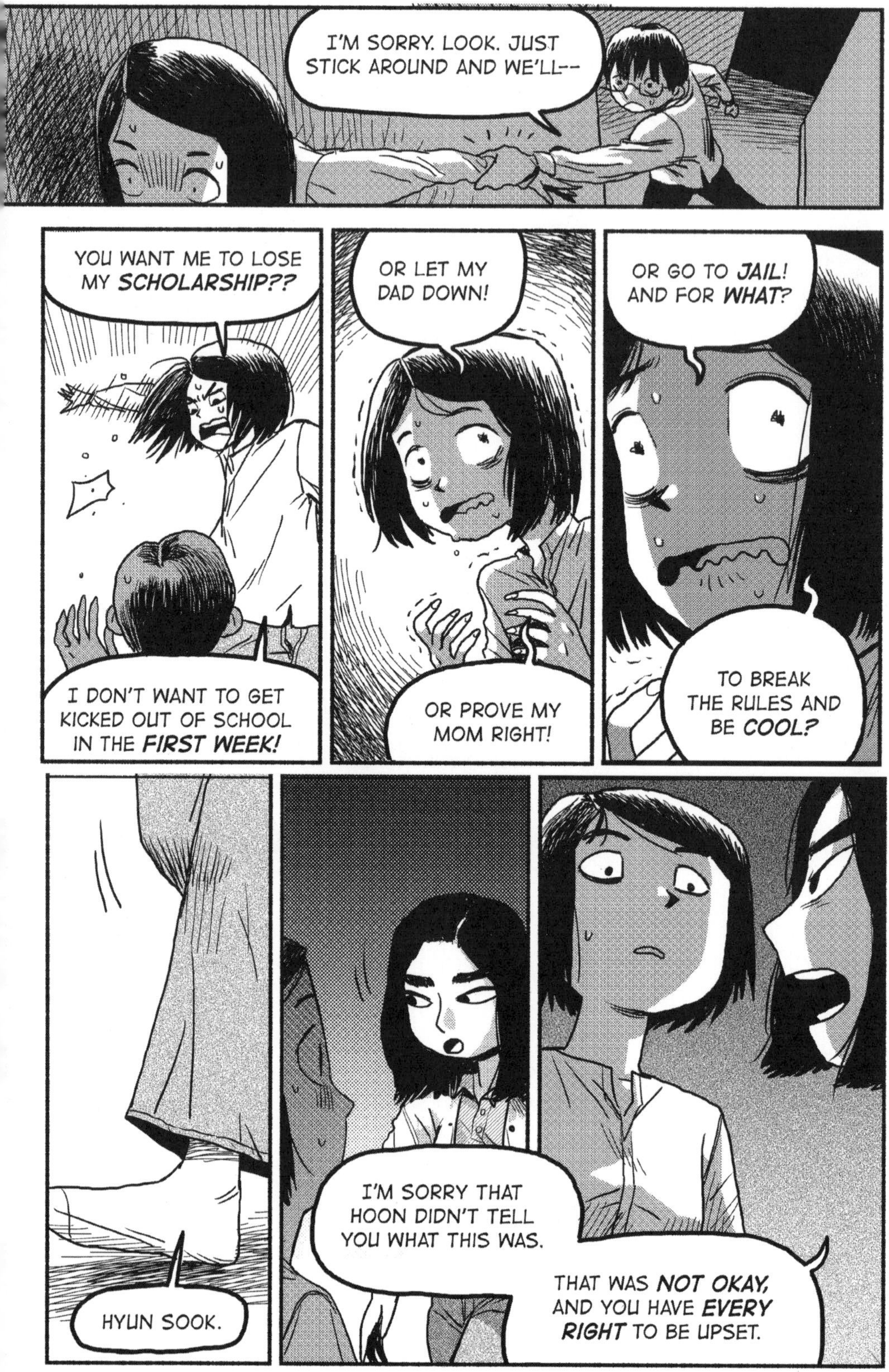
I'M SORRY. LOOK. JUST STICK AROUND AND WE'LL--
YOU WANT ME TO LOSE MY SCHOLARSHIP??
I DON'T WANT TO GET KICKED OUT OF SCHOOL IN THE FIRST WEEK!
OR LET MY DAD DOWN!
OR PROVE MY MOM RIGHT!
OR GO TO JAIL! AND FOR WHAT?
TO BREAK THE RULES AND BE COOL?
HYUN SOOK.
I'M SORRY THAT HOON DIDN'T TELL YOU WHAT THIS WAS.
THAT WAS NOT OKAY, AND YOU HAVE EVERY RIGHT TO BE UPSET.

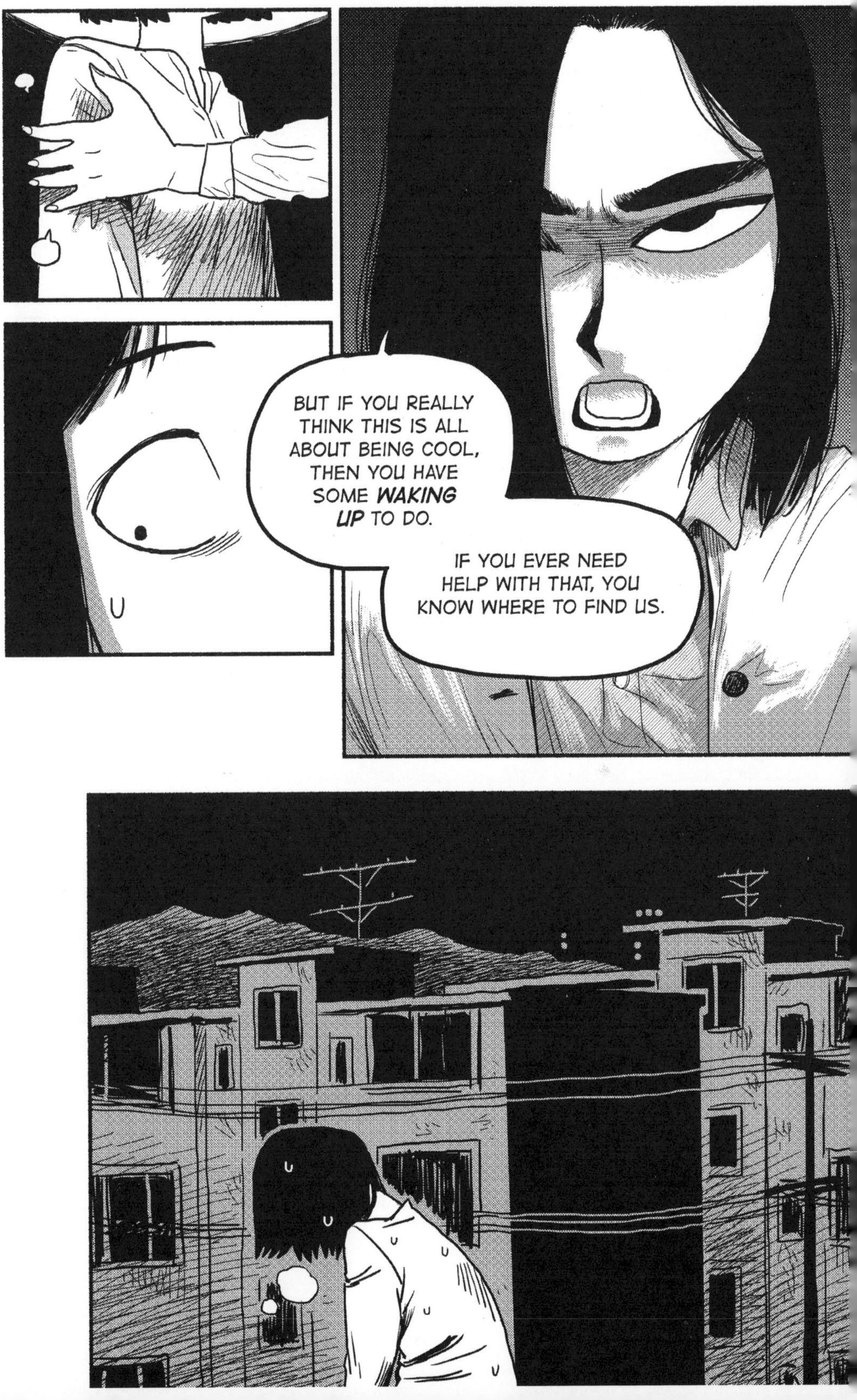
BUT IF YOU REALLY THINK THIS IS ALL ABOUT BEING COOL, THEN YOU HAVE SOME WAKING UP TO DO.
IF YOU EVER NEED HELP WITH THAT, YOU KNOW WHERE TO FIND US.

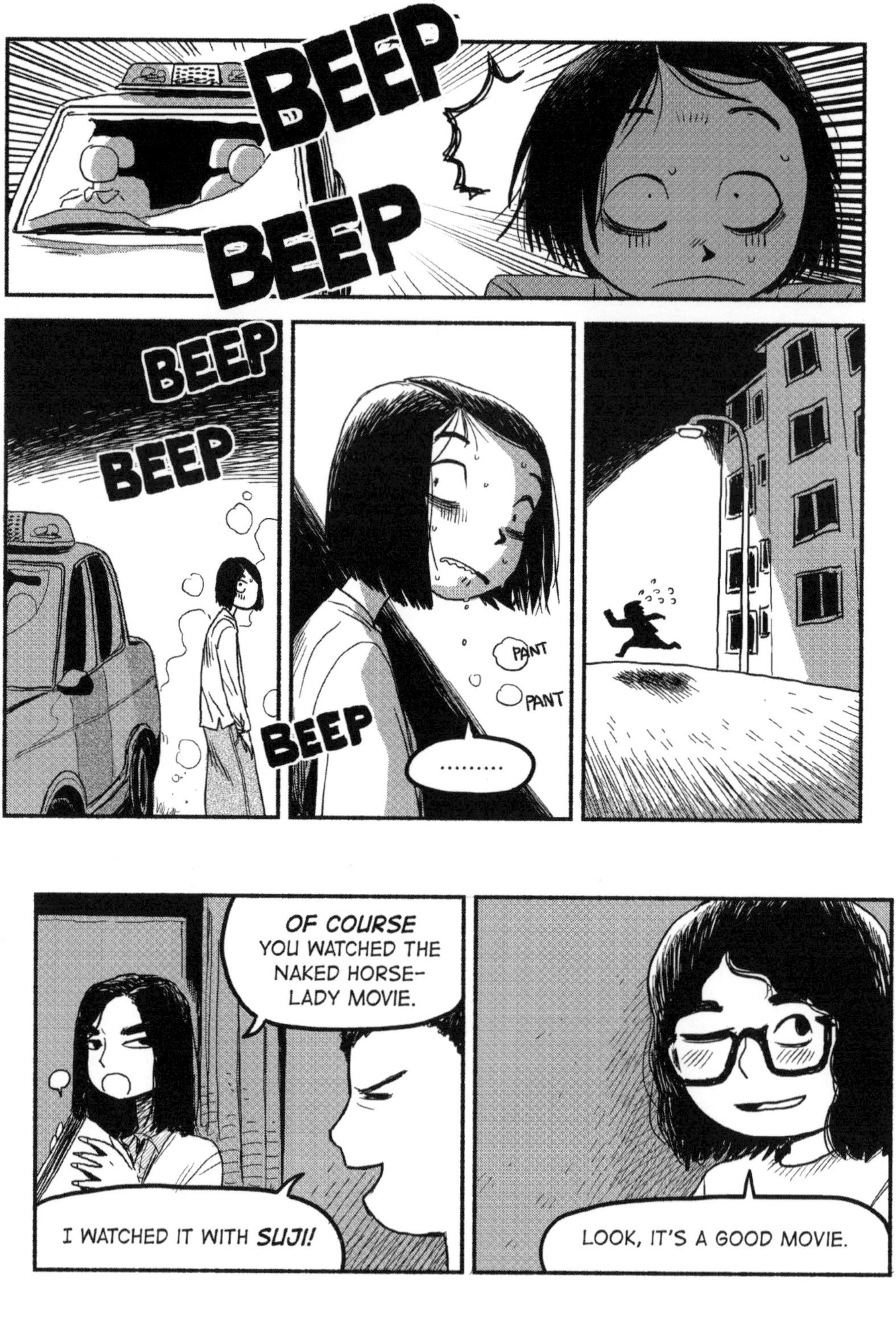
BEEP
BEEP
BEEP
BEEP
BEEP
PANT
PANT
....
OF COURSE YOU WATCHED THE NAKED HORSE-LADY MOVIE.
I WATCHED IT WITH SUJI!
LOOK, IT'S A GOOD MOVIE.

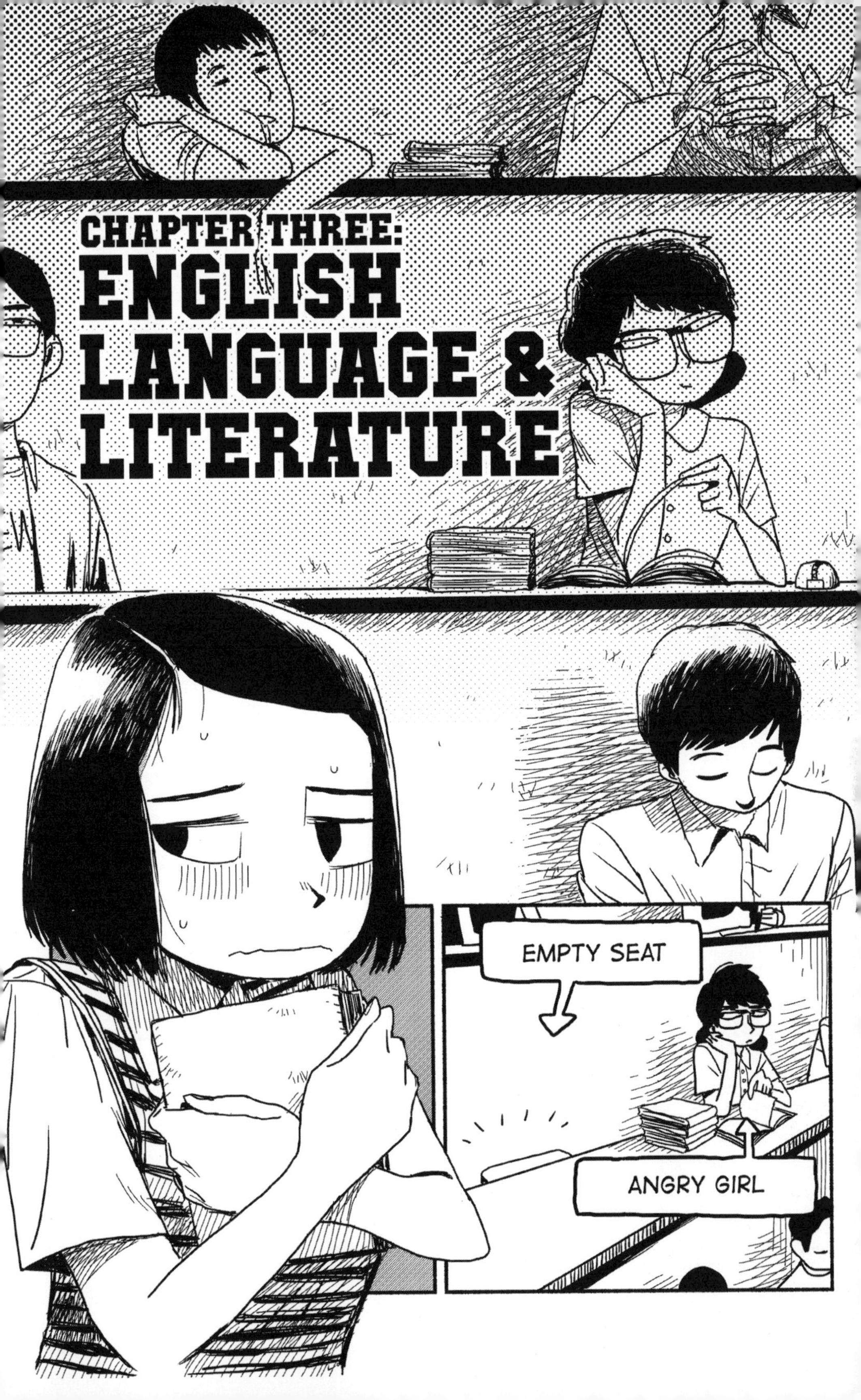
CHAPTER THREE:
ENGLISH LANGUAGE & LITERATURE
EMPTY SEAT
ANGRY GIRL

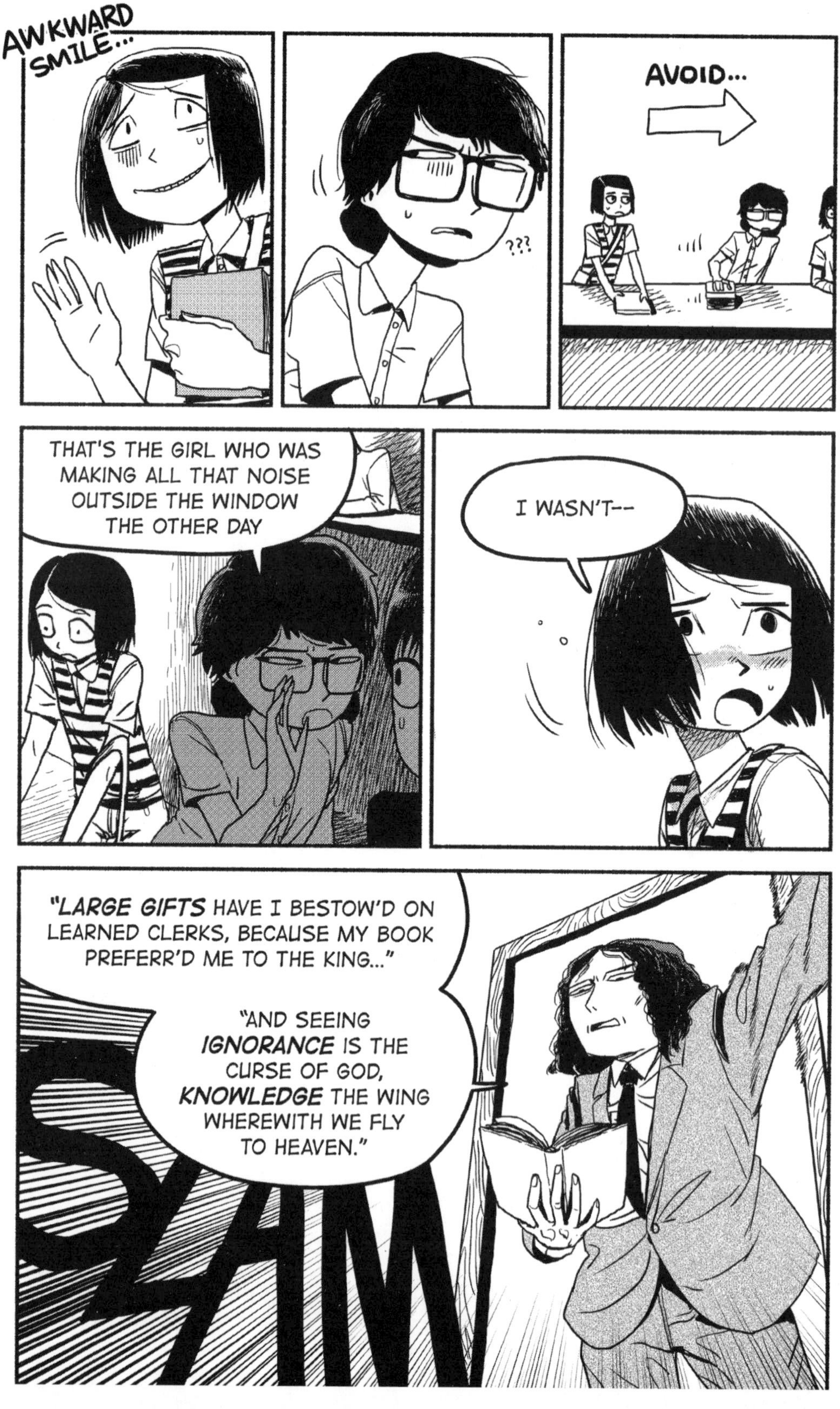
AWKWARD SMILE...
???
AVOID...
THAT'S THE GIRL WHO WAS MAKING ALL THAT NOISE OUTSIDE THE WINDOW THE OTHER DAY
I WASN'T--
"LARGE GIFTS HAVE I BESTOW'D ON LEARNED CLERKS, BECAUSE MY BOOK PREFERR'D ME TO THE KING..."
"AND SEEING IGNORANCE IS THE CURSE OF GOD, KNOWLEDGE THE WING WHEREWITH WE FLY TO HEAVEN."
SLAM

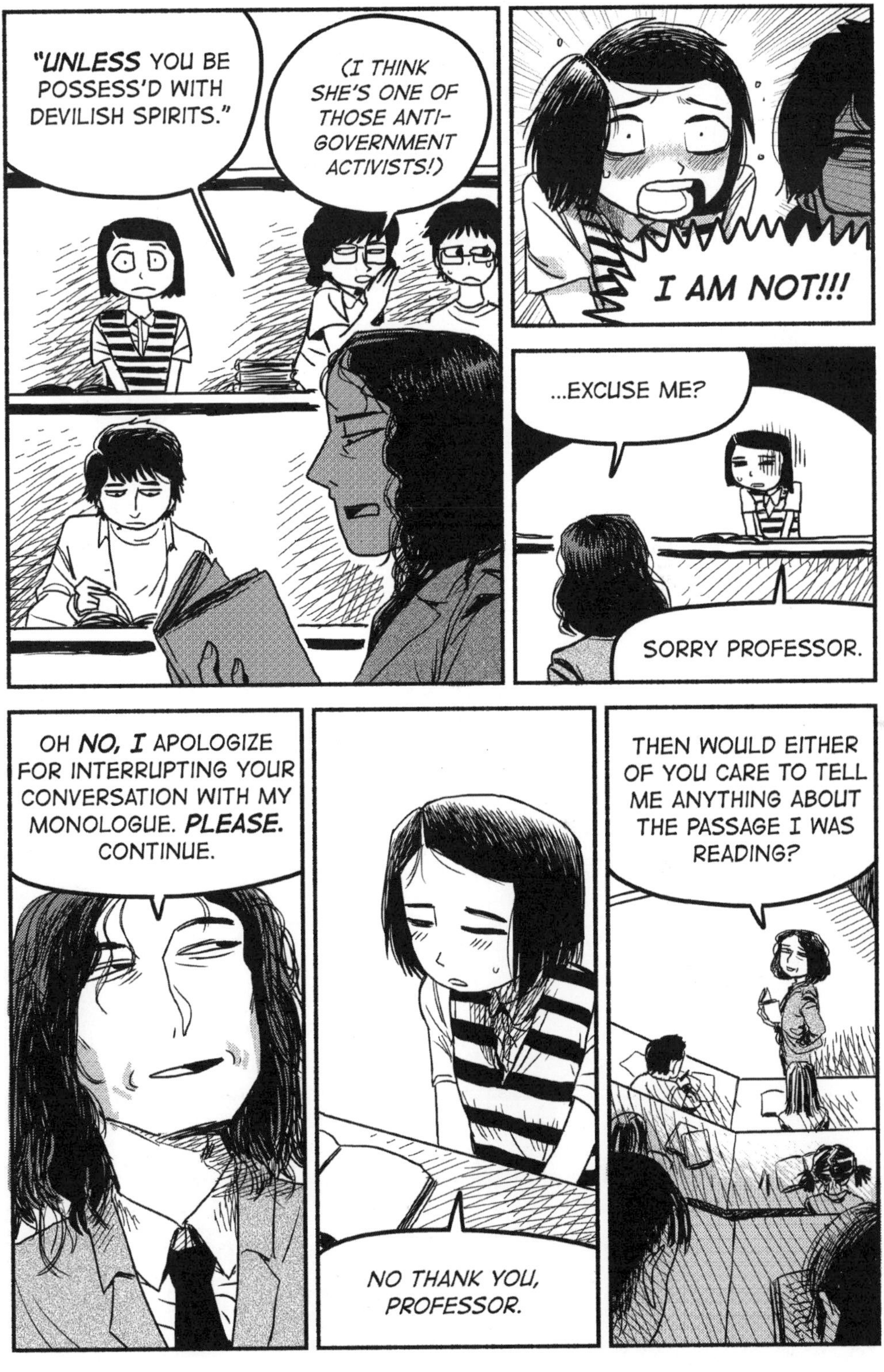
"UNLESS YOU BE POSSESS'D WITH DEVILISH SPIRITS."
(I THINK SHE'S ONE OF THOSE ANTI-GOVERNMENT ACTIVISTS!)
I AM NOT!!!
...EXCUSE ME?
SORRY PROFESSOR.
OH NO, I APOLOGIZE FOR INTERRUPTING YOUR CONVERSATION WITH MY MONOLOGUE. PLEASE. CONTINUE.
NO THANK YOU, PROFESSOR.
THEN WOULD EITHER OF YOU CARE TO TELL ME ANYTHING ABOUT THE PASSAGE I WAS READING?

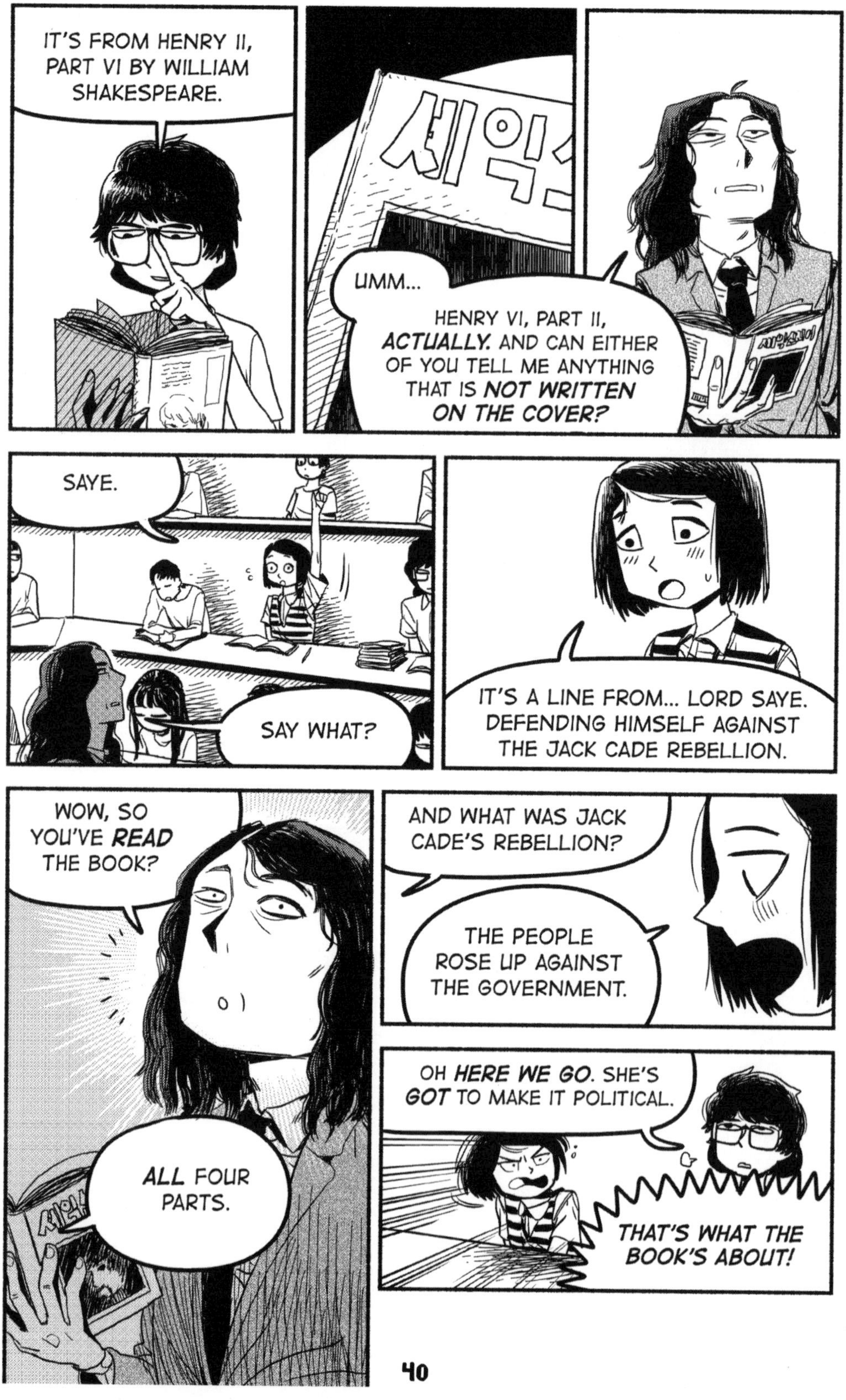
IT'S FROM HENRY II, PART VI BY WILLIAM SHAKESPEARE.
UMM...
HENRY VI, PART II, ACTUALLY. AND CAN EITHER OF YOU TELL ME ANYTHING THAT IS NOT WRITTEN ON THE COVER?
SAYE.
SAY WHAT?
IT'S A LINE FROM... LORD SAYE. DEFENDING HIMSELF AGAINST THE JACK CADE REBELLION.
WOW, SO YOU'VE READ THE BOOK?
ALL FOUR PARTS.
AND WHAT WAS JACK CADE'S REBELLION?
THE PEOPLE ROSE UP AGAINST THE GOVERNMENT.
OH HERE WE GO. SHE'S GOT TO MAKE IT POLITICAL.
THAT'S WHAT THE BOOK'S ABOUT!

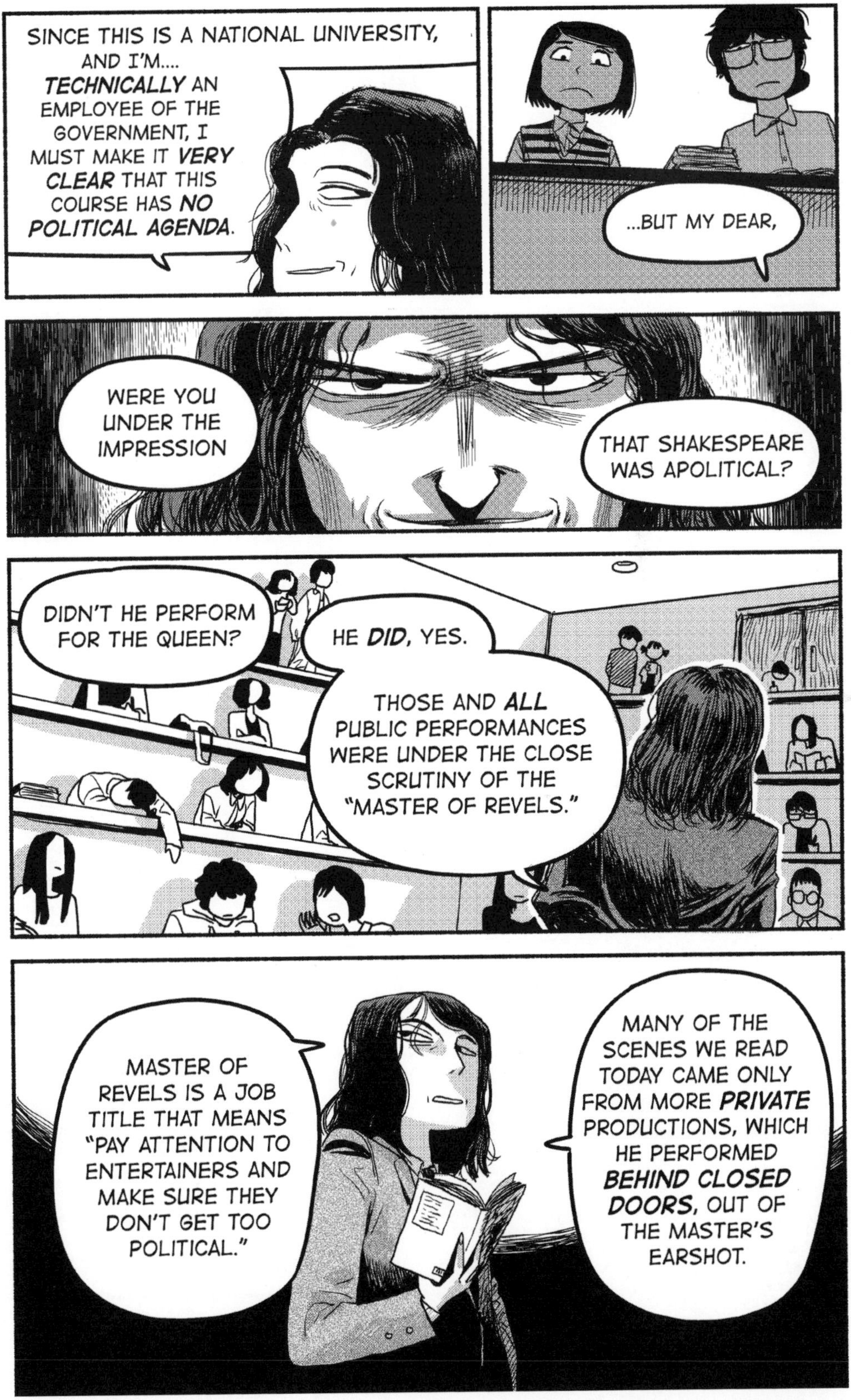
SINCE THIS IS A NATIONAL UNIVERSITY, AND I'M.... TECHNICALLY AN EMPLOYEE OF THE GOVERNMENT, I MUST MAKE IT VERY CLEAR THAT THIS COURSE HAS NO POLITICAL AGENDA.
...BUT MY DEAR,
WERE YOU UNDER THE IMPRESSION
THAT SHAKESPEARE WAS APOLITICAL?
DIDN'T HE PERFORM FOR THE QUEEN?
HE DID, YES.
THOSE AND ALL PUBLIC PERFORMANCES WERE UNDER THE CLOSE SCRUTINY OF THE "MASTER OF REVELS."
MASTER OF REVELS IS A JOB TITLE THAT MEANS "PAY ATTENTION TO ENTERTAINERS AND MAKE SURE THEY DON'T GET TOO POLITICAL."
MANY OF THE SCENES WE READ TODAY CAME ONLY FROM MORE PRIVATE PRODUCTIONS, WHICH HE PERFORMED BEHIND CLOSED DOORS, OUT OF THE MASTER'S EARSHOT.

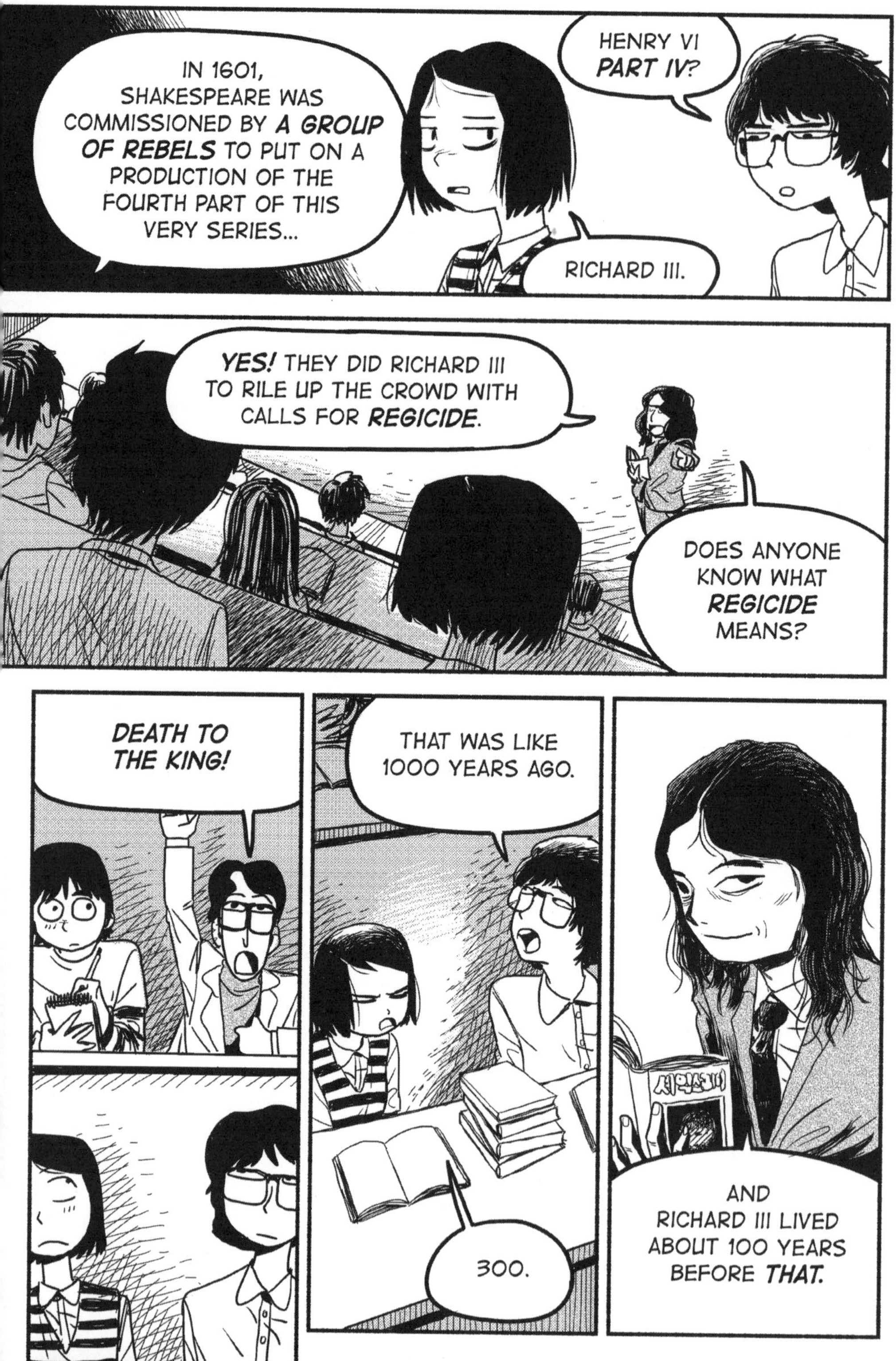
IN 1601, SHAKESPEARE WAS COMMISSIONED BY A GROUP OF REBELS TO PUT ON A PRODUCTION OF THE FOURTH PART OF THIS VERY SERIES...
HENRY VI PART IV?
RICHARD III.
YES! THEY DID RICHARD III TO RILE UP THE CROWD WITH CALLS FOR REGICIDE.
DOES ANYONE KNOW WHAT REGICIDE MEANS?
DEATH TO THE KING!
THAT WAS LIKE 1000 YEARS AGO.
300.
AND RICHARD III LIVED ABOUT 100 YEARS BEFORE THAT.

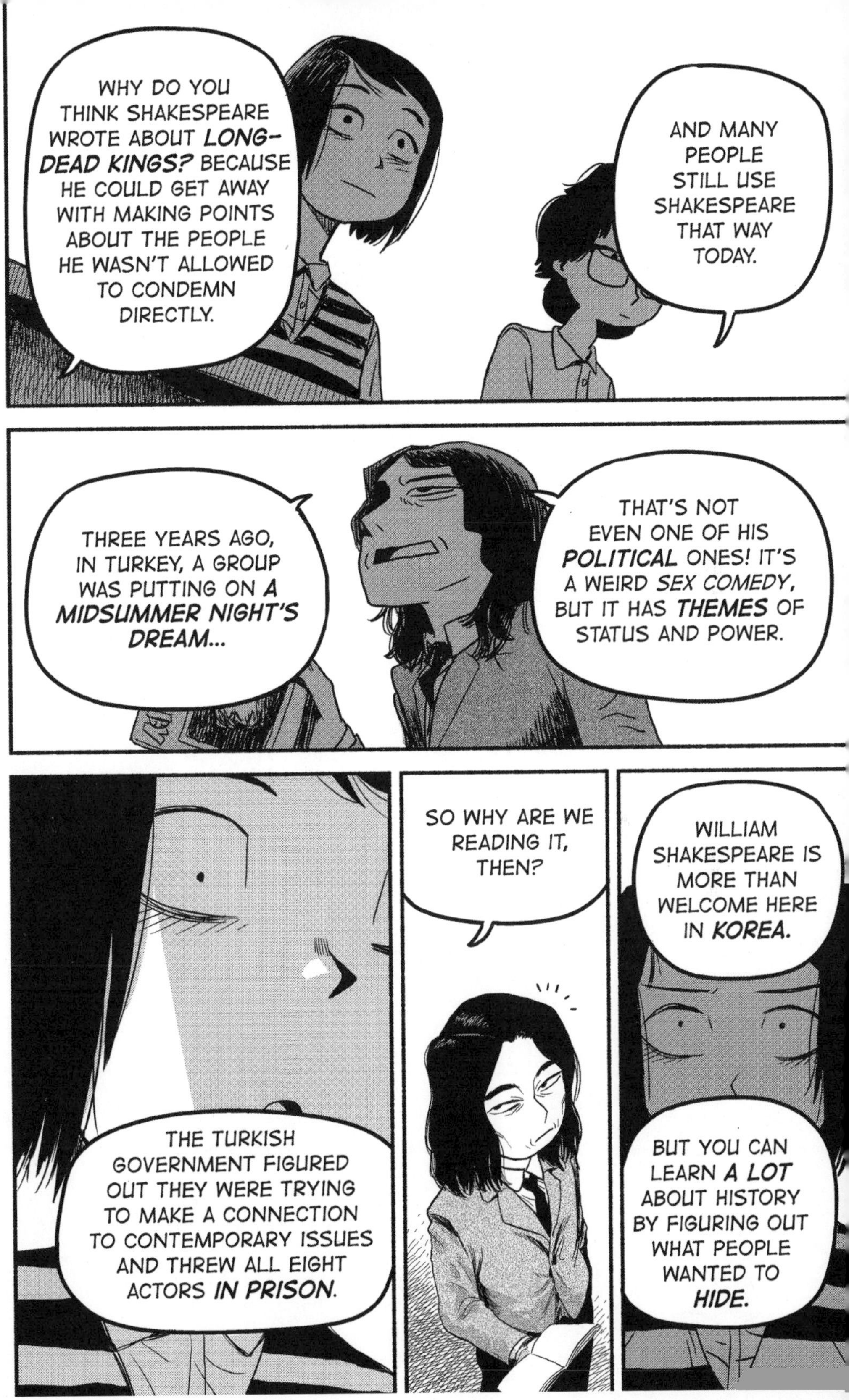
WHY DO YOU THINK SHAKESPEARE WROTE ABOUT LONG-DEAD KINGS? BECAUSE HE COULD GET AWAY WITH MAKING POINTS ABOUT THE PEOPLE HE WASN'T ALLOWED TO CONDEMN DIRECTLY.
AND MANY PEOPLE STILL USE SHAKESPEARE THAT WAY TODAY.
THREE YEARS AGO, IN TURKEY, A GROUP WAS PUTTING ON A MIDSUMMER NIGHT'S DREAM...
THAT'S NOT EVEN ONE OF HIS POLITICAL ONES! IT'S A WEIRD SEX COMEDY, BUT IT HAS THEMES OF STATUS AND POWER.
THE TURKISH GOVERNMENT FIGURED OUT THEY WERE TRYING TO MAKE A CONNECTION TO CONTEMPORARY ISSUES AND THREW ALL EIGHT ACTORS IN PRISON.
SO WHY ARE WE READING IT, THEN?
WILLIAM SHAKESPEARE IS MORE THAN WELCOME HERE IN KOREA.
BUT YOU CAN LEARN A LOT ABOUT HISTORY BY FIGURING OUT WHAT PEOPLE WANTED TO HIDE.

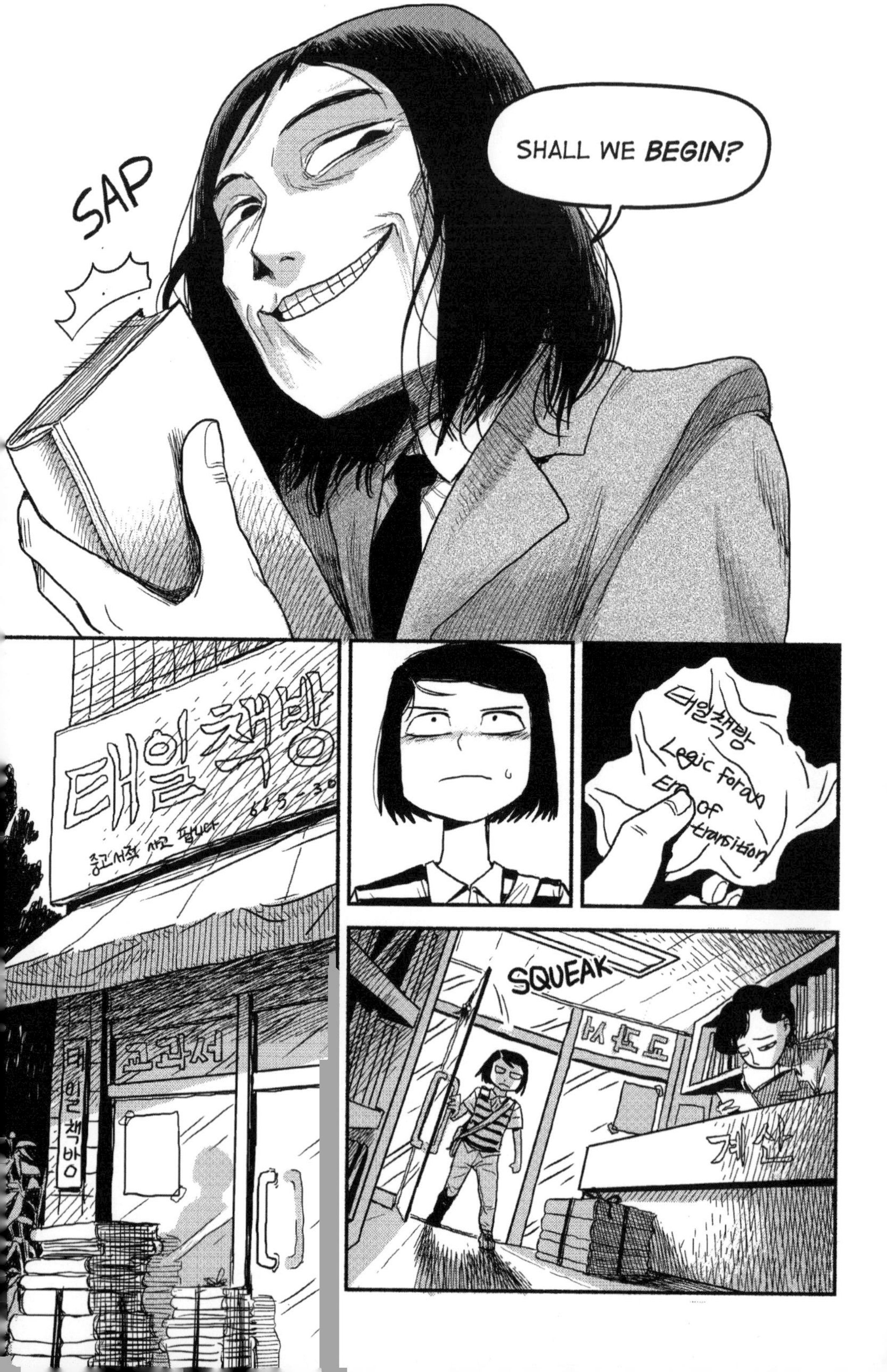
SAP
SHALL WE **BEGIN?**
태일책방
중고서적 사고 팝니다
교과서
태일책방
태일책방
Logic for an
of transition
SQUEAK
계산

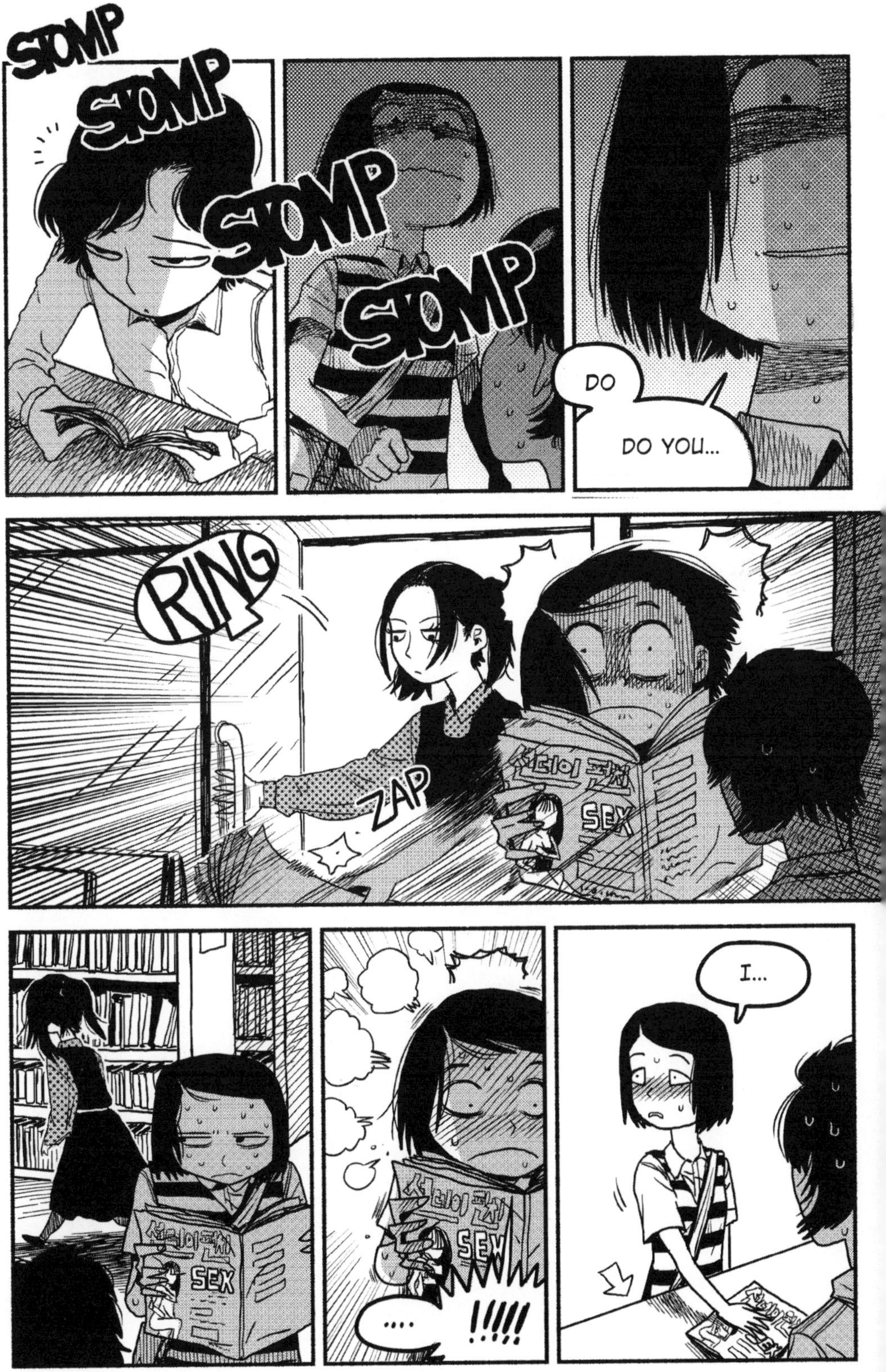
STOMP
STOMP
STOMP
STOMP
DO
DO YOU...
RING
ZAP
SEX
....
!!!!!
I...

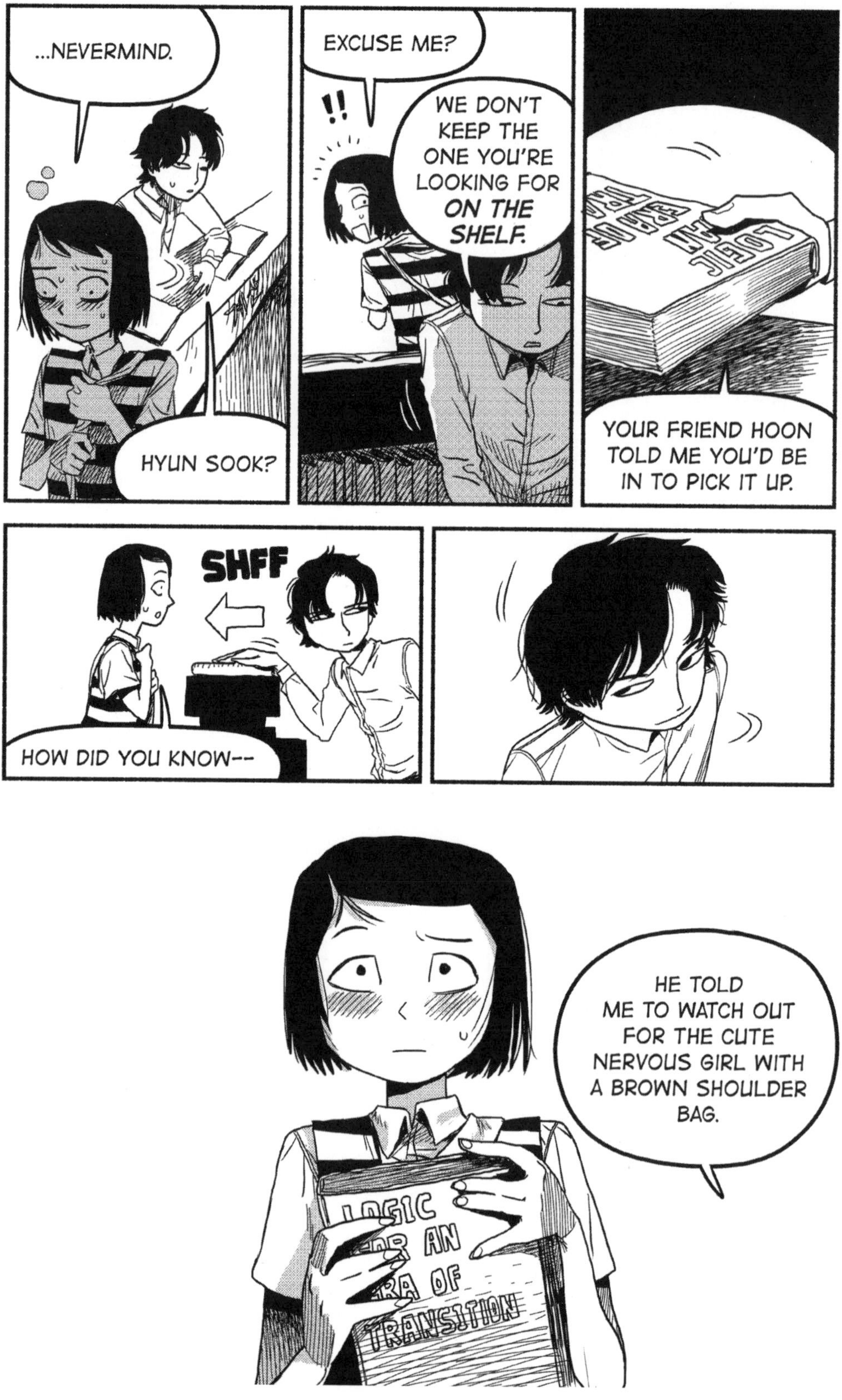
...NEVERMIND.
HYUN SOOK?
EXCUSE ME?
!!
WE DON'T KEEP THE ONE YOU'RE LOOKING FOR ON THE SHELF.
LOGIC FOR AN ERA OF TRANSITION
YOUR FRIEND HOON TOLD ME YOU'D BE IN TO PICK IT UP.
SHFF
HOW DID YOU KNOW--
HE TOLD ME TO WATCH OUT FOR THE CUTE NERVOUS GIRL WITH A BROWN SHOULDER BAG.
LOGIC FOR AN ERA OF TRANSITION

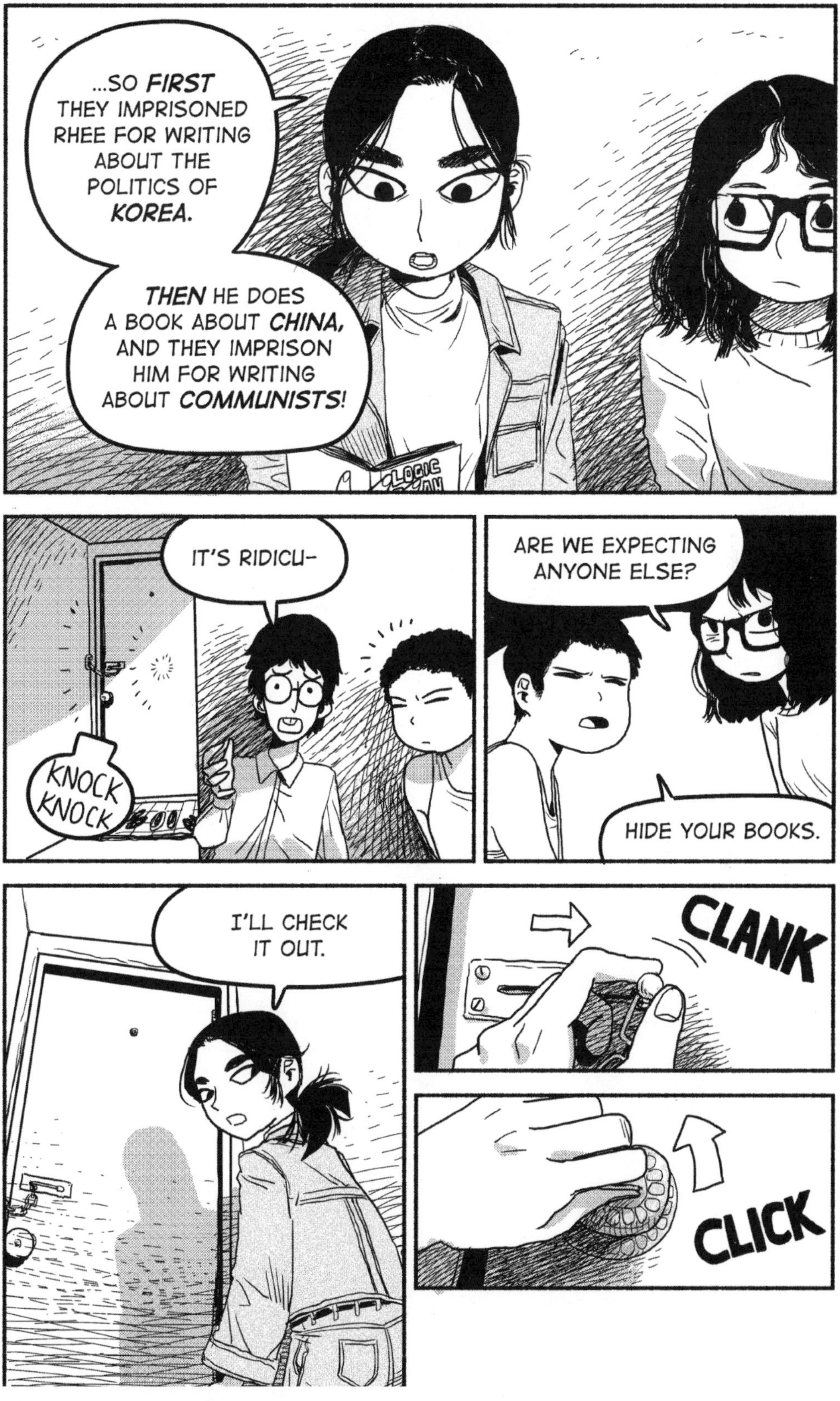
...SO FIRST THEY IMPRISONED RHEE FOR WRITING ABOUT THE POLITICS OF KOREA.
THEN HE DOES A BOOK ABOUT CHINA, AND THEY IMPRISON HIM FOR WRITING ABOUT COMMUNISTS!
LOGIC
IT'S RIDICU-
KNOCK KNOCK
ARE WE EXPECTING ANYONE ELSE?
HIDE YOUR BOOKS.
I'LL CHECK IT OUT.
CLANK
CLICK

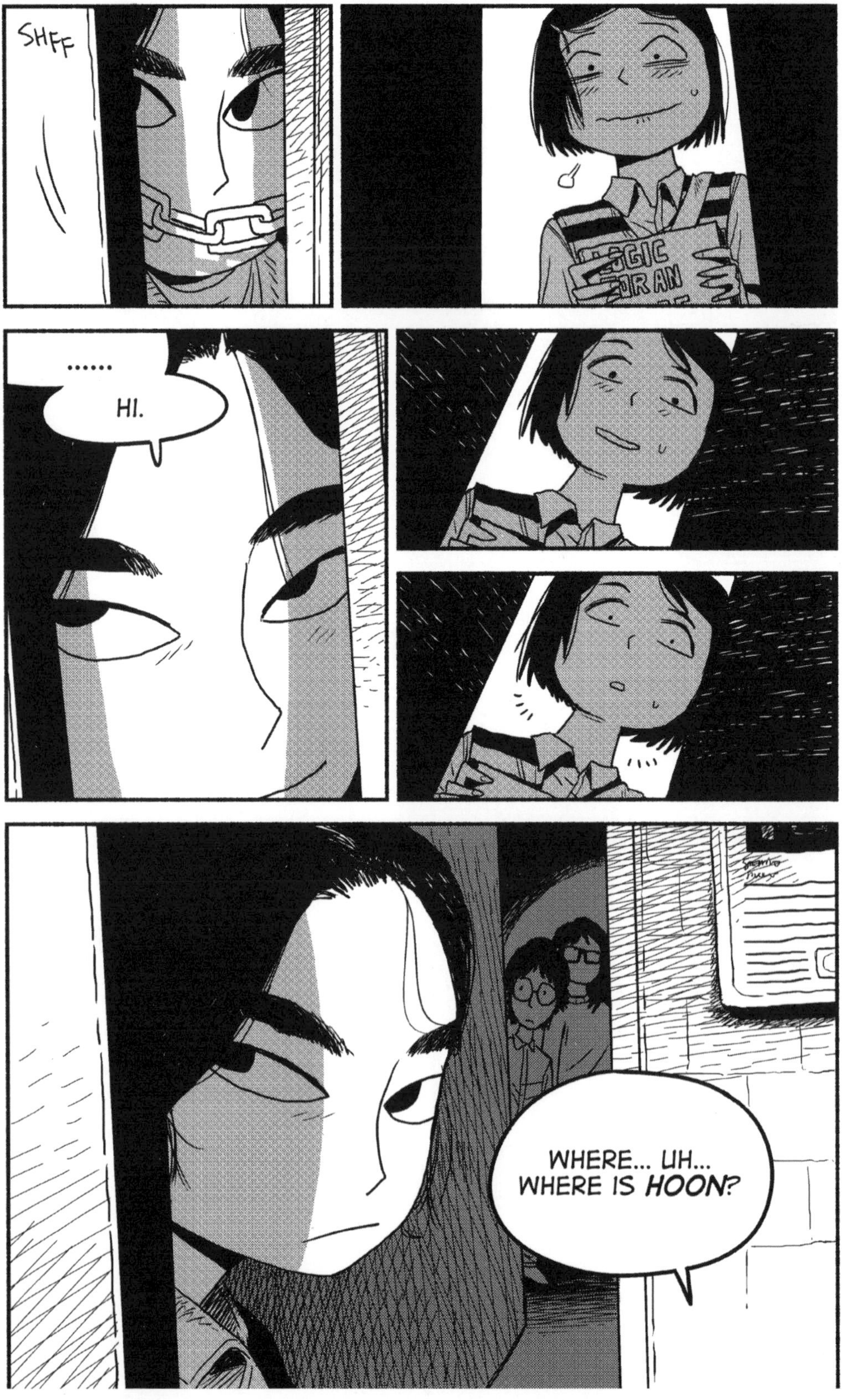
SHFF
......
HI.
WHERE... UH...
WHERE IS HOON?

CHAPTER FOUR: FILM STUDIES

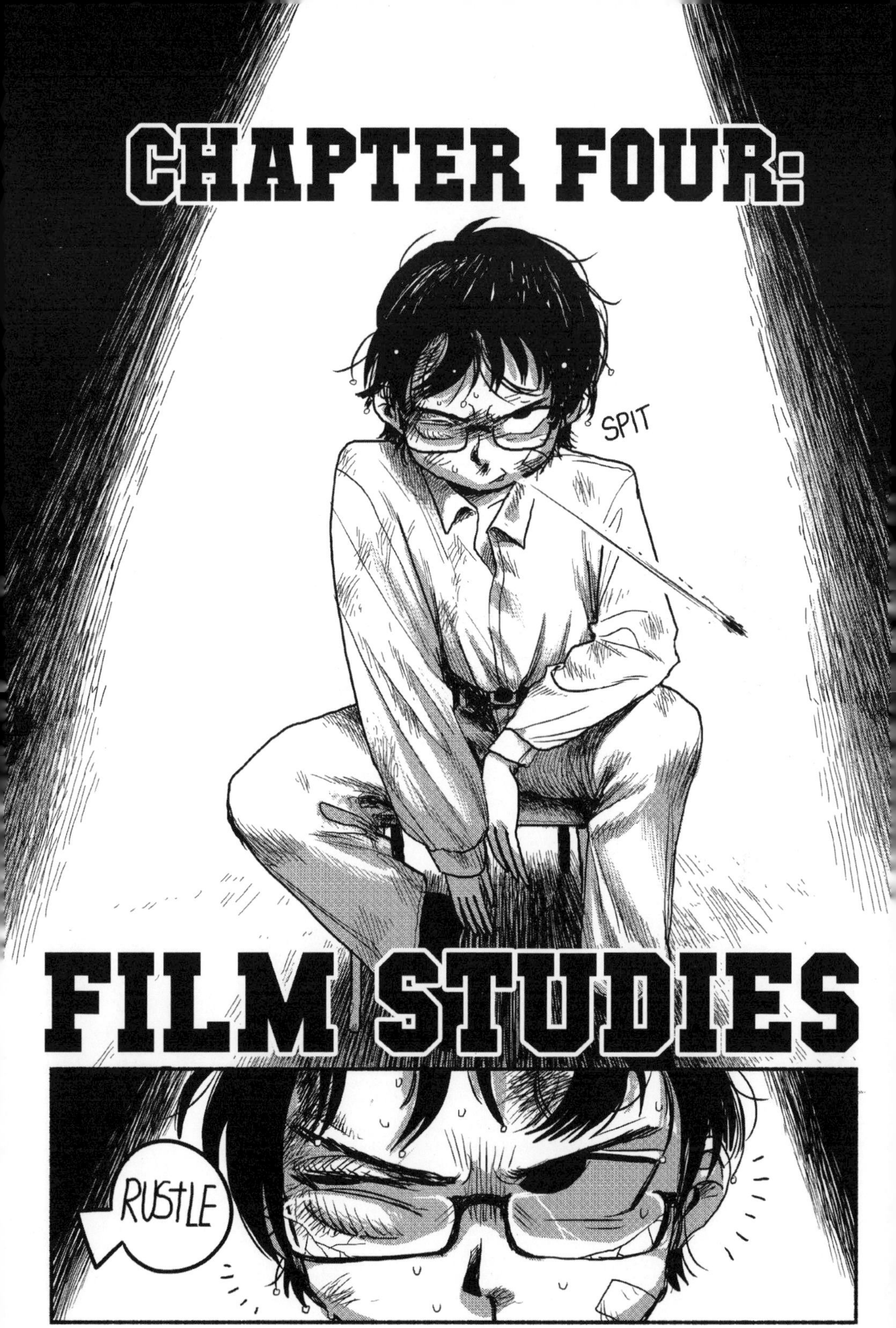
SPIT
RUSTLE

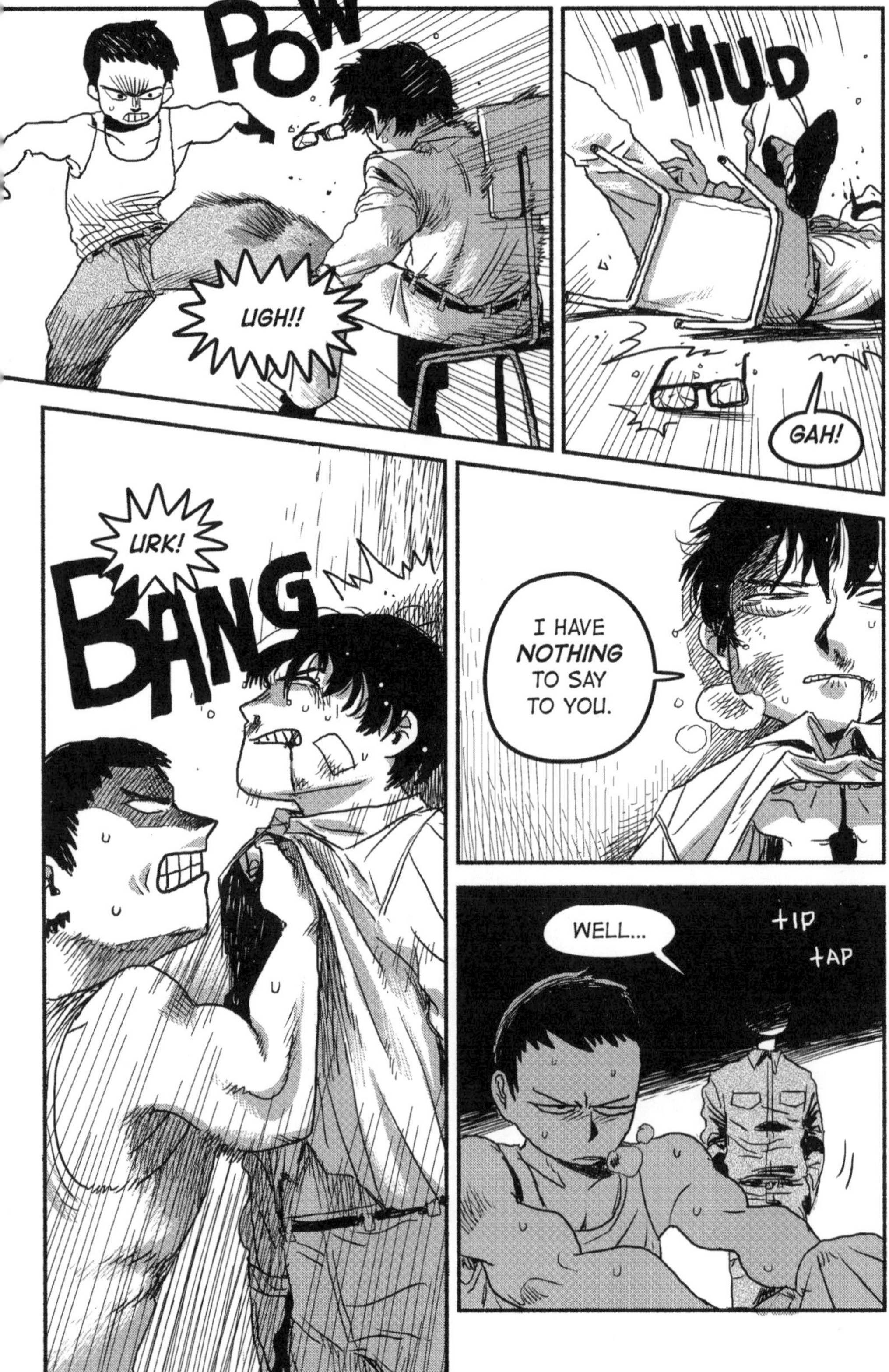
POW
UGH!!
THUD
GAH!
URK!
BANG
I HAVE NOTHING TO SAY TO YOU.
WELL...
tip
tap

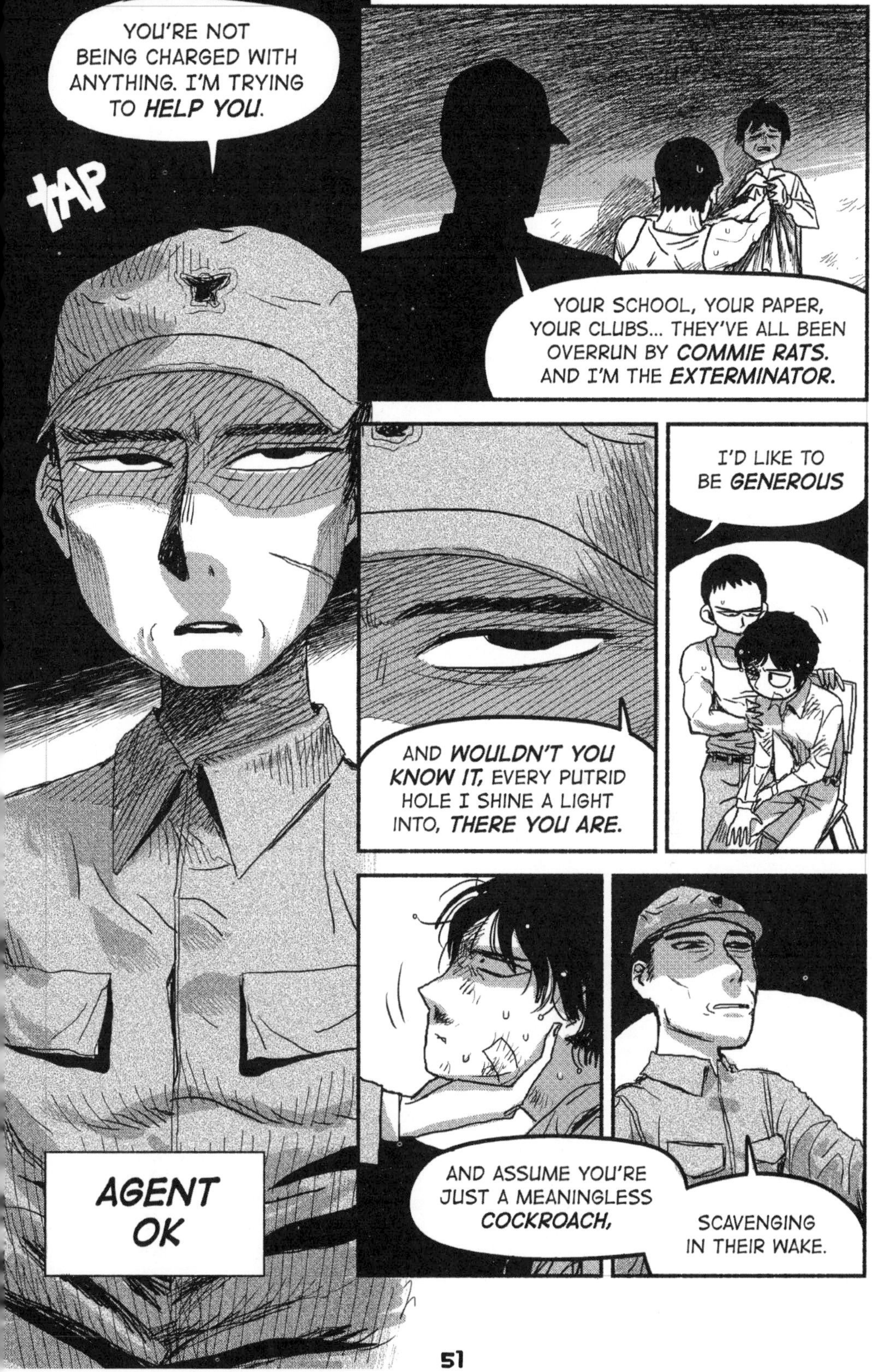
YOU'RE NOT BEING CHARGED WITH ANYTHING. I'M TRYING TO HELP YOU.
TAP
YOUR SCHOOL, YOUR PAPER, YOUR CLUBS... THEY'VE ALL BEEN OVERRUN BY COMMIE RATS. AND I'M THE EXTERMINATOR.
AGENT OK
AND WOULDN'T YOU KNOW IT, EVERY PUTRID HOLE I SHINE A LIGHT INTO, THERE YOU ARE.
I'D LIKE TO BE GENEROUS
AND ASSUME YOU'RE JUST A MEANINGLESS COCKROACH,
SCAVENGING IN THEIR WAKE.

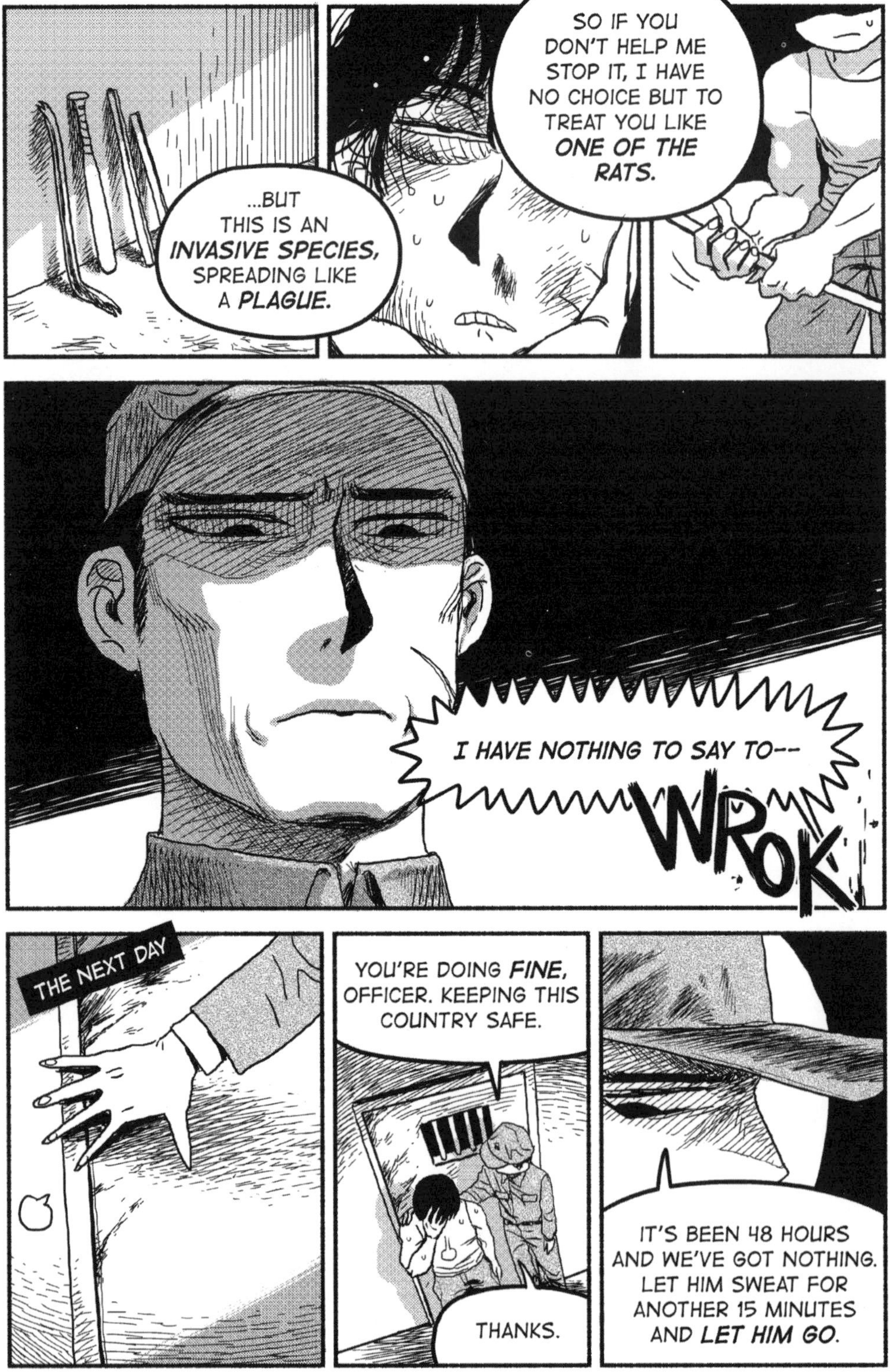
...BUT THIS IS AN INVASIVE SPECIES, SPREADING LIKE A PLAGUE.
SO IF YOU DON'T HELP ME STOP IT, I HAVE NO CHOICE BUT TO TREAT YOU LIKE ONE OF THE RATS.
I HAVE NOTHING TO SAY TO--
WROK
THE NEXT DAY
YOU'RE DOING FINE, OFFICER. KEEPING THIS COUNTRY SAFE.
THANKS.
IT'S BEEN 48 HOURS AND WE'VE GOT NOTHING. LET HIM SWEAT FOR ANOTHER 15 MINUTES AND LET HIM GO.

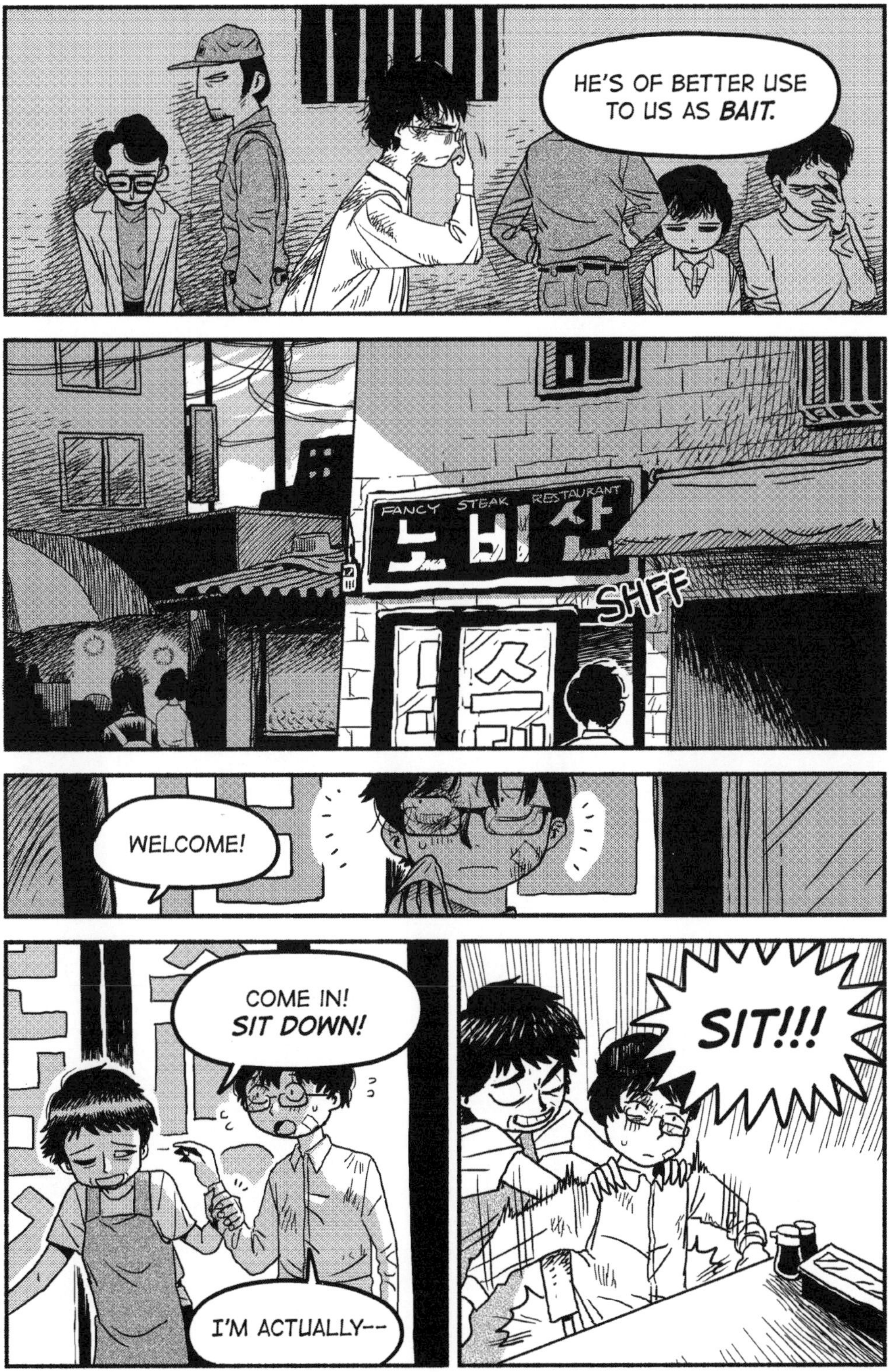
HE'S OF BETTER USE TO US AS BAIT.
FANCY STEAK RESTAURANT
SHFF
WELCOME!
COME IN! SIT DOWN!
I'M ACTUALLY--
SIT!!!

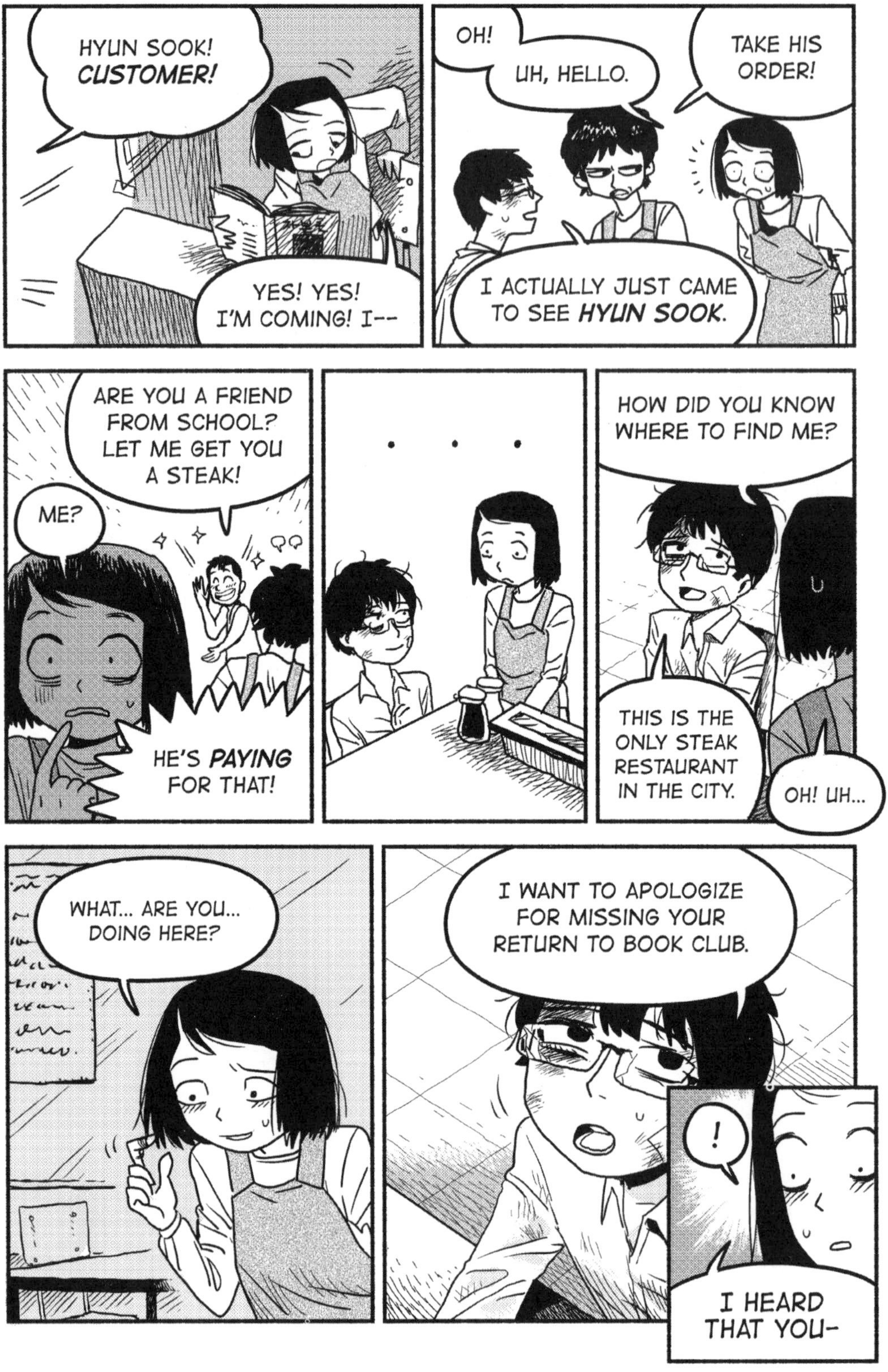
HYUN SOOK! **CUSTOMER!**
YES! YES! I'M COMING! I--
OH!
UH, HELLO.
TAKE HIS ORDER!
I ACTUALLY JUST CAME TO SEE **HYUN SOOK**.
ARE YOU A FRIEND FROM SCHOOL? LET ME GET YOU A STEAK!
ME?
HE'S **PAYING** FOR THAT!
. . .
HOW DID YOU KNOW WHERE TO FIND ME?
THIS IS THE ONLY STEAK RESTAURANT IN THE CITY.
OH! UH...
WHAT... ARE YOU... DOING HERE?
I WANT TO APOLOGIZE FOR MISSING YOUR RETURN TO BOOK CLUB.
!
I HEARD THAT YOU-

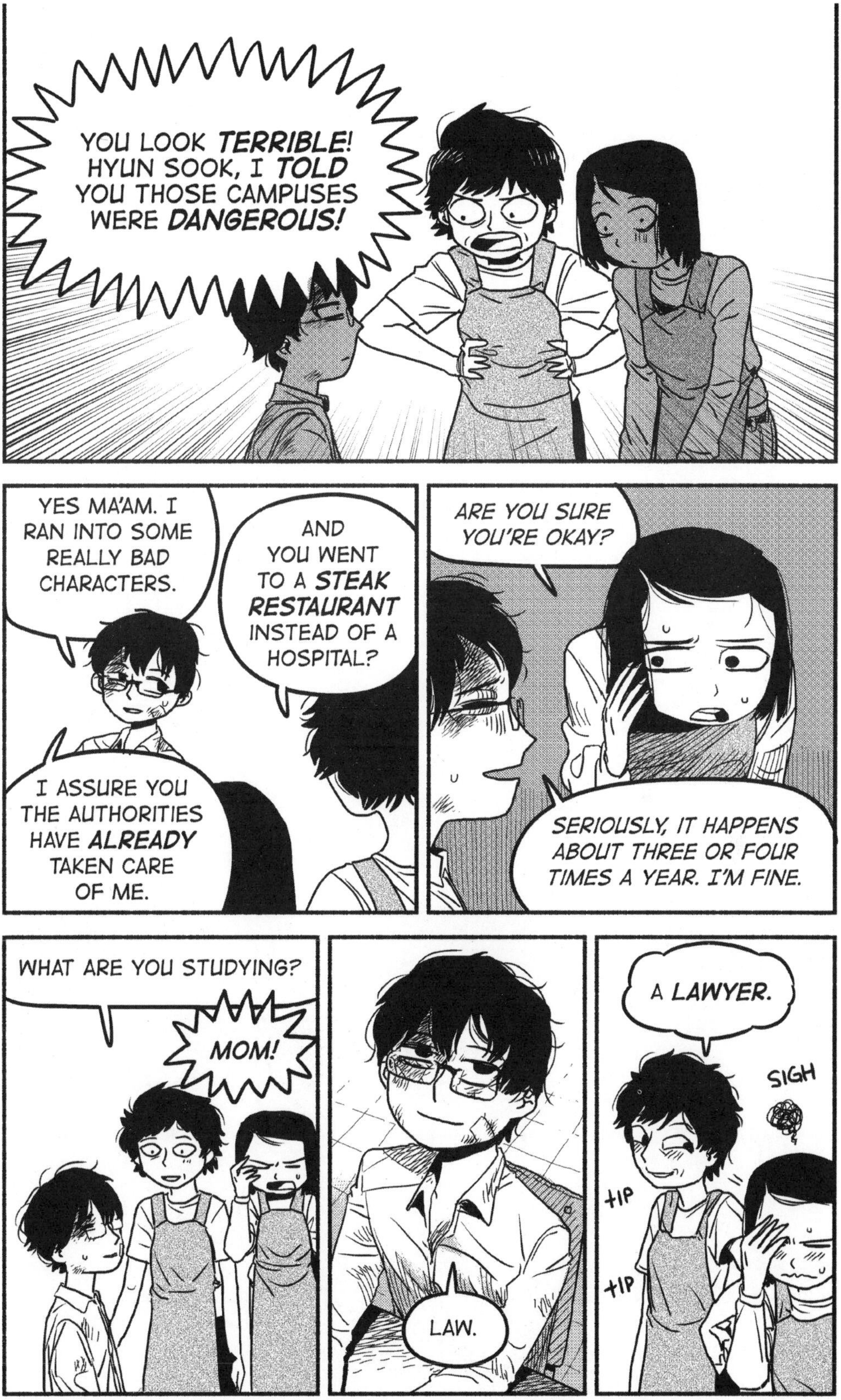
YOU LOOK TERRIBLE! HYUN SOOK, I TOLD YOU THOSE CAMPUSES WERE DANGEROUS!
YES MA'AM. I RAN INTO SOME REALLY BAD CHARACTERS.
AND YOU WENT TO A STEAK RESTAURANT INSTEAD OF A HOSPITAL?
I ASSURE YOU THE AUTHORITIES HAVE ALREADY TAKEN CARE OF ME.
ARE YOU SURE YOU'RE OKAY?
SERIOUSLY, IT HAPPENS ABOUT THREE OR FOUR TIMES A YEAR. I'M FINE.
WHAT ARE YOU STUDYING?
MOM!
LAW.
A LAWYER.
SIGH
TIP
TIP

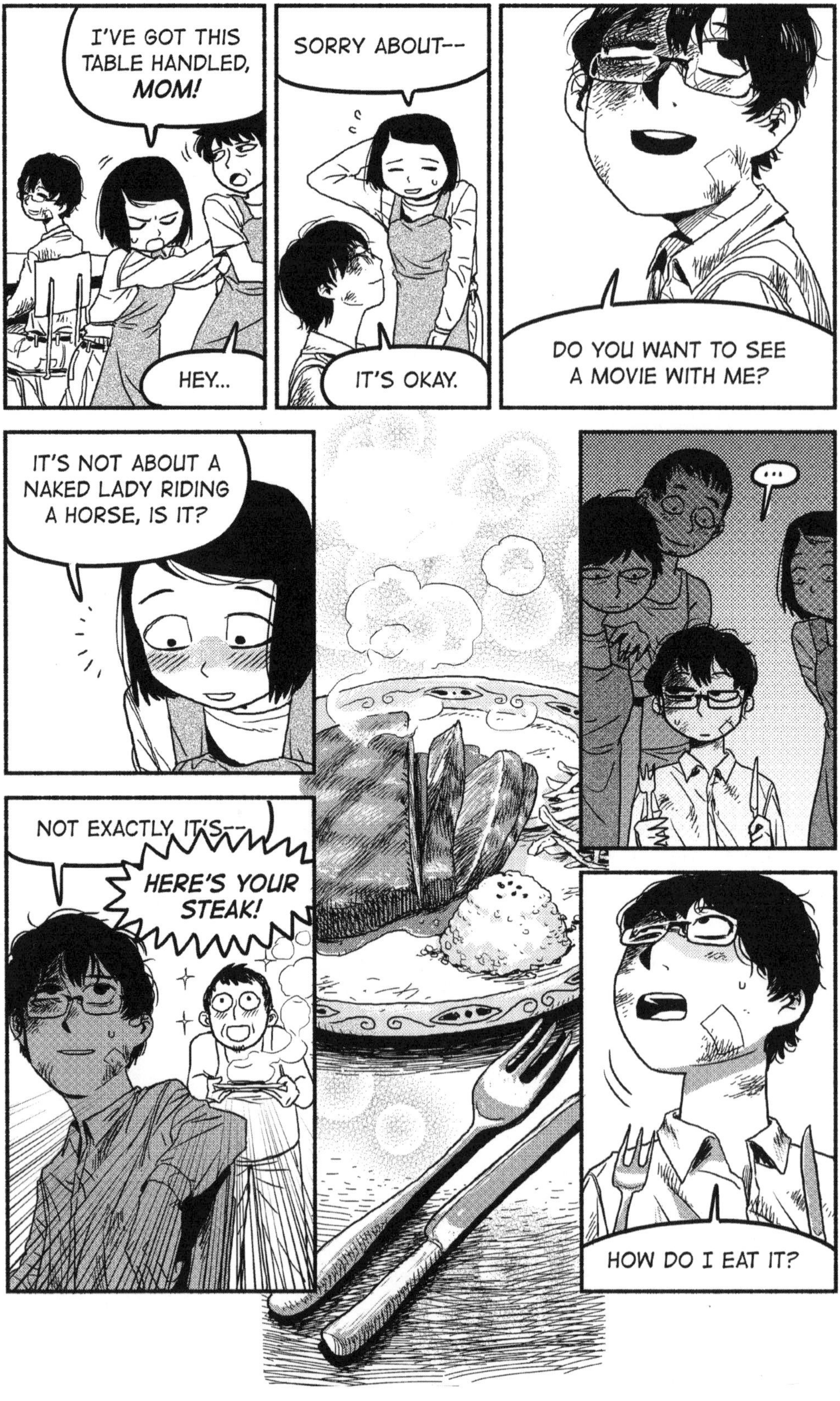
I'VE GOT THIS TABLE HANDLED, MOM!
HEY...
SORRY ABOUT--
IT'S OKAY.
DO YOU WANT TO SEE A MOVIE WITH ME?
IT'S NOT ABOUT A NAKED LADY RIDING A HORSE, IS IT?
NOT EXACTLY. IT'S--
HERE'S YOUR STEAK!
...
HOW DO I EAT IT?

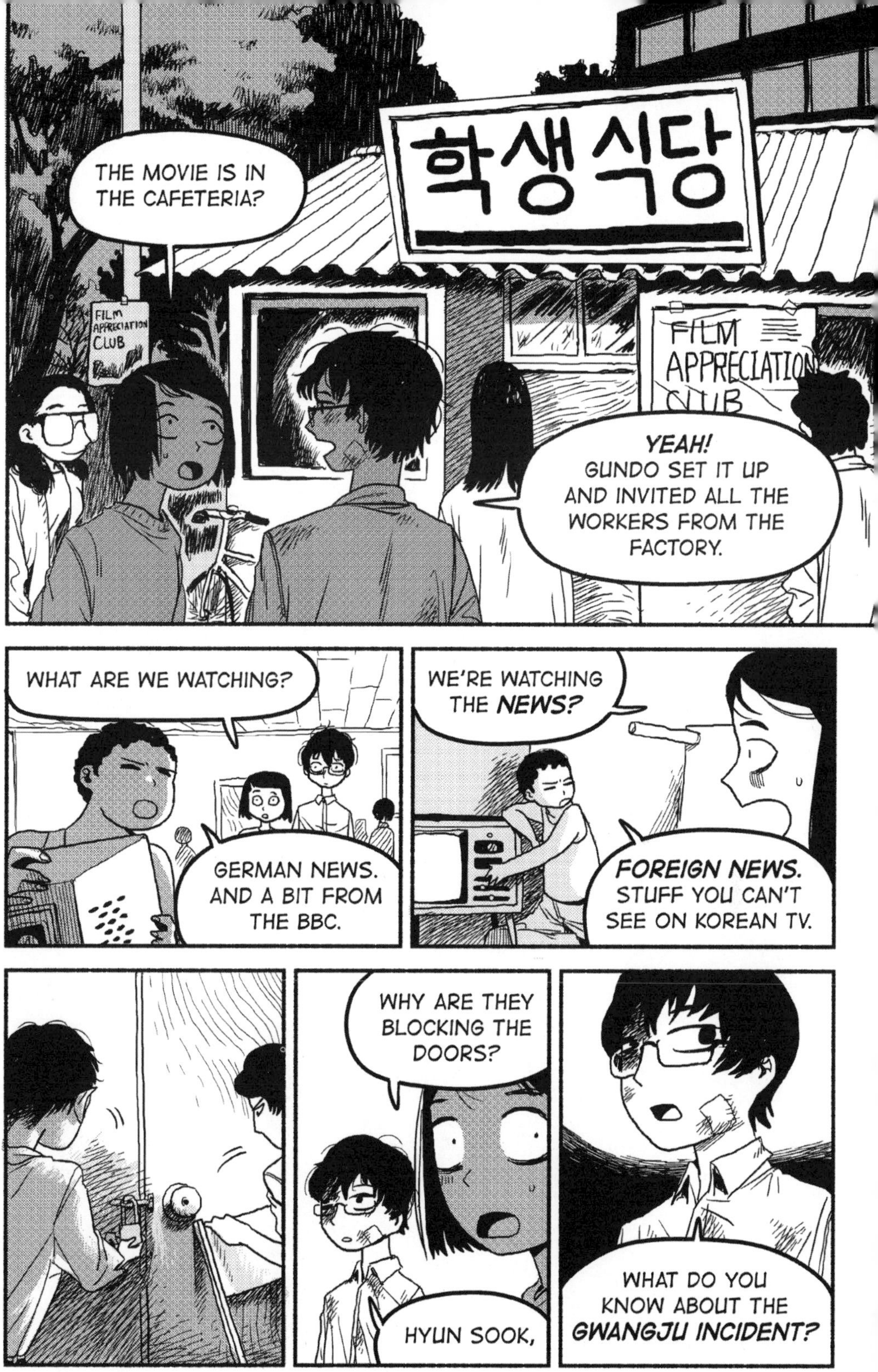
학생식당
THE MOVIE IS IN THE CAFETERIA?
FILM APPRECIATION CLUB
FILM APPRECIATION CLUB
YEAH! GUNDO SET IT UP AND INVITED ALL THE WORKERS FROM THE FACTORY.
WHAT ARE WE WATCHING?
GERMAN NEWS. AND A BIT FROM THE BBC.
WE'RE WATCHING THE NEWS?
FOREIGN NEWS. STUFF YOU CAN'T SEE ON KOREAN TV.
WHY ARE THEY BLOCKING THE DOORS?
HYUN SOOK,
WHAT DO YOU KNOW ABOUT THE GWANGJU INCIDENT?

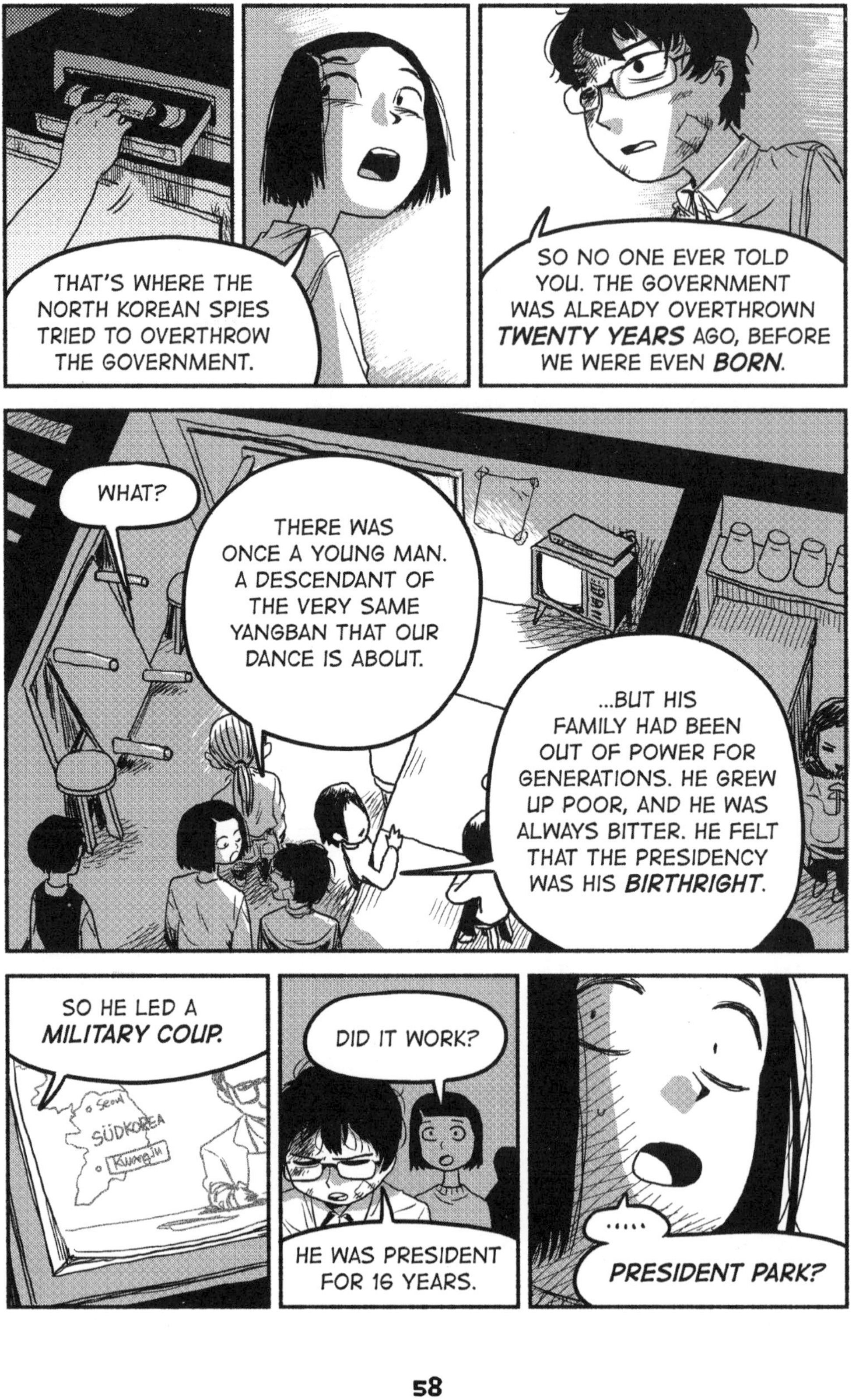
THAT'S WHERE THE NORTH KOREAN SPIES TRIED TO OVERTHROW THE GOVERNMENT.
SO NO ONE EVER TOLD YOU. THE GOVERNMENT WAS ALREADY OVERTHROWN TWENTY YEARS AGO, BEFORE WE WERE EVEN BORN.
WHAT?
THERE WAS ONCE A YOUNG MAN. A DESCENDANT OF THE VERY SAME YANGBAN THAT OUR DANCE IS ABOUT.
...BUT HIS FAMILY HAD BEEN OUT OF POWER FOR GENERATIONS. HE GREW UP POOR, AND HE WAS ALWAYS BITTER. HE FELT THAT THE PRESIDENCY WAS HIS BIRTHRIGHT.
SO HE LED A MILITARY COUP.
Seoul
SÜDKOREA
Kwangju
DID IT WORK?
HE WAS PRESIDENT FOR 16 YEARS.
.....
PRESIDENT PARK?

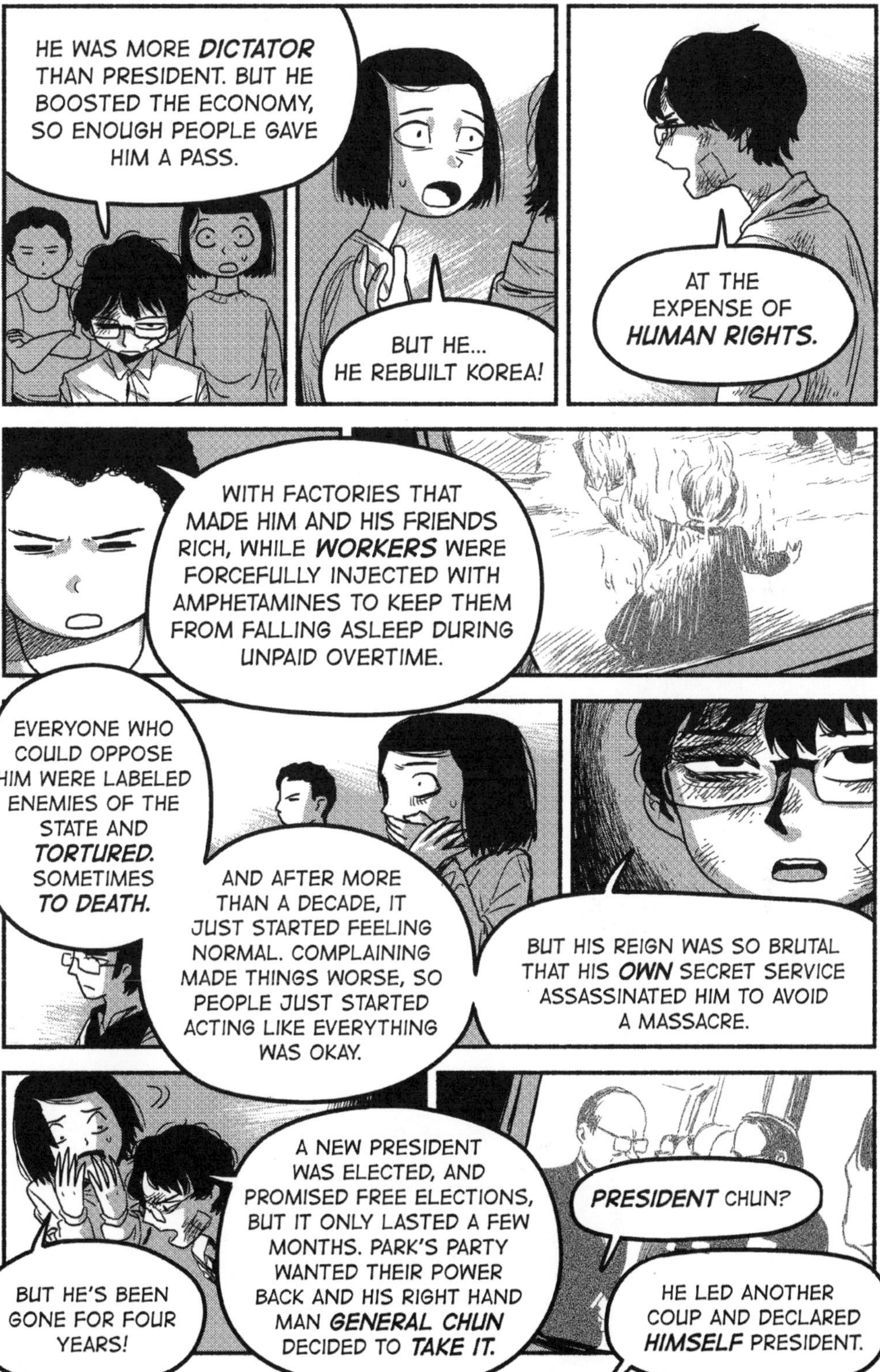

HE WAS MORE DICTATOR THAN PRESIDENT. BUT HE BOOSTED THE ECONOMY, SO ENOUGH PEOPLE GAVE HIM A PASS.
BUT HE... HE REBUILT KOREA!
AT THE EXPENSE OF HUMAN RIGHTS.
WITH FACTORIES THAT MADE HIM AND HIS FRIENDS RICH, WHILE WORKERS WERE FORCEFULLY INJECTED WITH AMPHETAMINES TO KEEP THEM FROM FALLING ASLEEP DURING UNPAID OVERTIME.
EVERYONE WHO COULD OPPOSE HIM WERE LABELED ENEMIES OF THE STATE AND TORTURED. SOMETIMES TO DEATH.
AND AFTER MORE THAN A DECADE, IT JUST STARTED FEELING NORMAL. COMPLAINING MADE THINGS WORSE, SO PEOPLE JUST STARTED ACTING LIKE EVERYTHING WAS OKAY.
BUT HIS REIGN WAS SO BRUTAL THAT HIS OWN SECRET SERVICE ASSASSINATED HIM TO AVOID A MASSACRE.
BUT HE'S BEEN GONE FOR FOUR YEARS!
A NEW PRESIDENT WAS ELECTED, AND PROMISED FREE ELECTIONS, BUT IT ONLY LASTED A FEW MONTHS. PARK'S PARTY WANTED THEIR POWER BACK AND HIS RIGHT HAND MAN GENERAL CHUN DECIDED TO TAKE IT.
PRESIDENT CHUN?
HE LED ANOTHER COUP AND DECLARED HIMSELF PRESIDENT.

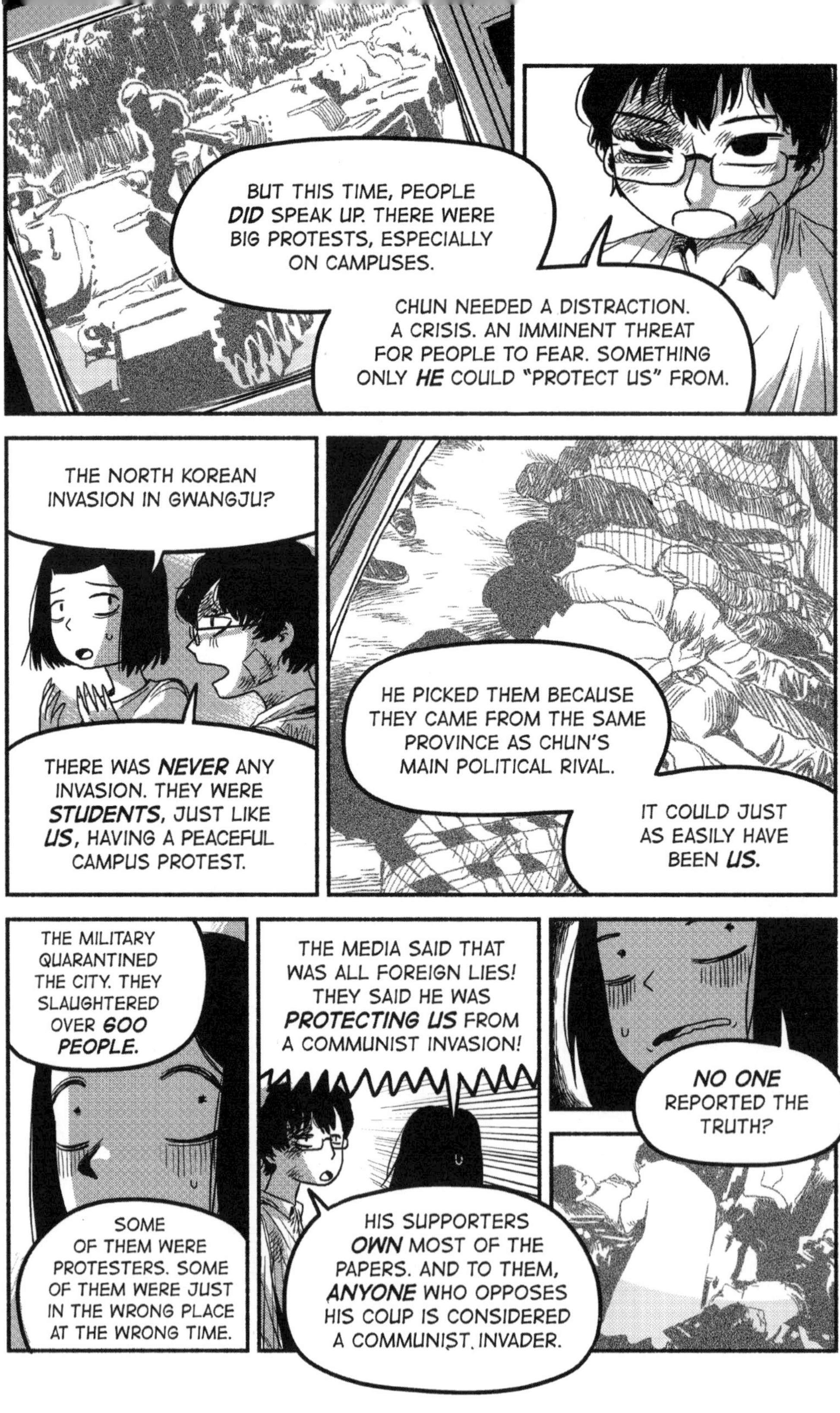
BUT THIS TIME, PEOPLE DID SPEAK UP. THERE WERE BIG PROTESTS, ESPECIALLY ON CAMPUSES.
CHUN NEEDED A DISTRACTION. A CRISIS. AN IMMINENT THREAT FOR PEOPLE TO FEAR. SOMETHING ONLY HE COULD "PROTECT US" FROM.
THE NORTH KOREAN INVASION IN GWANGJU?
THERE WAS NEVER ANY INVASION. THEY WERE STUDENTS, JUST LIKE US, HAVING A PEACEFUL CAMPUS PROTEST.
HE PICKED THEM BECAUSE THEY CAME FROM THE SAME PROVINCE AS CHUN'S MAIN POLITICAL RIVAL.
IT COULD JUST AS EASILY HAVE BEEN US.
THE MILITARY QUARANTINED THE CITY. THEY SLAUGHTERED OVER 600 PEOPLE.
SOME OF THEM WERE PROTESTERS. SOME OF THEM WERE JUST IN THE WRONG PLACE AT THE WRONG TIME.
THE MEDIA SAID THAT WAS ALL FOREIGN LIES! THEY SAID HE WAS PROTECTING US FROM A COMMUNIST INVASION!
HIS SUPPORTERS OWN MOST OF THE PAPERS. AND TO THEM, ANYONE WHO OPPOSES HIS COUP IS CONSIDERED A COMMUNIST INVADER.
NO ONE REPORTED THE TRUTH?

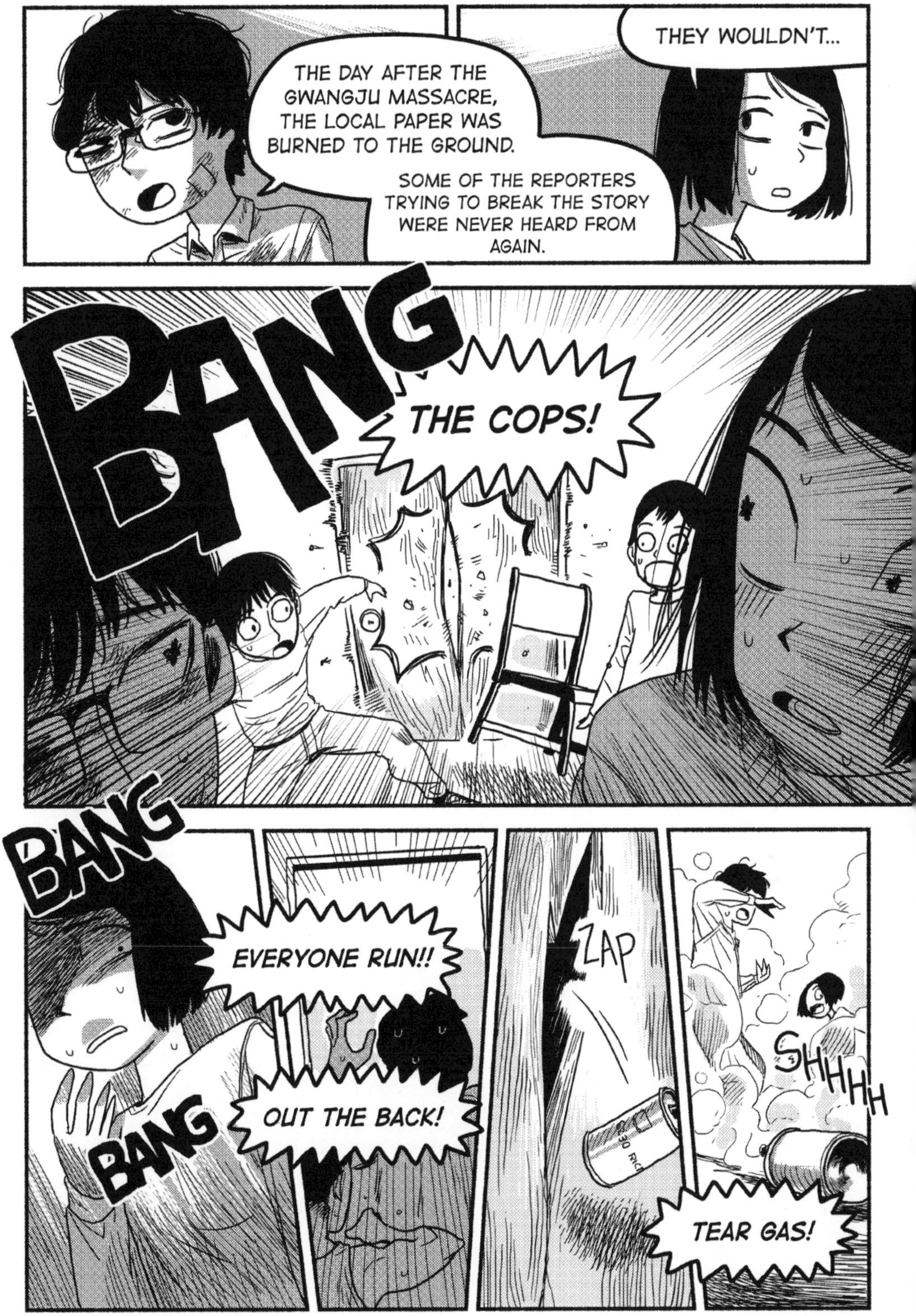
THE DAY AFTER THE GWANGJU MASSACRE, THE LOCAL PAPER WAS BURNED TO THE GROUND.
SOME OF THE REPORTERS TRYING TO BREAK THE STORY WERE NEVER HEARD FROM AGAIN.
THEY WOULDN'T...
BANG
THE COPS!
BANG
EVERYONE RUN!!
BANG
OUT THE BACK!
ZAP
SHHHHH
TEAR GAS!

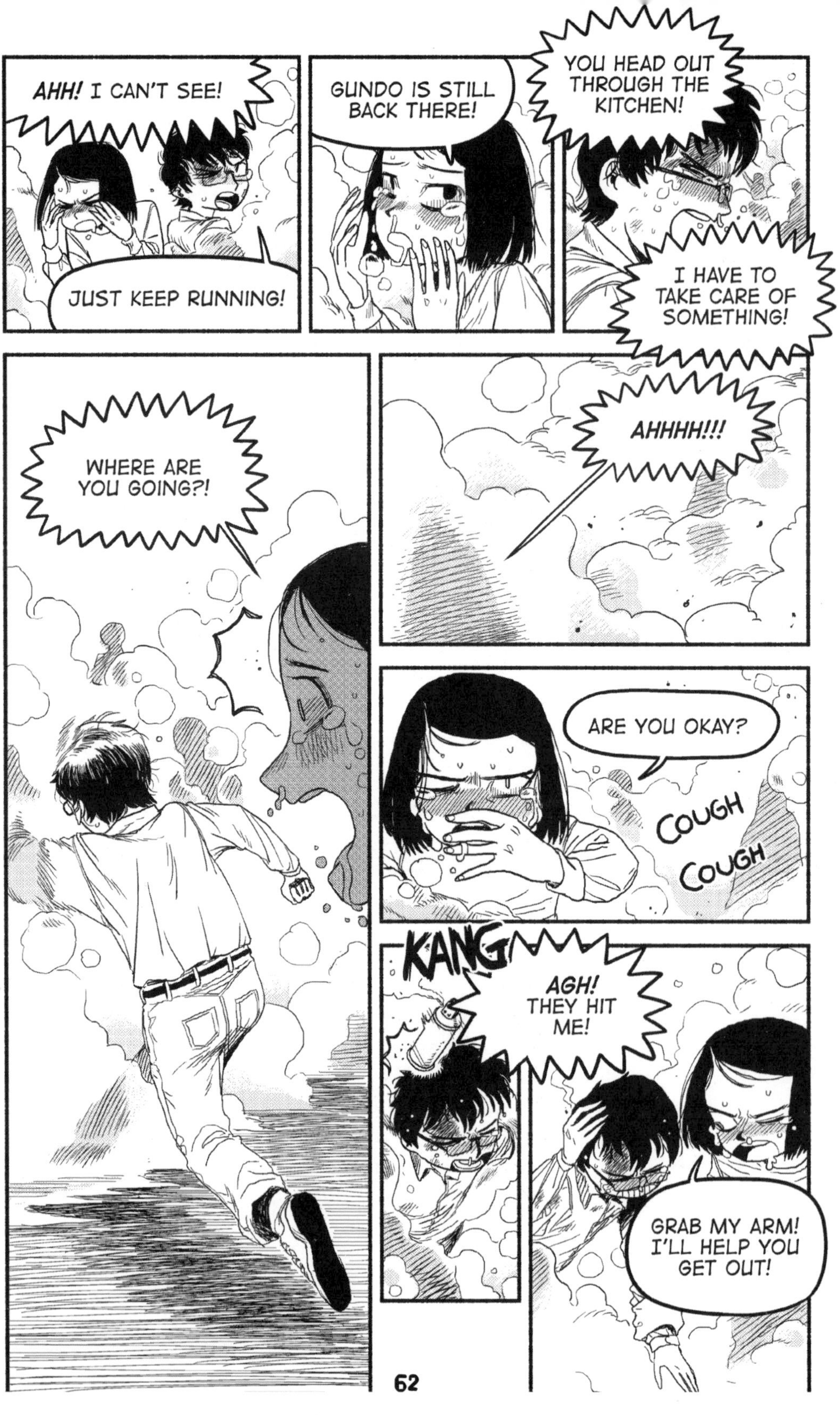
AHH! I CAN'T SEE!
JUST KEEP RUNNING!
GUNDO IS STILL BACK THERE!
YOU HEAD OUT THROUGH THE KITCHEN!
I HAVE TO TAKE CARE OF SOMETHING!
WHERE ARE YOU GOING?!
AHHHH!!!
ARE YOU OKAY?
COUGH
COUGH
KANG
AGH! THEY HIT ME!
GRAB MY ARM! I'LL HELP YOU GET OUT!

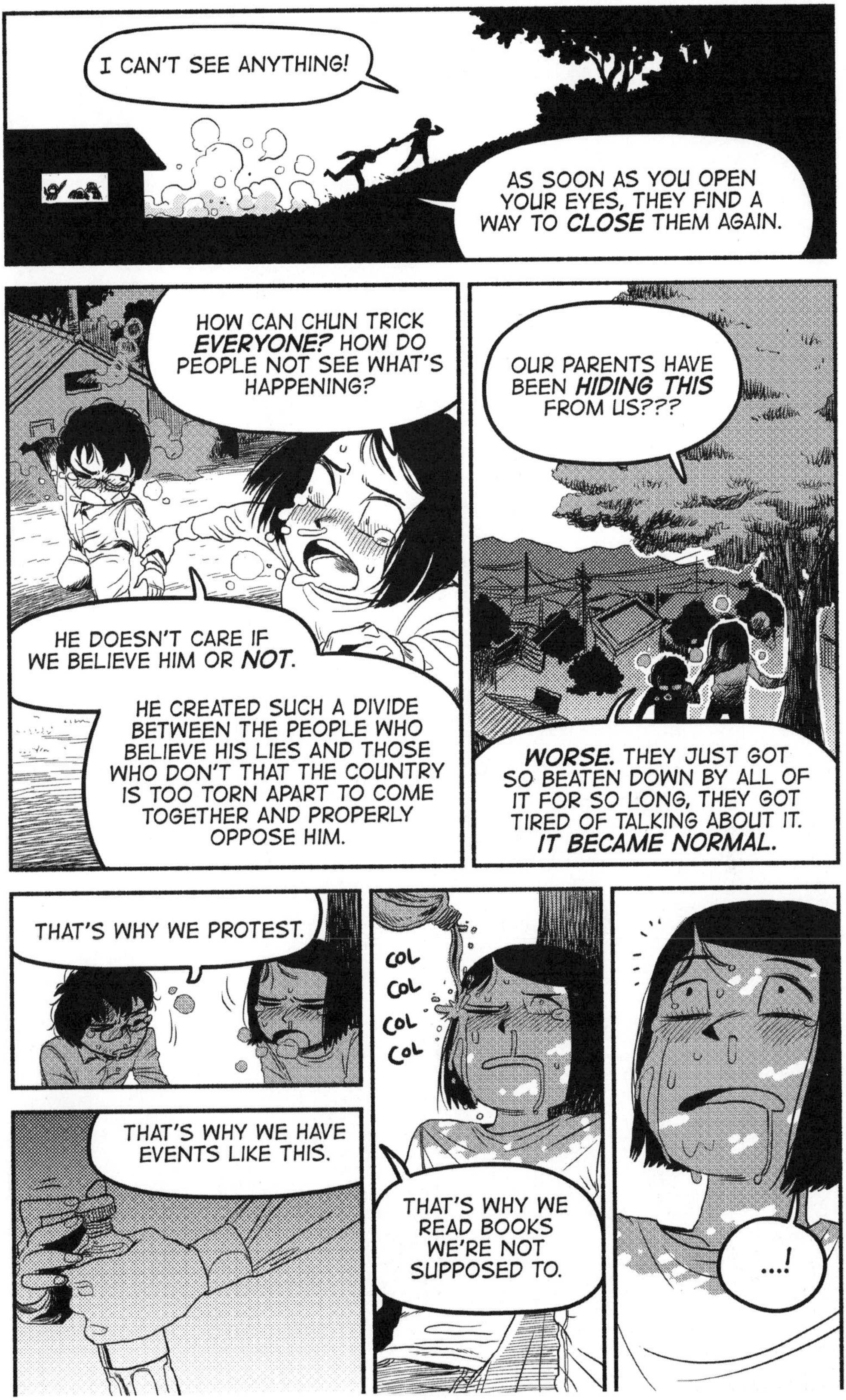
I CAN'T SEE ANYTHING!
AS SOON AS YOU OPEN YOUR EYES, THEY FIND A WAY TO *CLOSE* THEM AGAIN.
HOW CAN CHUN TRICK *EVERYONE?* HOW DO PEOPLE NOT SEE WHAT'S HAPPENING?
HE DOESN'T CARE IF WE BELIEVE HIM OR *NOT*.
HE CREATED SUCH A DIVIDE BETWEEN THE PEOPLE WHO BELIEVE HIS LIES AND THOSE WHO DON'T THAT THE COUNTRY IS TOO TORN APART TO COME TOGETHER AND PROPERLY OPPOSE HIM.
OUR PARENTS HAVE BEEN *HIDING THIS* FROM US???
WORSE. THEY JUST GOT SO BEATEN DOWN BY ALL OF IT FOR SO LONG, THEY GOT TIRED OF TALKING ABOUT IT. *IT BECAME NORMAL.*
THAT'S WHY WE PROTEST.
THAT'S WHY WE HAVE EVENTS LIKE THIS.
COL
COL
COL
COL
THAT'S WHY WE READ BOOKS WE'RE NOT SUPPOSED TO.
...!

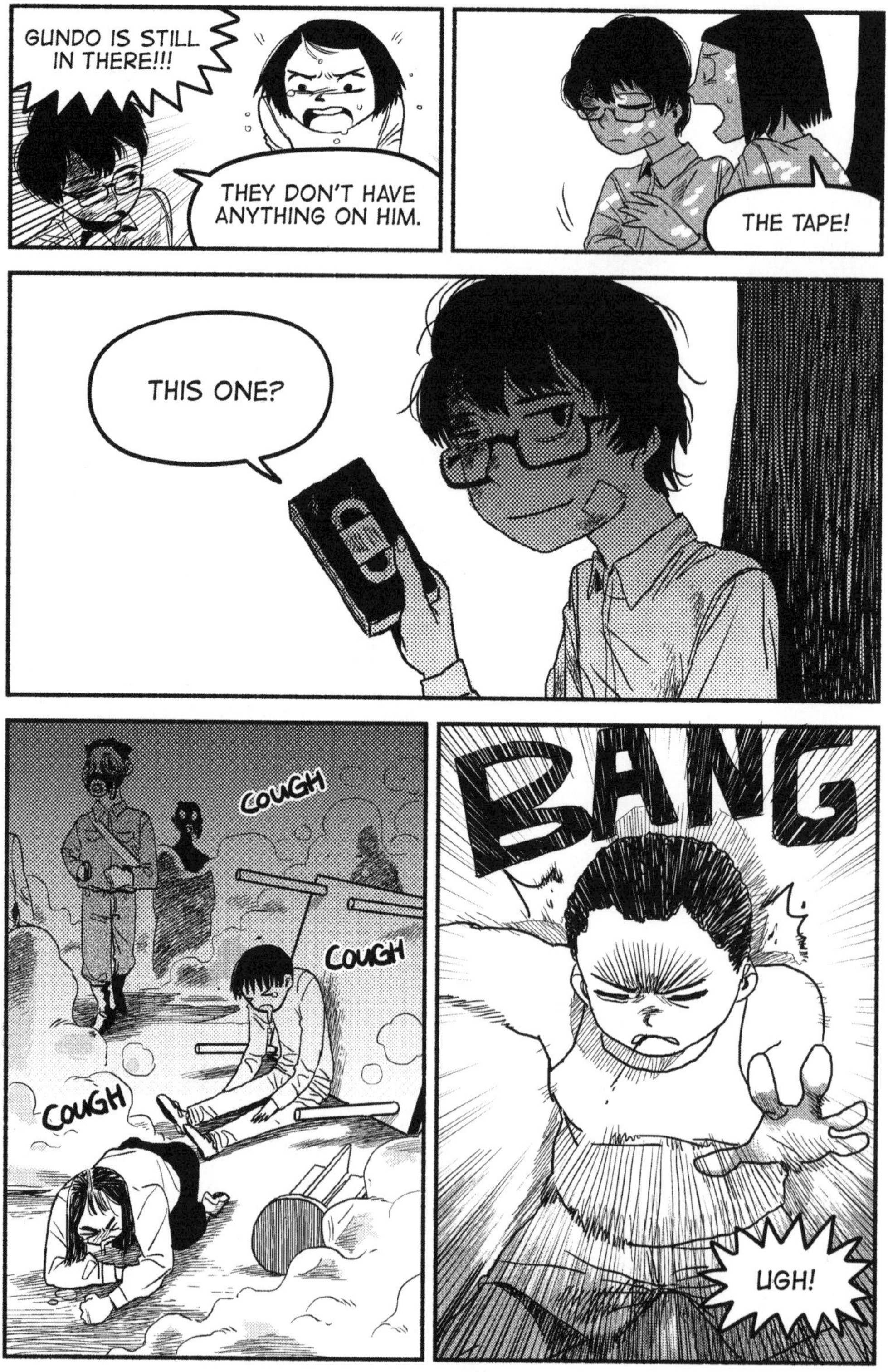
GUNDO IS STILL IN THERE!!!
THEY DON'T HAVE ANYTHING ON HIM.
THE TAPE!
THIS ONE?
COUGH
COUGH
COUGH
BANG
UGH!

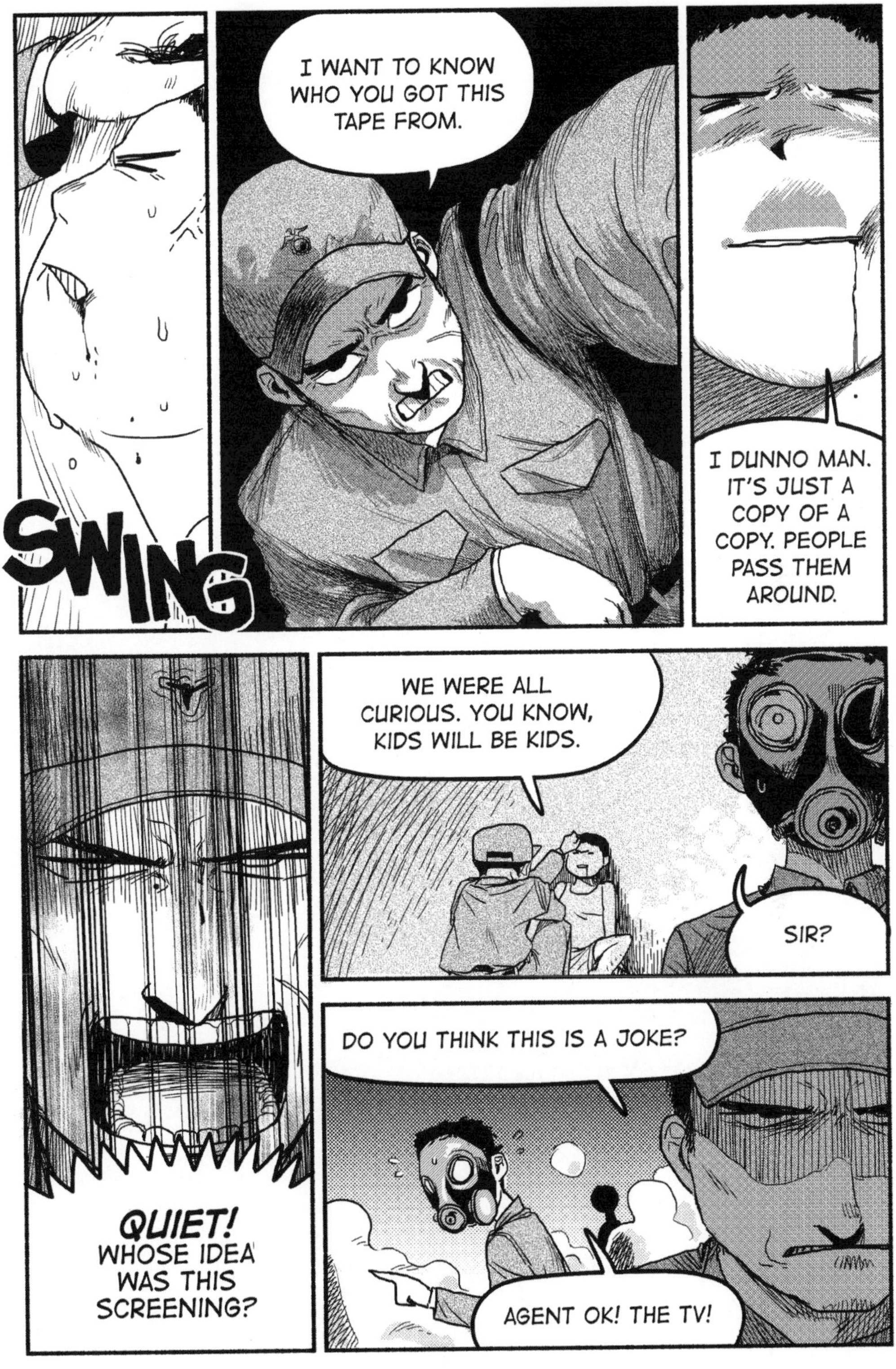
SWING
I WANT TO KNOW WHO YOU GOT THIS TAPE FROM.
I DUNNO MAN. IT'S JUST A COPY OF A COPY. PEOPLE PASS THEM AROUND.
WE WERE ALL CURIOUS. YOU KNOW, KIDS WILL BE KIDS.
SIR?
QUIET! WHOSE IDEA WAS THIS SCREENING?
DO YOU THINK THIS IS A JOKE?
AGENT OK! THE TV!

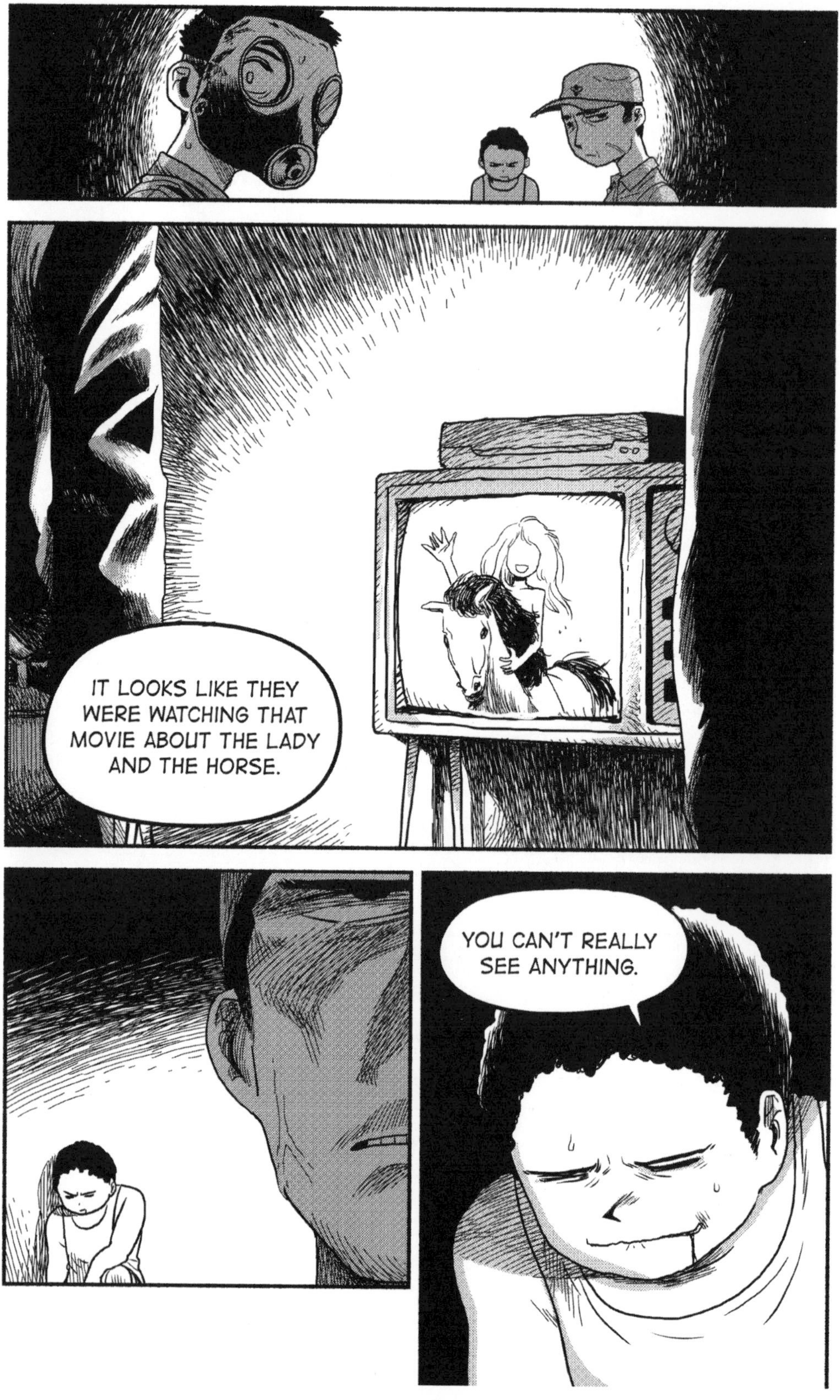
IT LOOKS LIKE THEY WERE WATCHING THAT MOVIE ABOUT THE LADY AND THE HORSE.
YOU CAN'T REALLY SEE ANYTHING.

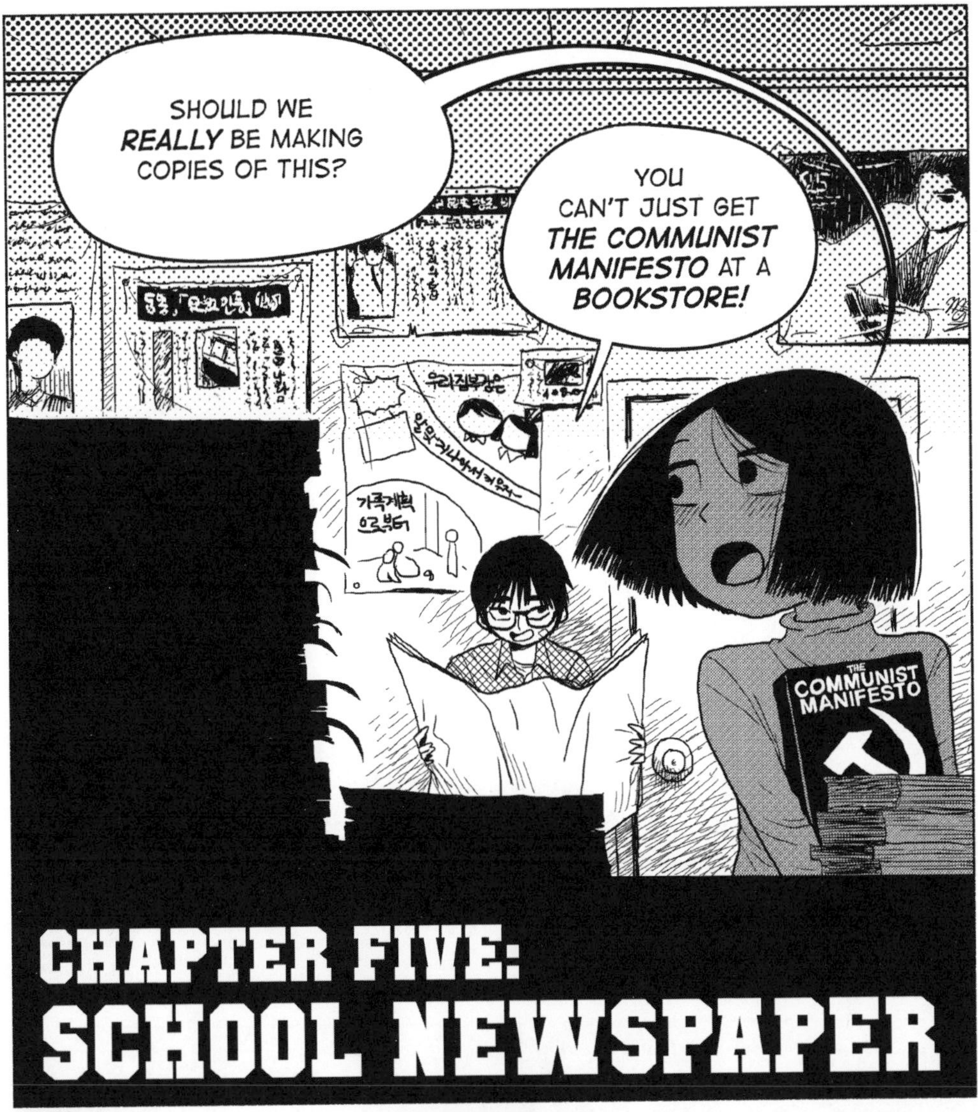
SHOULD WE REALLY BE MAKING COPIES OF THIS?
YOU CAN'T JUST GET THE COMMUNIST MANIFESTO AT A BOOKSTORE!
THE COMMUNIST MANIFESTO

CHAPTER FIVE: SCHOOL NEWSPAPER

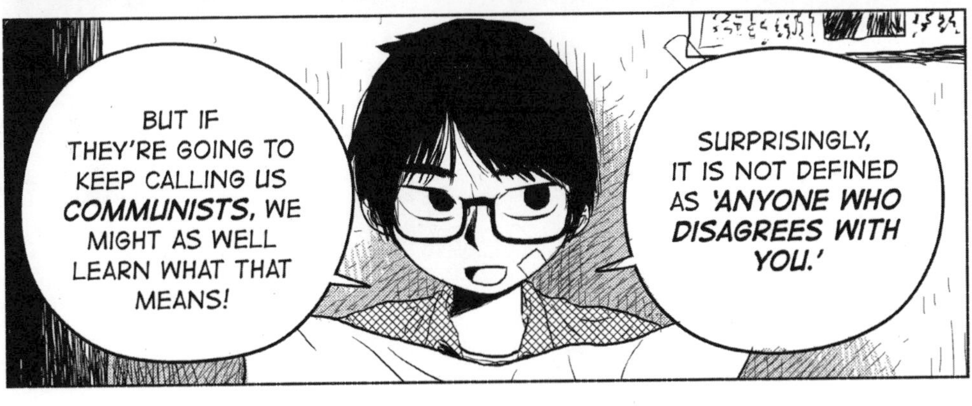
BUT IF THEY'RE GOING TO KEEP CALLING US COMMUNISTS, WE MIGHT AS WELL LEARN WHAT THAT MEANS!
SURPRISINGLY, IT IS NOT DEFINED AS 'ANYONE WHO DISAGREES WITH YOU.'

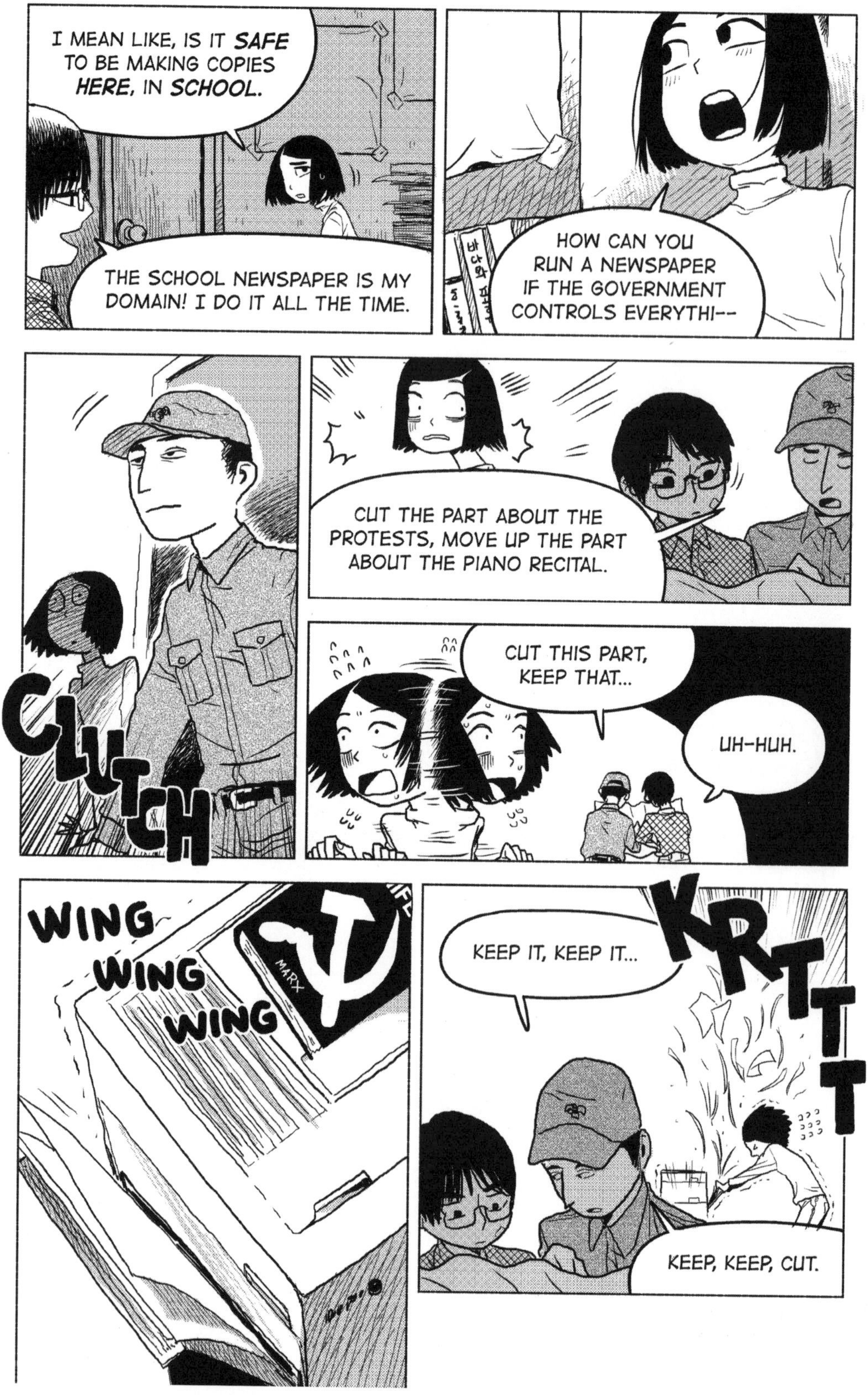
I MEAN LIKE, IS IT SAFE TO BE MAKING COPIES HERE, IN SCHOOL.
THE SCHOOL NEWSPAPER IS MY DOMAIN! I DO IT ALL THE TIME.
HOW CAN YOU RUN A NEWSPAPER IF THE GOVERNMENT CONTROLS EVERYTHI--
CLUTCH
CUT THE PART ABOUT THE PROTESTS, MOVE UP THE PART ABOUT THE PIANO RECITAL.
CUT THIS PART, KEEP THAT...
UH-HUH.
WING
WING
WING
MARX
KEEP IT, KEEP IT...
KRTTT
KEEP, KEEP, CUT.

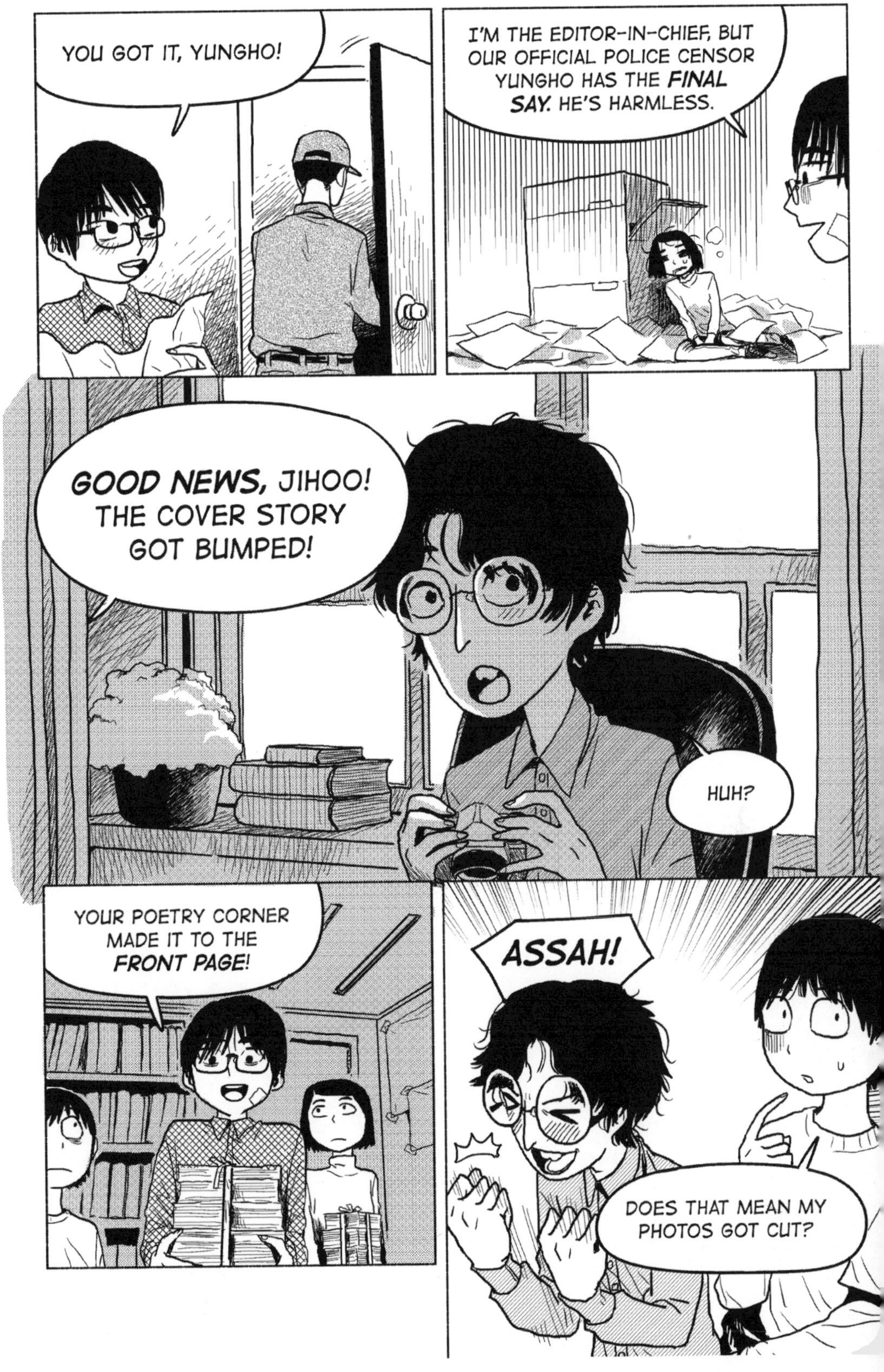
YOU GOT IT, YUNGHO!
I'M THE EDITOR-IN-CHIEF, BUT OUR OFFICIAL POLICE CENSOR YUNGHO HAS THE FINAL SAY. HE'S HARMLESS.
GOOD NEWS, JIHOO! THE COVER STORY GOT BUMPED!
HUH?
YOUR POETRY CORNER MADE IT TO THE FRONT PAGE!
ASSAH!
DOES THAT MEAN MY PHOTOS GOT CUT?

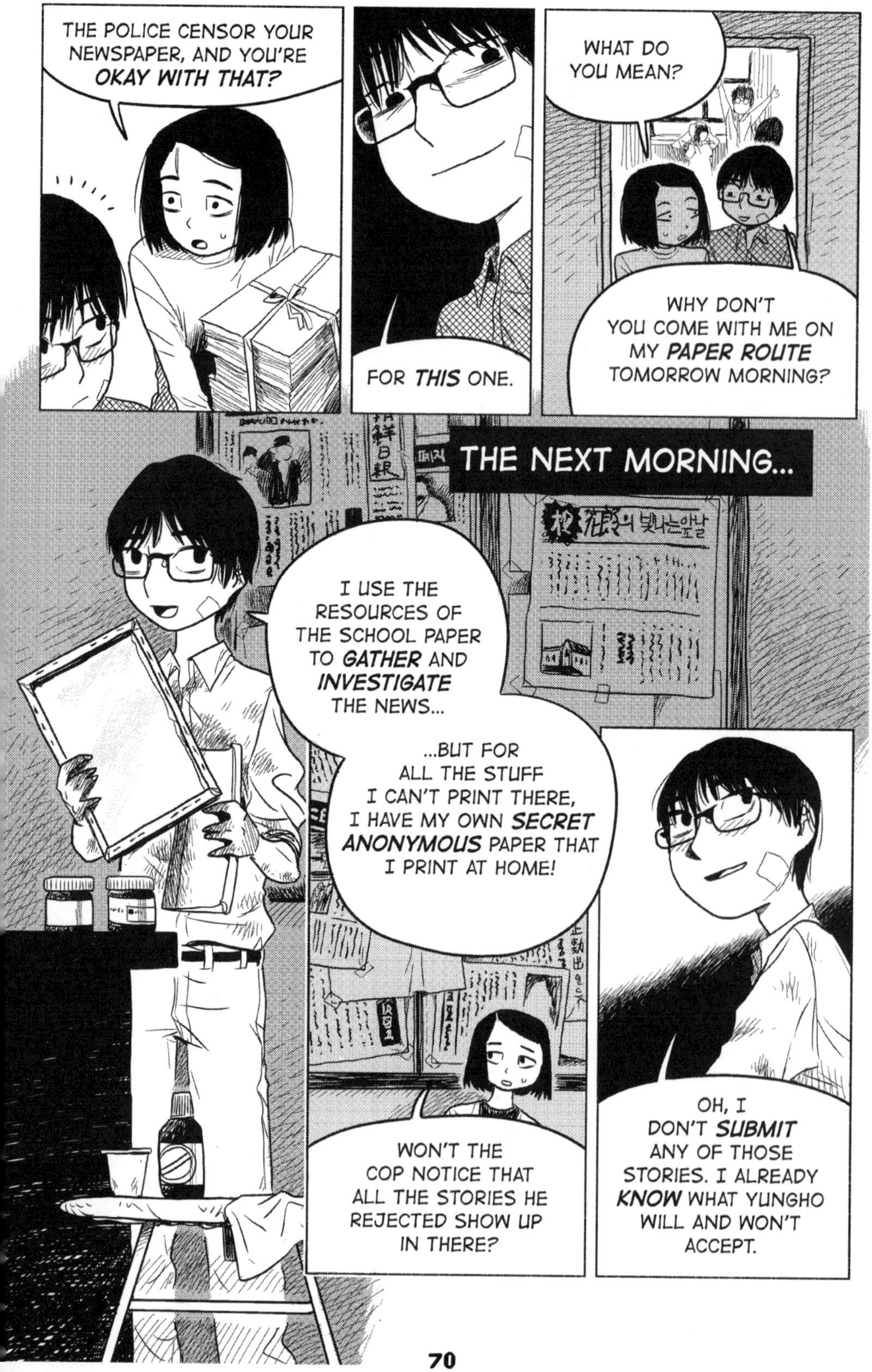

THE POLICE CENSOR YOUR NEWSPAPER, AND YOU'RE OKAY WITH THAT?
FOR THIS ONE.
WHAT DO YOU MEAN?
WHY DON'T YOU COME WITH ME ON MY PAPER ROUTE TOMORROW MORNING?
THE NEXT MORNING...
I USE THE RESOURCES OF THE SCHOOL PAPER TO GATHER AND INVESTIGATE THE NEWS...
...BUT FOR ALL THE STUFF I CAN'T PRINT THERE, I HAVE MY OWN SECRET ANONYMOUS PAPER THAT I PRINT AT HOME!
WON'T THE COP NOTICE THAT ALL THE STORIES HE REJECTED SHOW UP IN THERE?
OH, I DON'T SUBMIT ANY OF THOSE STORIES. I ALREADY KNOW WHAT YUNGHO WILL AND WON'T ACCEPT.

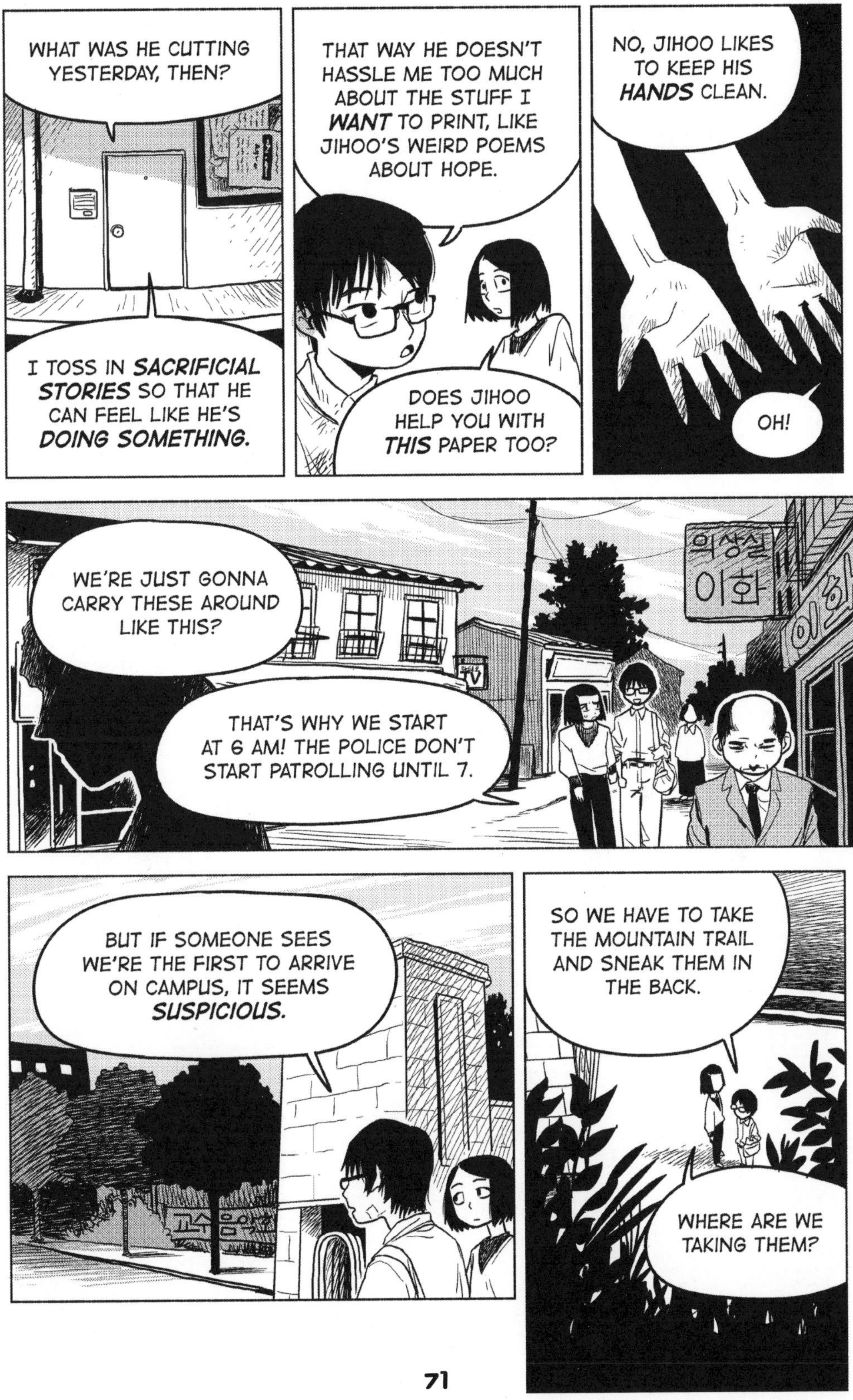
WHAT WAS HE CUTTING YESTERDAY, THEN?
I TOSS IN SACRIFICIAL STORIES SO THAT HE CAN FEEL LIKE HE'S DOING SOMETHING.
THAT WAY HE DOESN'T HASSLE ME TOO MUCH ABOUT THE STUFF I WANT TO PRINT, LIKE JIHOO'S WEIRD POEMS ABOUT HOPE.
DOES JIHOO HELP YOU WITH THIS PAPER TOO?
NO, JIHOO LIKES TO KEEP HIS HANDS CLEAN.
OH!
의상실
이화
이화
WE'RE JUST GONNA CARRY THESE AROUND LIKE THIS?
THAT'S WHY WE START AT 6 AM! THE POLICE DON'T START PATROLLING UNTIL 7.
BUT IF SOMEONE SEES WE'RE THE FIRST TO ARRIVE ON CAMPUS, IT SEEMS SUSPICIOUS.
SO WE HAVE TO TAKE THE MOUNTAIN TRAIL AND SNEAK THEM IN THE BACK.
WHERE ARE WE TAKING THEM?

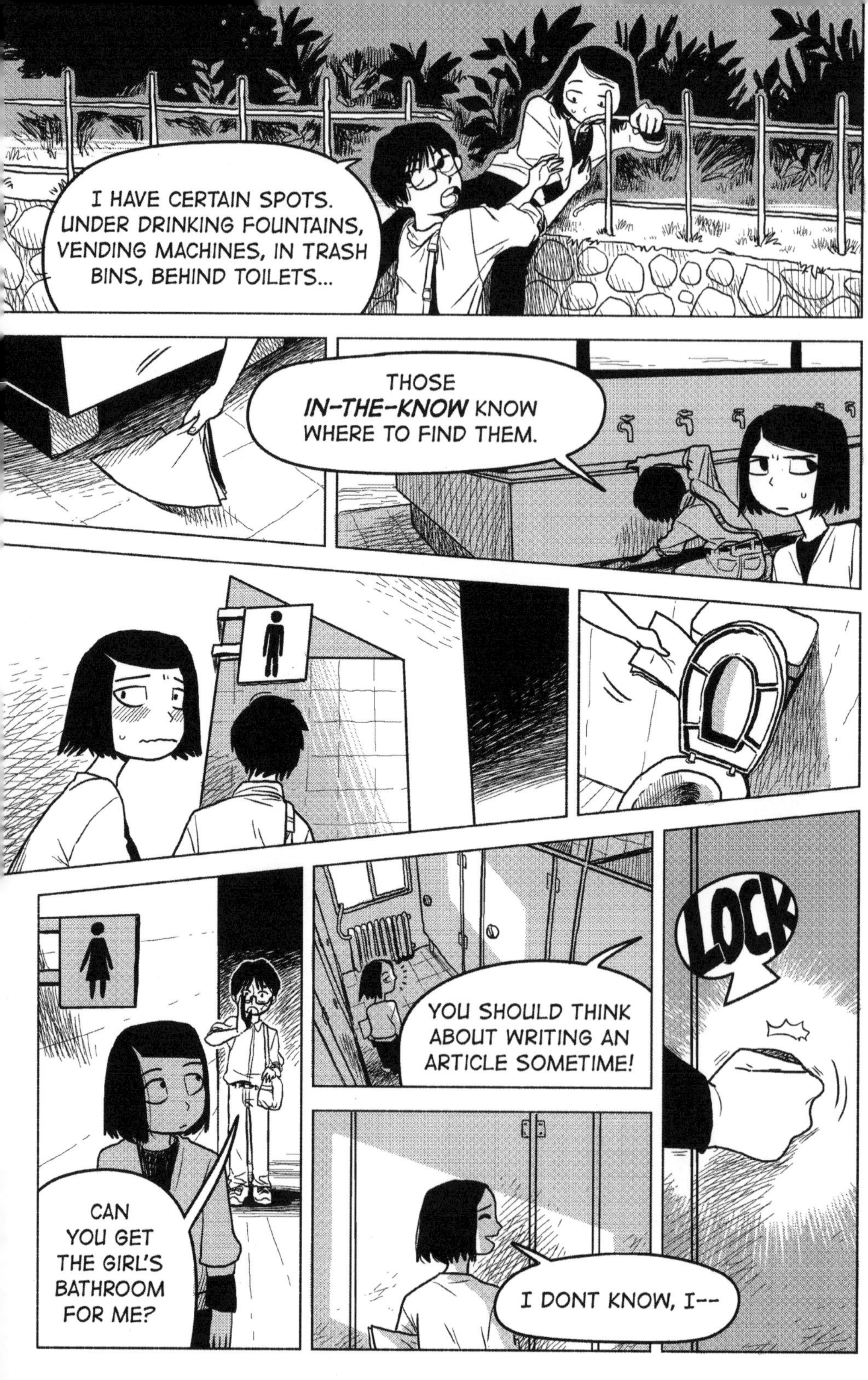
I HAVE CERTAIN SPOTS. UNDER DRINKING FOUNTAINS, VENDING MACHINES, IN TRASH BINS, BEHIND TOILETS...
THOSE *IN-THE-KNOW* KNOW WHERE TO FIND THEM.
CAN YOU GET THE GIRL'S BATHROOM FOR ME?
YOU SHOULD THINK ABOUT WRITING AN ARTICLE SOMETIME!
I DONT KNOW, I--
LOCK

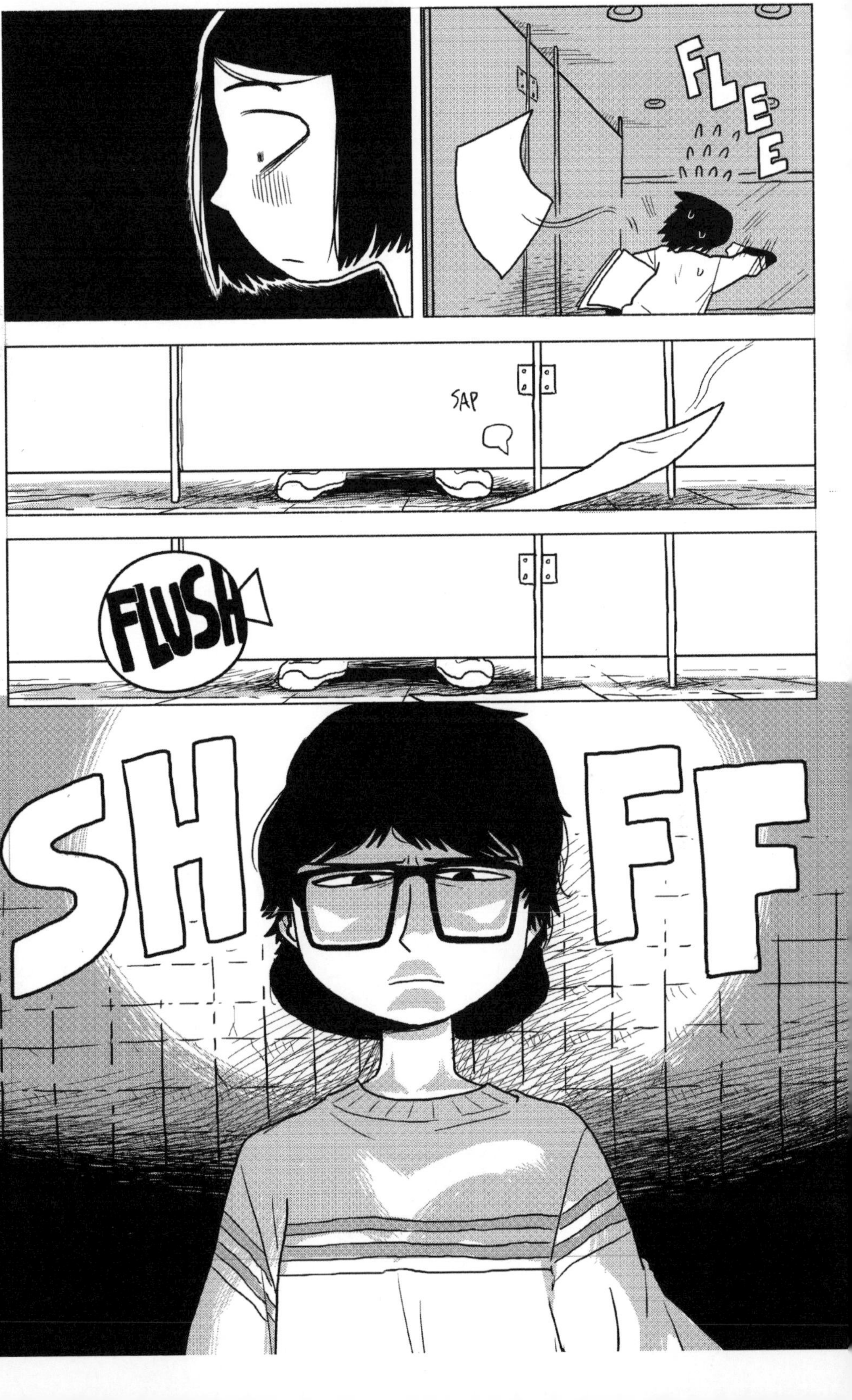
FLEE
SAP
FLUSH
SH FF

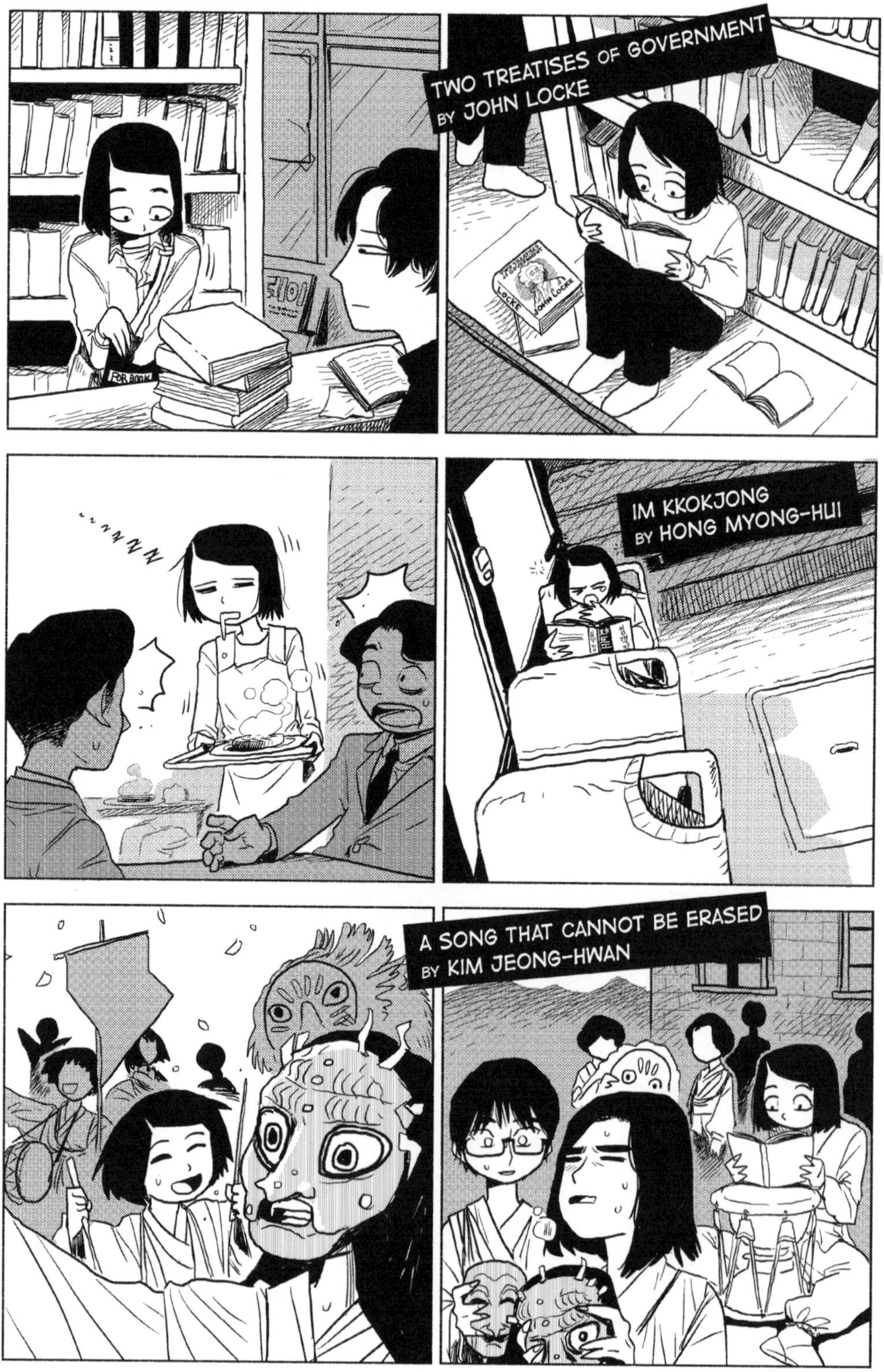
FOR BOOK
TWO TREATISES OF GOVERNMENT
BY JOHN LOCKE
JOHN LOCKE
LOCKE
IM KKOKJONG
BY HONG MYONG-HUI
A SONG THAT CANNOT BE ERASED
BY KIM JEONG-HWAN

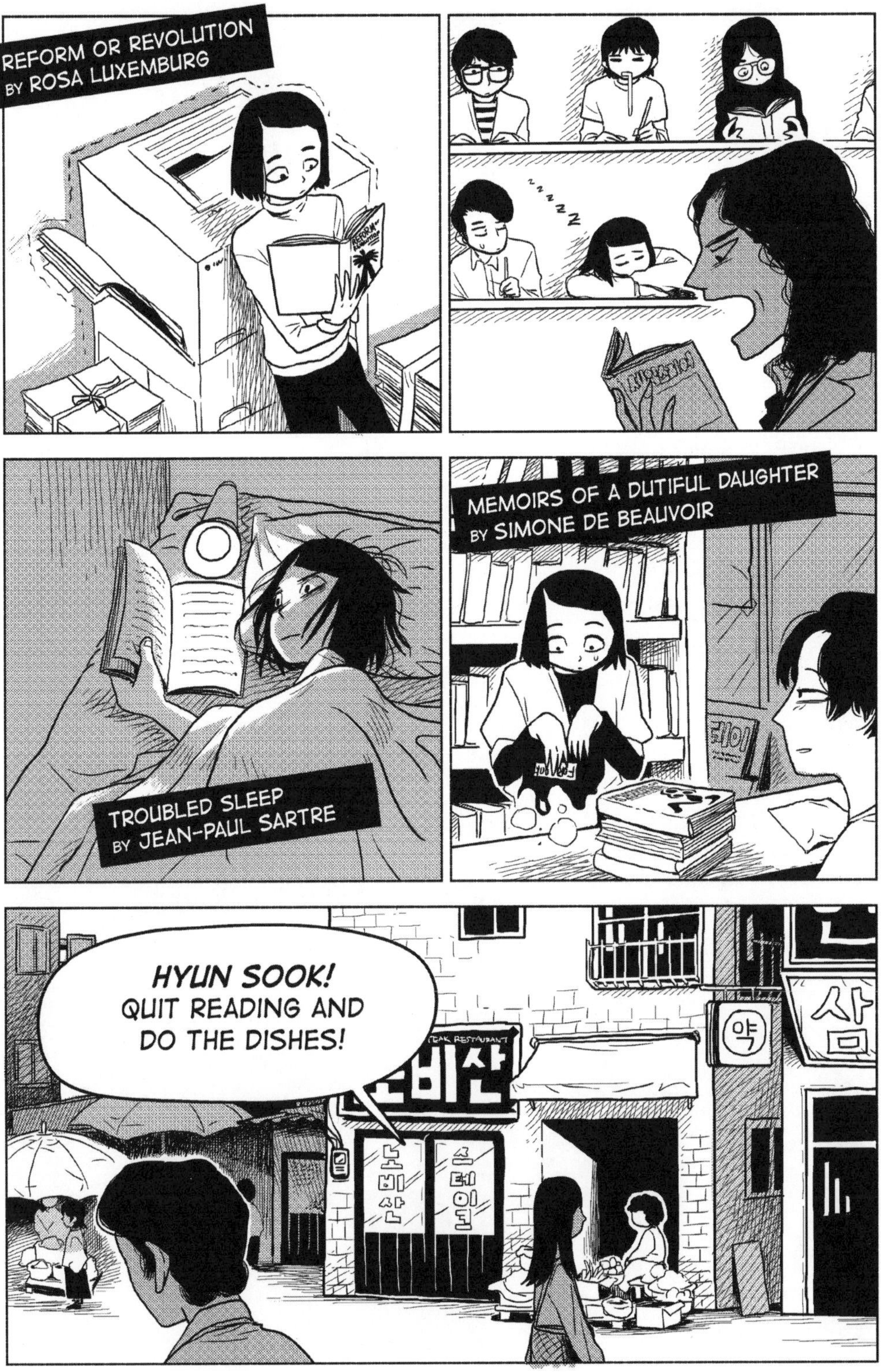
REFORM OR REVOLUTION
BY ROSA LUXEMBURG
TROUBLED SLEEP
BY JEAN-PAUL SARTRE
MEMOIRS OF A DUTIFUL DAUGHTER
BY SIMONE DE BEAUVOIR
HYUN SOOK! QUIT READING AND DO THE DISHES!
약

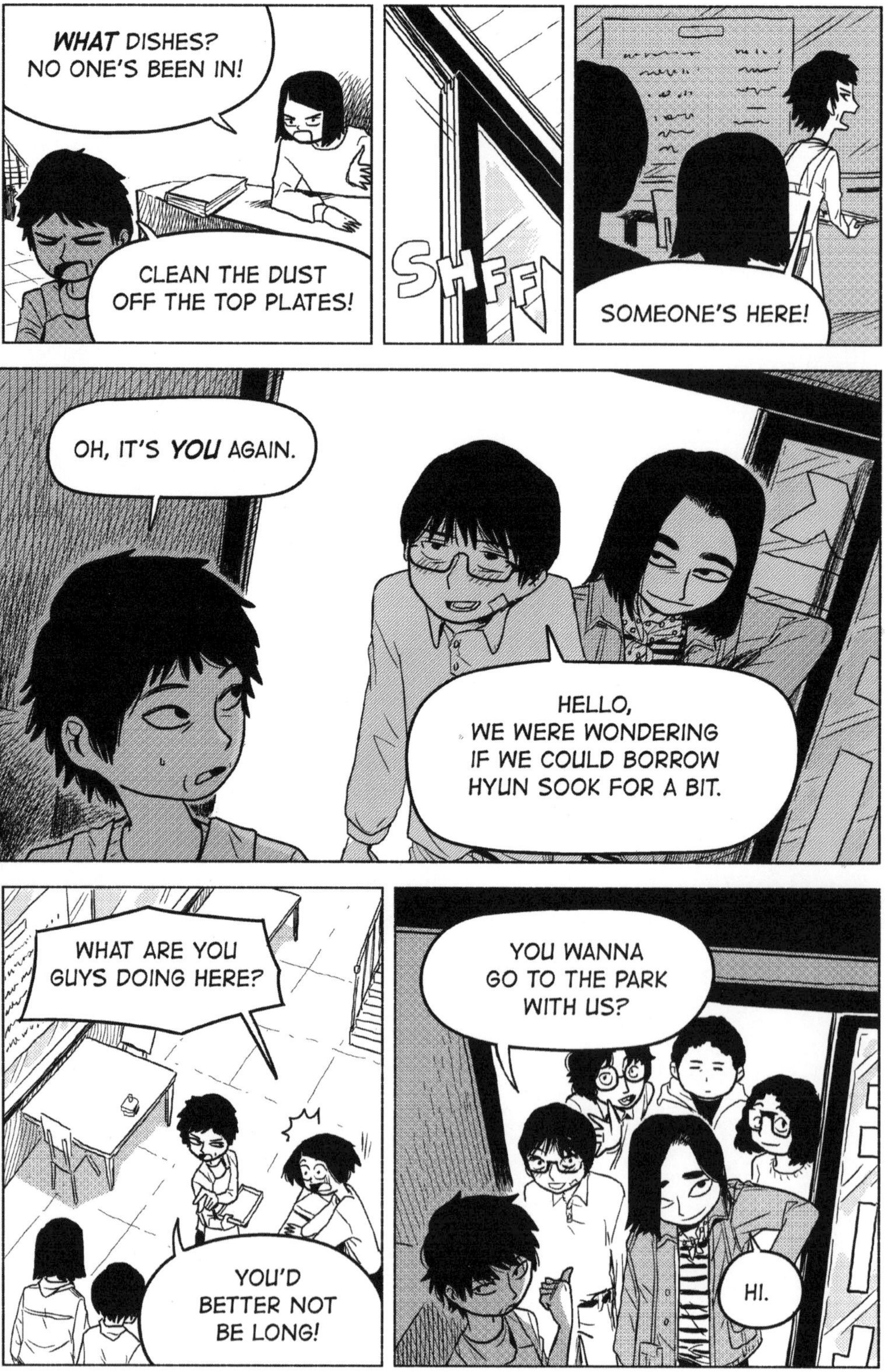
WHAT DISHES? NO ONE'S BEEN IN!
CLEAN THE DUST OFF THE TOP PLATES!
SHFF
SOMEONE'S HERE!
OH, IT'S YOU AGAIN.
HELLO, WE WERE WONDERING IF WE COULD BORROW HYUN SOOK FOR A BIT.
WHAT ARE YOU GUYS DOING HERE?
YOU'D BETTER NOT BE LONG!
YOU WANNA GO TO THE PARK WITH US?
HI.

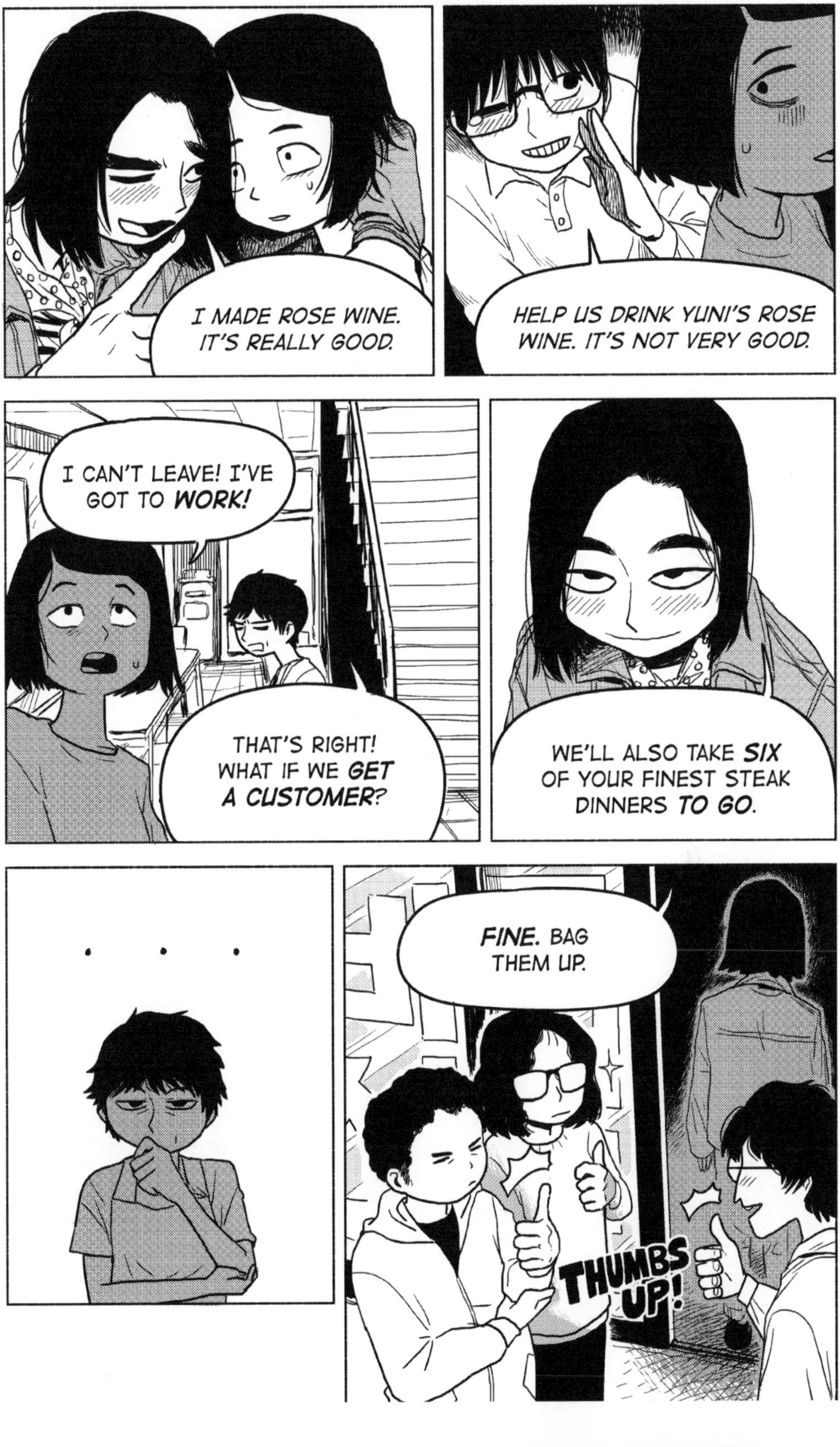
I MADE ROSE WINE. IT'S REALLY GOOD.
HELP US DRINK YUNI'S ROSE WINE. IT'S NOT VERY GOOD.
I CAN'T LEAVE! I'VE GOT TO WORK!
THAT'S RIGHT! WHAT IF WE GET A CUSTOMER?
WE'LL ALSO TAKE SIX OF YOUR FINEST STEAK DINNERS TO GO.
. . .
FINE. BAG THEM UP.
THUMBS UP!

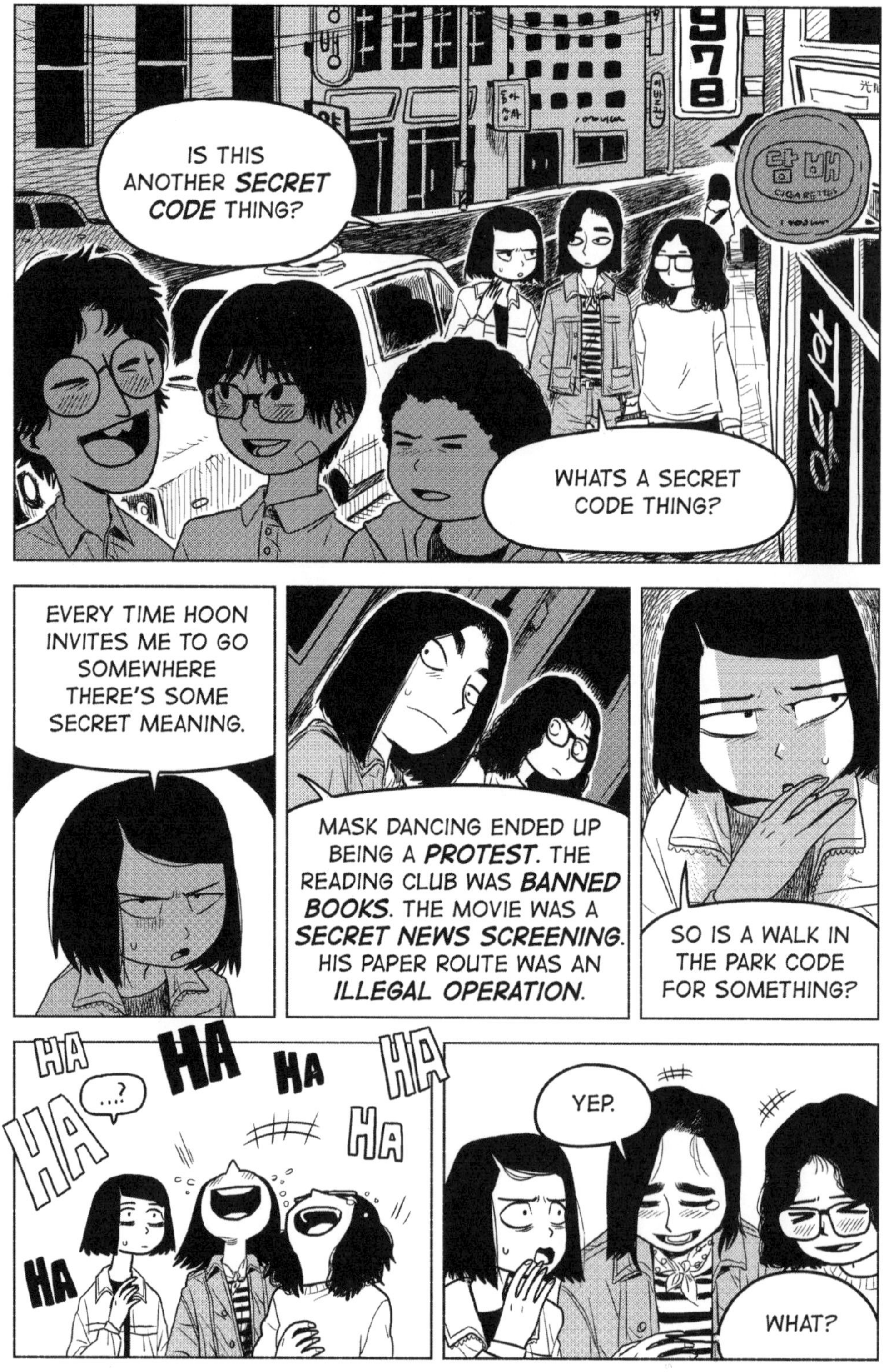
IS THIS ANOTHER SECRET CODE THING?
WHATS A SECRET CODE THING?
EVERY TIME HOON INVITES ME TO GO SOMEWHERE THERE'S SOME SECRET MEANING.
MASK DANCING ENDED UP BEING A PROTEST. THE READING CLUB WAS BANNED BOOKS. THE MOVIE WAS A SECRET NEWS SCREENING. HIS PAPER ROUTE WAS AN ILLEGAL OPERATION.
SO IS A WALK IN THE PARK CODE FOR SOMETHING?
HA HA HA HA HA HA HA HA
...?
YEP.
WHAT?

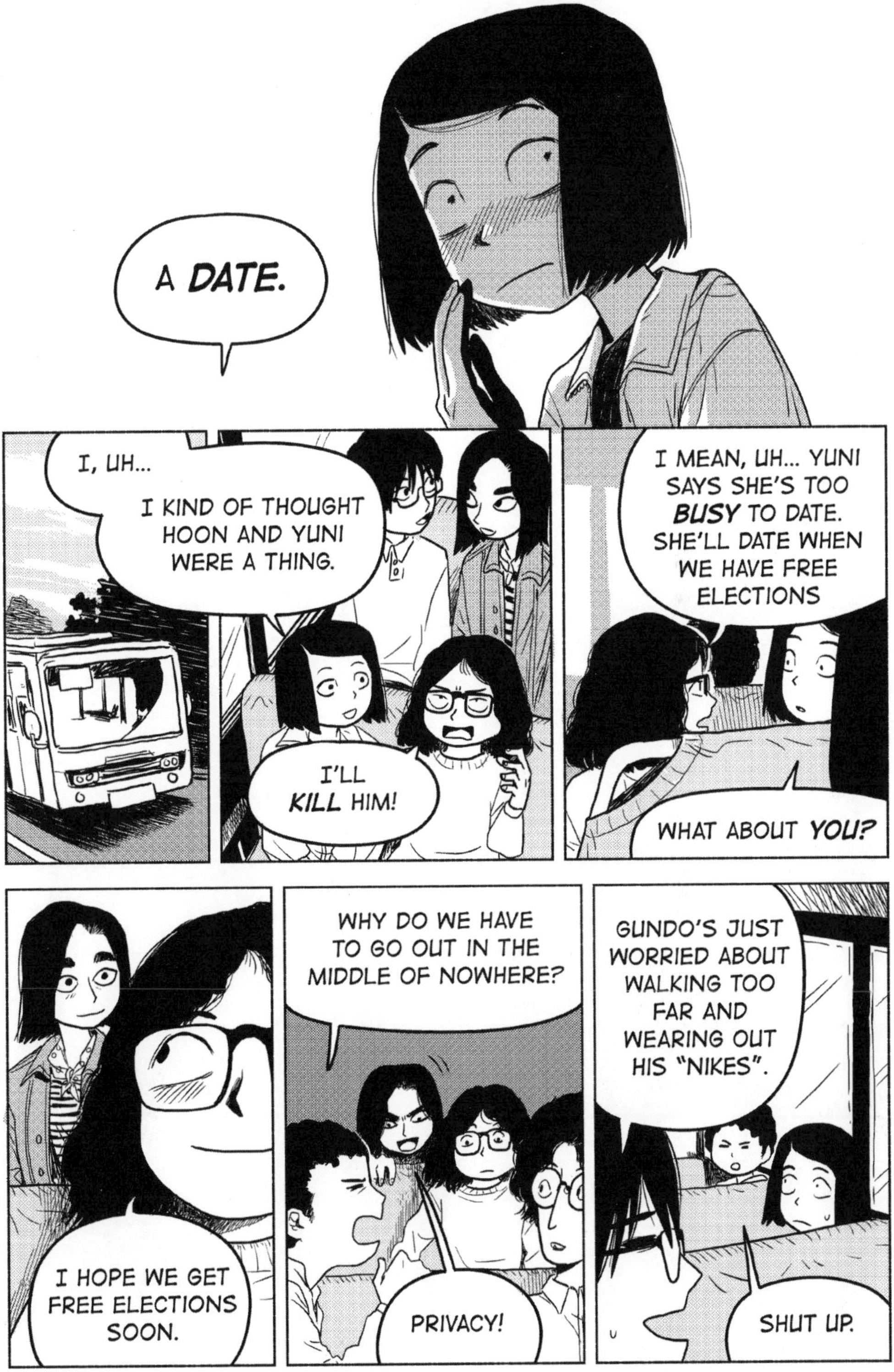
A DATE.
I, UH...
I KIND OF THOUGHT HOON AND YUNI WERE A THING.
I'LL KILL HIM!
I MEAN, UH... YUNI SAYS SHE'S TOO BUSY TO DATE. SHE'LL DATE WHEN WE HAVE FREE ELECTIONS
WHAT ABOUT YOU?
I HOPE WE GET FREE ELECTIONS SOON.
WHY DO WE HAVE TO GO OUT IN THE MIDDLE OF NOWHERE?
PRIVACY!
GUNDO'S JUST WORRIED ABOUT WALKING TOO FAR AND WEARING OUT HIS "NIKES".
SHUT UP.

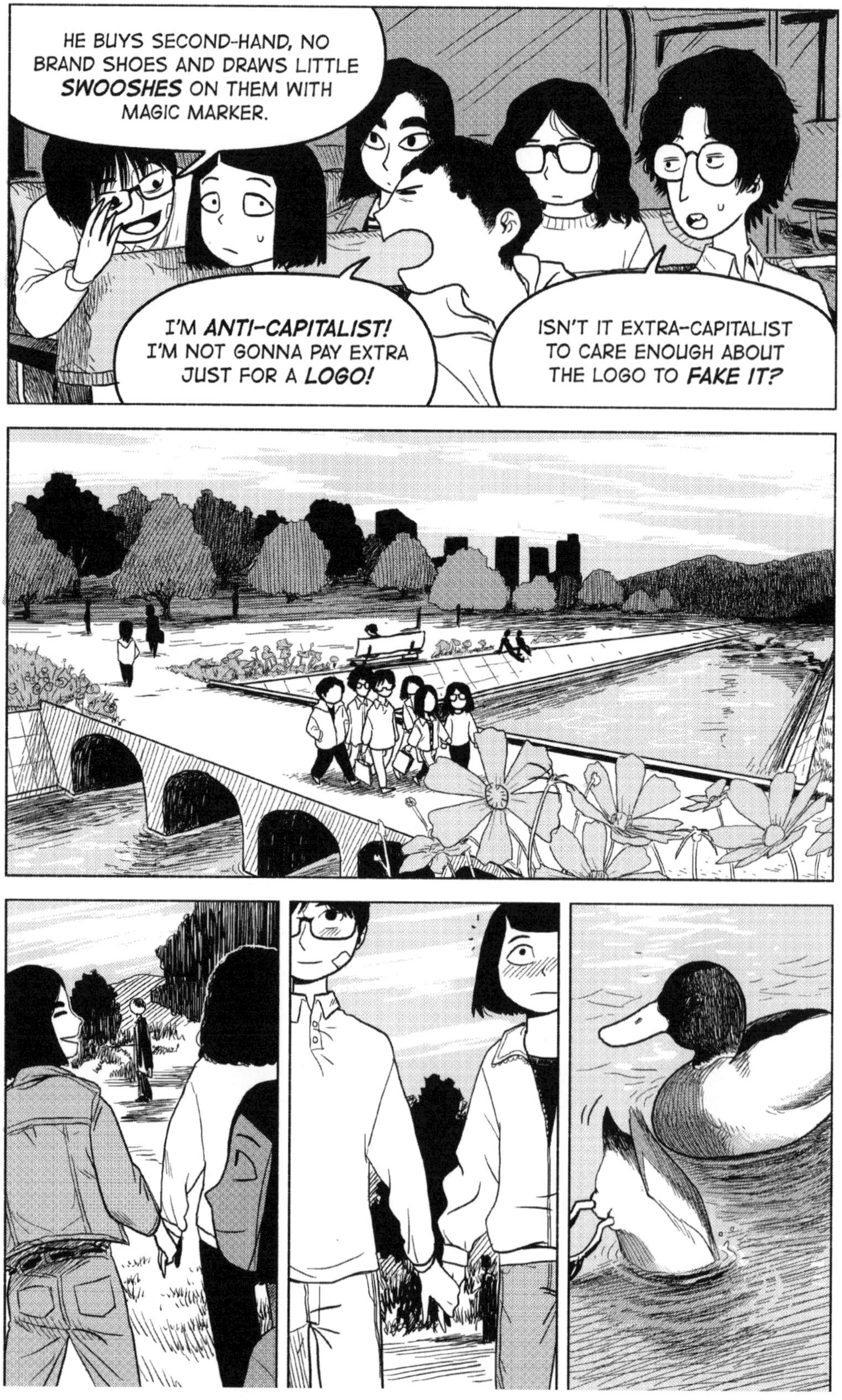
HE BUYS SECOND-HAND, NO BRAND SHOES AND DRAWS LITTLE **SWOOSHES** ON THEM WITH MAGIC MARKER.
I'M **ANTI-CAPITALIST!** I'M NOT GONNA PAY EXTRA JUST FOR A **LOGO!**
ISN'T IT EXTRA-CAPITALIST TO CARE ENOUGH ABOUT THE LOGO TO **FAKE IT?**

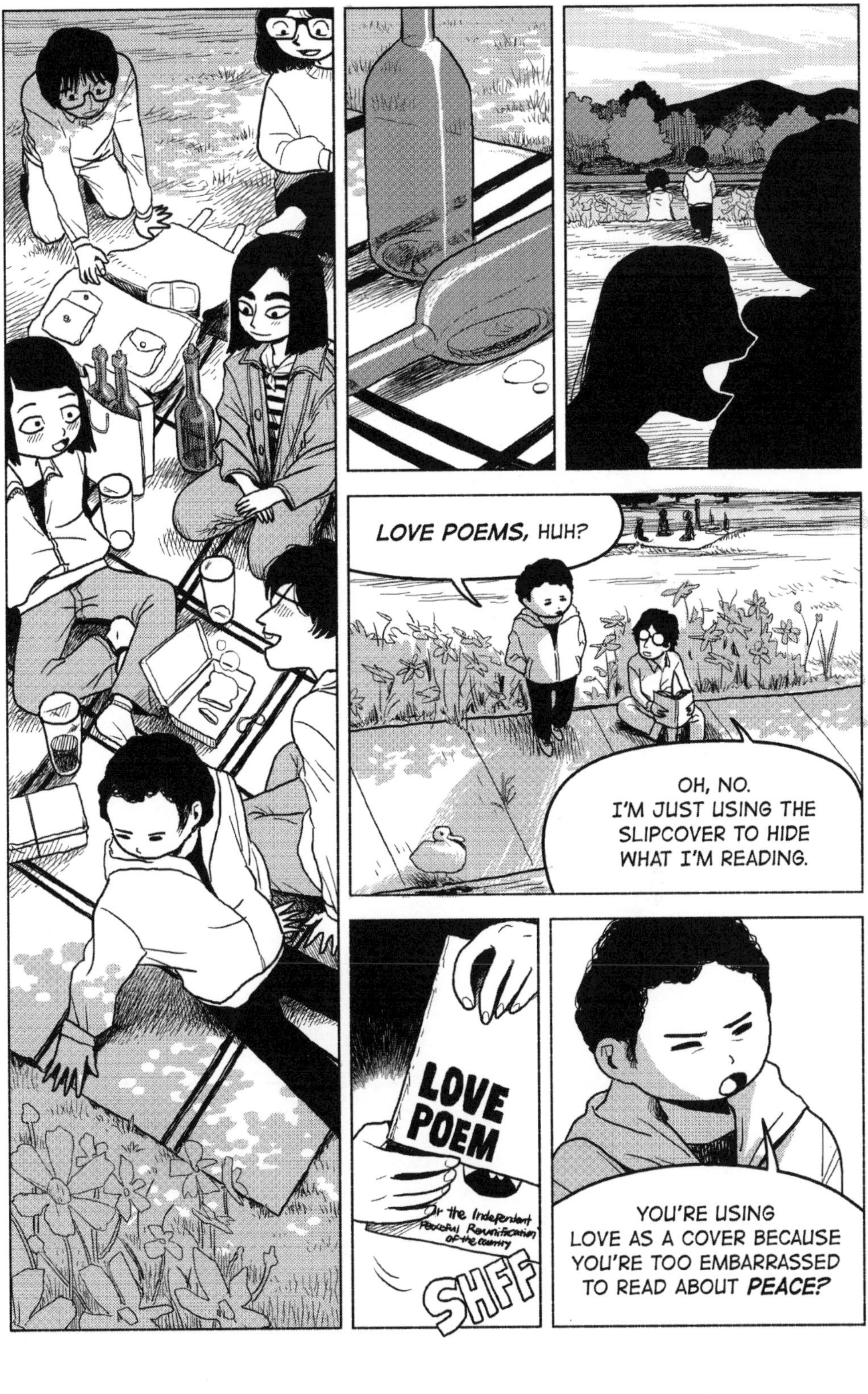
LOVE POEMS, HUH?
OH, NO. I'M JUST USING THE SLIPCOVER TO HIDE WHAT I'M READING.
LOVE POEM
Or the Independent Peaceful Reunification of the country
SHFF
YOU'RE USING LOVE AS A COVER BECAUSE YOU'RE TOO EMBARRASSED TO READ ABOUT PEACE?

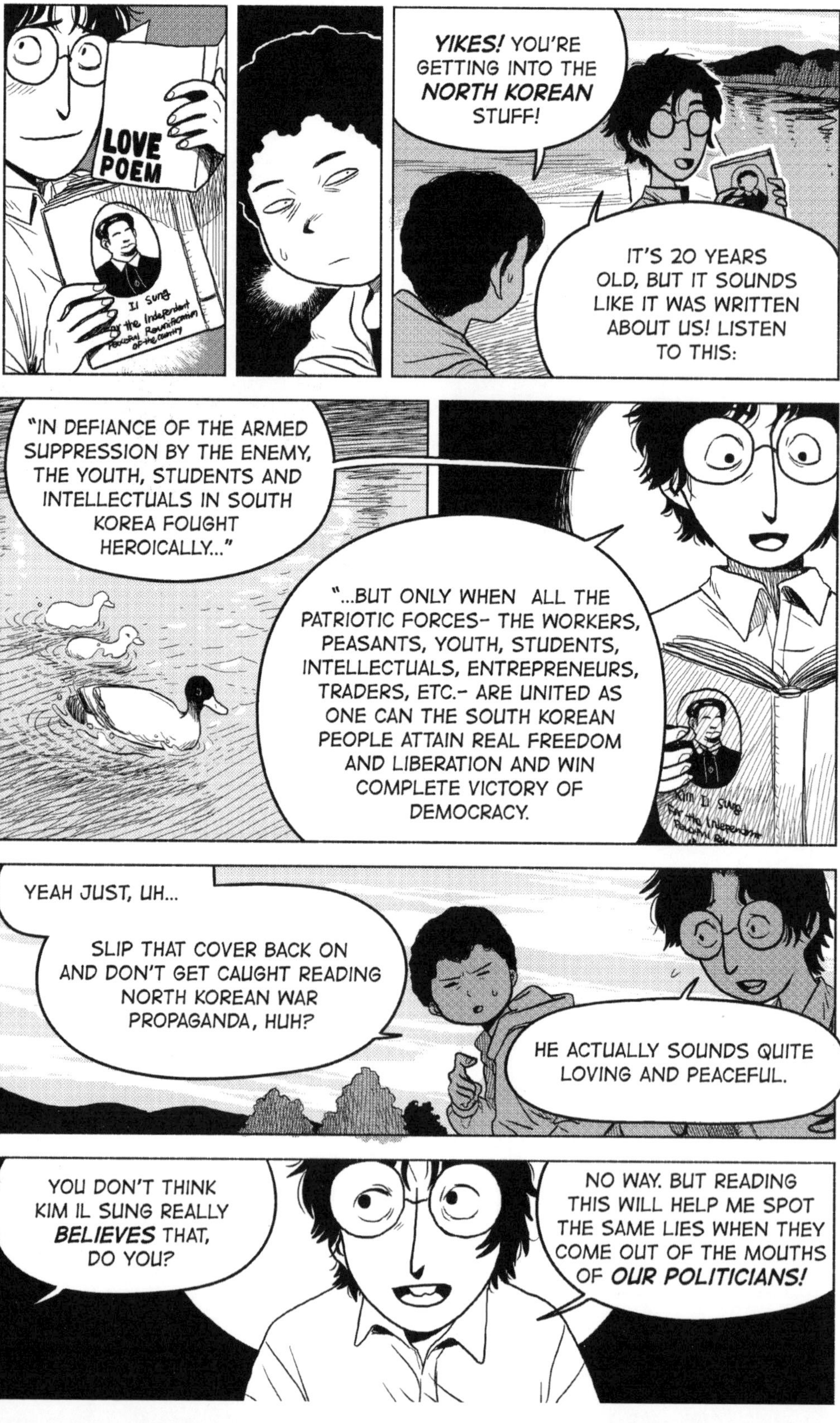

LOVE POEM
YIKES! YOU'RE GETTING INTO THE NORTH KOREAN STUFF!
IT'S 20 YEARS OLD, BUT IT SOUNDS LIKE IT WAS WRITTEN ABOUT US! LISTEN TO THIS:
"IN DEFIANCE OF THE ARMED SUPPRESSION BY THE ENEMY, THE YOUTH, STUDENTS AND INTELLECTUALS IN SOUTH KOREA FOUGHT HEROICALLY..."
"...BUT ONLY WHEN ALL THE PATRIOTIC FORCES- THE WORKERS, PEASANTS, YOUTH, STUDENTS, INTELLECTUALS, ENTREPRENEURS, TRADERS, ETC.- ARE UNITED AS ONE CAN THE SOUTH KOREAN PEOPLE ATTAIN REAL FREEDOM AND LIBERATION AND WIN COMPLETE VICTORY OF DEMOCRACY.
Kim Il Sung
YEAH JUST, UH...
SLIP THAT COVER BACK ON AND DON'T GET CAUGHT READING NORTH KOREAN WAR PROPAGANDA, HUH?
HE ACTUALLY SOUNDS QUITE LOVING AND PEACEFUL.
YOU DON'T THINK KIM IL SUNG REALLY BELIEVES THAT, DO YOU?
NO WAY. BUT READING THIS WILL HELP ME SPOT THE SAME LIES WHEN THEY COME OUT OF THE MOUTHS OF OUR POLITICIANS!

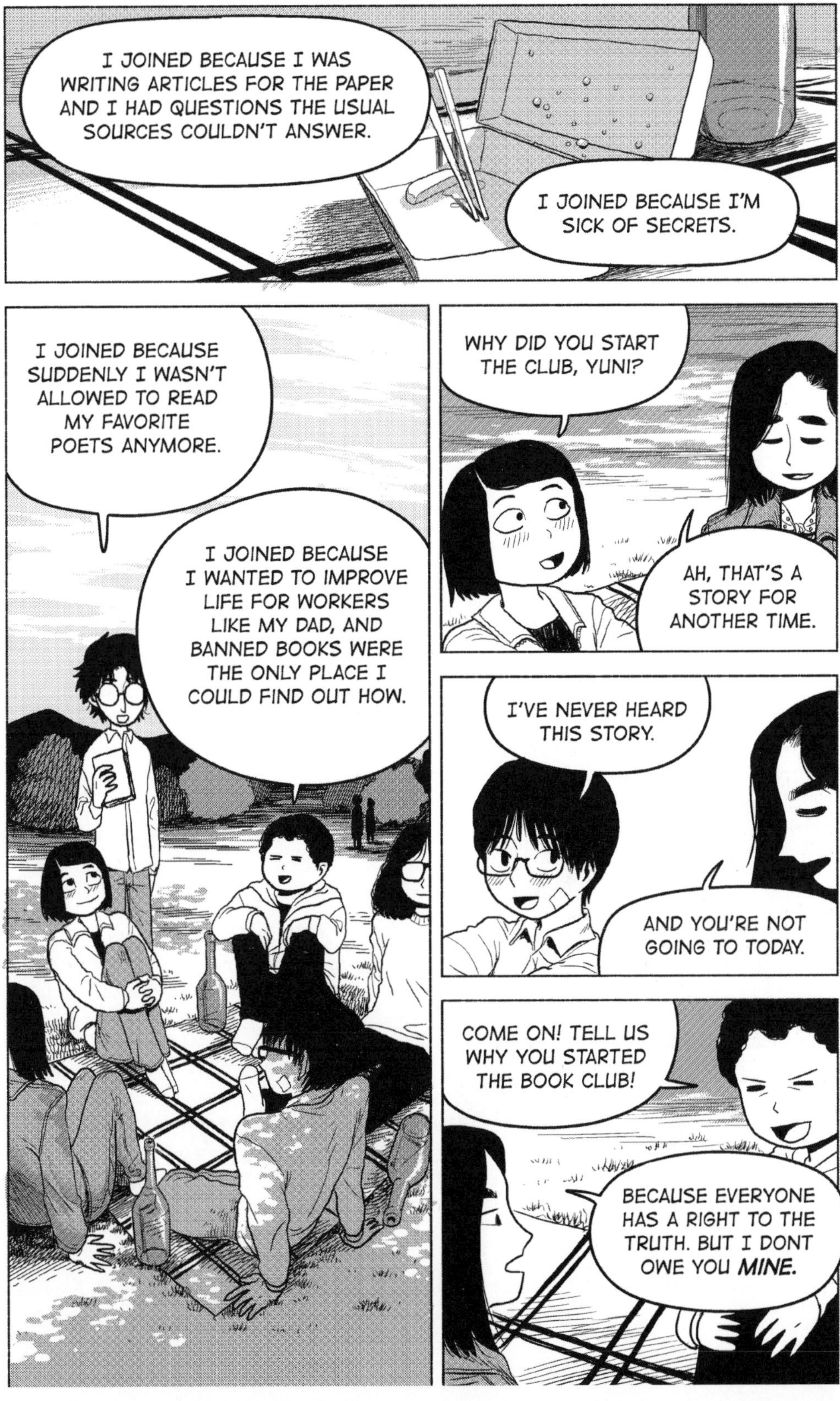
I JOINED BECAUSE I WAS WRITING ARTICLES FOR THE PAPER AND I HAD QUESTIONS THE USUAL SOURCES COULDN'T ANSWER.
I JOINED BECAUSE I'M SICK OF SECRETS.
I JOINED BECAUSE SUDDENLY I WASN'T ALLOWED TO READ MY FAVORITE POETS ANYMORE.
I JOINED BECAUSE I WANTED TO IMPROVE LIFE FOR WORKERS LIKE MY DAD, AND BANNED BOOKS WERE THE ONLY PLACE I COULD FIND OUT HOW.
WHY DID YOU START THE CLUB, YUNI?
AH, THAT'S A STORY FOR ANOTHER TIME.
I'VE NEVER HEARD THIS STORY.
AND YOU'RE NOT GOING TO TODAY.
COME ON! TELL US WHY YOU STARTED THE BOOK CLUB!
BECAUSE EVERYONE HAS A RIGHT TO THE TRUTH. BUT I DONT OWE YOU *MINE.*

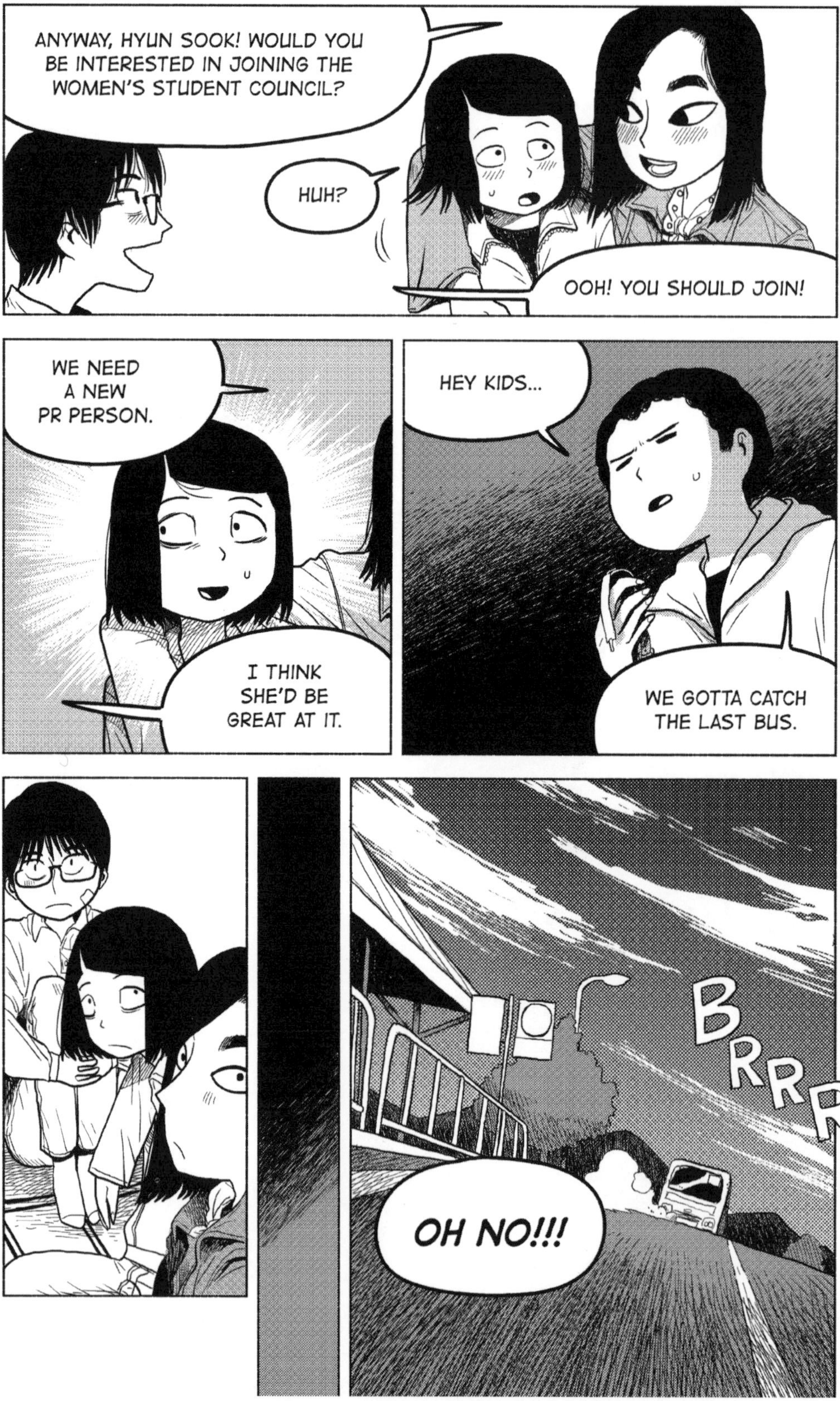
ANYWAY, HYUN SOOK! WOULD YOU BE INTERESTED IN JOINING THE WOMEN'S STUDENT COUNCIL?
HUH?
OOH! YOU SHOULD JOIN!
WE NEED A NEW PR PERSON.
I THINK SHE'D BE GREAT AT IT.
HEY KIDS...
WE GOTTA CATCH THE LAST BUS.
BRRRR
OH NO!!!

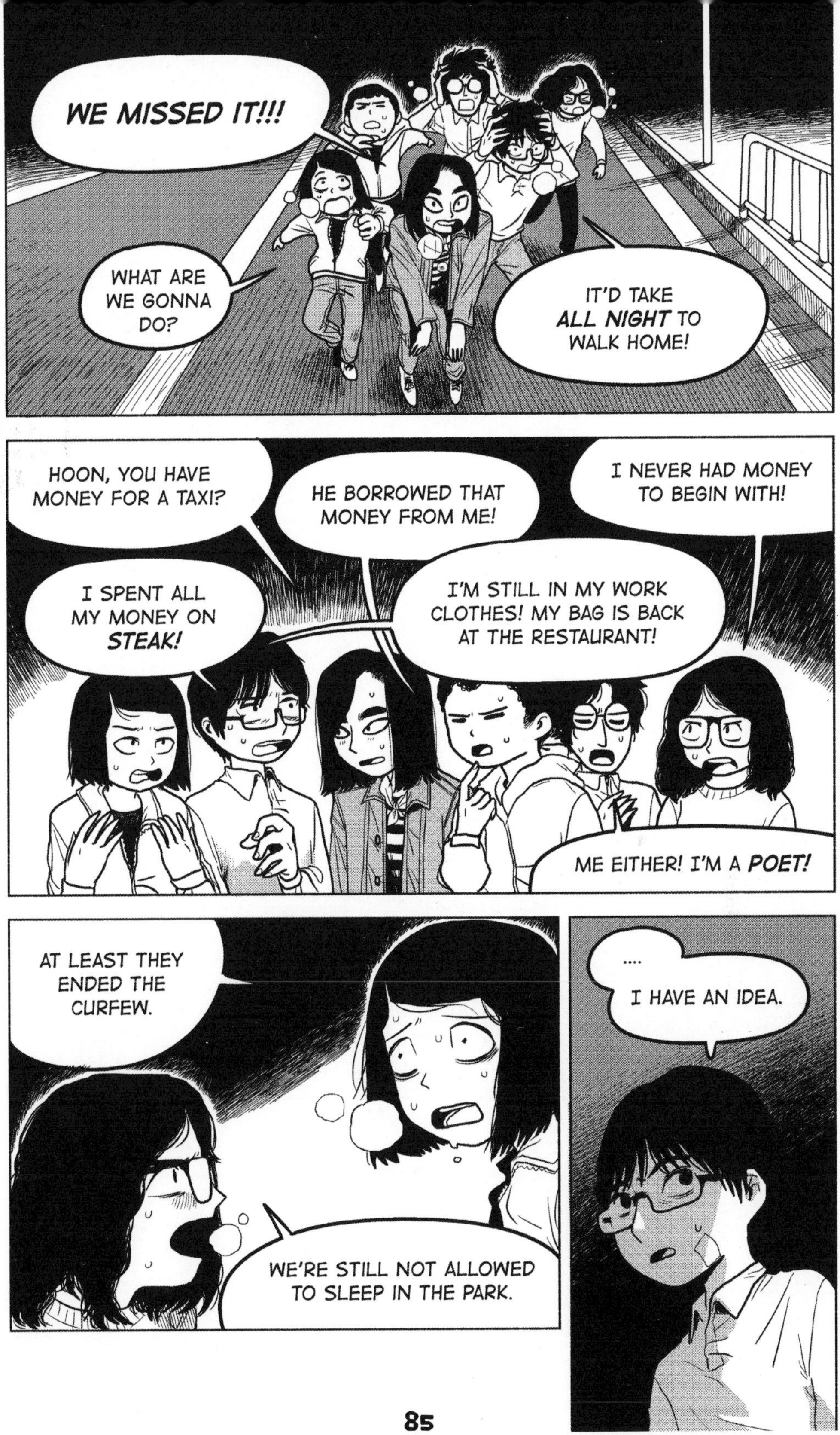
WE MISSED IT!!!
WHAT ARE WE GONNA DO?
IT'D TAKE ALL NIGHT TO WALK HOME!
HOON, YOU HAVE MONEY FOR A TAXI!?
HE BORROWED THAT MONEY FROM ME!
I NEVER HAD MONEY TO BEGIN WITH!
I SPENT ALL MY MONEY ON STEAK!
I'M STILL IN MY WORK CLOTHES! MY BAG IS BACK AT THE RESTAURANT!
ME EITHER! I'M A POET!
AT LEAST THEY ENDED THE CURFEW.
WE'RE STILL NOT ALLOWED TO SLEEP IN THE PARK.
....
I HAVE AN IDEA.

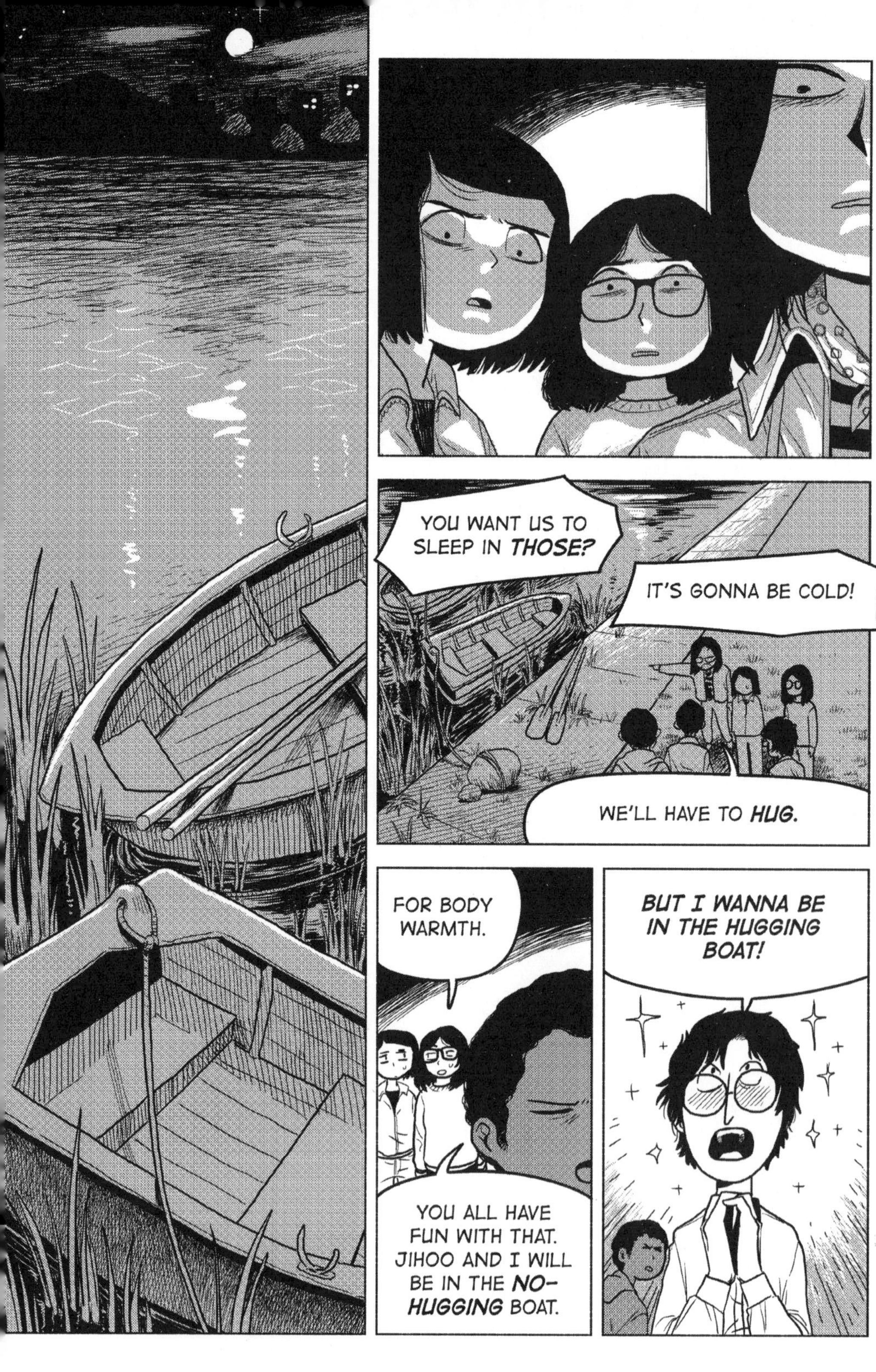

YOU WANT US TO SLEEP IN *THOSE?*
IT'S GONNA BE COLD!
WE'LL HAVE TO *HUG.*
FOR BODY WARMTH.
YOU ALL HAVE FUN WITH THAT. JIHOO AND I WILL BE IN THE *NO-HUGGING* BOAT.
BUT I WANNA BE IN THE HUGGING BOAT!

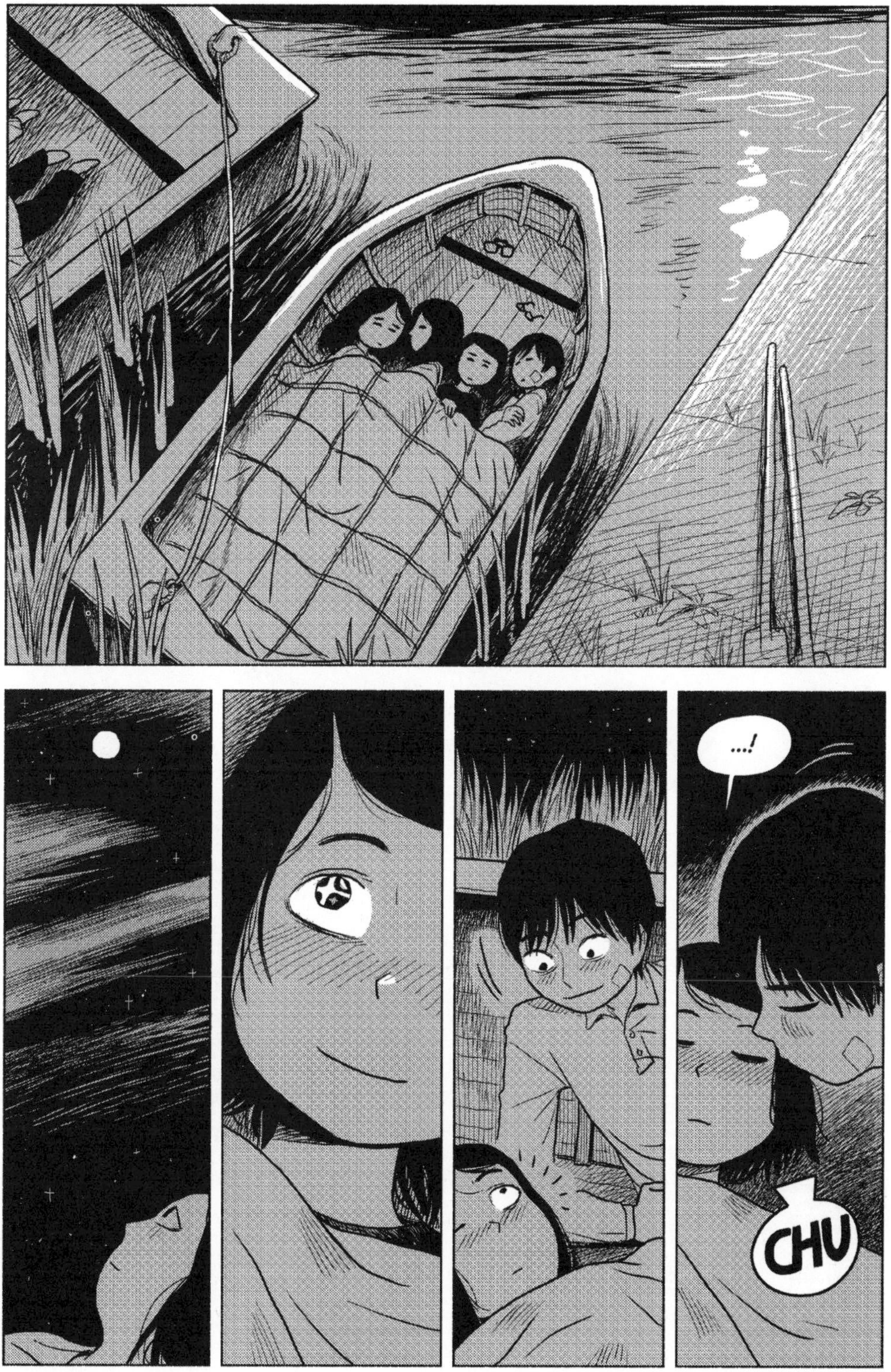
...!
CHU

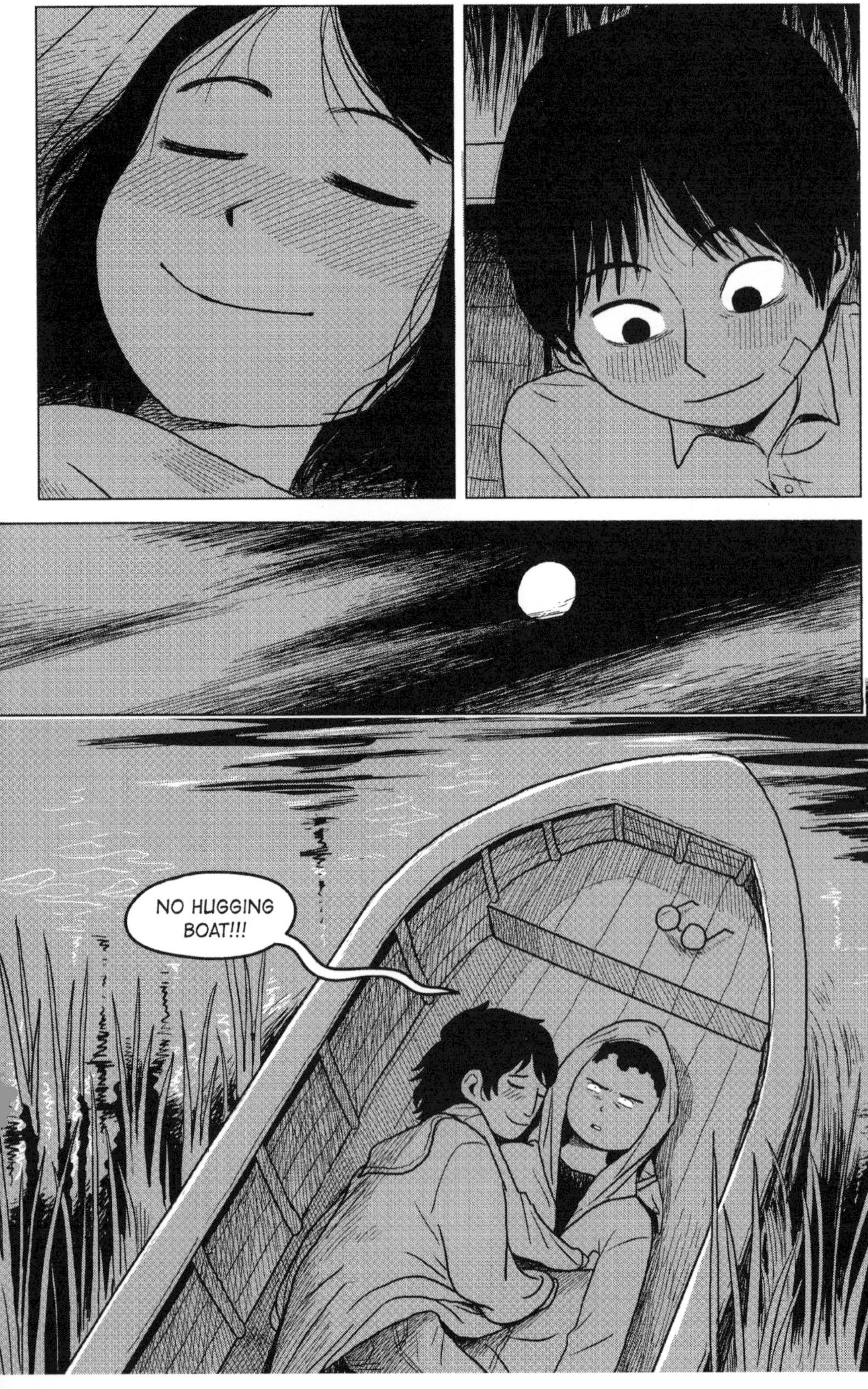
NO HUGGING BOAT!!!

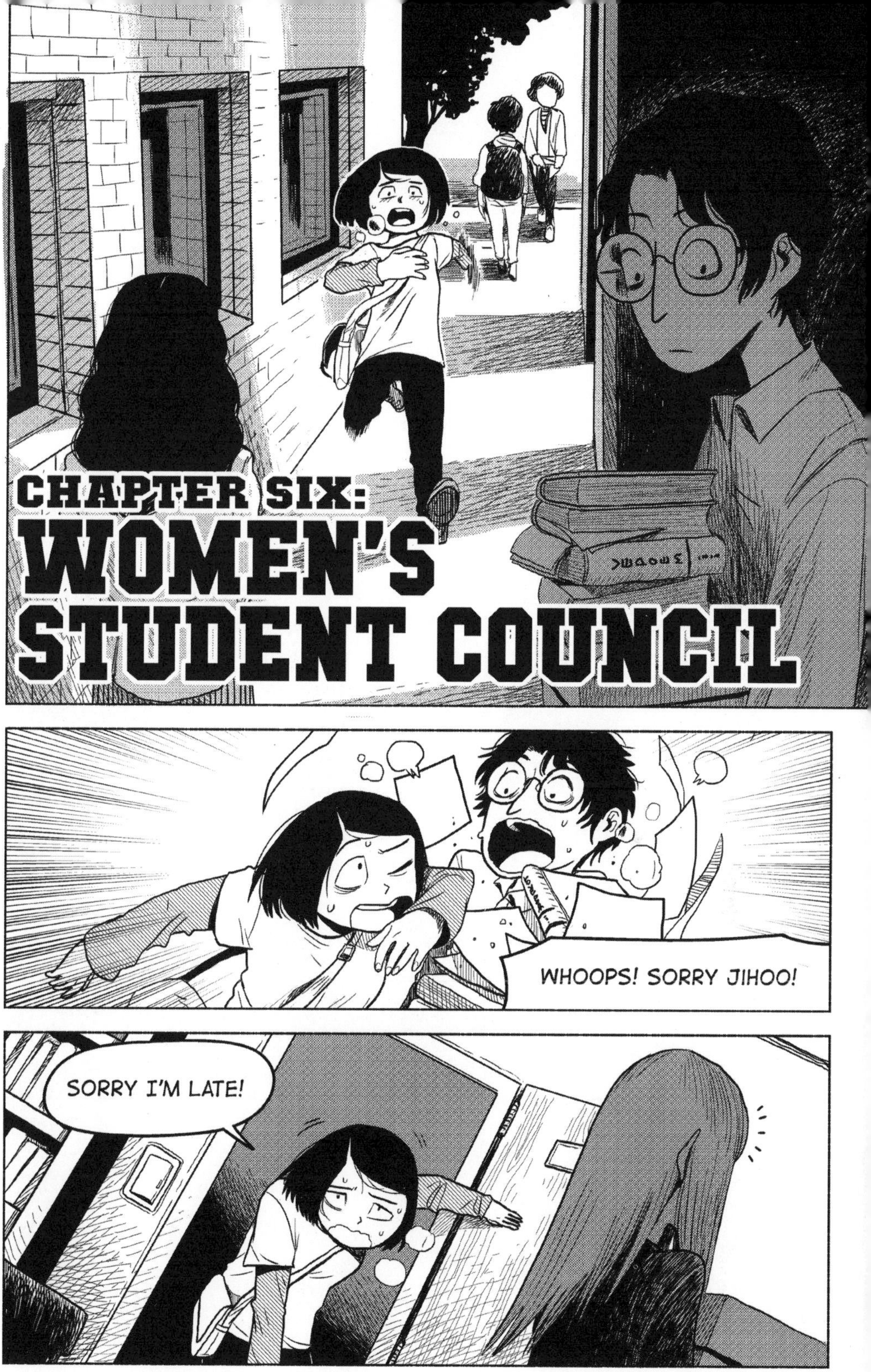
CHAPTER SIX:
WOMEN'S
STUDENT COUNCIL
WHOOPS! SORRY JIHOO!
SORRY I'M LATE!

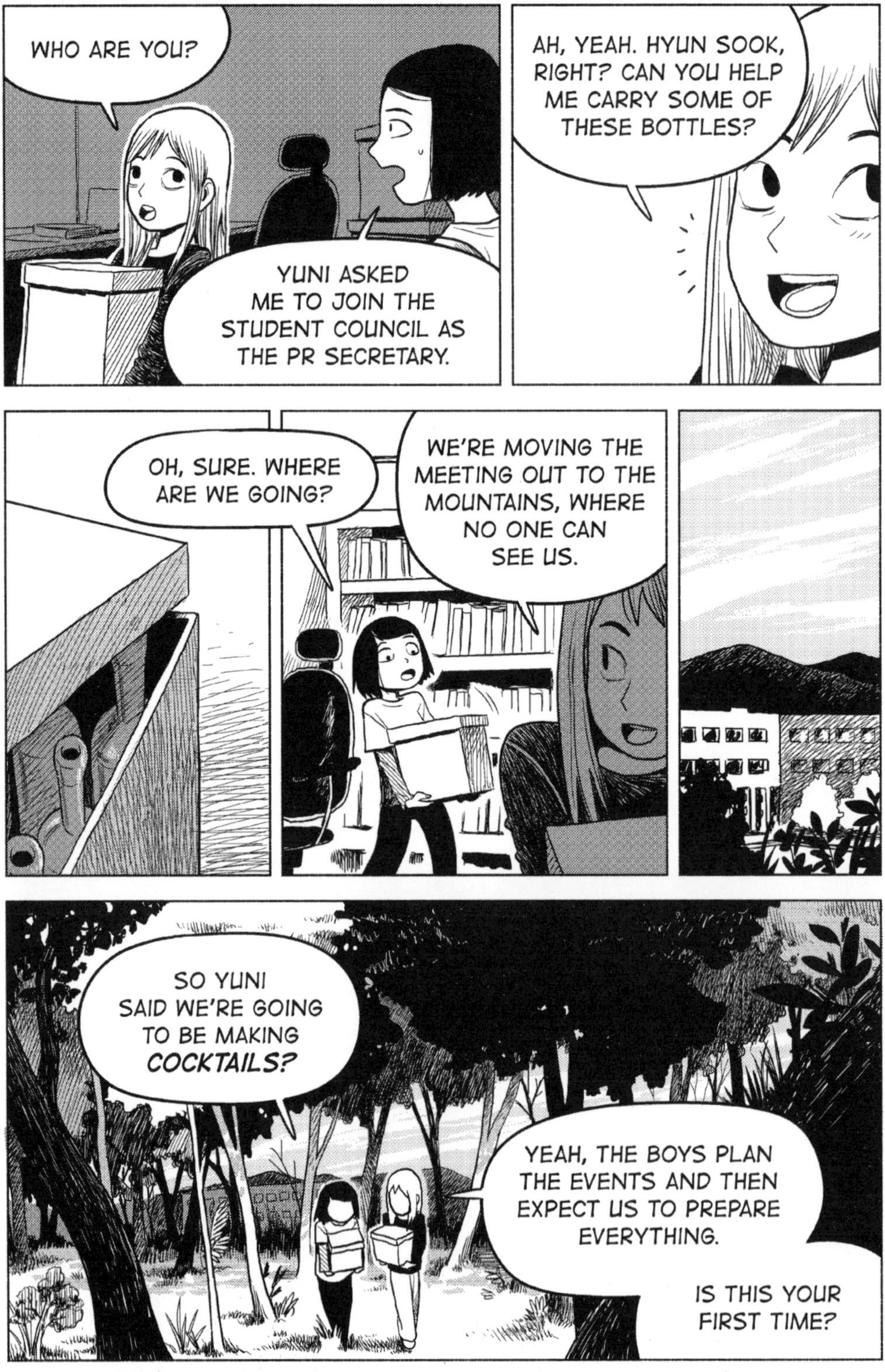
WHO ARE YOU?
YUNI ASKED ME TO JOIN THE STUDENT COUNCIL AS THE PR SECRETARY.
AH, YEAH. HYUN SOOK, RIGHT? CAN YOU HELP ME CARRY SOME OF THESE BOTTLES?
OH, SURE. WHERE ARE WE GOING?
WE'RE MOVING THE MEETING OUT TO THE MOUNTAINS, WHERE NO ONE CAN SEE US.
SO YUNI SAID WE'RE GOING TO BE MAKING *COCKTAILS?*
YEAH, THE BOYS PLAN THE EVENTS AND THEN EXPECT US TO PREPARE EVERYTHING.
IS THIS YOUR FIRST TIME?

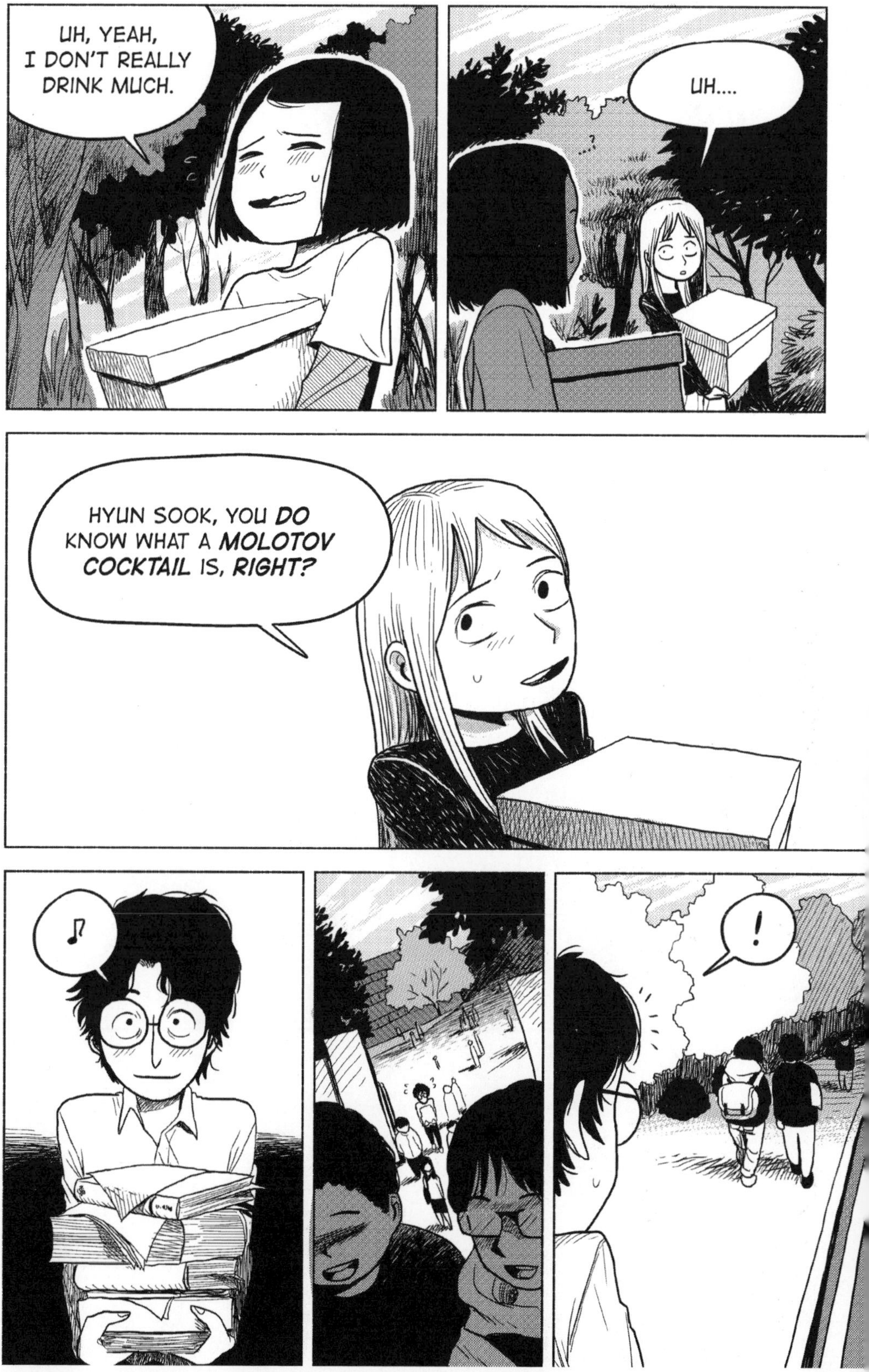
UH, YEAH, I DON'T REALLY DRINK MUCH.
UH....
HYUN SOOK, YOU DO KNOW WHAT A MOLOTOV COCKTAIL IS, RIGHT?
♫
!

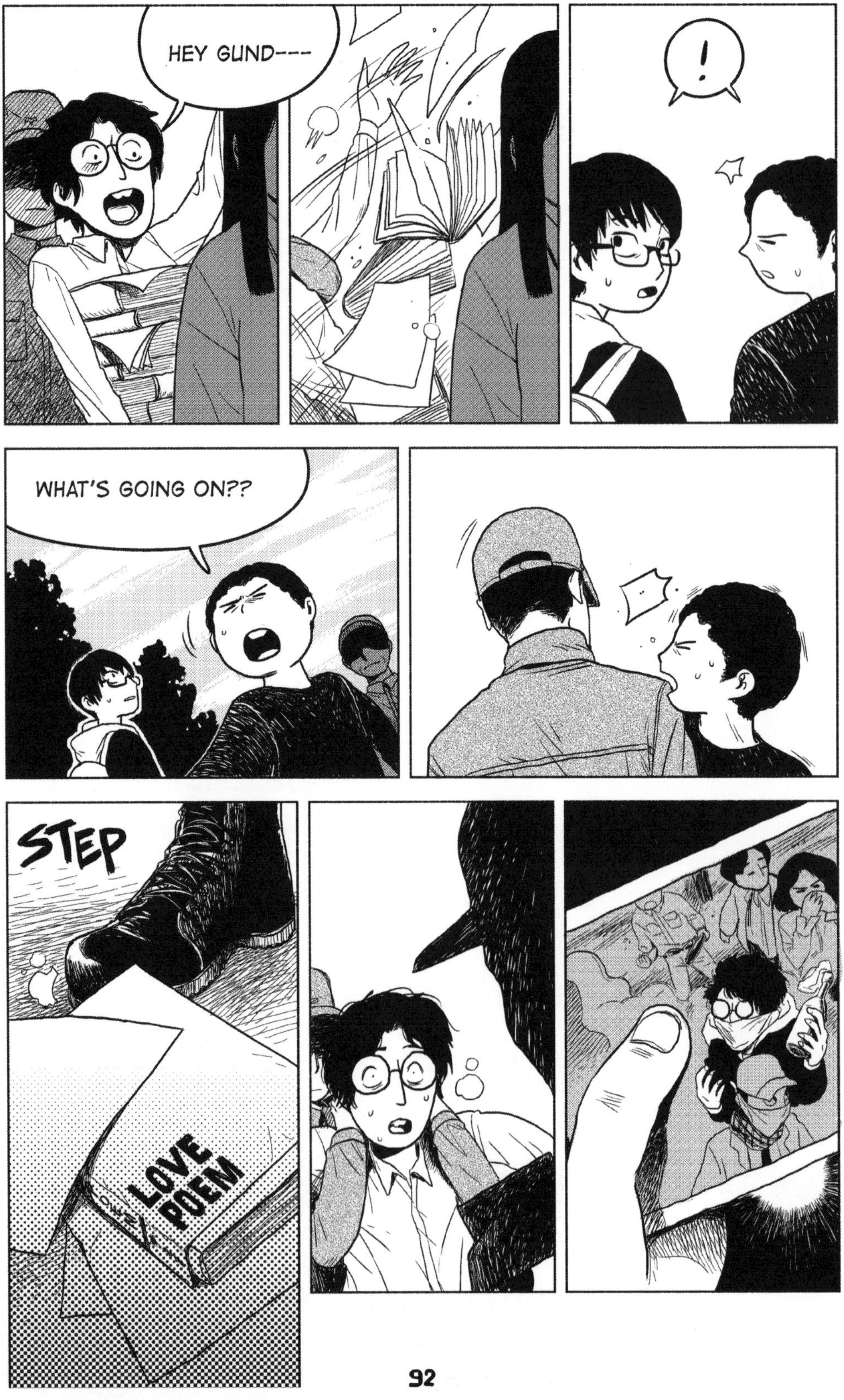
HEY GUND---
!
WHAT'S GOING ON??
STEP
LOVE POEM

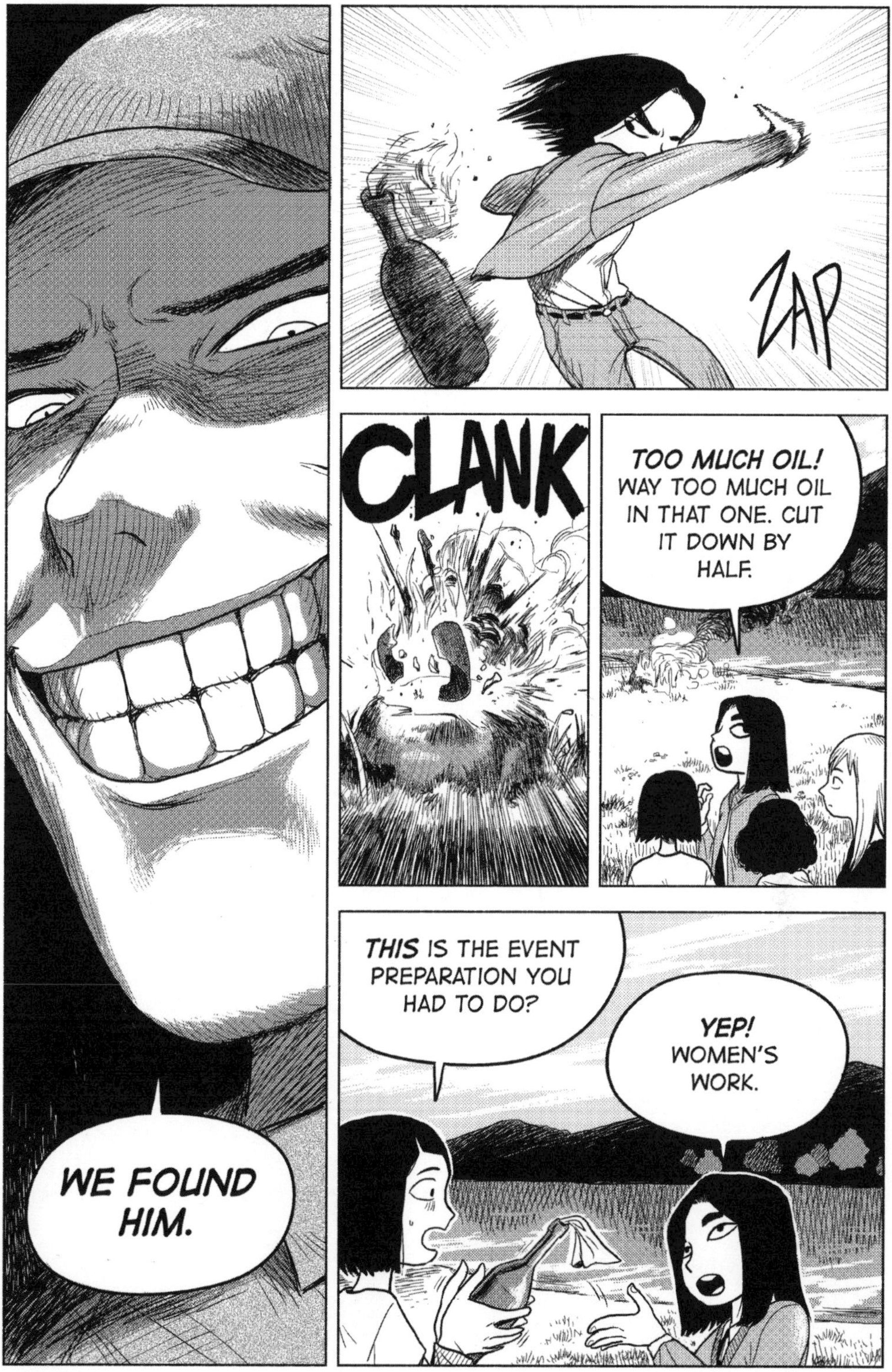

WE FOUND HIM.
ZAP
CLANK
TOO MUCH OIL! WAY TOO MUCH OIL IN THAT ONE. CUT IT DOWN BY HALF.
THIS IS THE EVENT PREPARATION YOU HAD TO DO?
YEP! WOMEN'S WORK.

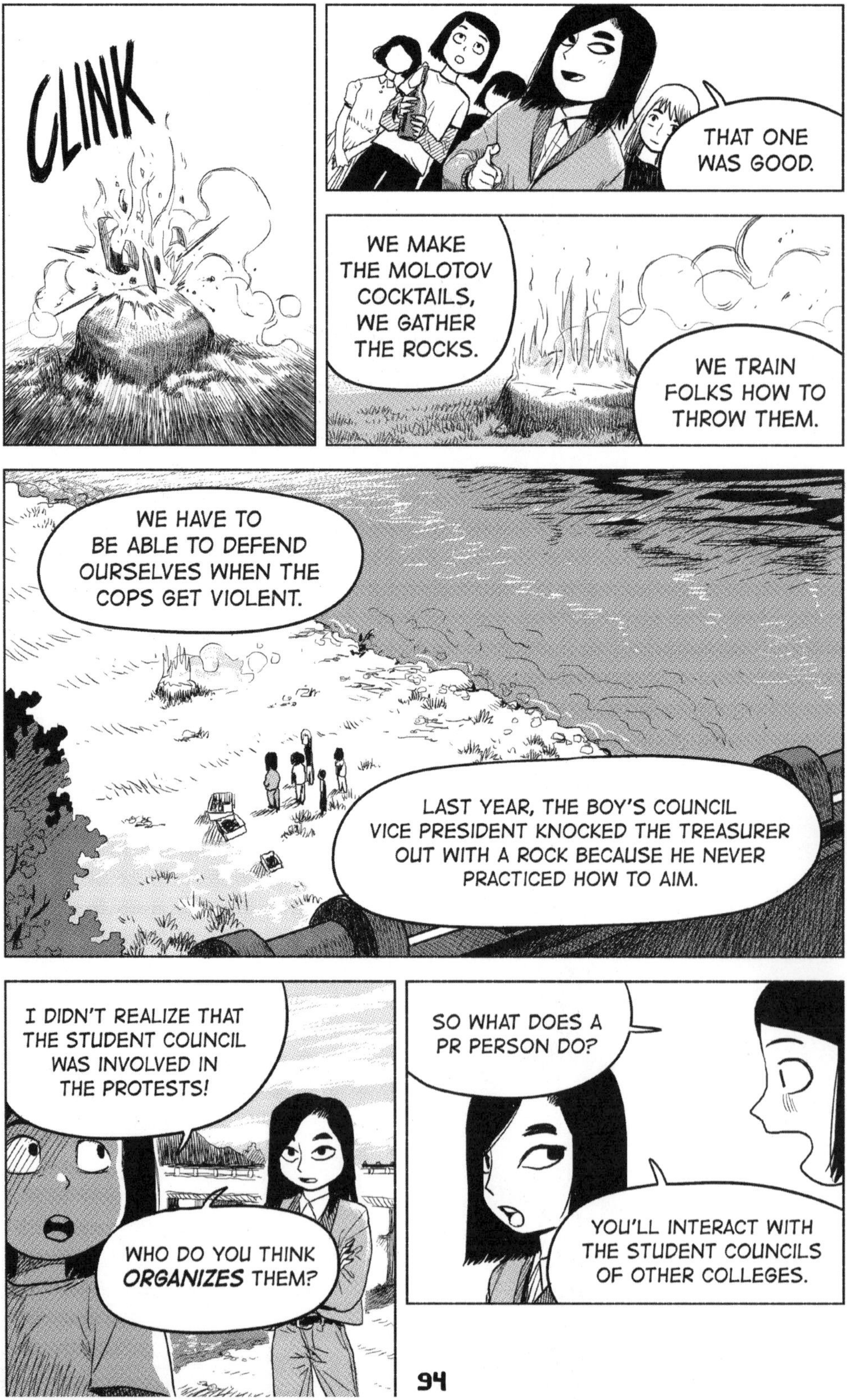
CLINK
THAT ONE WAS GOOD.
WE MAKE THE MOLOTOV COCKTAILS, WE GATHER THE ROCKS.
WE TRAIN FOLKS HOW TO THROW THEM.
WE HAVE TO BE ABLE TO DEFEND OURSELVES WHEN THE COPS GET VIOLENT.
LAST YEAR, THE BOY'S COUNCIL VICE PRESIDENT KNOCKED THE TREASURER OUT WITH A ROCK BECAUSE HE NEVER PRACTICED HOW TO AIM.
I DIDN'T REALIZE THAT THE STUDENT COUNCIL WAS INVOLVED IN THE PROTESTS!
WHO DO YOU THINK *ORGANIZES* THEM?
SO WHAT DOES A PR PERSON DO?
YOU'LL INTERACT WITH THE STUDENT COUNCILS OF OTHER COLLEGES.

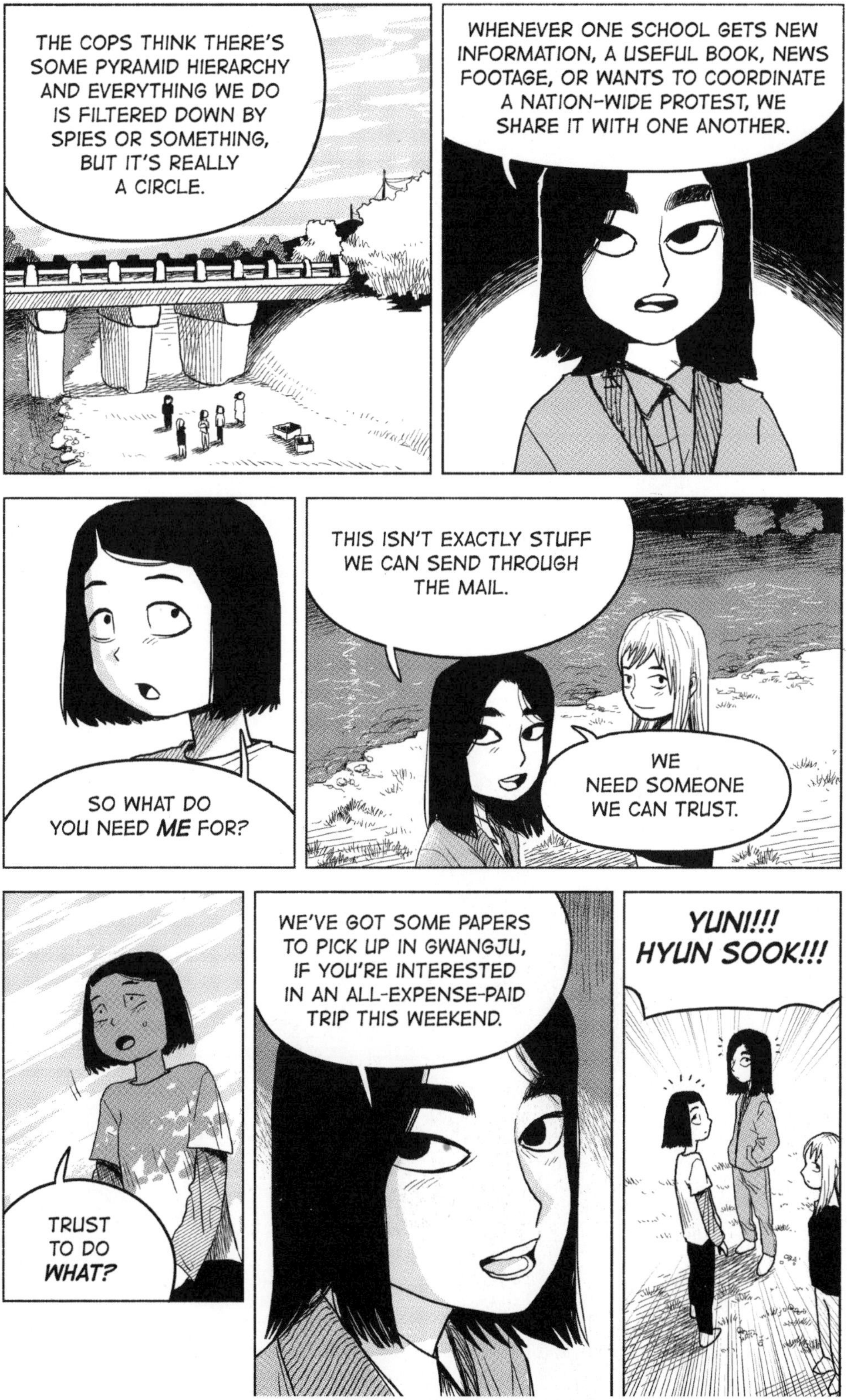
THE COPS THINK THERE'S SOME PYRAMID HIERARCHY AND EVERYTHING WE DO IS FILTERED DOWN BY SPIES OR SOMETHING, BUT IT'S REALLY A CIRCLE.
WHENEVER ONE SCHOOL GETS NEW INFORMATION, A USEFUL BOOK, NEWS FOOTAGE, OR WANTS TO COORDINATE A NATION-WIDE PROTEST, WE SHARE IT WITH ONE ANOTHER.
SO WHAT DO YOU NEED *ME* FOR?
THIS ISN'T EXACTLY STUFF WE CAN SEND THROUGH THE MAIL.
WE NEED SOMEONE WE CAN TRUST.
TRUST TO DO *WHAT?*
WE'VE GOT SOME PAPERS TO PICK UP IN GWANGJU, IF YOU'RE INTERESTED IN AN ALL-EXPENSE-PAID TRIP THIS WEEKEND.
YUNI!!! HYUN SOOK!!!

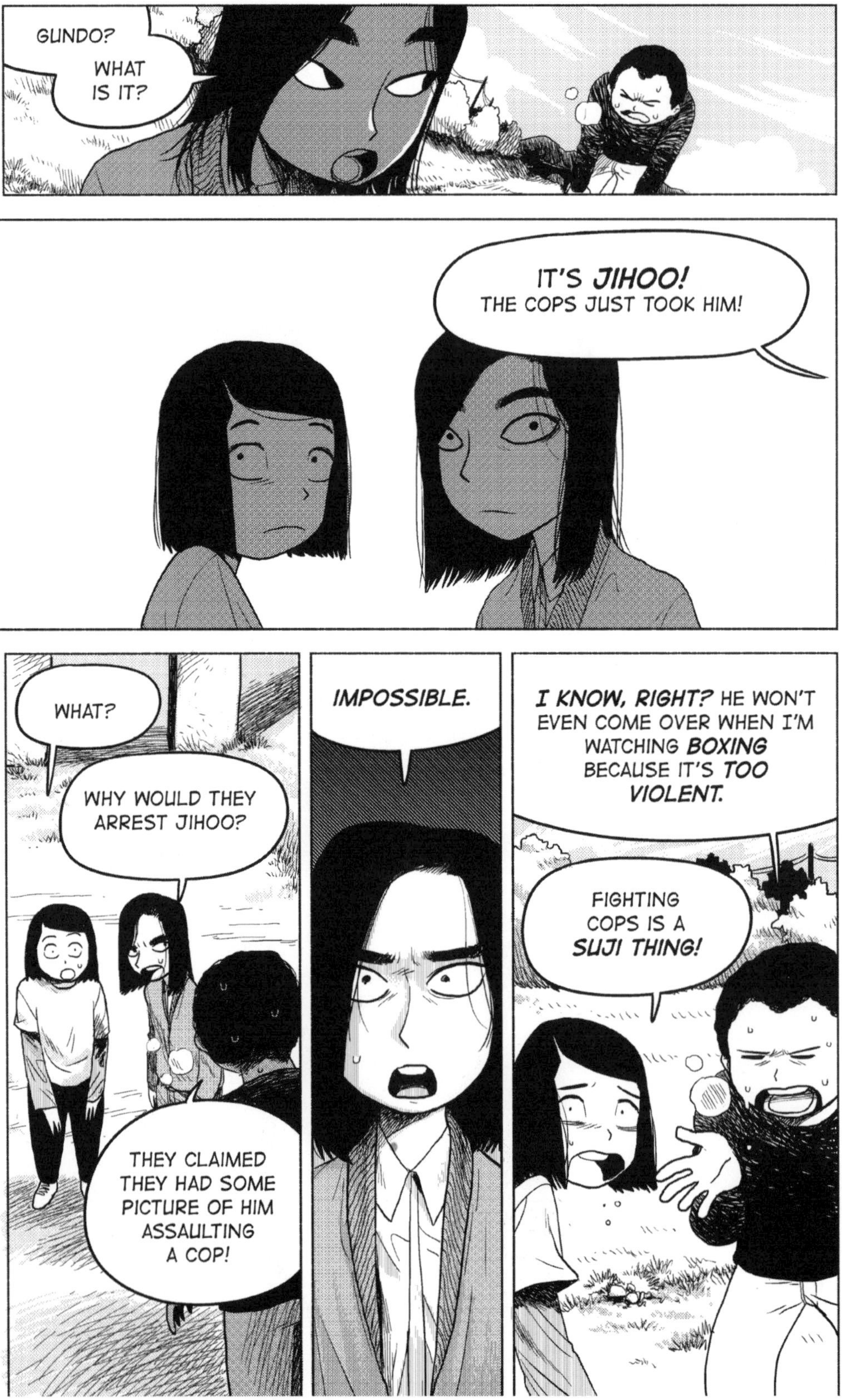
GUNDO?
WHAT IS IT?
IT'S JIHOO! THE COPS JUST TOOK HIM!
WHAT?
WHY WOULD THEY ARREST JIHOO?
THEY CLAIMED THEY HAD SOME PICTURE OF HIM ASSAULTING A COP!
IMPOSSIBLE.
I KNOW, RIGHT? HE WON'T EVEN COME OVER WHEN I'M WATCHING BOXING BECAUSE IT'S TOO VIOLENT.
FIGHTING COPS IS A SUJI THING!

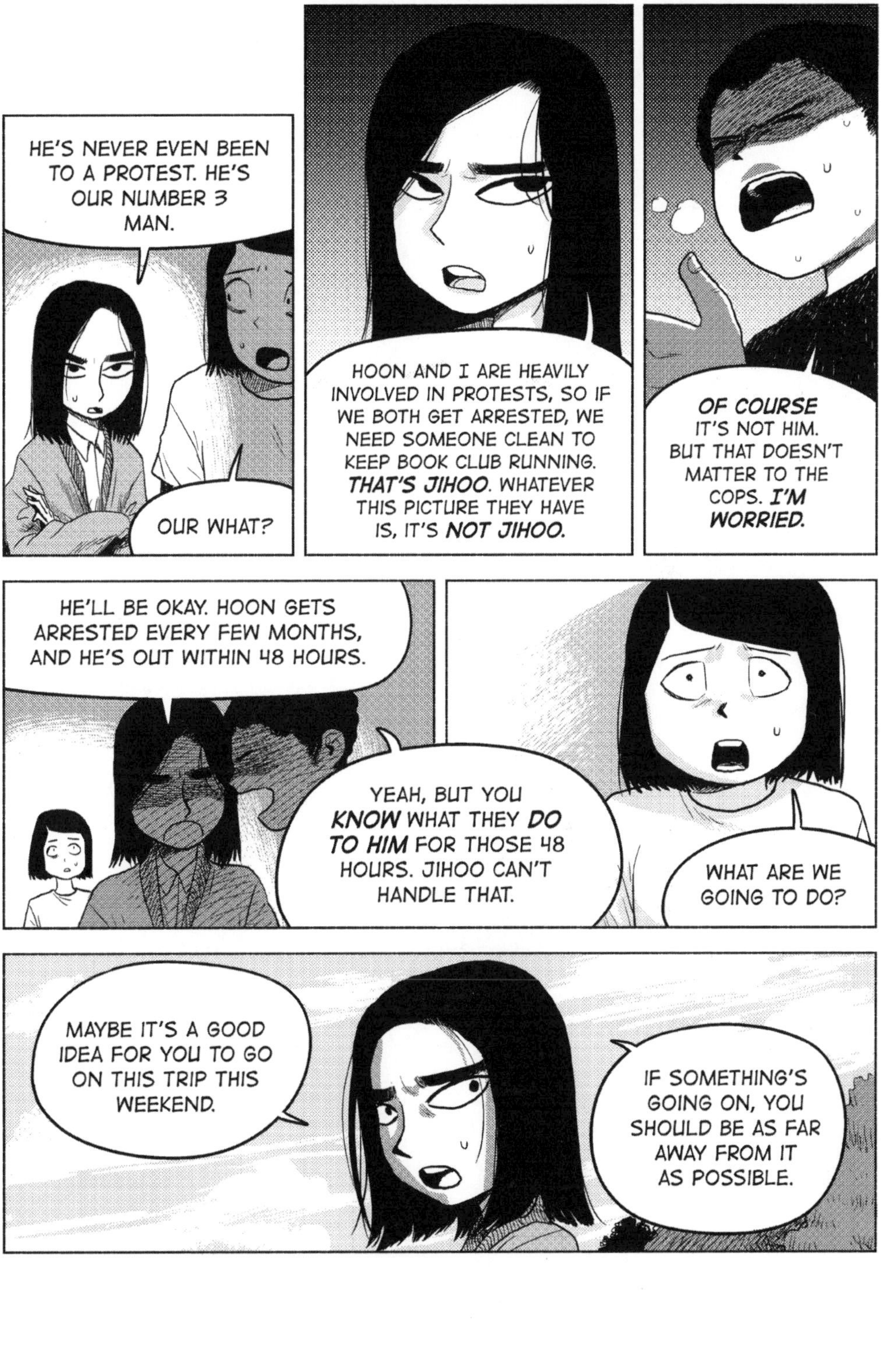
HE'S NEVER EVEN BEEN TO A PROTEST. HE'S OUR NUMBER 3 MAN.
OUR WHAT?
HOON AND I ARE HEAVILY INVOLVED IN PROTESTS, SO IF WE BOTH GET ARRESTED, WE NEED SOMEONE CLEAN TO KEEP BOOK CLUB RUNNING. THAT'S JIHOO. WHATEVER THIS PICTURE THEY HAVE IS, IT'S NOT JIHOO.
OF COURSE IT'S NOT HIM. BUT THAT DOESN'T MATTER TO THE COPS. I'M WORRIED.
HE'LL BE OKAY. HOON GETS ARRESTED EVERY FEW MONTHS, AND HE'S OUT WITHIN 48 HOURS.
YEAH, BUT YOU KNOW WHAT THEY DO TO HIM FOR THOSE 48 HOURS. JIHOO CAN'T HANDLE THAT.
WHAT ARE WE GOING TO DO?
MAYBE IT'S A GOOD IDEA FOR YOU TO GO ON THIS TRIP THIS WEEKEND.
IF SOMETHING'S GOING ON, YOU SHOULD BE AS FAR AWAY FROM IT AS POSSIBLE.

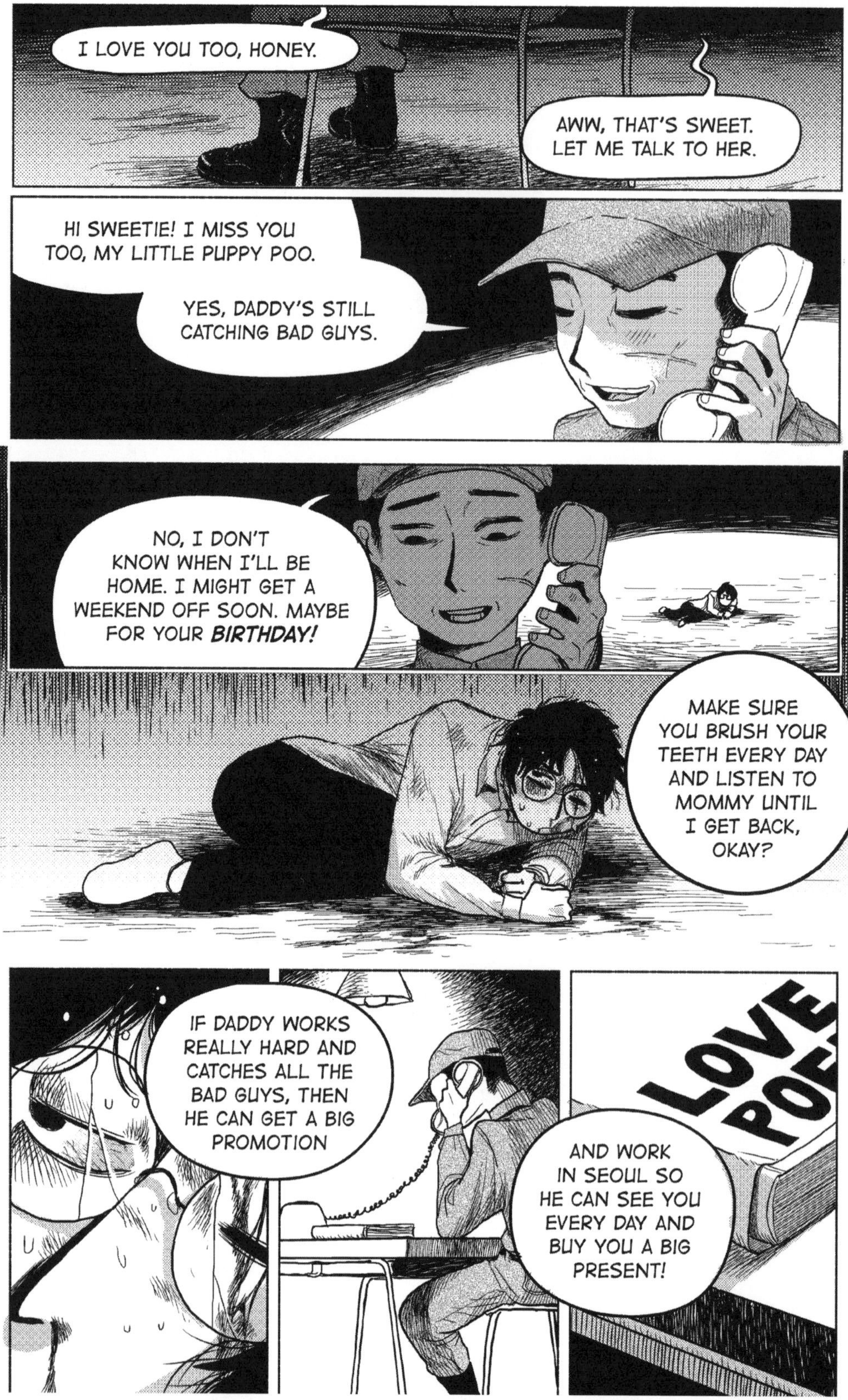
I LOVE YOU TOO, HONEY.
AWW, THAT'S SWEET. LET ME TALK TO HER.
HI SWEETIE! I MISS YOU TOO, MY LITTLE PUPPY POO.
YES, DADDY'S STILL CATCHING BAD GUYS.
NO, I DON'T KNOW WHEN I'LL BE HOME. I MIGHT GET A WEEKEND OFF SOON. MAYBE FOR YOUR **BIRTHDAY!**
MAKE SURE YOU BRUSH YOUR TEETH EVERY DAY AND LISTEN TO MOMMY UNTIL I GET BACK, OKAY?
IF DADDY WORKS REALLY HARD AND CATCHES ALL THE BAD GUYS, THEN HE CAN GET A BIG PROMOTION
AND WORK IN SEOUL SO HE CAN SEE YOU EVERY DAY AND BUY YOU A BIG PRESENT!
LOVE

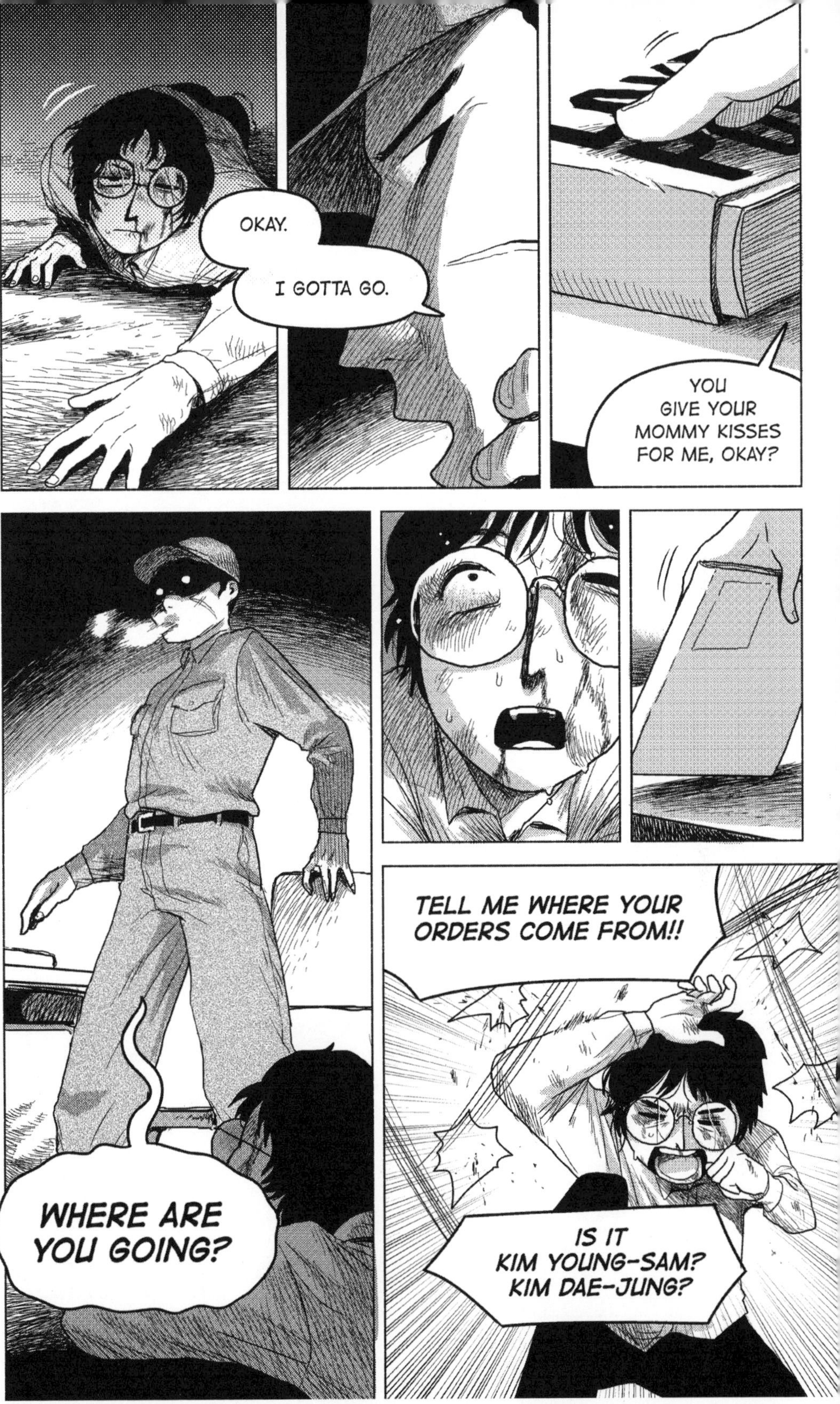
OKAY.
I GOTTA GO.
YOU GIVE YOUR MOMMY KISSES FOR ME, OKAY?
WHERE ARE YOU GOING?
TELL ME WHERE YOUR ORDERS COME FROM!!
IS IT KIM YOUNG-SAM? KIM DAE-JUNG?

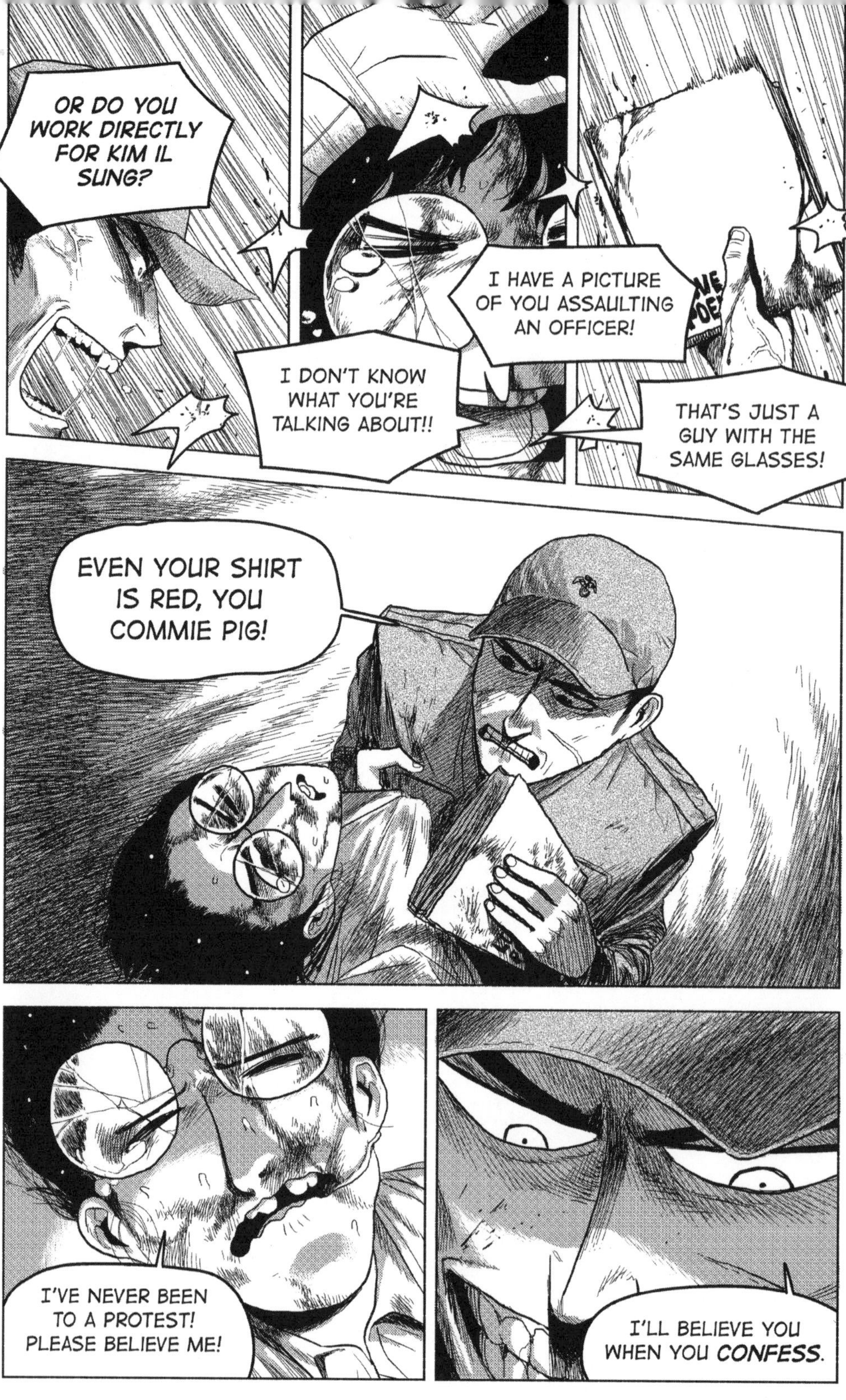
OR DO YOU WORK DIRECTLY FOR KIM IL SUNG?
I DON'T KNOW WHAT YOU'RE TALKING ABOUT!!
I HAVE A PICTURE OF YOU ASSAULTING AN OFFICER!
THAT'S JUST A GUY WITH THE SAME GLASSES!
EVEN YOUR SHIRT IS RED, YOU COMMIE PIG!
I'VE NEVER BEEN TO A PROTEST! PLEASE BELIEVE ME!
I'LL BELIEVE YOU WHEN YOU CONFESS.

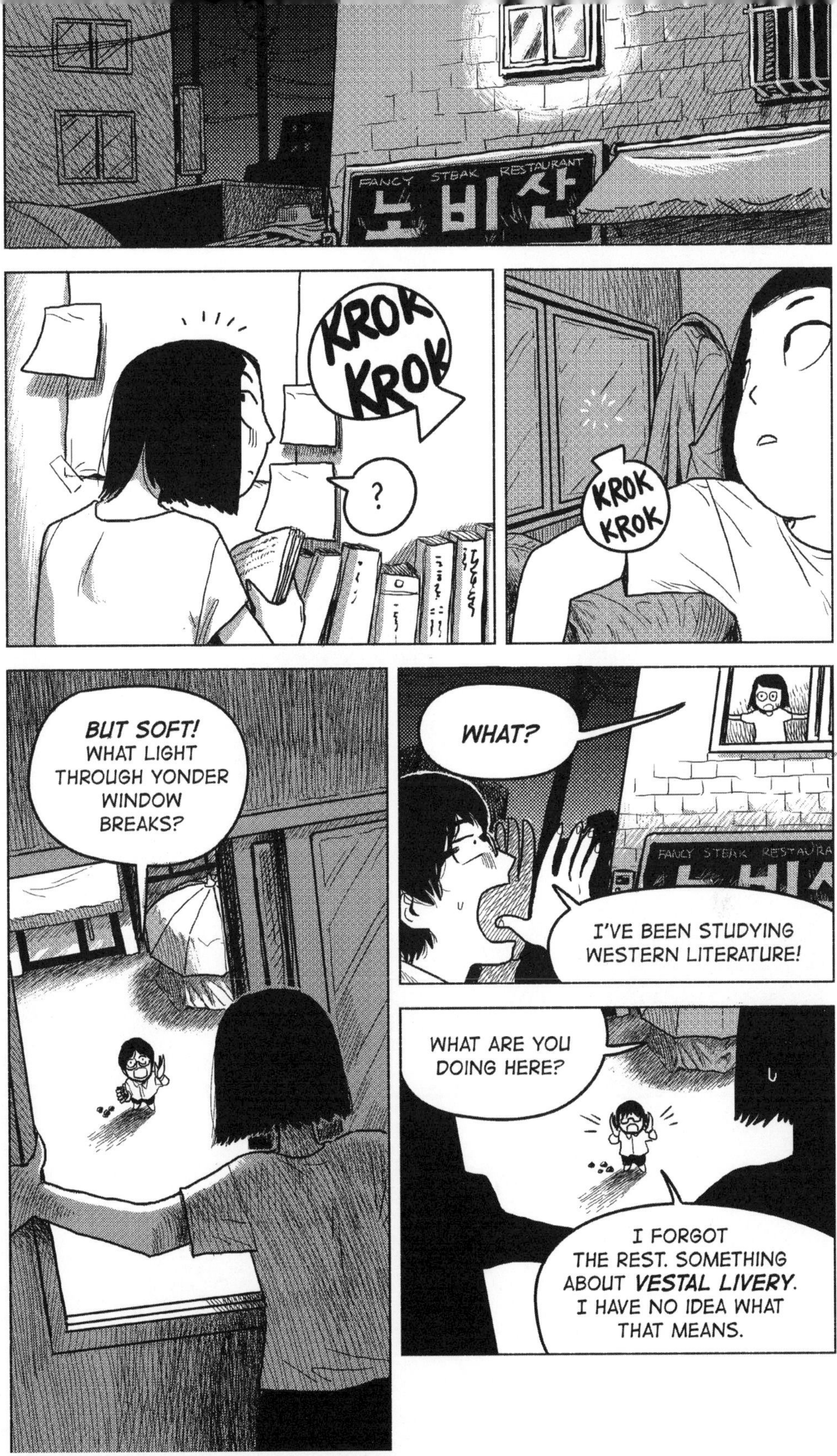

FANCY STBAK RESTAURANT
노비산
KROK KROK
?
KROK KROK
BUT SOFT! WHAT LIGHT THROUGH YONDER WINDOW BREAKS?
WHAT?
FANCY STBAK RESTAURA
I'VE BEEN STUDYING WESTERN LITERATURE!
WHAT ARE YOU DOING HERE?
I FORGOT THE REST. SOMETHING ABOUT VESTAL LIVERY. I HAVE NO IDEA WHAT THAT MEANS.

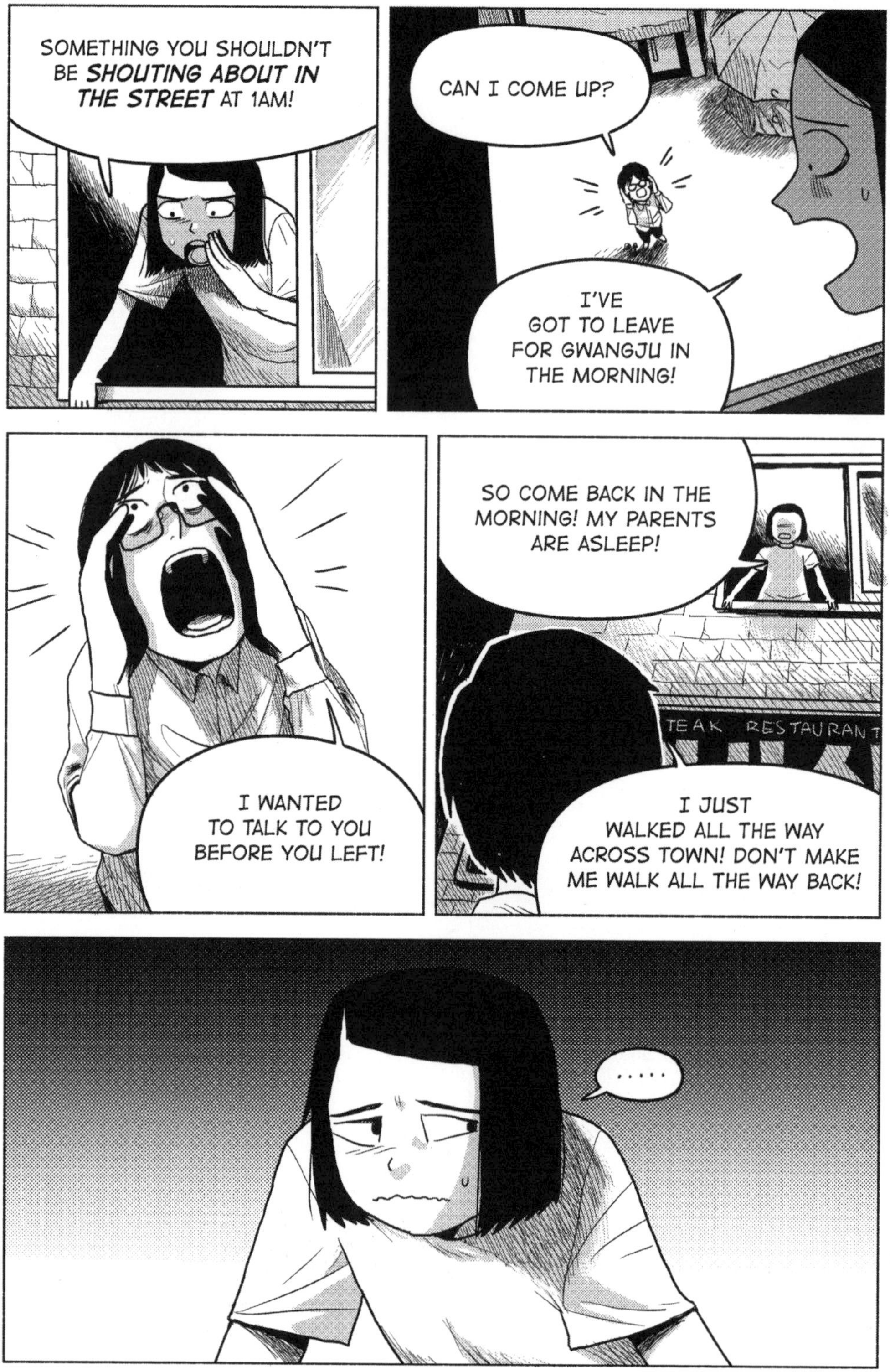
SOMETHING YOU SHOULDN'T BE ***SHOUTING ABOUT IN THE STREET*** AT 1AM!
CAN I COME UP?
I'VE GOT TO LEAVE FOR GWANGJU IN THE MORNING!
I WANTED TO TALK TO YOU BEFORE YOU LEFT!
SO COME BACK IN THE MORNING! MY PARENTS ARE ASLEEP!
TEAK RESTAURANT
I JUST WALKED ALL THE WAY ACROSS TOWN! DON'T MAKE ME WALK ALL THE WAY BACK!
......

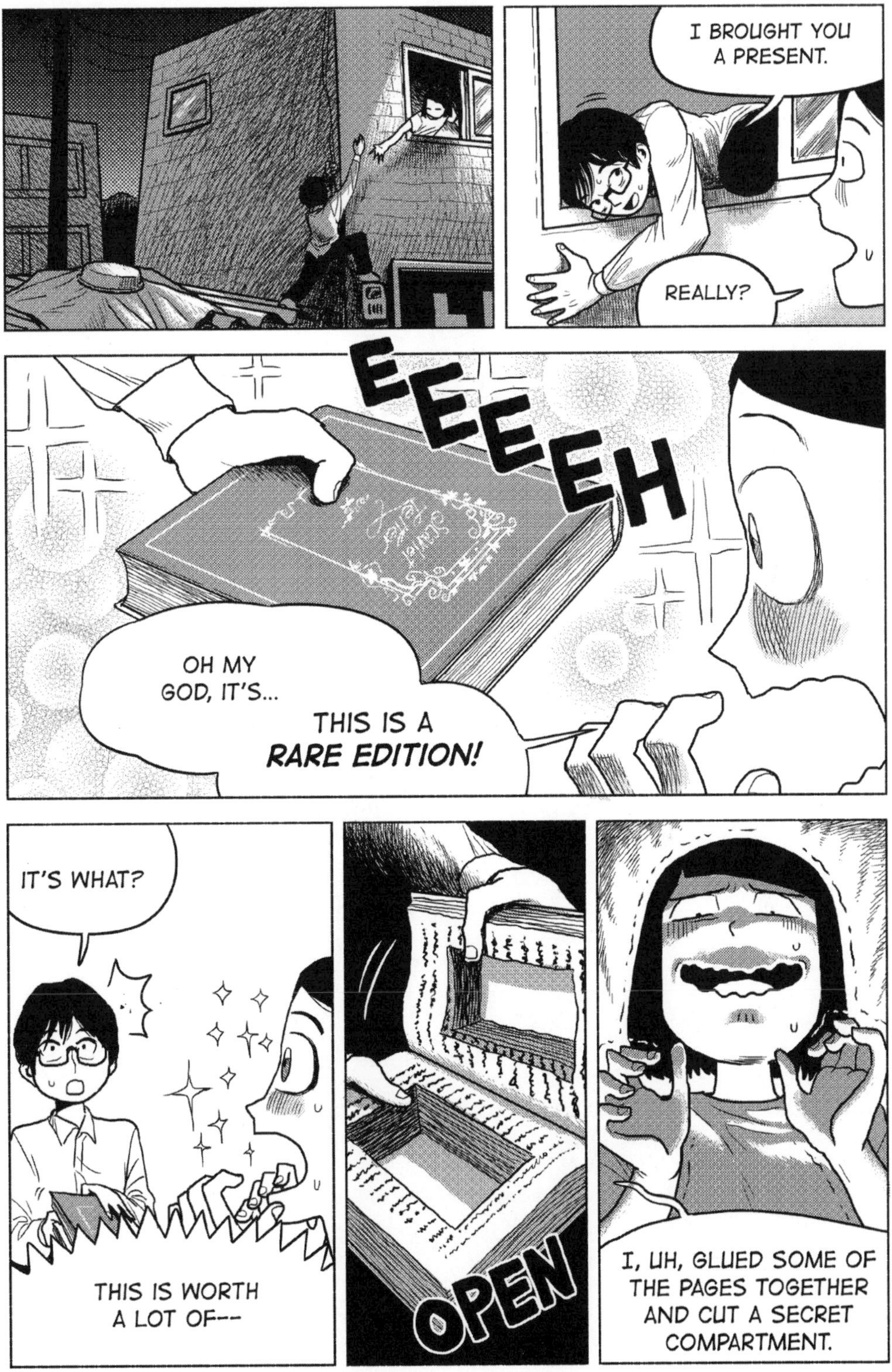
I BROUGHT YOU A PRESENT.
REALLY?
EEEEEH
OH MY GOD, IT'S...
THIS IS A *RARE EDITION!*
IT'S WHAT?
THIS IS WORTH A LOT OF--
OPEN
I, UH, GLUED SOME OF THE PAGES TOGETHER AND CUT A SECRET COMPARTMENT.

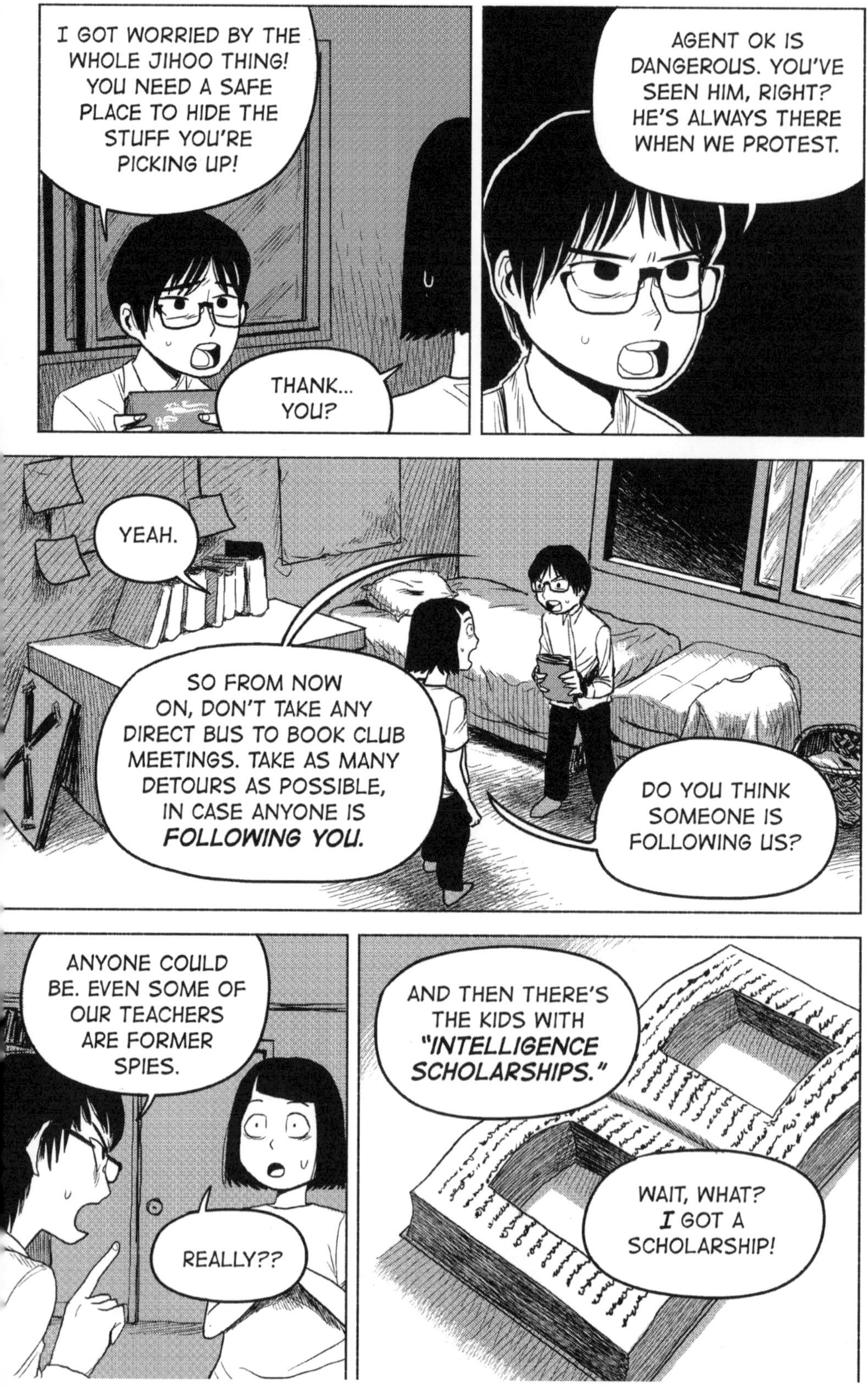
I GOT WORRIED BY THE WHOLE JIHOO THING! YOU NEED A SAFE PLACE TO HIDE THE STUFF YOU'RE PICKING UP!
THANK... YOU?
AGENT OK IS DANGEROUS. YOU'VE SEEN HIM, RIGHT? HE'S ALWAYS THERE WHEN WE PROTEST.
YEAH.
SO FROM NOW ON, DON'T TAKE ANY DIRECT BUS TO BOOK CLUB MEETINGS. TAKE AS MANY DETOURS AS POSSIBLE, IN CASE ANYONE IS ***FOLLOWING YOU.***
DO YOU THINK SOMEONE IS FOLLOWING US?
ANYONE COULD BE. EVEN SOME OF OUR TEACHERS ARE FORMER SPIES.
REALLY??
AND THEN THERE'S THE KIDS WITH ***"INTELLIGENCE SCHOLARSHIPS."***
WAIT, WHAT? *I* GOT A SCHOLARSHIP!

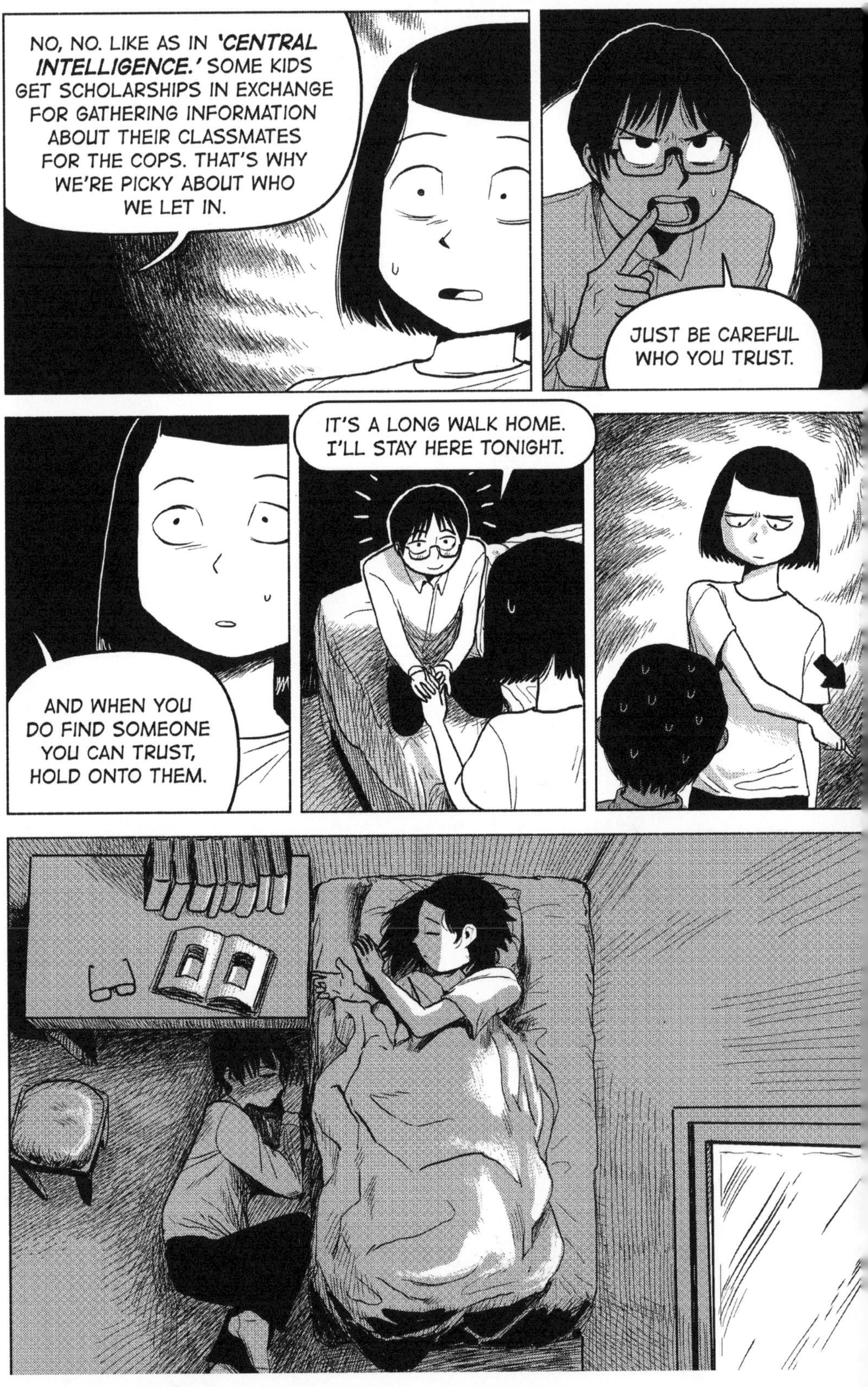
NO, NO. LIKE AS IN 'CENTRAL INTELLIGENCE.' SOME KIDS GET SCHOLARSHIPS IN EXCHANGE FOR GATHERING INFORMATION ABOUT THEIR CLASSMATES FOR THE COPS. THAT'S WHY WE'RE PICKY ABOUT WHO WE LET IN.
JUST BE CAREFUL WHO YOU TRUST.
AND WHEN YOU DO FIND SOMEONE YOU CAN TRUST, HOLD ONTO THEM.
IT'S A LONG WALK HOME. I'LL STAY HERE TONIGHT.

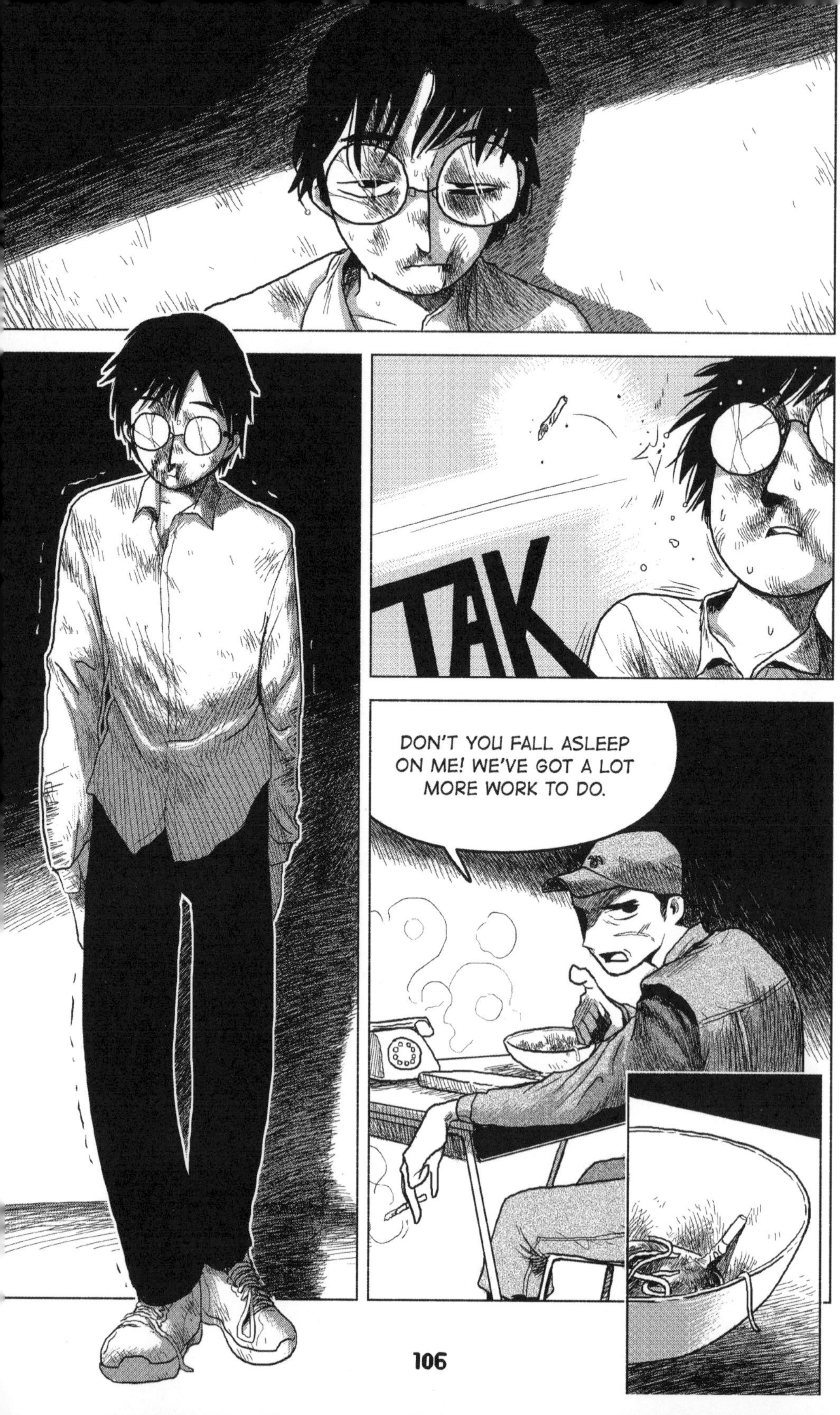
TAK
DON'T YOU FALL ASLEEP ON ME! WE'VE GOT A LOT MORE WORK TO DO.

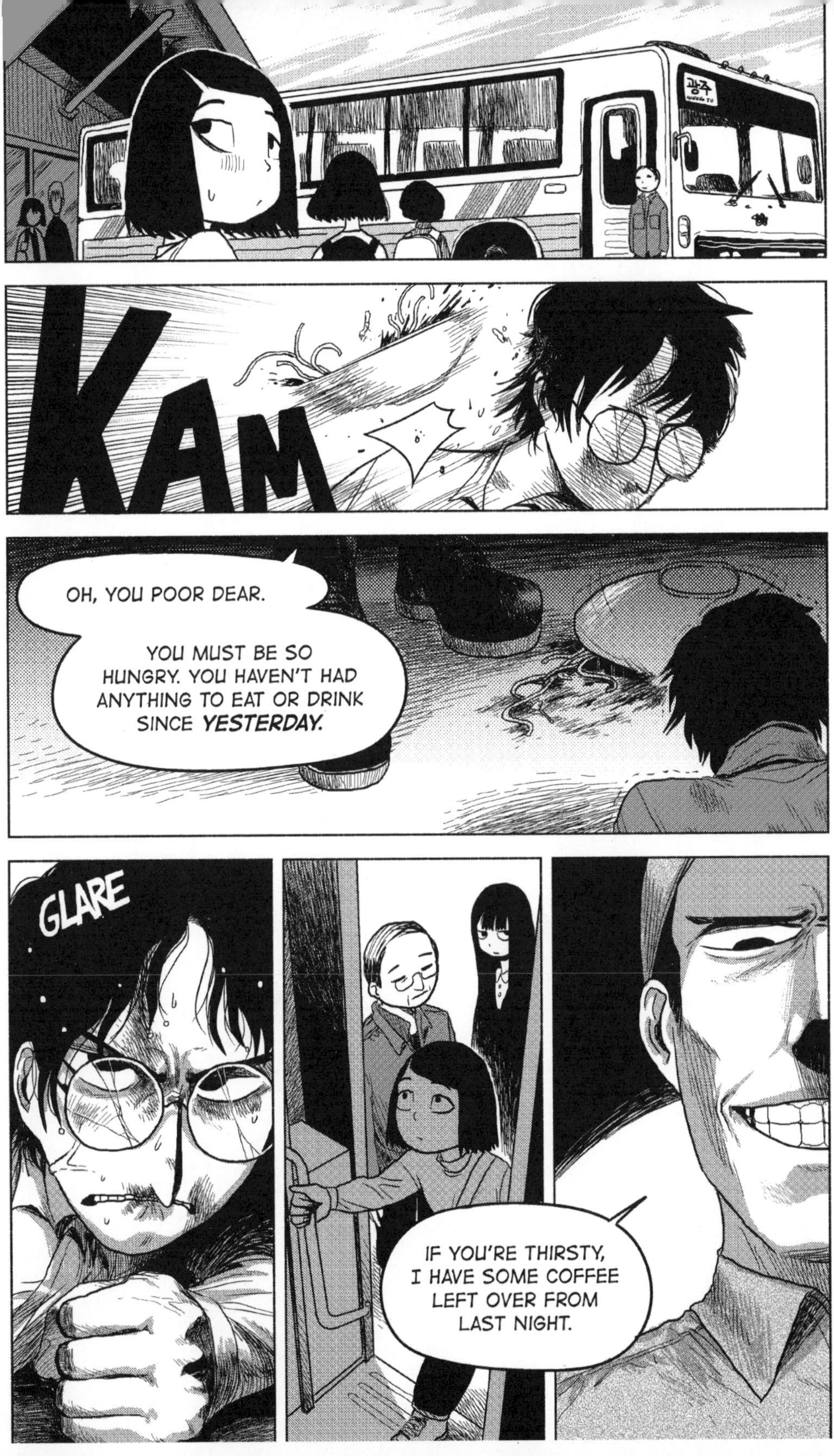
광주
KAM
OH, YOU POOR DEAR.
YOU MUST BE SO HUNGRY. YOU HAVEN'T HAD ANYTHING TO EAT OR DRINK SINCE *YESTERDAY.*
GLARE
IF YOU'RE THIRSTY, I HAVE SOME COFFEE LEFT OVER FROM LAST NIGHT.

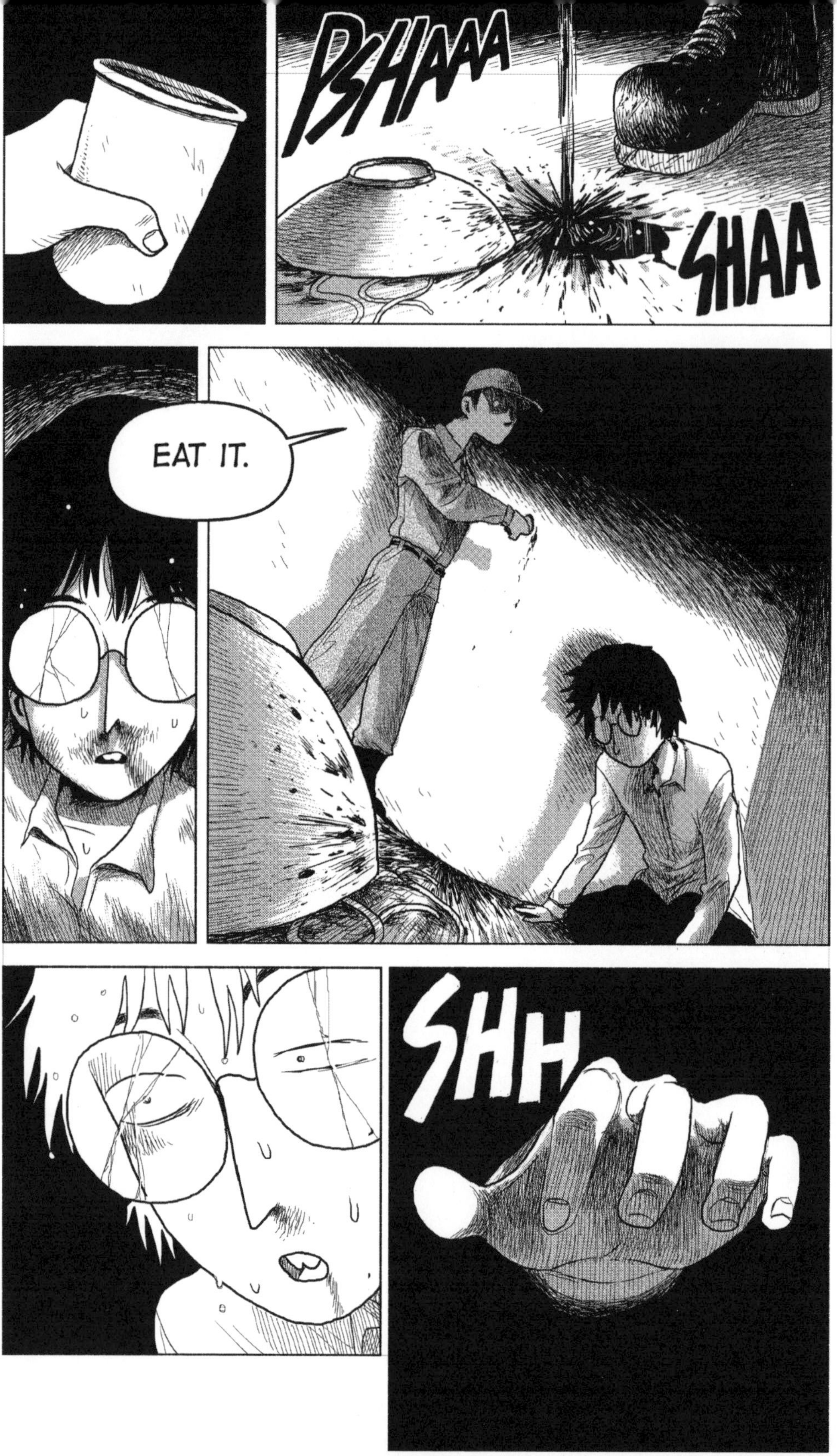
PSHAAA
SHAA
EAT IT.
SHH

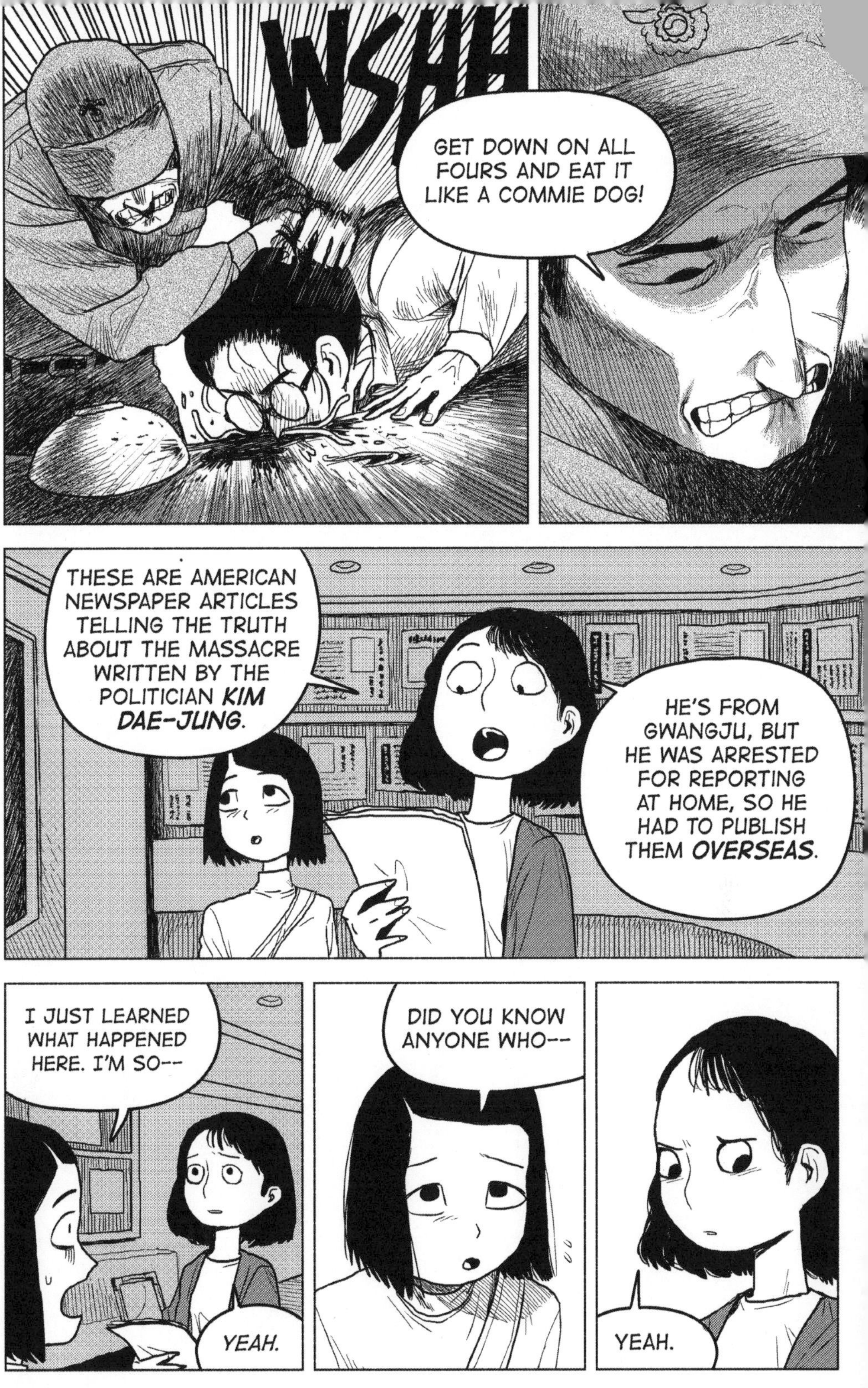
WSHH
GET DOWN ON ALL FOURS AND EAT IT LIKE A COMMIE DOG!
THESE ARE AMERICAN NEWSPAPER ARTICLES TELLING THE TRUTH ABOUT THE MASSACRE WRITTEN BY THE POLITICIAN KIM DAE-JUNG.
HE'S FROM GWANGJU, BUT HE WAS ARRESTED FOR REPORTING AT HOME, SO HE HAD TO PUBLISH THEM OVERSEAS.
I JUST LEARNED WHAT HAPPENED HERE. I'M SO--
YEAH.
DID YOU KNOW ANYONE WHO--
YEAH.

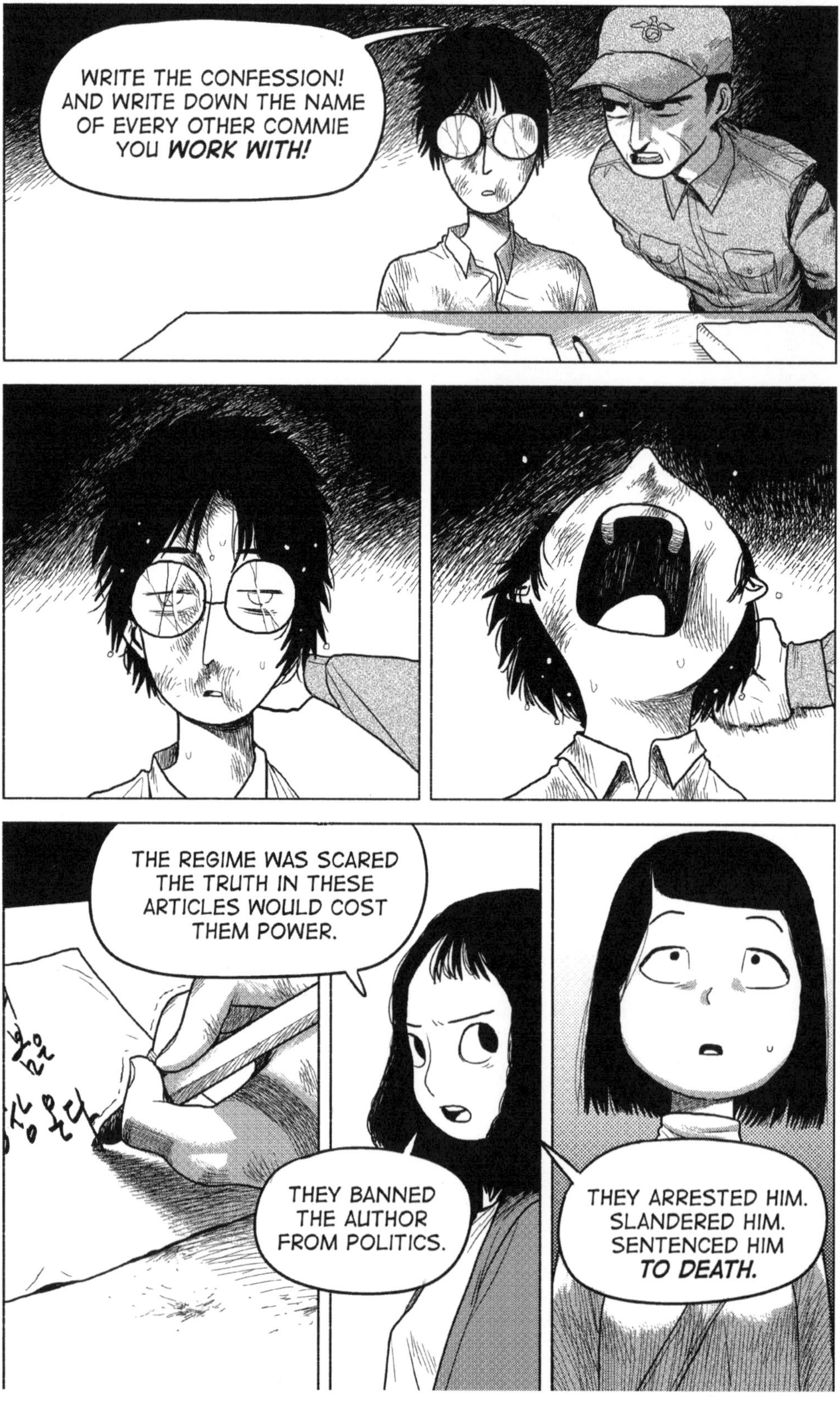
WRITE THE CONFESSION! AND WRITE DOWN THE NAME OF EVERY OTHER COMMIE YOU **WORK WITH!**
THE REGIME WAS SCARED THE TRUTH IN THESE ARTICLES WOULD COST THEM POWER.
THEY BANNED THE AUTHOR FROM POLITICS.
THEY ARRESTED HIM. SLANDERED HIM. SENTENCED HIM **TO DEATH.**

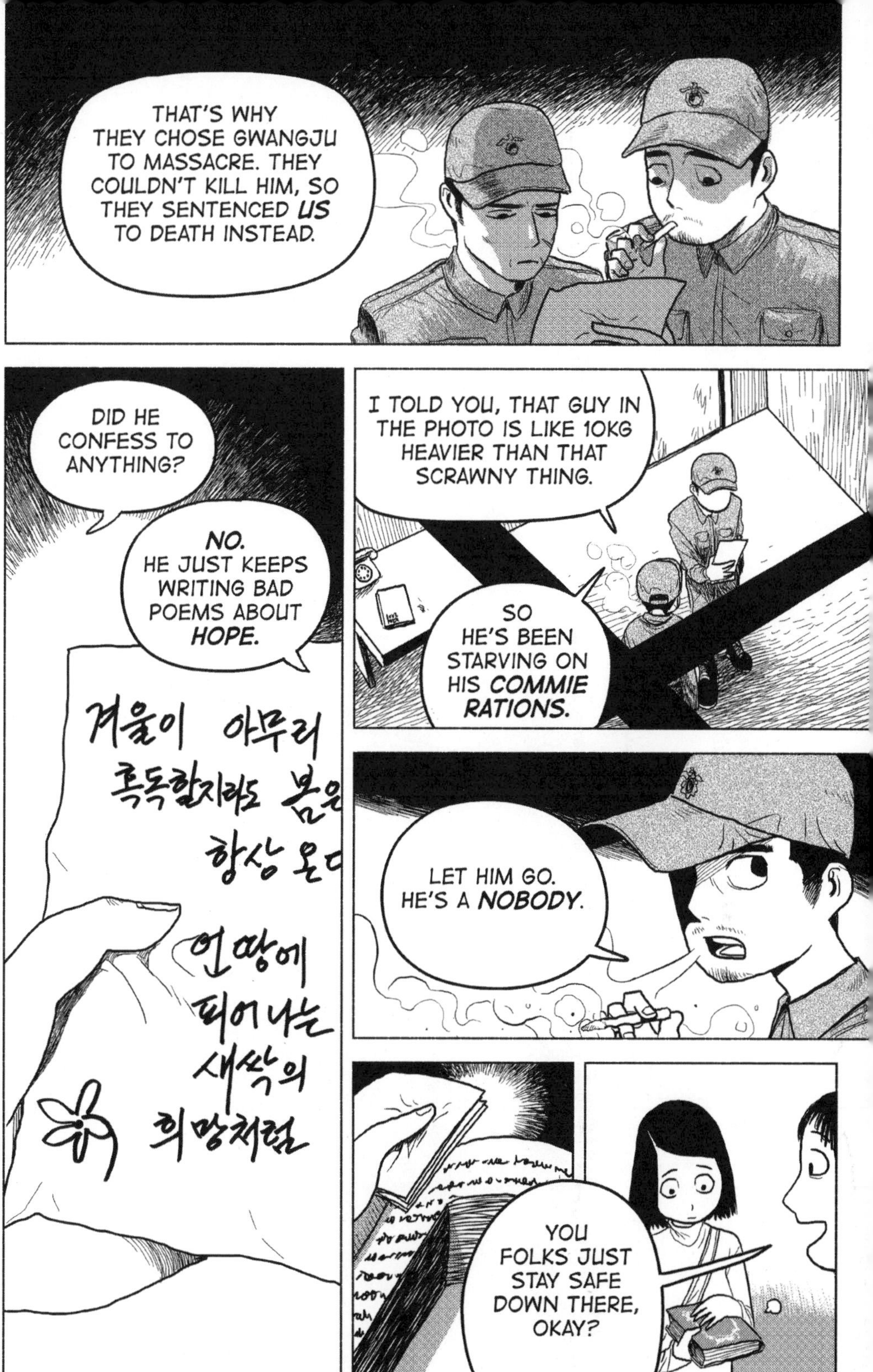
THAT'S WHY THEY CHOSE GWANGJU TO MASSACRE. THEY COULDN'T KILL HIM, SO THEY SENTENCED *US* TO DEATH INSTEAD.
DID HE CONFESS TO ANYTHING?
NO. HE JUST KEEPS WRITING BAD POEMS ABOUT *HOPE.*
겨울이 아무리
혹독할지라도 봄은
항상 온
언땅에
피어나는
새싹의
희망처럼
I TOLD YOU, THAT GUY IN THE PHOTO IS LIKE 10KG HEAVIER THAN THAT SCRAWNY THING.
SO HE'S BEEN STARVING ON HIS *COMMIE RATIONS.*
LET HIM GO. HE'S A *NOBODY.*
YOU FOLKS JUST STAY SAFE DOWN THERE, OKAY?

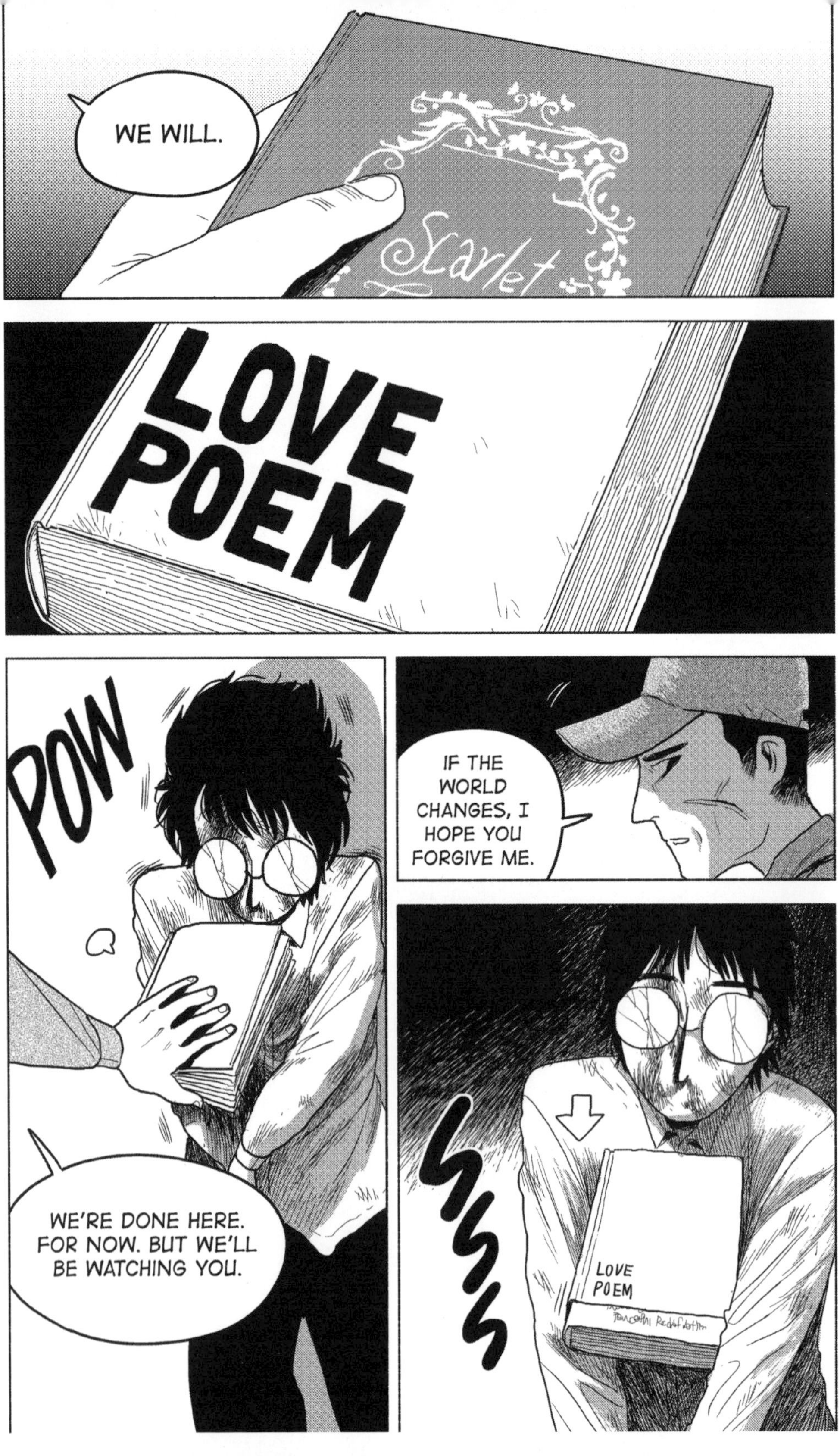
WE WILL.
Scarlet
LOVE POEM
POW
WE'RE DONE HERE. FOR NOW. BUT WE'LL BE WATCHING YOU.
IF THE WORLD CHANGES, I HOPE YOU FORGIVE ME.
LOVE POEM

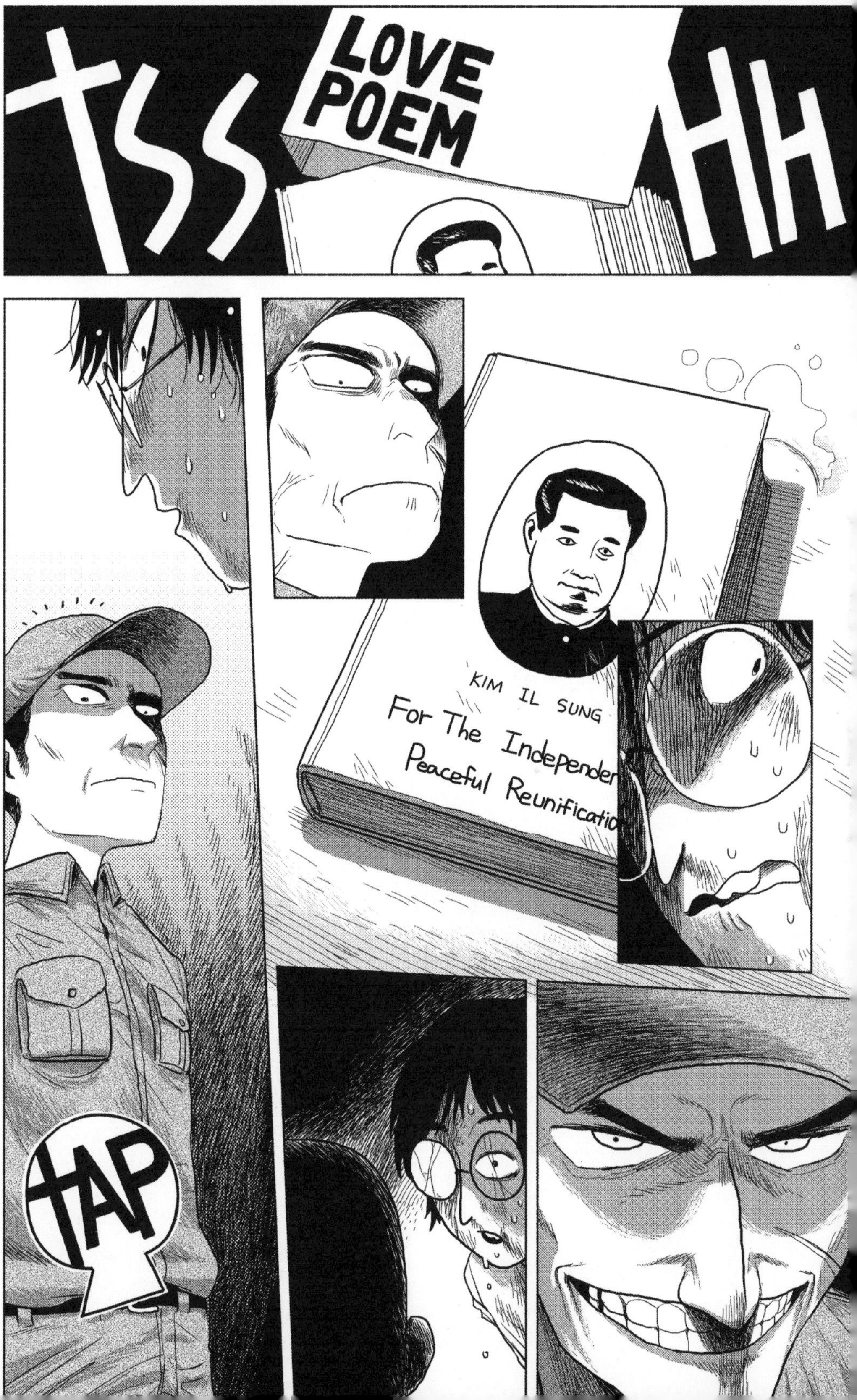
TSSHH
LOVE POEM
KIM IL SUNG
For The Independen
Peaceful Reunificatio
TAP

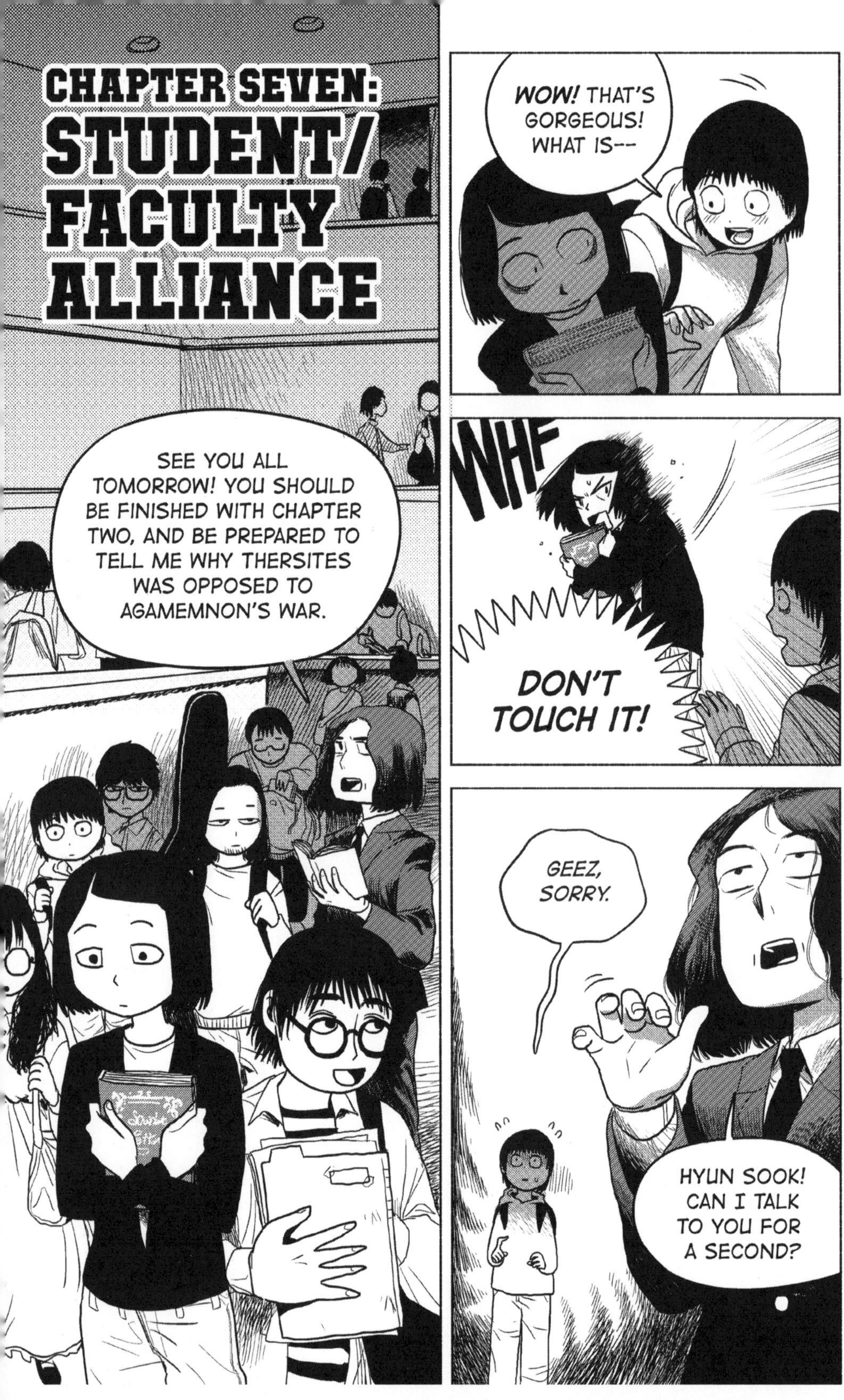
CHAPTER SEVEN: STUDENT/FACULTY ALLIANCE
SEE YOU ALL TOMORROW! YOU SHOULD BE FINISHED WITH CHAPTER TWO, AND BE PREPARED TO TELL ME WHY THERSITES WAS OPPOSED TO AGAMEMNON'S WAR.
WOW! THAT'S GORGEOUS! WHAT IS--
WHF
DON'T TOUCH IT!
GEEZ, SORRY.
HYUN SOOK! CAN I TALK TO YOU FOR A SECOND?

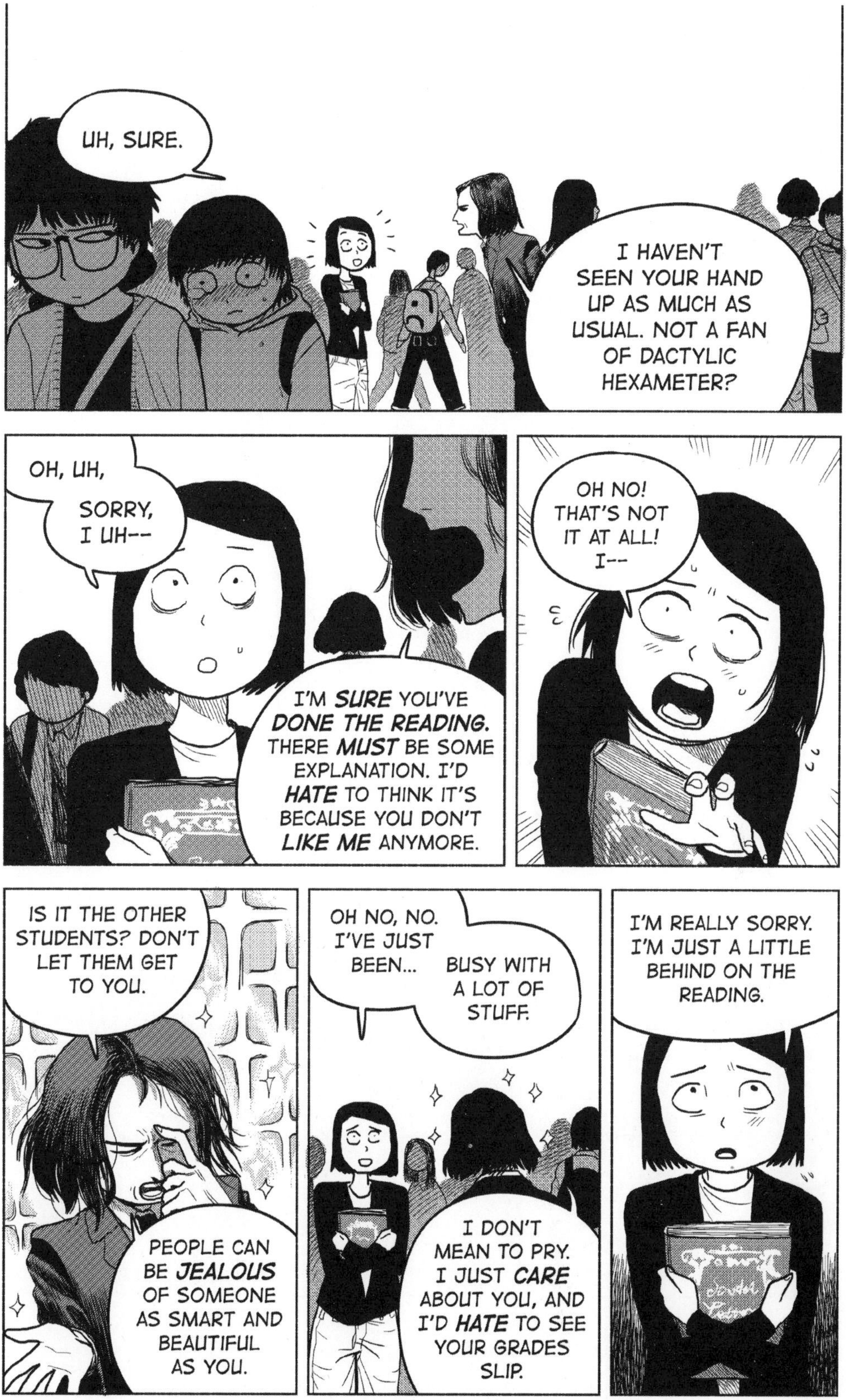
UH, SURE.
I HAVEN'T SEEN YOUR HAND UP AS MUCH AS USUAL. NOT A FAN OF DACTYLIC HEXAMETER?
OH, UH,
SORRY, I UH--
I'M SURE YOU'VE DONE THE READING. THERE MUST BE SOME EXPLANATION. I'D HATE TO THINK IT'S BECAUSE YOU DON'T LIKE ME ANYMORE.
OH NO! THAT'S NOT IT AT ALL! I--
IS IT THE OTHER STUDENTS? DON'T LET THEM GET TO YOU.
PEOPLE CAN BE JEALOUS OF SOMEONE AS SMART AND BEAUTIFUL AS YOU.
OH NO, NO. I'VE JUST BEEN...
BUSY WITH A LOT OF STUFF.
I DON'T MEAN TO PRY. I JUST CARE ABOUT YOU, AND I'D HATE TO SEE YOUR GRADES SLIP.
I'M REALLY SORRY. I'M JUST A LITTLE BEHIND ON THE READING.

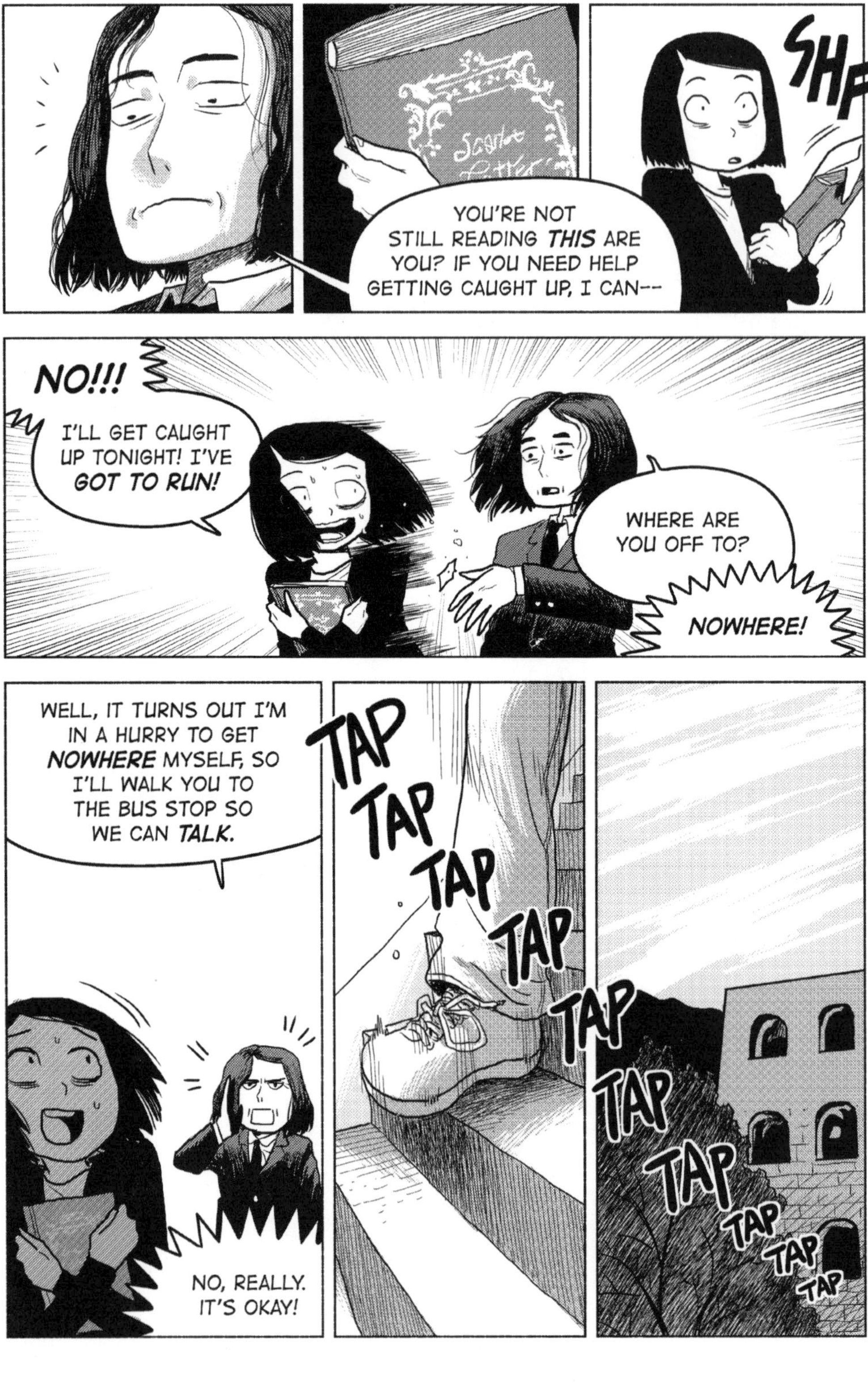
SHF
YOU'RE NOT STILL READING THIS ARE YOU? IF YOU NEED HELP GETTING CAUGHT UP, I CAN--
NO!!!
I'LL GET CAUGHT UP TONIGHT! I'VE GOT TO RUN!
WHERE ARE YOU OFF TO?
NOWHERE!
WELL, IT TURNS OUT I'M IN A HURRY TO GET NOWHERE MYSELF, SO I'LL WALK YOU TO THE BUS STOP SO WE CAN TALK.
NO, REALLY. IT'S OKAY!
TAP TAP TAP TAP TAP TAP TAP TAP TAP TAP

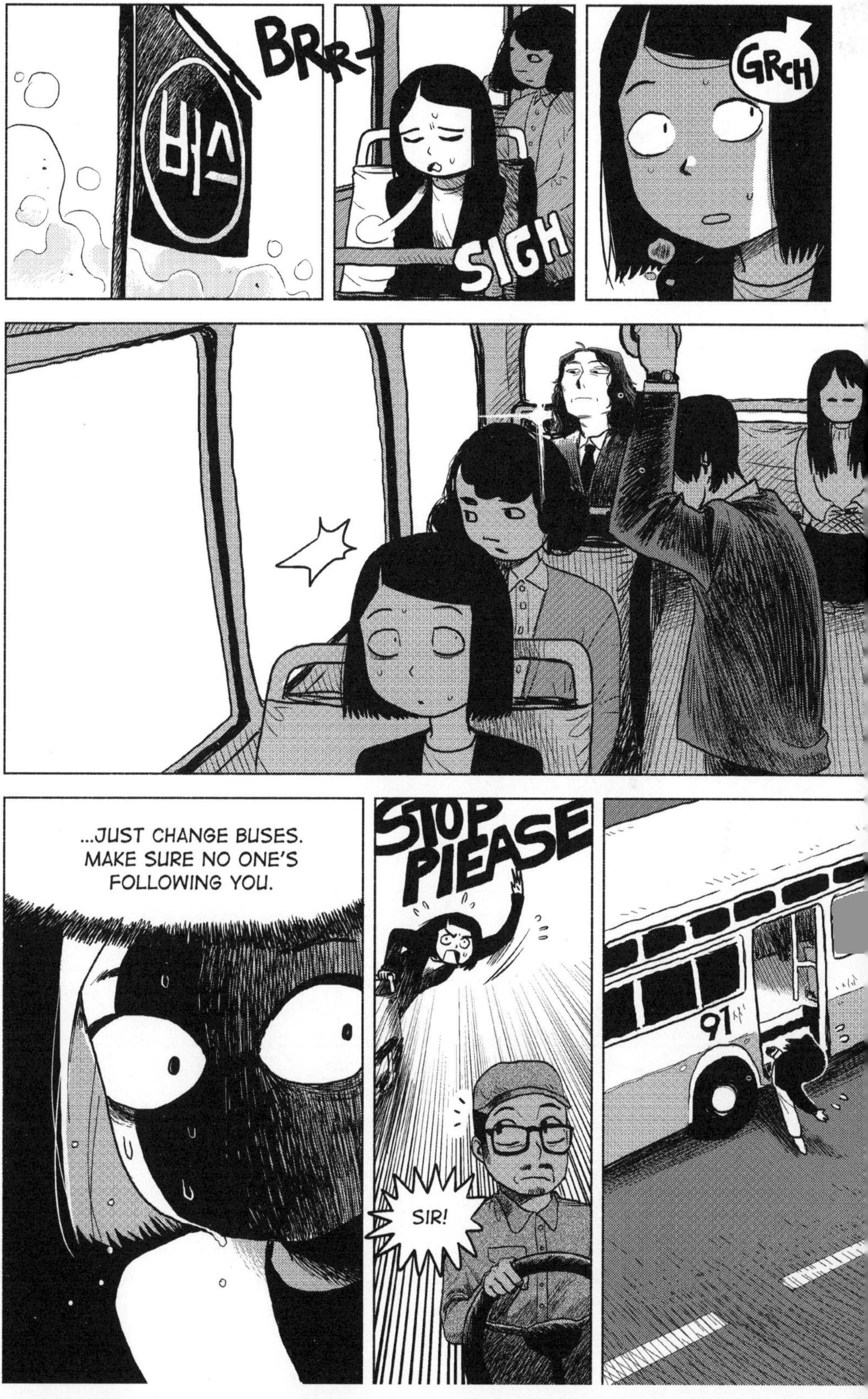
버스
BRRR-
SIGH
GRCH
...JUST CHANGE BUSES. MAKE SURE NO ONE'S FOLLOWING YOU.
STOP PlEASE
SIR!
91

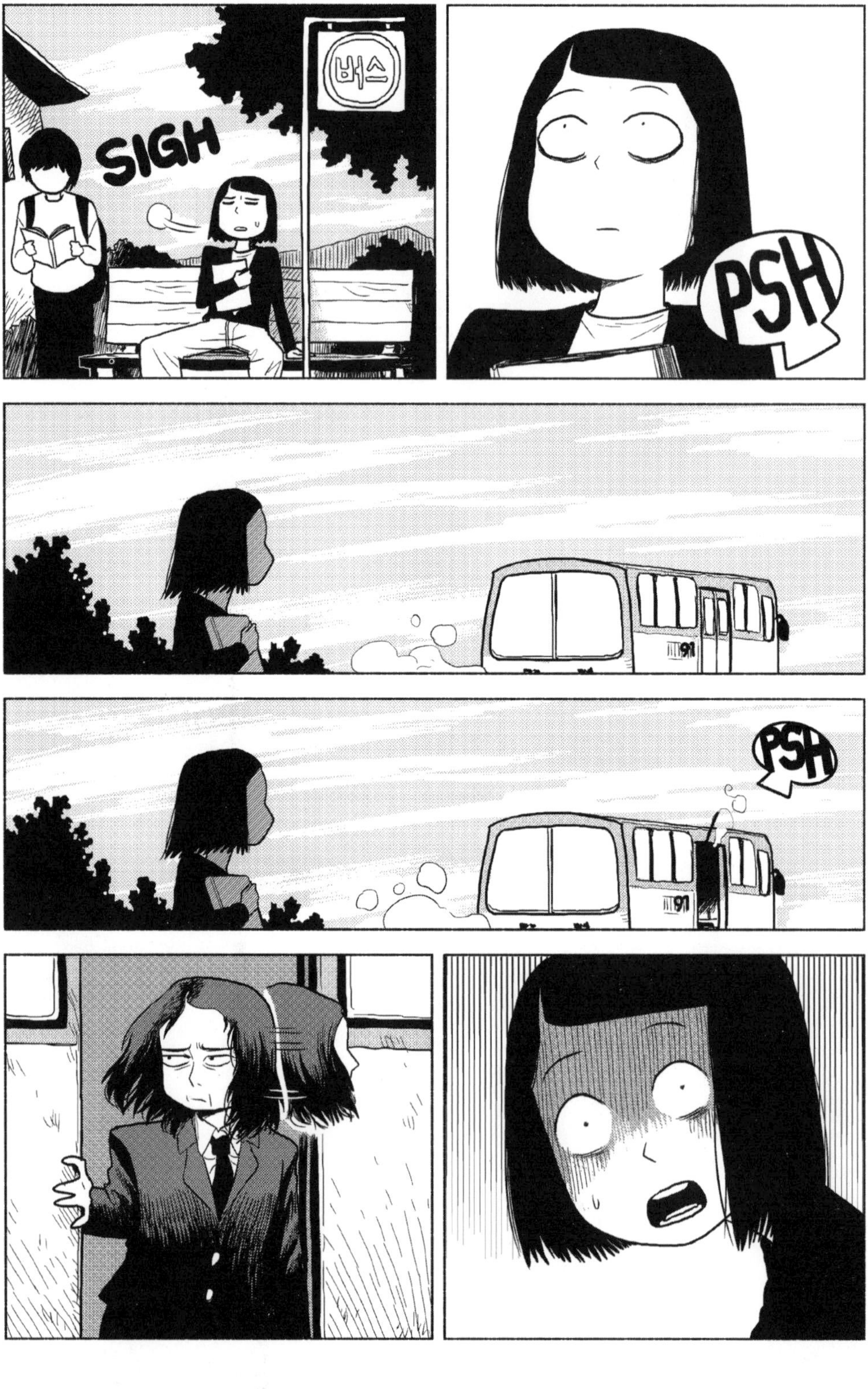
버스
SIGH
PSH
PSH

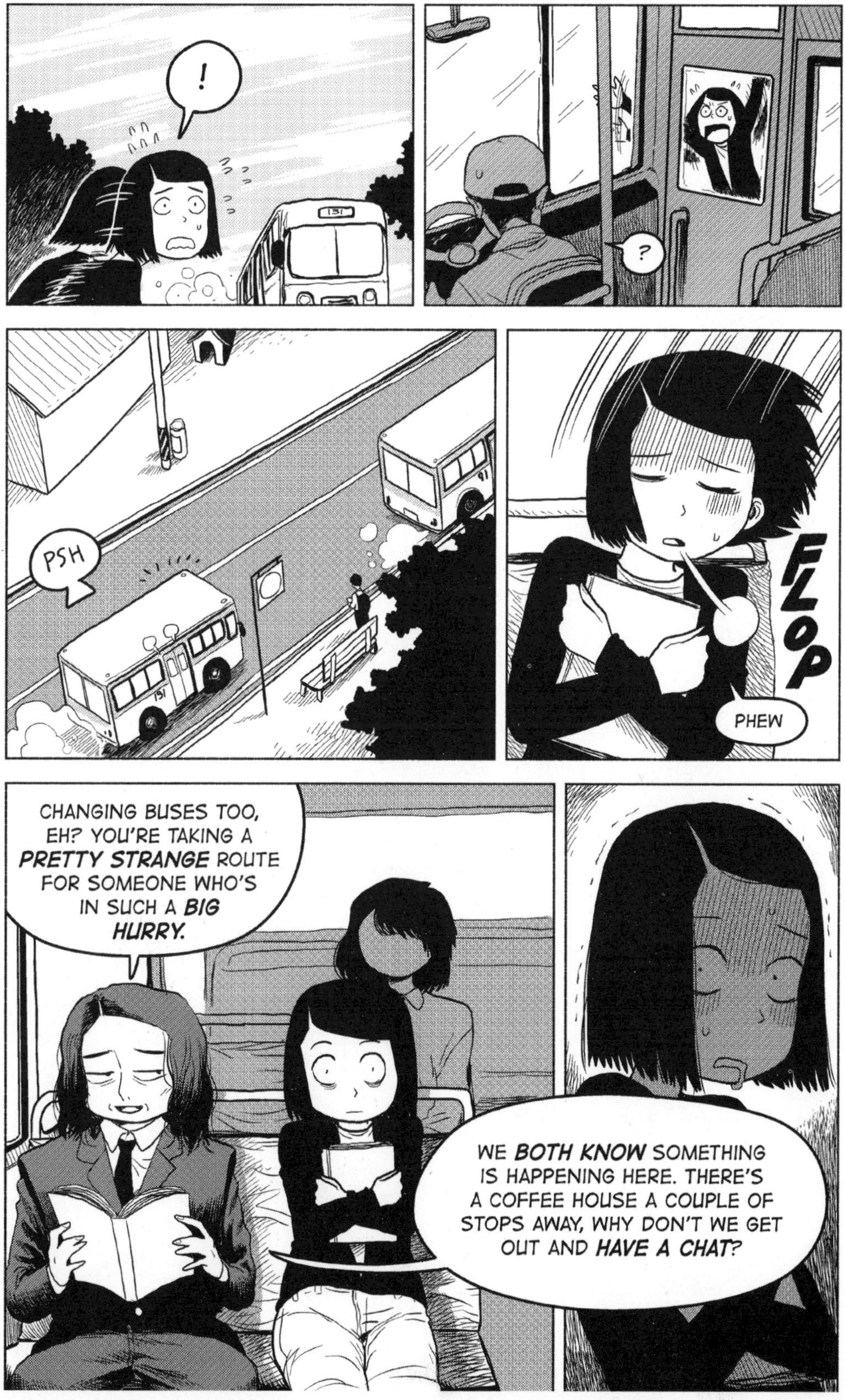

!
?
PSH
FLOP
PHEW
CHANGING BUSES TOO, EH? YOU'RE TAKING A PRETTY STRANGE ROUTE FOR SOMEONE WHO'S IN SUCH A BIG HURRY.
WE BOTH KNOW SOMETHING IS HAPPENING HERE. THERE'S A COFFEE HOUSE A COUPLE OF STOPS AWAY, WHY DON'T WE GET OUT AND HAVE A CHAT?

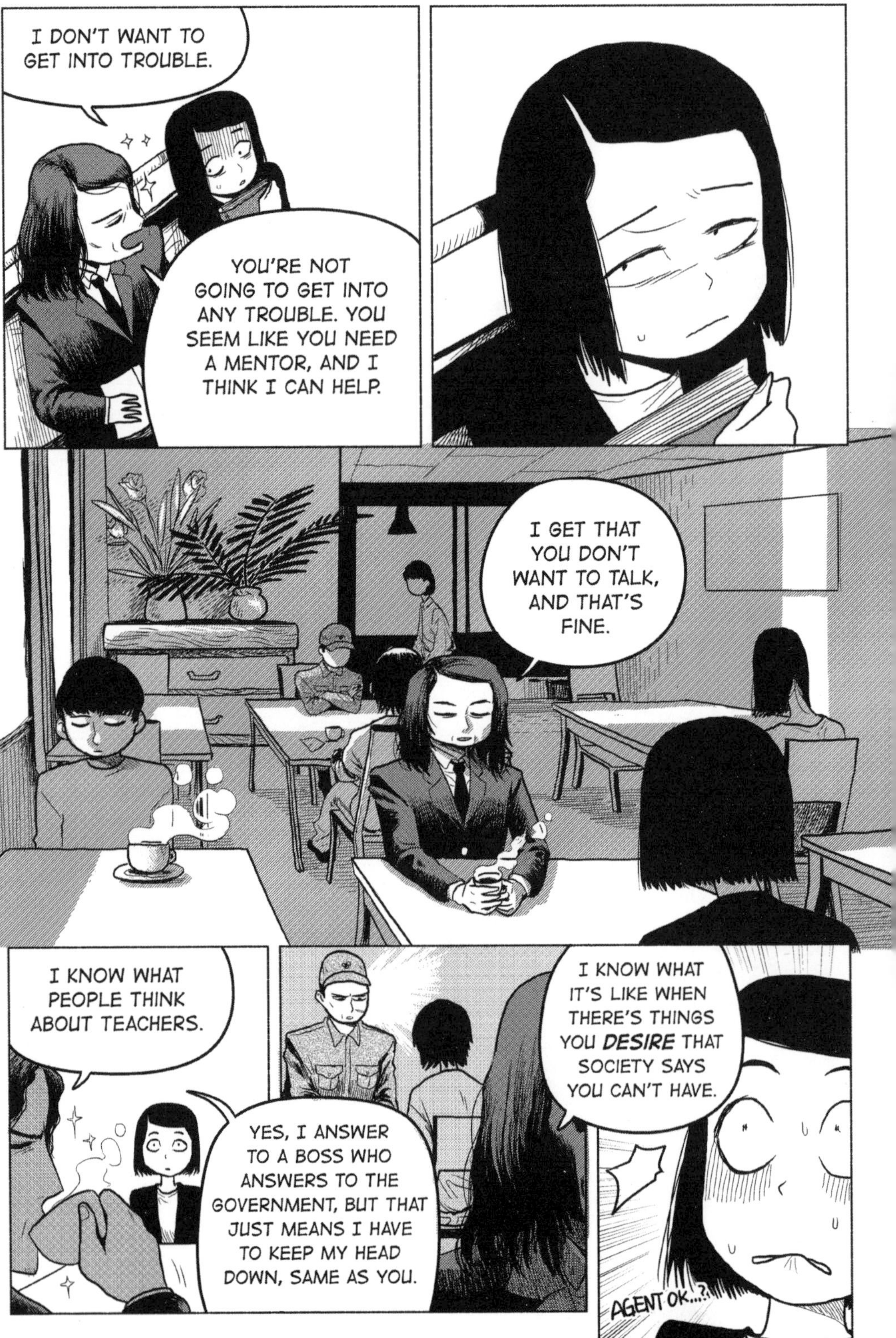
I DON'T WANT TO GET INTO TROUBLE.
YOU'RE NOT GOING TO GET INTO ANY TROUBLE. YOU SEEM LIKE YOU NEED A MENTOR, AND I THINK I CAN HELP.
I GET THAT YOU DON'T WANT TO TALK, AND THAT'S FINE.
I KNOW WHAT PEOPLE THINK ABOUT TEACHERS.
YES, I ANSWER TO A BOSS WHO ANSWERS TO THE GOVERNMENT, BUT THAT JUST MEANS I HAVE TO KEEP MY HEAD DOWN, SAME AS YOU.
I KNOW WHAT IT'S LIKE WHEN THERE'S THINGS YOU ***DESIRE*** THAT SOCIETY SAYS YOU CAN'T HAVE.
AGENT OK...?

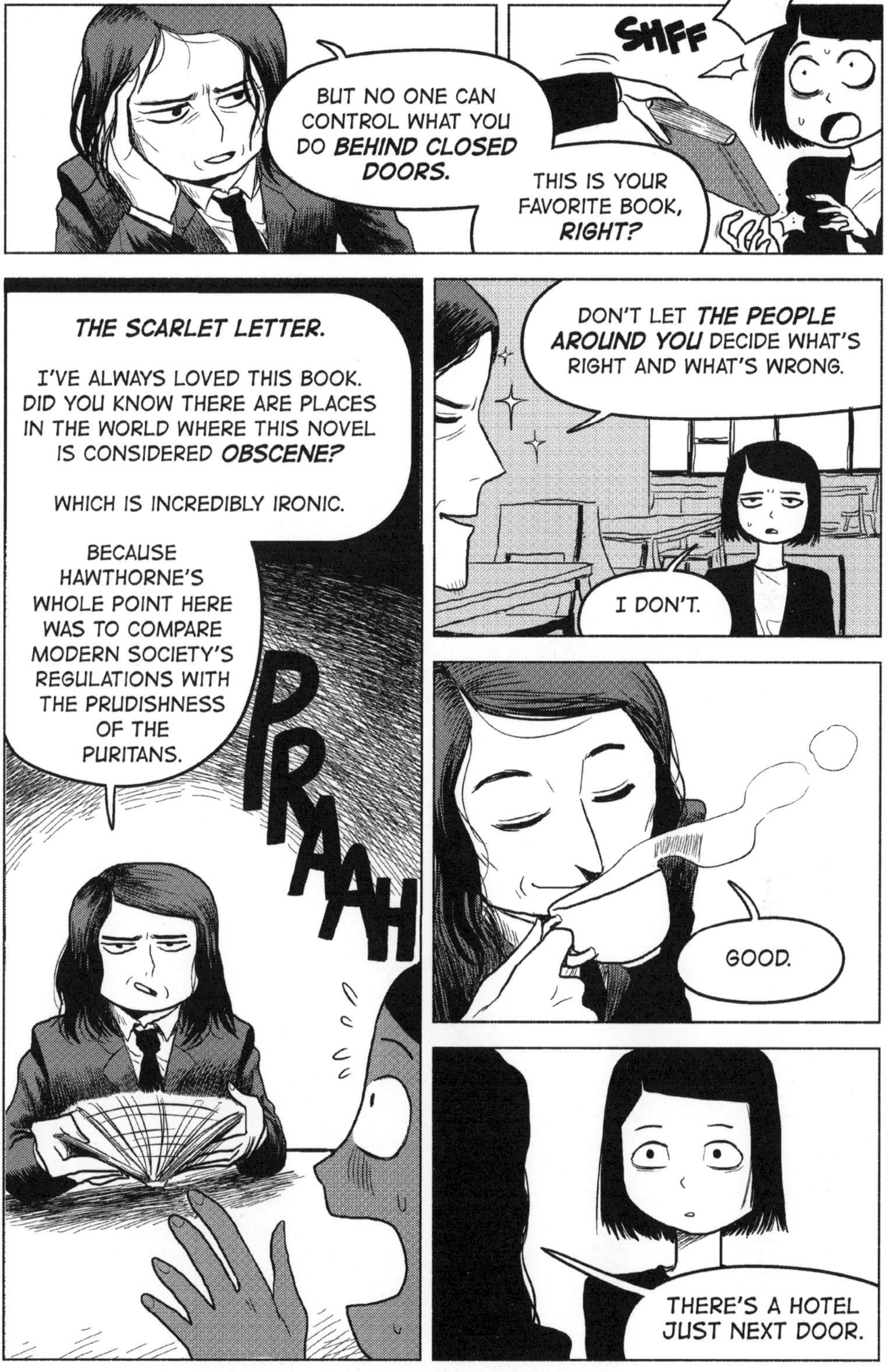
BUT NO ONE CAN CONTROL WHAT YOU DO BEHIND CLOSED DOORS.
SHFF
THIS IS YOUR FAVORITE BOOK, RIGHT?
THE SCARLET LETTER.
I'VE ALWAYS LOVED THIS BOOK. DID YOU KNOW THERE ARE PLACES IN THE WORLD WHERE THIS NOVEL IS CONSIDERED OBSCENE?
WHICH IS INCREDIBLY IRONIC.
BECAUSE HAWTHORNE'S WHOLE POINT HERE WAS TO COMPARE MODERN SOCIETY'S REGULATIONS WITH THE PRUDISHNESS OF THE PURITANS.
PRAAAH
DON'T LET THE PEOPLE AROUND YOU DECIDE WHAT'S RIGHT AND WHAT'S WRONG.
I DON'T.
GOOD.
THERE'S A HOTEL JUST NEXT DOOR.

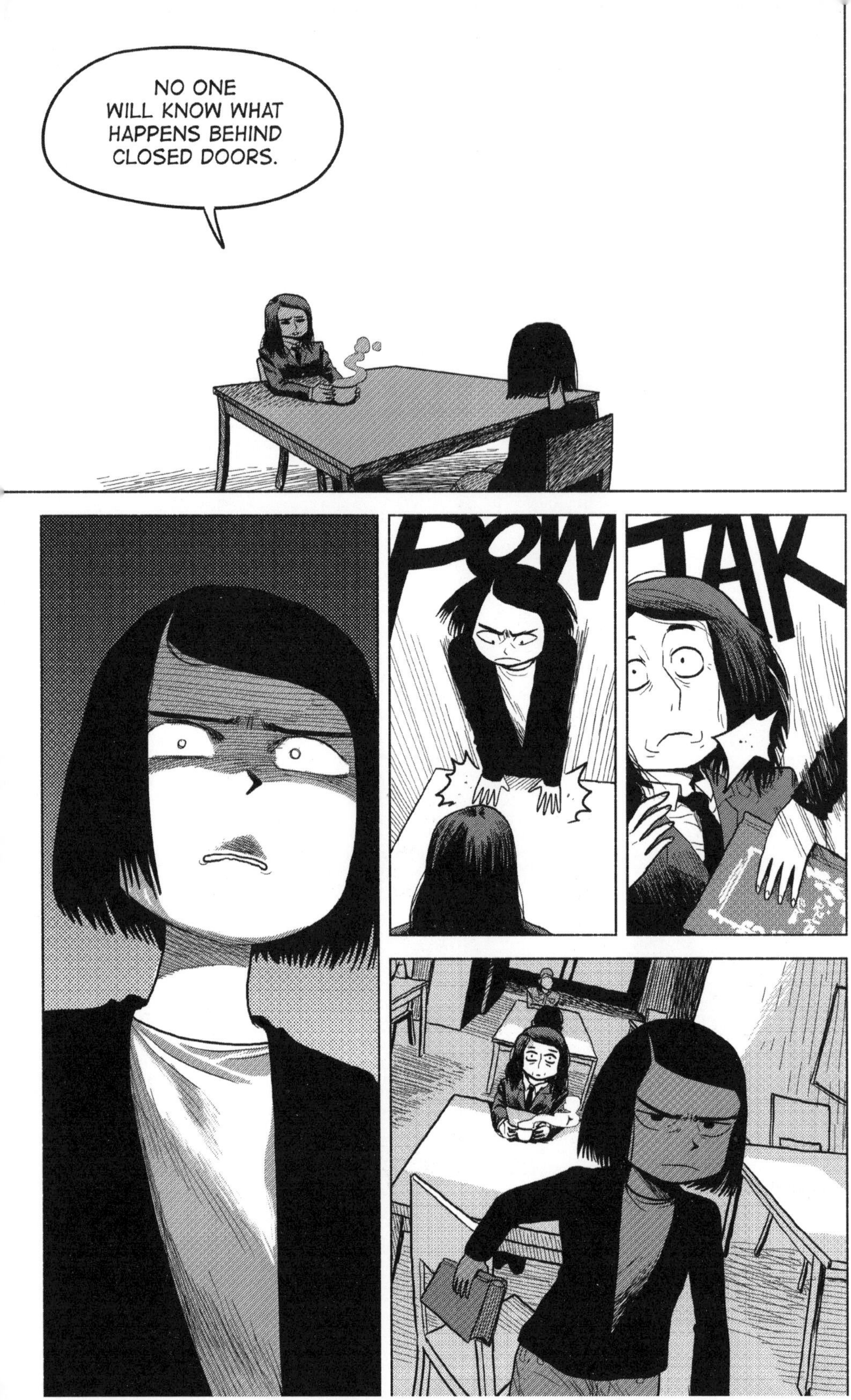
NO ONE WILL KNOW WHAT HAPPENS BEHIND CLOSED DOORS.
POW
TAK

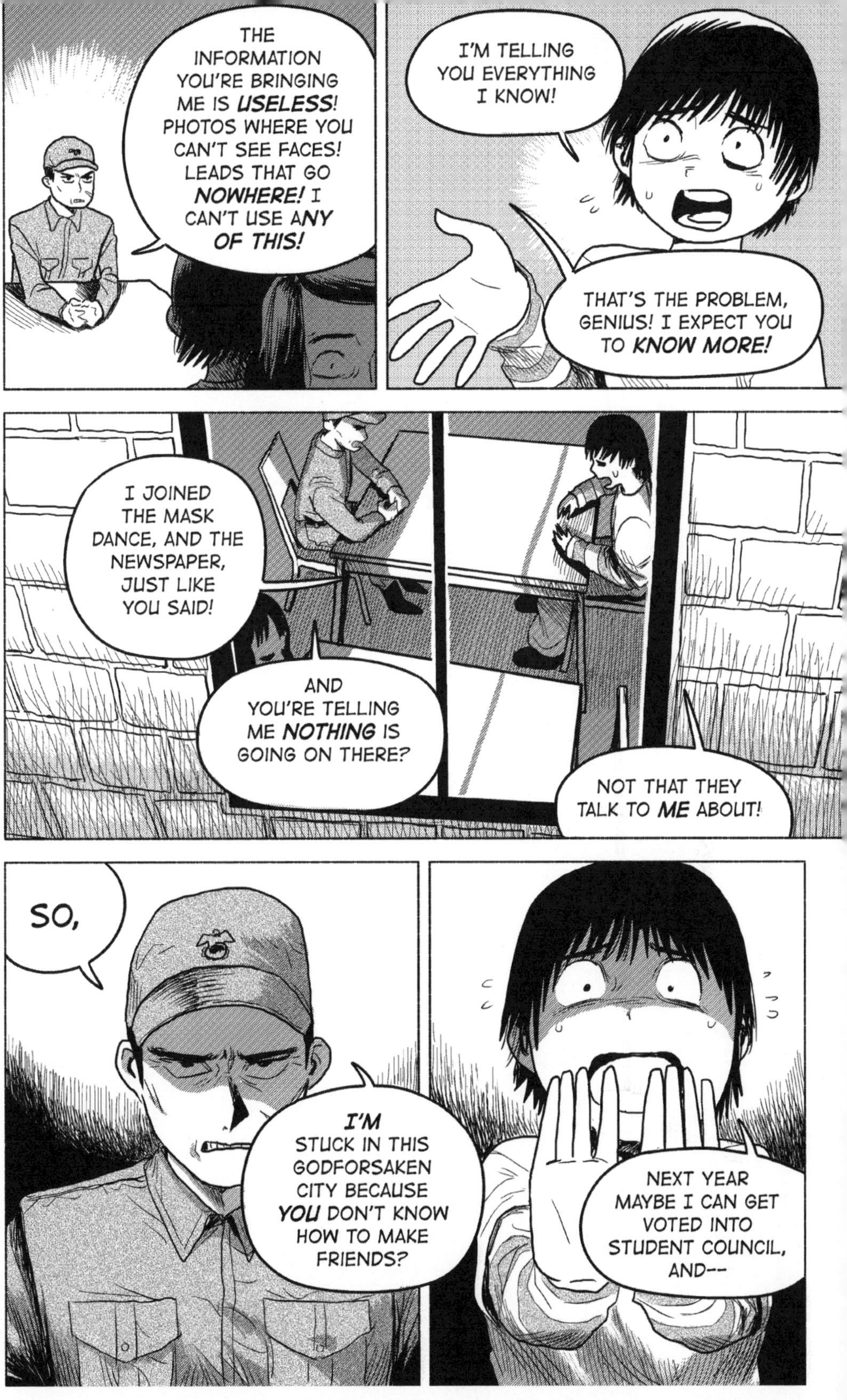
THE INFORMATION YOU'RE BRINGING ME IS USELESS! PHOTOS WHERE YOU CAN'T SEE FACES! LEADS THAT GO NOWHERE! I CAN'T USE ANY OF THIS!
I'M TELLING YOU EVERYTHING I KNOW!
THAT'S THE PROBLEM, GENIUS! I EXPECT YOU TO KNOW MORE!
I JOINED THE MASK DANCE, AND THE NEWSPAPER, JUST LIKE YOU SAID!
AND YOU'RE TELLING ME NOTHING IS GOING ON THERE?
NOT THAT THEY TALK TO ME ABOUT!
SO,
I'M STUCK IN THIS GODFORSAKEN CITY BECAUSE YOU DON'T KNOW HOW TO MAKE FRIENDS?
NEXT YEAR MAYBE I CAN GET VOTED INTO STUDENT COUNCIL, AND--

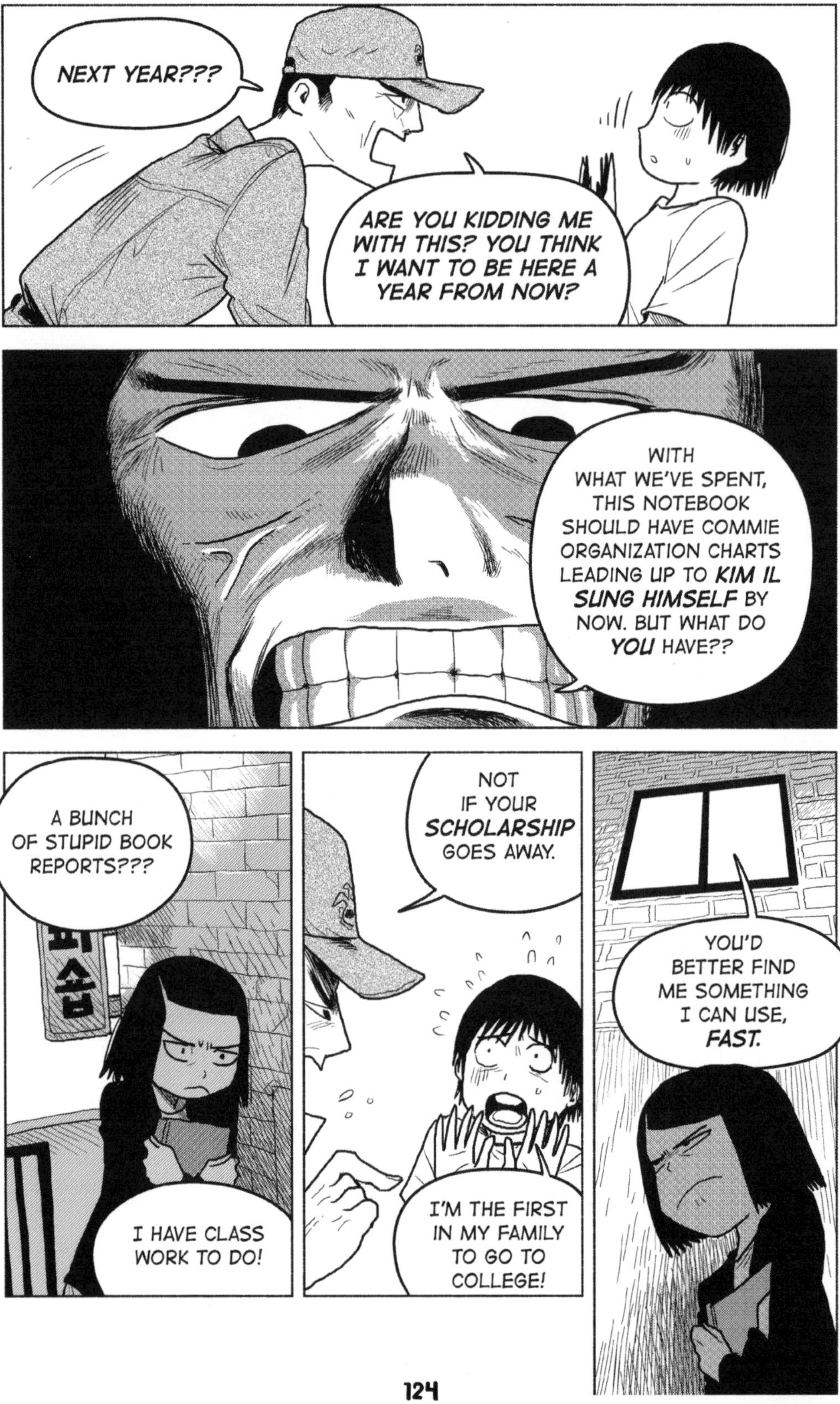
NEXT YEAR???
ARE YOU KIDDING ME WITH THIS? YOU THINK I WANT TO BE HERE A YEAR FROM NOW?
WITH WHAT WE'VE SPENT, THIS NOTEBOOK SHOULD HAVE COMMIE ORGANIZATION CHARTS LEADING UP TO KIM IL SUNG HIMSELF BY NOW. BUT WHAT DO YOU HAVE??
A BUNCH OF STUPID BOOK REPORTS???
I HAVE CLASS WORK TO DO!
NOT IF YOUR SCHOLARSHIP GOES AWAY.
I'M THE FIRST IN MY FAMILY TO GO TO COLLEGE!
YOU'D BETTER FIND ME SOMETHING I CAN USE, FAST.

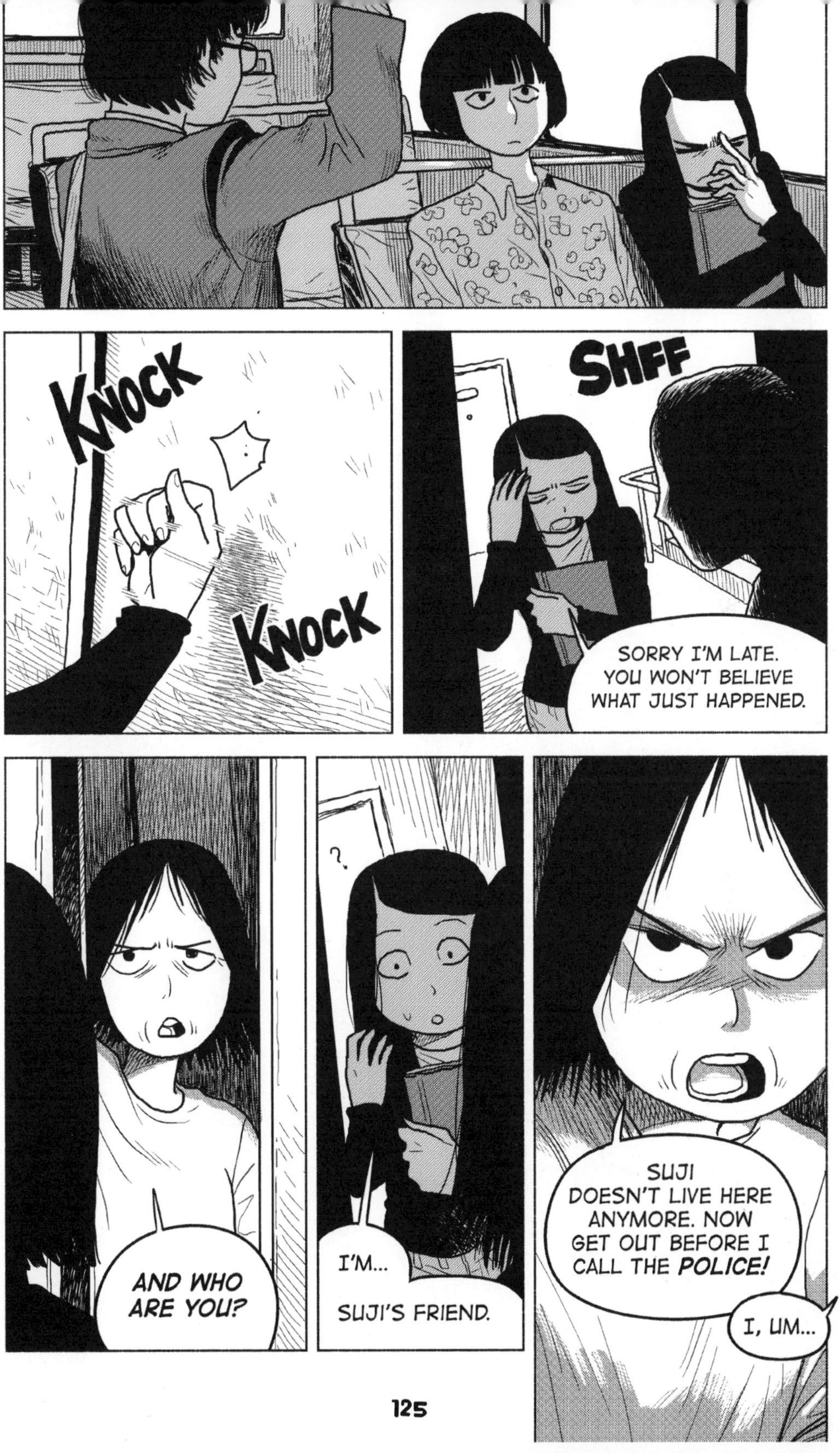
KNOCK
KNOCK
SHFF
SORRY I'M LATE. YOU WON'T BELIEVE WHAT JUST HAPPENED.
AND WHO ARE YOU?
I'M...
SUJI'S FRIEND.
SUJI DOESN'T LIVE HERE ANYMORE. NOW GET OUT BEFORE I CALL THE *POLICE!*
I, UM...

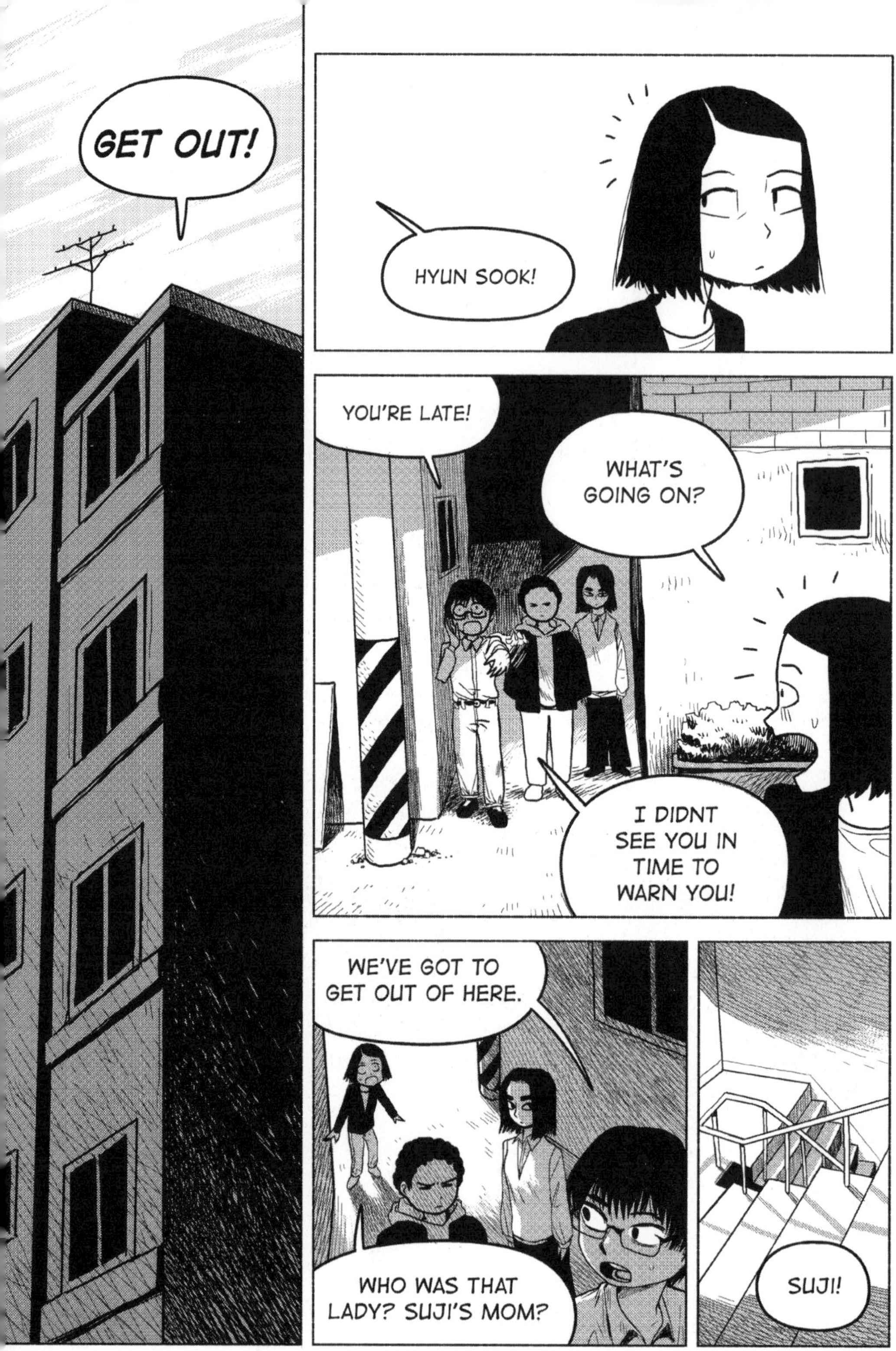
GET OUT!
HYUN SOOK!
YOU'RE LATE!
WHAT'S GOING ON?
I DIDNT SEE YOU IN TIME TO WARN YOU!
WE'VE GOT TO GET OUT OF HERE.
WHO WAS THAT LADY? SUJI'S MOM?
SUJI!

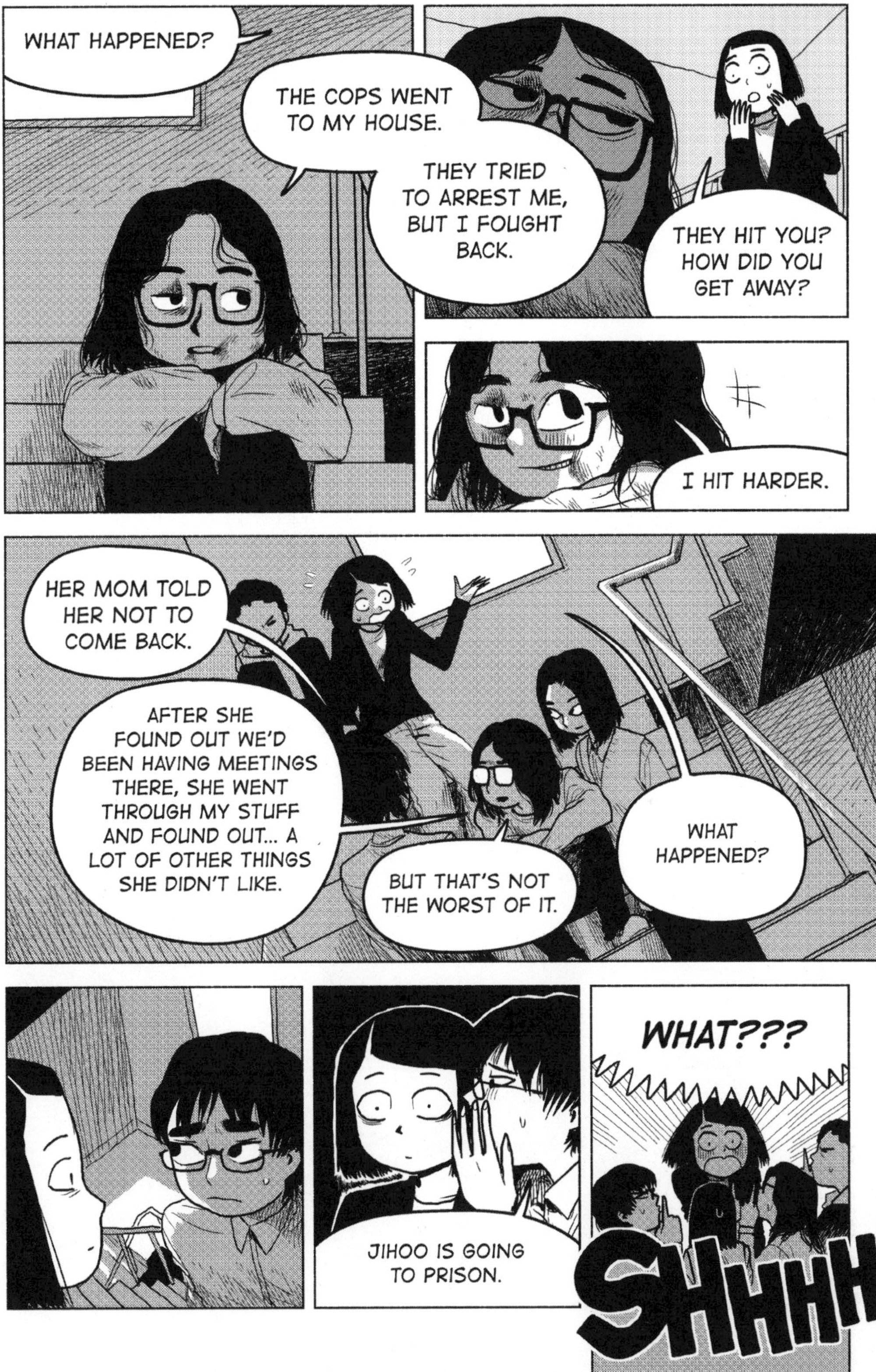
WHAT HAPPENED?
THE COPS WENT TO MY HOUSE.
THEY TRIED TO ARREST ME, BUT I FOUGHT BACK.
THEY HIT YOU? HOW DID YOU GET AWAY?
I HIT HARDER.
HER MOM TOLD HER NOT TO COME BACK.
AFTER SHE FOUND OUT WE'D BEEN HAVING MEETINGS THERE, SHE WENT THROUGH MY STUFF AND FOUND OUT... A LOT OF OTHER THINGS SHE DIDN'T LIKE.
WHAT HAPPENED?
BUT THAT'S NOT THE WORST OF IT.
JIHOO IS GOING TO PRISON.
WHAT???
SHHHH

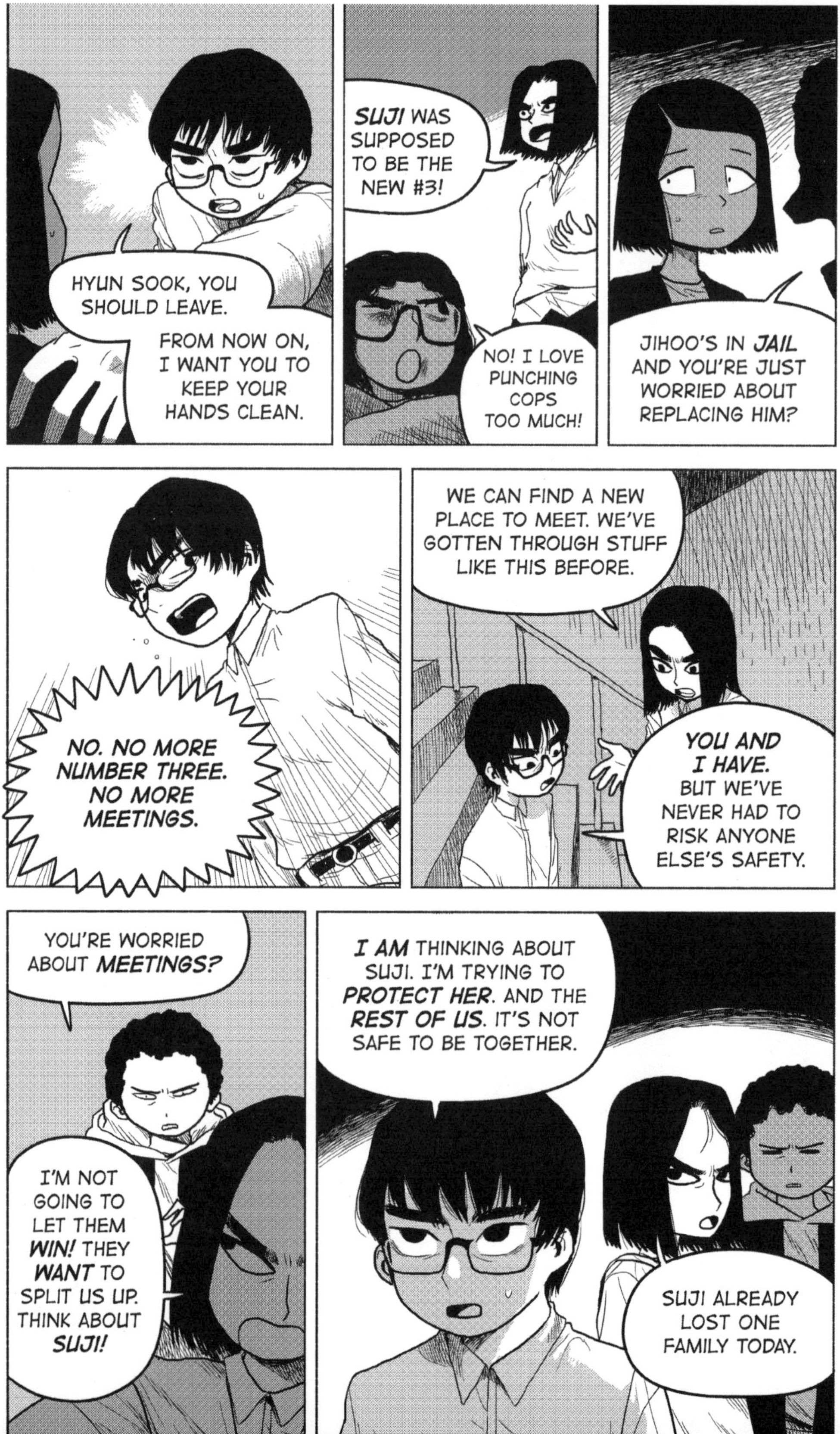
HYUN SOOK, YOU SHOULD LEAVE.
FROM NOW ON, I WANT YOU TO KEEP YOUR HANDS CLEAN.
SUJI WAS SUPPOSED TO BE THE NEW #3!
NO! I LOVE PUNCHING COPS TOO MUCH!
JIHOO'S IN JAIL AND YOU'RE JUST WORRIED ABOUT REPLACING HIM?
NO. NO MORE NUMBER THREE. NO MORE MEETINGS.
WE CAN FIND A NEW PLACE TO MEET. WE'VE GOTTEN THROUGH STUFF LIKE THIS BEFORE.
YOU AND I HAVE. BUT WE'VE NEVER HAD TO RISK ANYONE ELSE'S SAFETY.
YOU'RE WORRIED ABOUT MEETINGS?
I'M NOT GOING TO LET THEM WIN! THEY WANT TO SPLIT US UP. THINK ABOUT SUJI!
I AM THINKING ABOUT SUJI. I'M TRYING TO PROTECT HER. AND THE REST OF US. IT'S NOT SAFE TO BE TOGETHER.
SUJI ALREADY LOST ONE FAMILY TODAY.

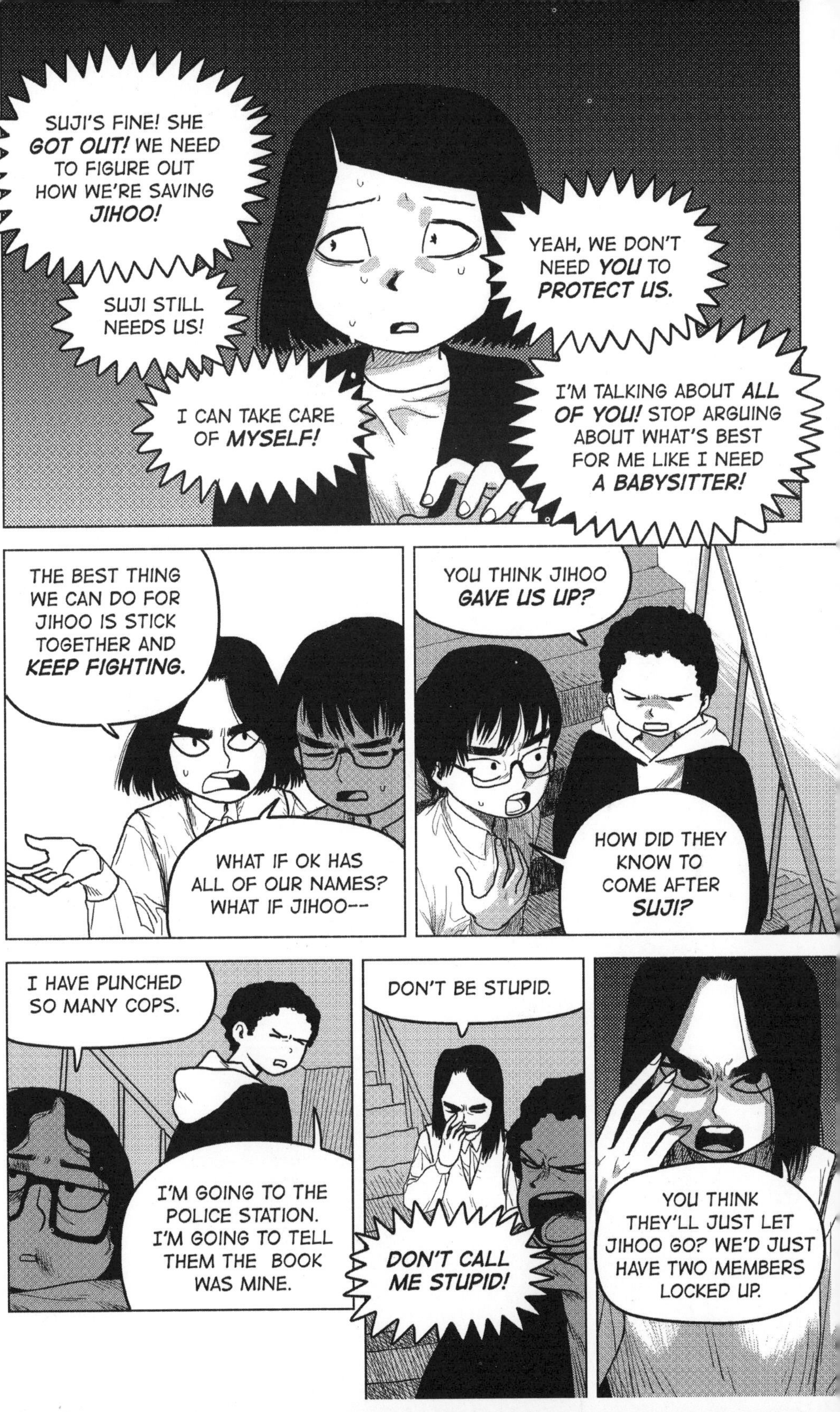
SUJI'S FINE! SHE GOT OUT! WE NEED TO FIGURE OUT HOW WE'RE SAVING JIHOO!
SUJI STILL NEEDS US!
YEAH, WE DON'T NEED YOU TO PROTECT US.
I CAN TAKE CARE OF MYSELF!
I'M TALKING ABOUT ALL OF YOU! STOP ARGUING ABOUT WHAT'S BEST FOR ME LIKE I NEED A BABYSITTER!
THE BEST THING WE CAN DO FOR JIHOO IS STICK TOGETHER AND KEEP FIGHTING.
WHAT IF OK HAS ALL OF OUR NAMES? WHAT IF JIHOO--
YOU THINK JIHOO GAVE US UP?
HOW DID THEY KNOW TO COME AFTER SUJI?
I HAVE PUNCHED SO MANY COPS.
I'M GOING TO THE POLICE STATION. I'M GOING TO TELL THEM THE BOOK WAS MINE.
DON'T BE STUPID.
DON'T CALL ME STUPID!
YOU THINK THEY'LL JUST LET JIHOO GO? WE'D JUST HAVE TWO MEMBERS LOCKED UP.

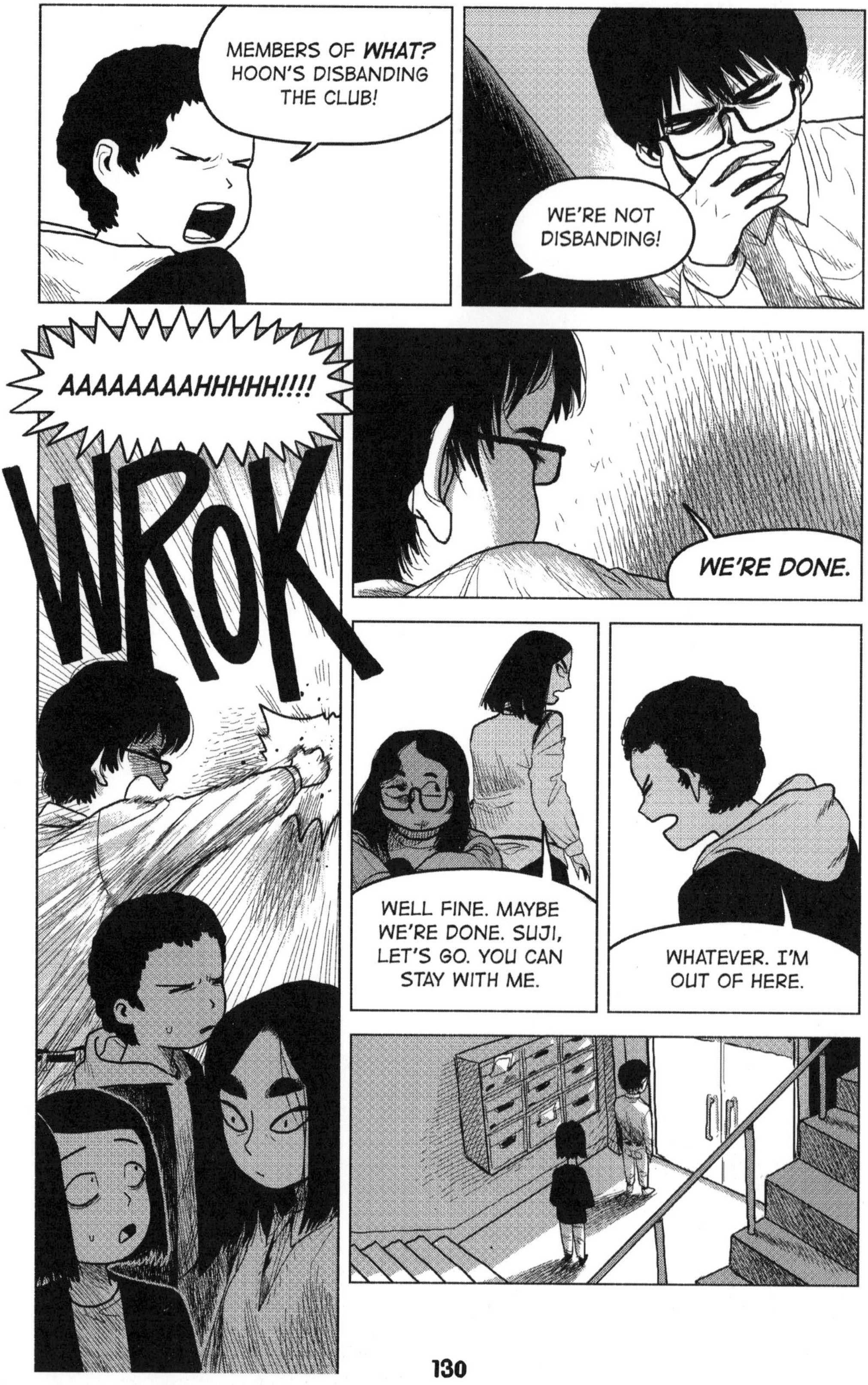
MEMBERS OF *WHAT?* HOON'S DISBANDING THE CLUB!
WE'RE NOT DISBANDING!
AAAAAAAAHHHHH!!!!
WROK
WE'RE DONE.
WELL FINE. MAYBE WE'RE DONE. SUJI, LET'S GO. YOU CAN STAY WITH ME.
WHATEVER. I'M OUT OF HERE.

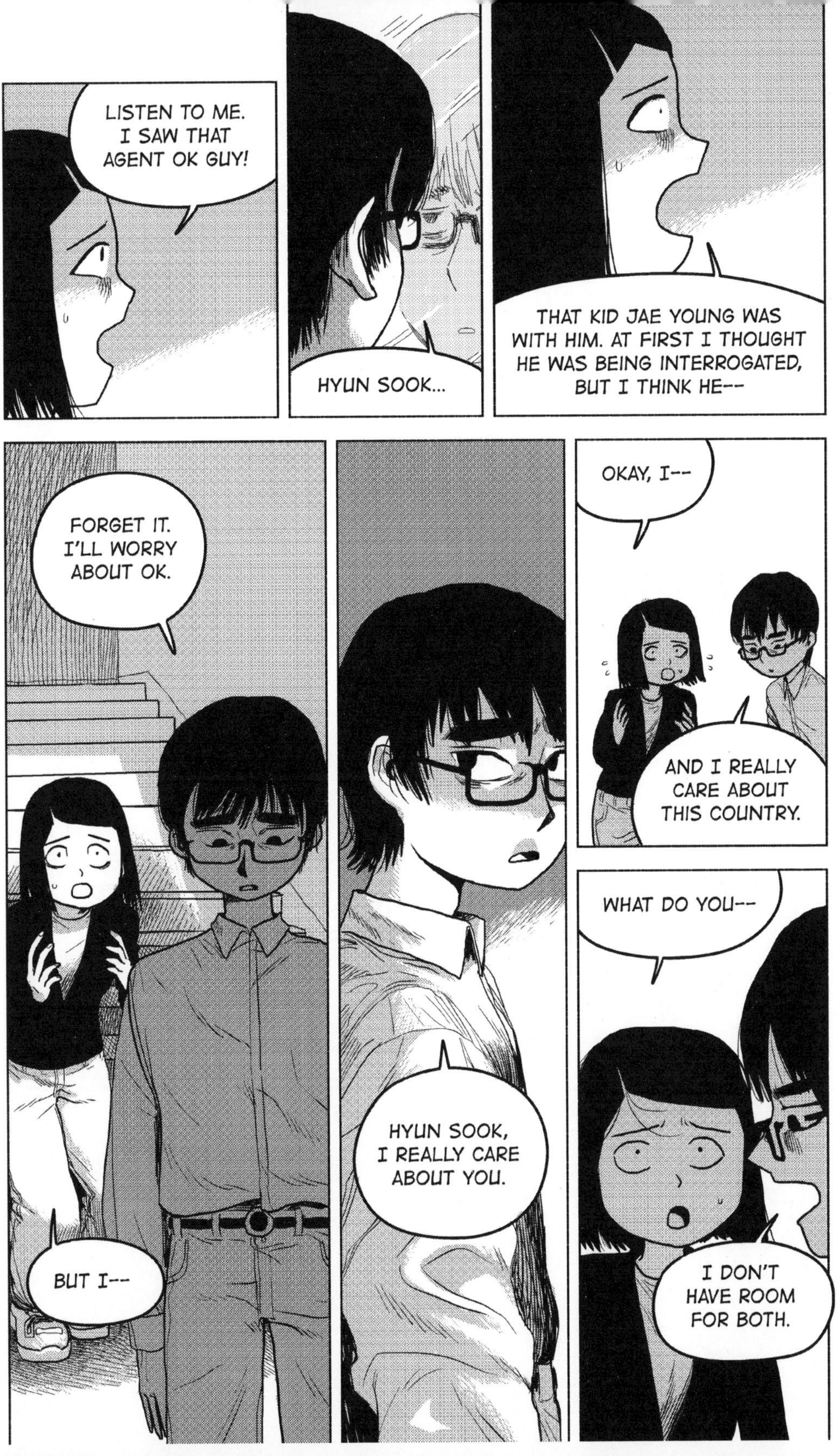
LISTEN TO ME. I SAW THAT AGENT OK GUY!
HYUN SOOK...
THAT KID JAE YOUNG WAS WITH HIM. AT FIRST I THOUGHT HE WAS BEING INTERROGATED, BUT I THINK HE--
FORGET IT. I'LL WORRY ABOUT OK.
BUT I--
HYUN SOOK, I REALLY CARE ABOUT YOU.
OKAY, I--
AND I REALLY CARE ABOUT THIS COUNTRY.
WHAT DO YOU--
I DON'T HAVE ROOM FOR BOTH.

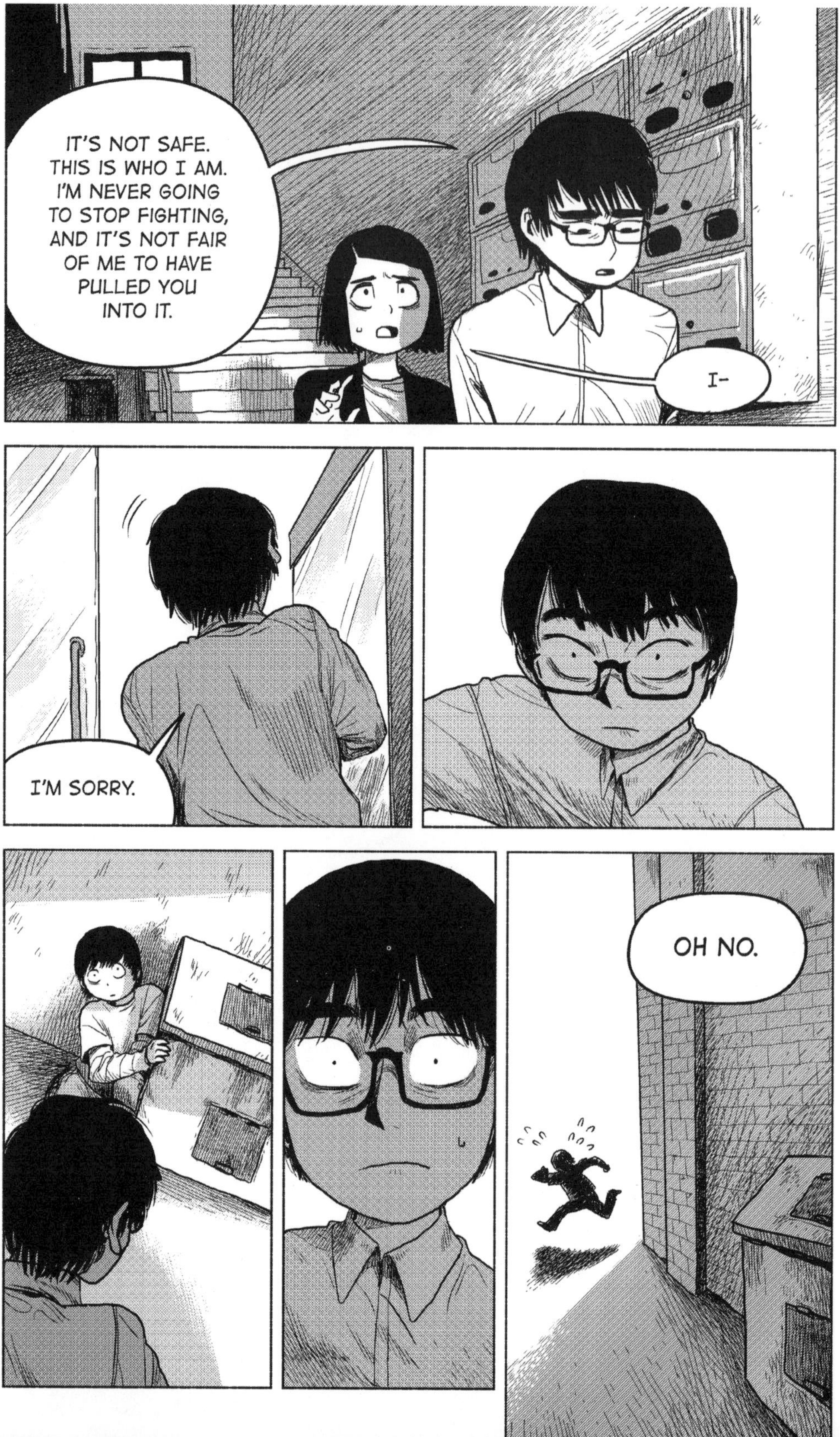
IT'S NOT SAFE. THIS IS WHO I AM. I'M NEVER GOING TO STOP FIGHTING, AND IT'S NOT FAIR OF ME TO HAVE PULLED YOU INTO IT.
I-
I'M SORRY.
OH NO.

CHAPTER EIGHT: CAMPUS SECURITY

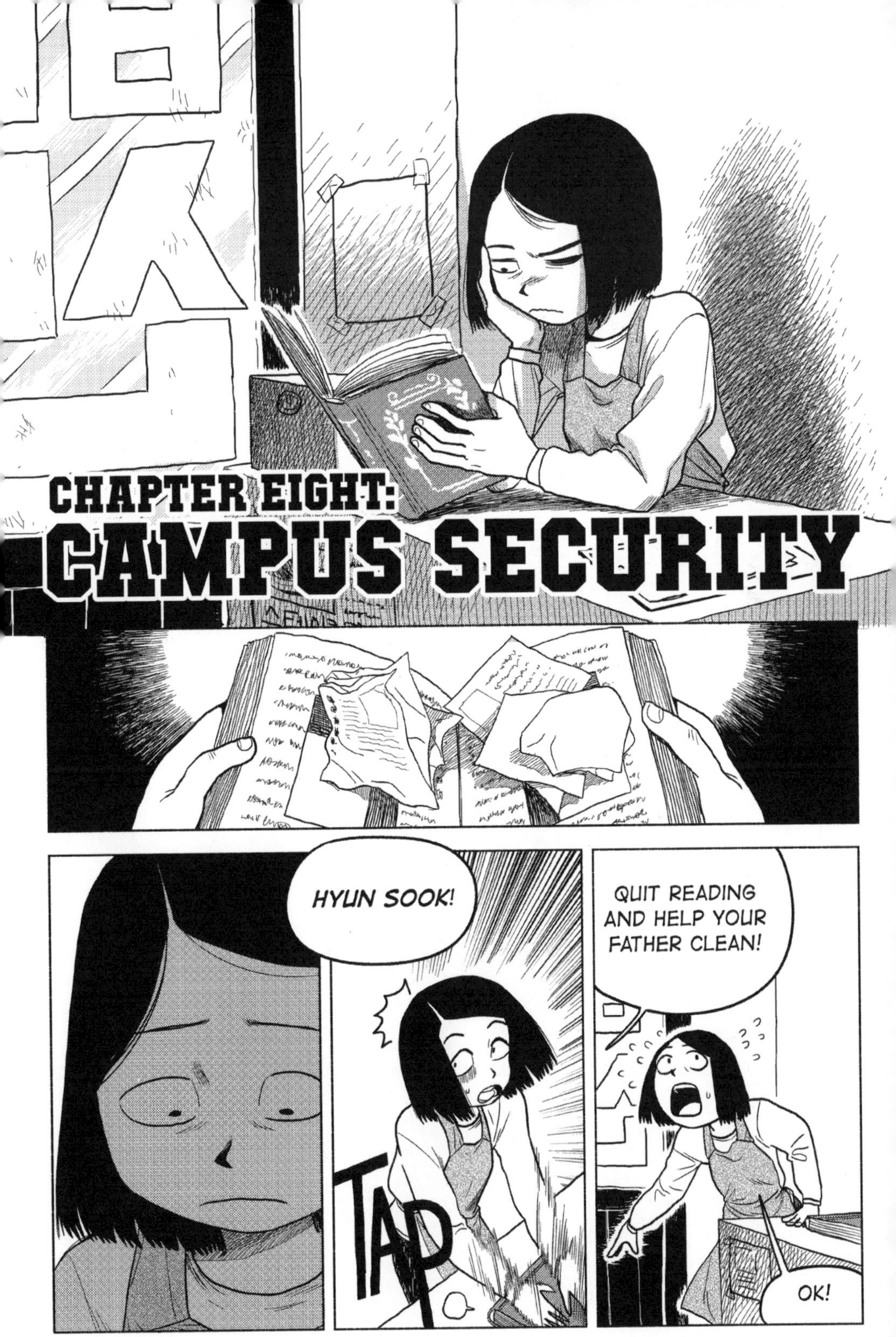
HYUN SOOK!
TAP
QUIT READING AND HELP YOUR FATHER CLEAN!
OK!

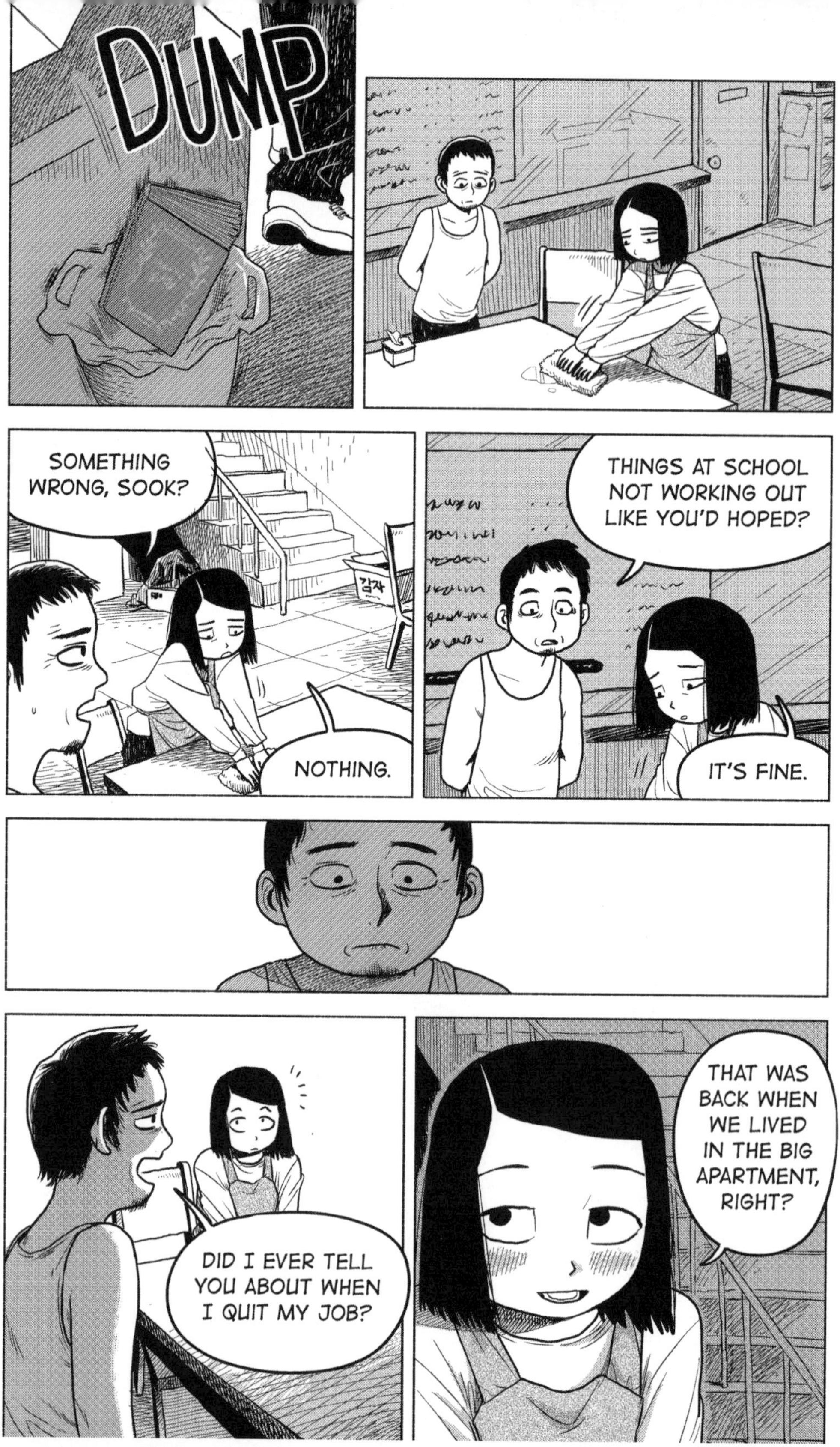
DUMP
SOMETHING WRONG, SOOK?
NOTHING.
THINGS AT SCHOOL NOT WORKING OUT LIKE YOU'D HOPED?
IT'S FINE.
DID I EVER TELL YOU ABOUT WHEN I QUIT MY JOB?
THAT WAS BACK WHEN WE LIVED IN THE BIG APARTMENT, RIGHT?

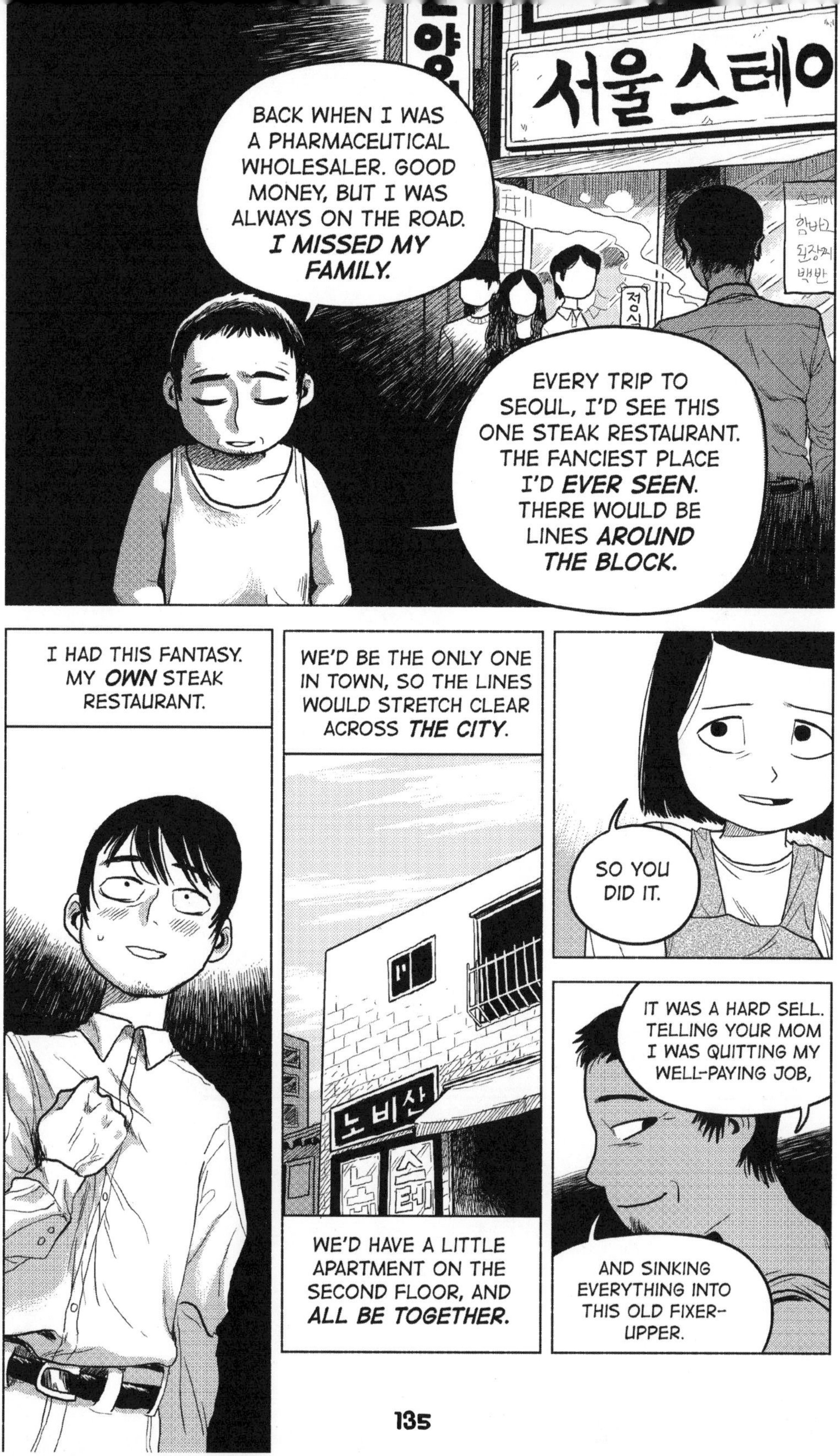
서울스테이
BACK WHEN I WAS A PHARMACEUTICAL WHOLESALER. GOOD MONEY, BUT I WAS ALWAYS ON THE ROAD. *I MISSED MY FAMILY.*
EVERY TRIP TO SEOUL, I'D SEE THIS ONE STEAK RESTAURANT. THE FANCIEST PLACE I'D *EVER SEEN*. THERE WOULD BE LINES *AROUND THE BLOCK*.
I HAD THIS FANTASY. MY *OWN* STEAK RESTAURANT.
WE'D BE THE ONLY ONE IN TOWN, SO THE LINES WOULD STRETCH CLEAR ACROSS *THE CITY*.
노비산
WE'D HAVE A LITTLE APARTMENT ON THE SECOND FLOOR, AND *ALL BE TOGETHER*.
SO YOU DID IT.
IT WAS A HARD SELL. TELLING YOUR MOM I WAS QUITTING MY WELL-PAYING JOB,
AND SINKING EVERYTHING INTO THIS OLD FIXER-UPPER.

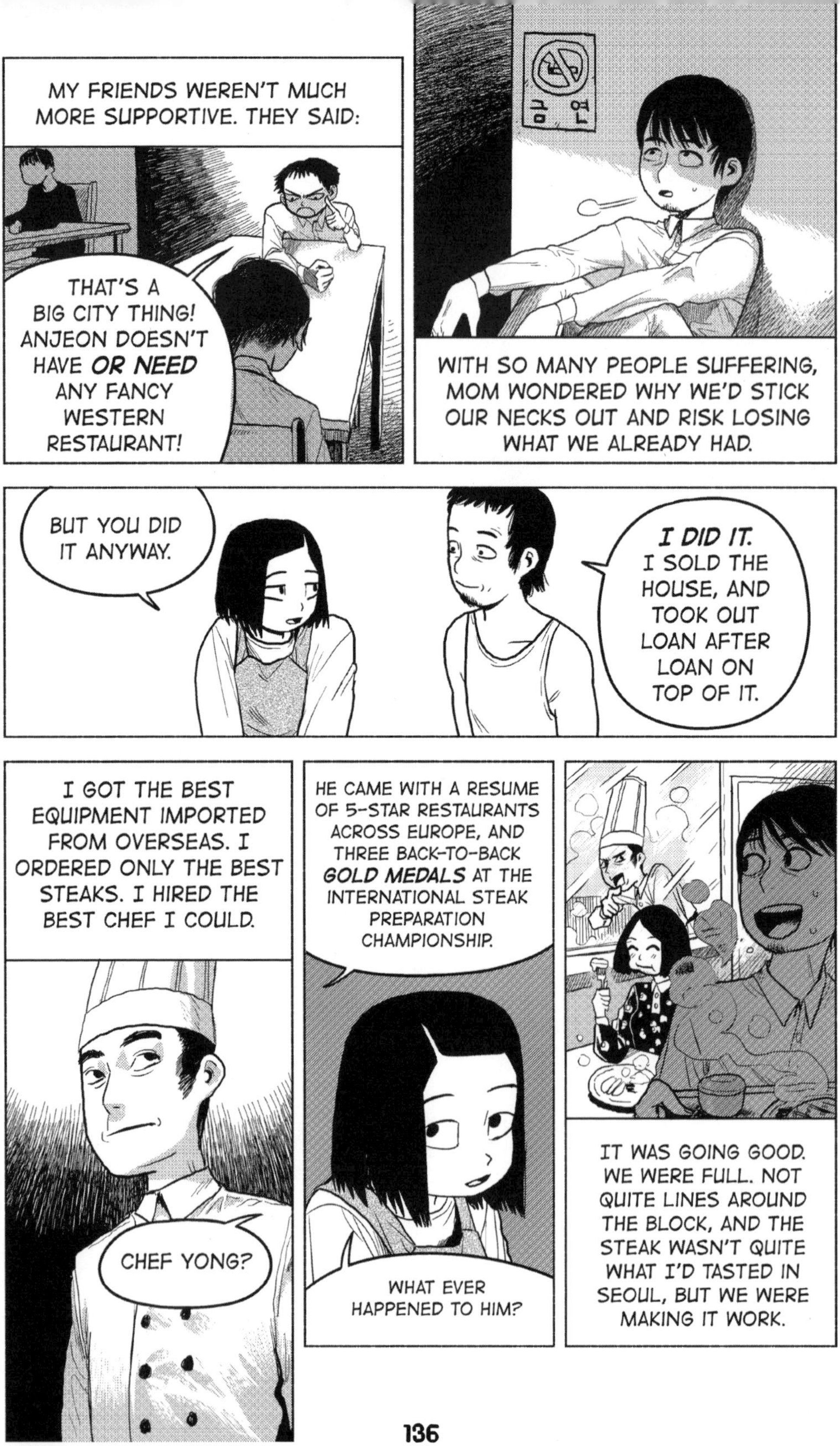
MY FRIENDS WEREN'T MUCH MORE SUPPORTIVE. THEY SAID:
THAT'S A BIG CITY THING! ANJEON DOESN'T HAVE ***OR NEED*** ANY FANCY WESTERN RESTAURANT!
금연
WITH SO MANY PEOPLE SUFFERING, MOM WONDERED WHY WE'D STICK OUR NECKS OUT AND RISK LOSING WHAT WE ALREADY HAD.
BUT YOU DID IT ANYWAY.
I DID IT. I SOLD THE HOUSE, AND TOOK OUT LOAN AFTER LOAN ON TOP OF IT.
I GOT THE BEST EQUIPMENT IMPORTED FROM OVERSEAS. I ORDERED ONLY THE BEST STEAKS. I HIRED THE BEST CHEF I COULD.
CHEF YONG?
HE CAME WITH A RESUME OF 5-STAR RESTAURANTS ACROSS EUROPE, AND THREE BACK-TO-BACK ***GOLD MEDALS*** AT THE INTERNATIONAL STEAK PREPARATION CHAMPIONSHIP.
WHAT EVER HAPPENED TO HIM?
IT WAS GOING GOOD. WE WERE FULL. NOT QUITE LINES AROUND THE BLOCK, AND THE STEAK WASN'T QUITE WHAT I'D TASTED IN SEOUL, BUT WE WERE MAKING IT WORK.

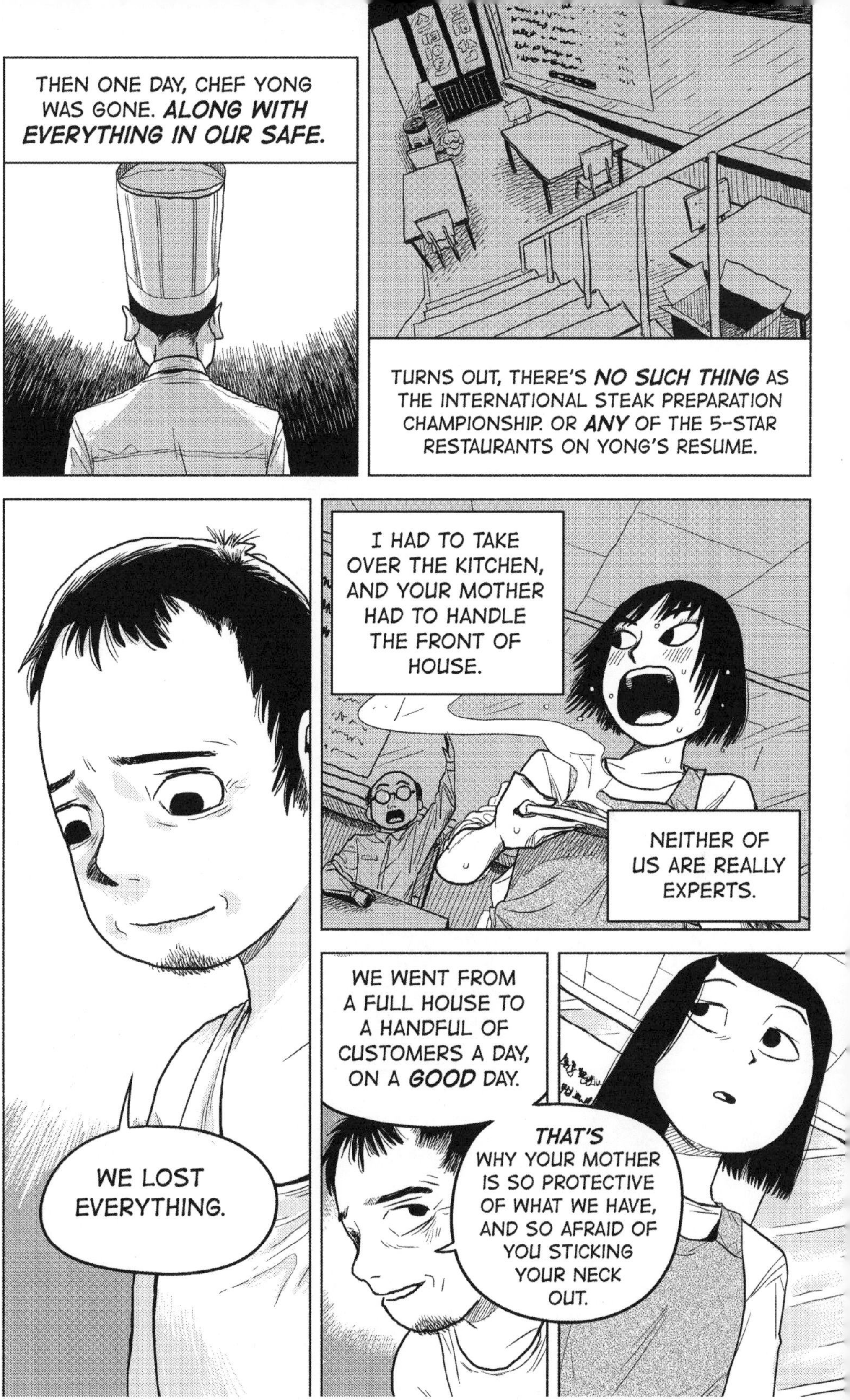
THEN ONE DAY, CHEF YONG WAS GONE. ALONG WITH EVERYTHING IN OUR SAFE.
TURNS OUT, THERE'S NO SUCH THING AS THE INTERNATIONAL STEAK PREPARATION CHAMPIONSHIP. OR ANY OF THE 5-STAR RESTAURANTS ON YONG'S RESUME.
WE LOST EVERYTHING.
I HAD TO TAKE OVER THE KITCHEN, AND YOUR MOTHER HAD TO HANDLE THE FRONT OF HOUSE.
NEITHER OF US ARE REALLY EXPERTS.
WE WENT FROM A FULL HOUSE TO A HANDFUL OF CUSTOMERS A DAY, ON A GOOD DAY.
THAT'S WHY YOUR MOTHER IS SO PROTECTIVE OF WHAT WE HAVE, AND SO AFRAID OF YOU STICKING YOUR NECK OUT.

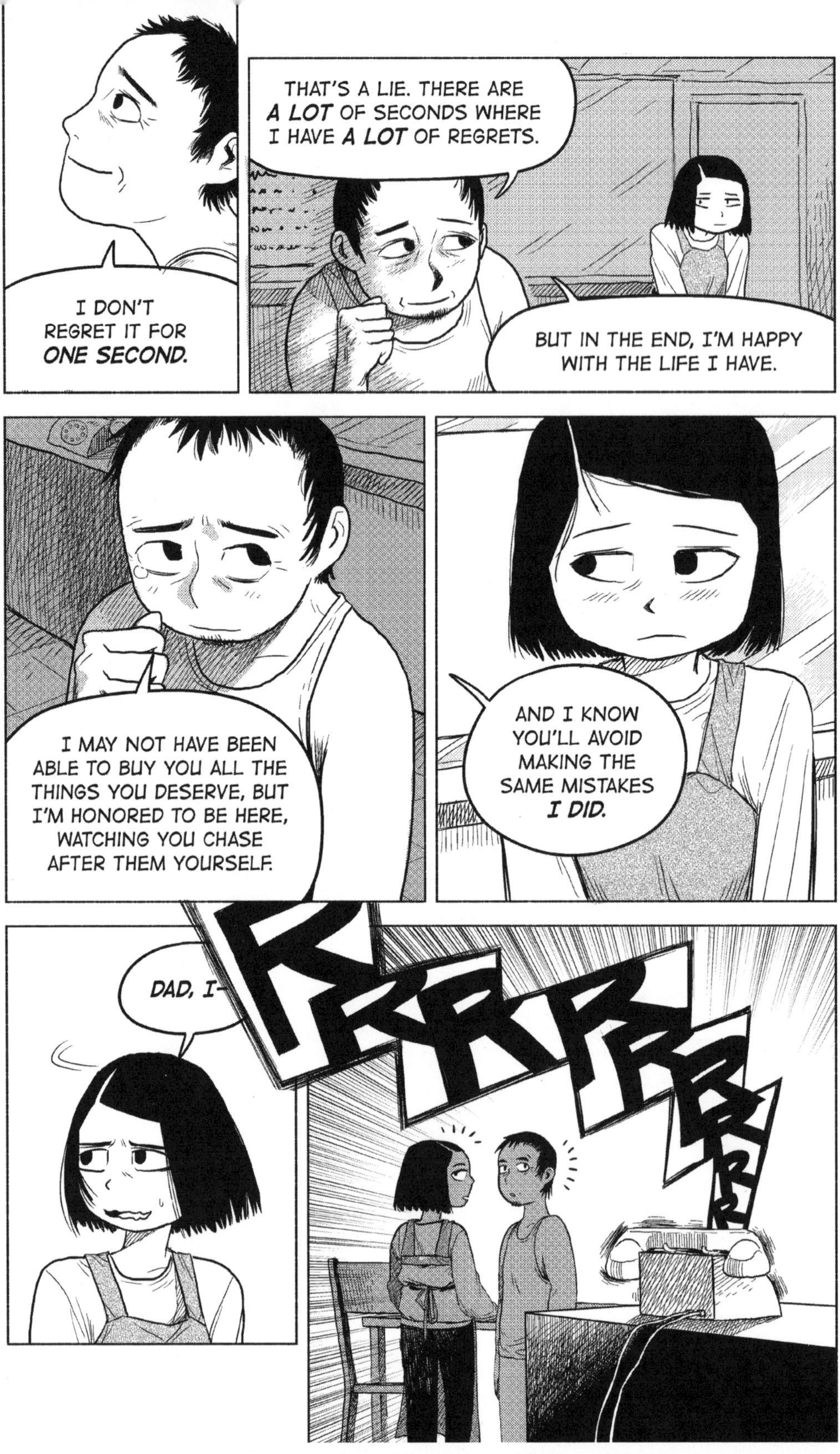
I DON'T REGRET IT FOR ONE SECOND.
THAT'S A LIE. THERE ARE A LOT OF SECONDS WHERE I HAVE A LOT OF REGRETS.
BUT IN THE END, I'M HAPPY WITH THE LIFE I HAVE.
I MAY NOT HAVE BEEN ABLE TO BUY YOU ALL THE THINGS YOU DESERVE, BUT I'M HONORED TO BE HERE, WATCHING YOU CHASE AFTER THEM YOURSELF.
AND I KNOW YOU'LL AVOID MAKING THE SAME MISTAKES I DID.
DAD, I-
RRRRRRRR

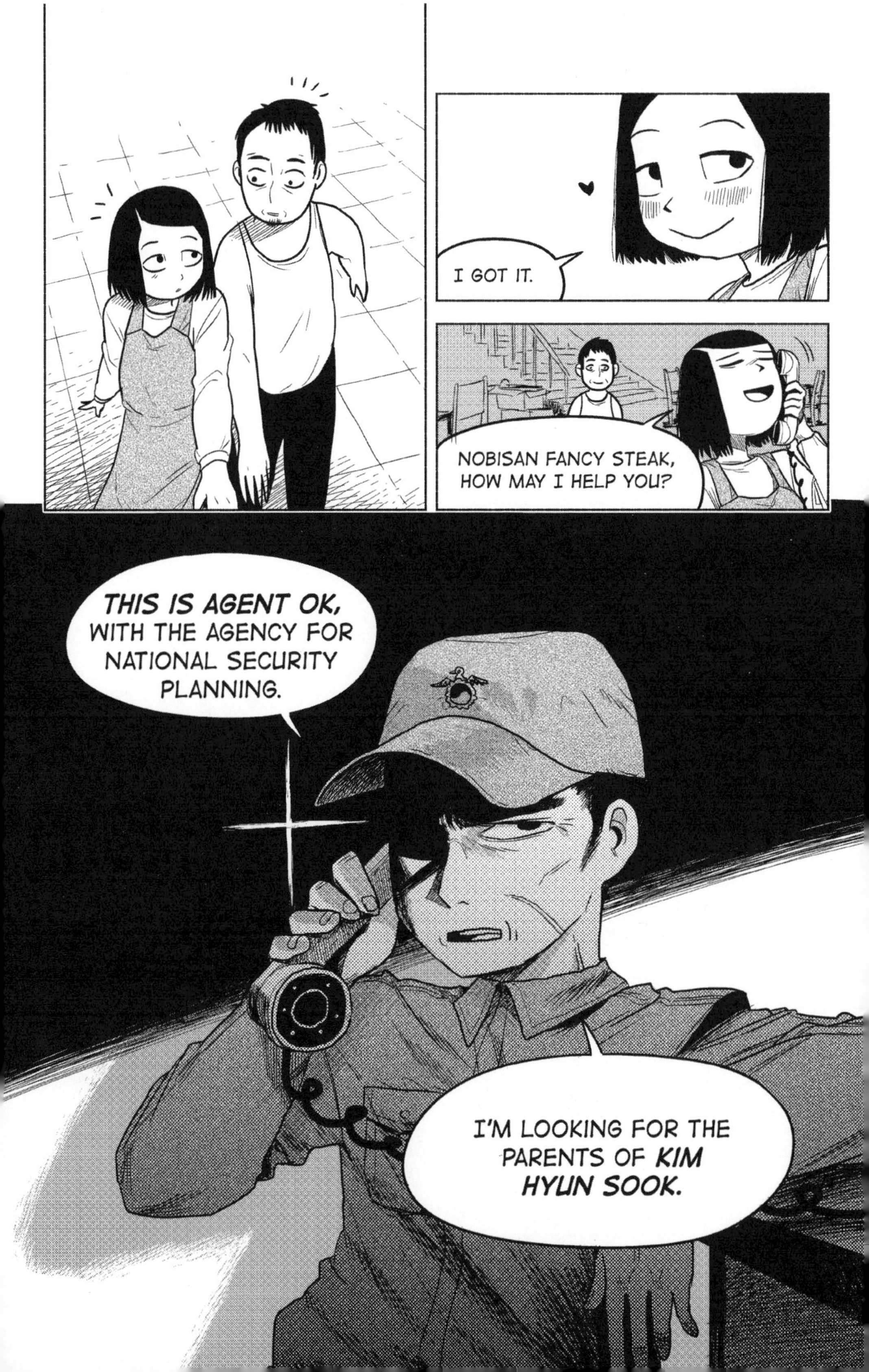
I GOT IT.
NOBISAN FANCY STEAK, HOW MAY I HELP YOU?
THIS IS AGENT OK, WITH THE AGENCY FOR NATIONAL SECURITY PLANNING.
I'M LOOKING FOR THE PARENTS OF KIM HYUN SOOK.

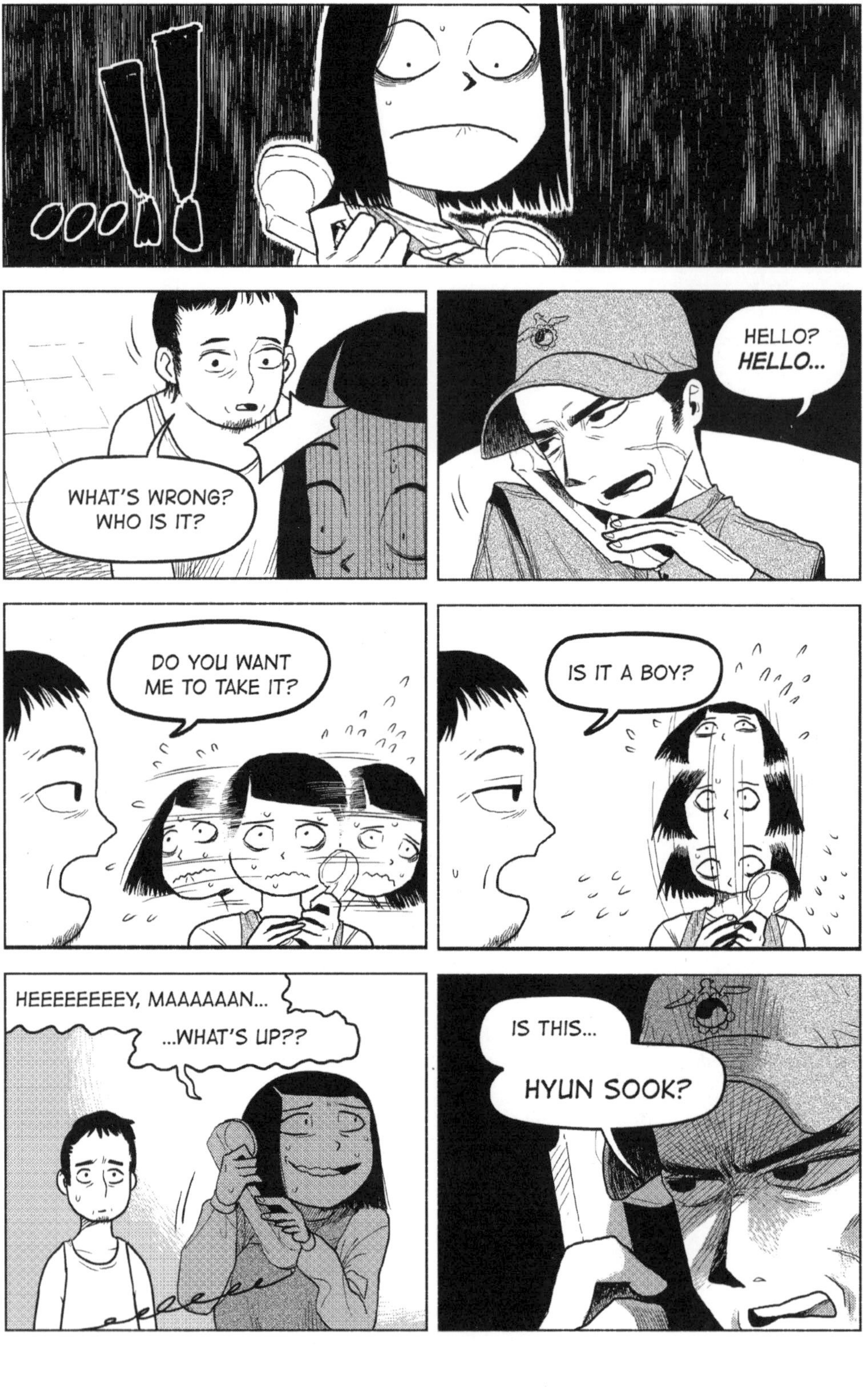
OOO!!
WHAT'S WRONG? WHO IS IT?
HELLO? HELLO...
DO YOU WANT ME TO TAKE IT?
IS IT A BOY?
HEEEEEEEEY, MAAAAAAN... ...WHAT'S UP??
IS THIS... HYUN SOOK?

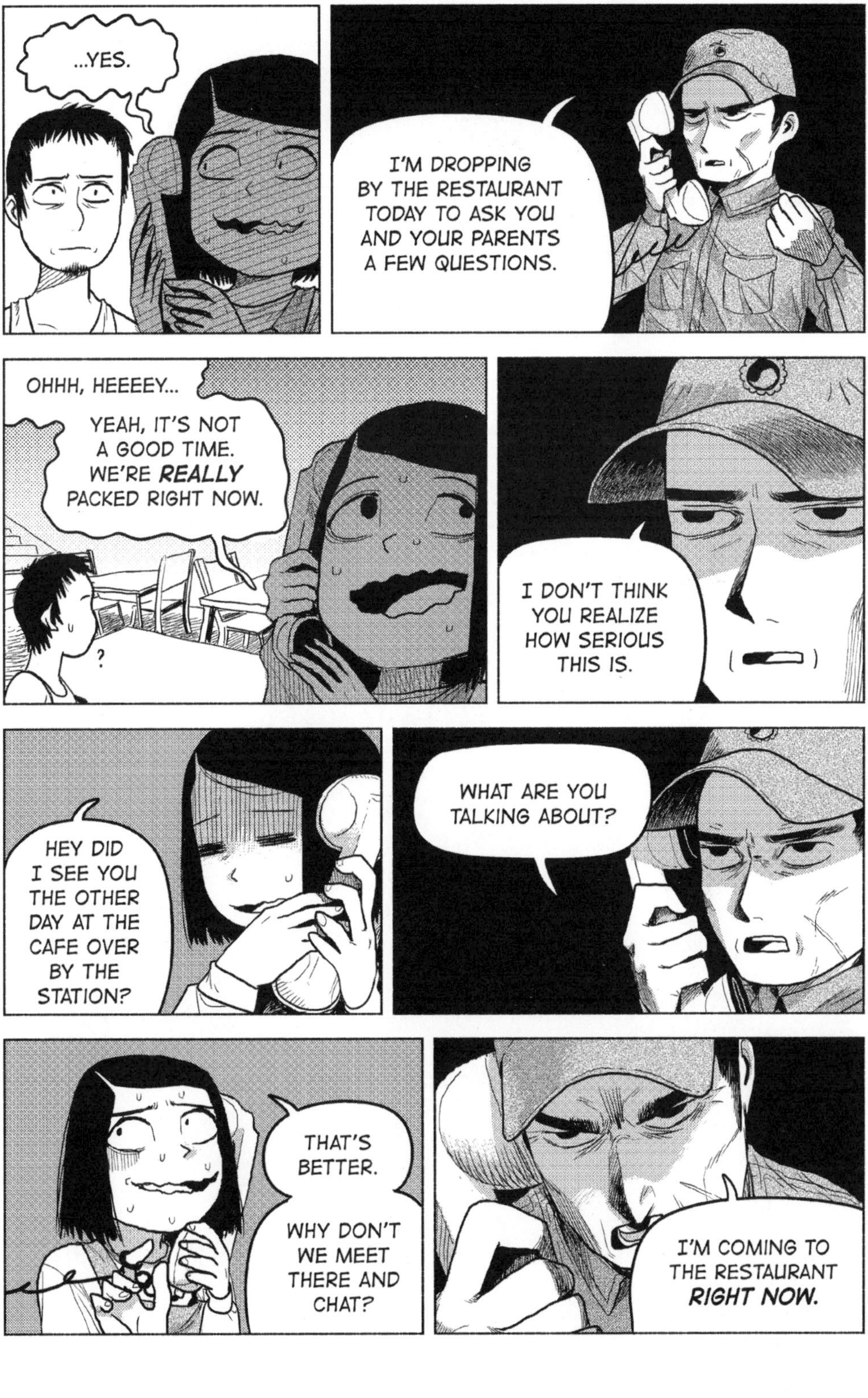
...YES.
I'M DROPPING BY THE RESTAURANT TODAY TO ASK YOU AND YOUR PARENTS A FEW QUESTIONS.
OHHH, HEEEEY...
YEAH, IT'S NOT A GOOD TIME. WE'RE *REALLY* PACKED RIGHT NOW.
?
I DON'T THINK YOU REALIZE HOW SERIOUS THIS IS.
HEY DID I SEE YOU THE OTHER DAY AT THE CAFE OVER BY THE STATION?
WHAT ARE YOU TALKING ABOUT?
THAT'S BETTER.
WHY DON'T WE MEET THERE AND CHAT?
I'M COMING TO THE RESTAURANT *RIGHT NOW.*

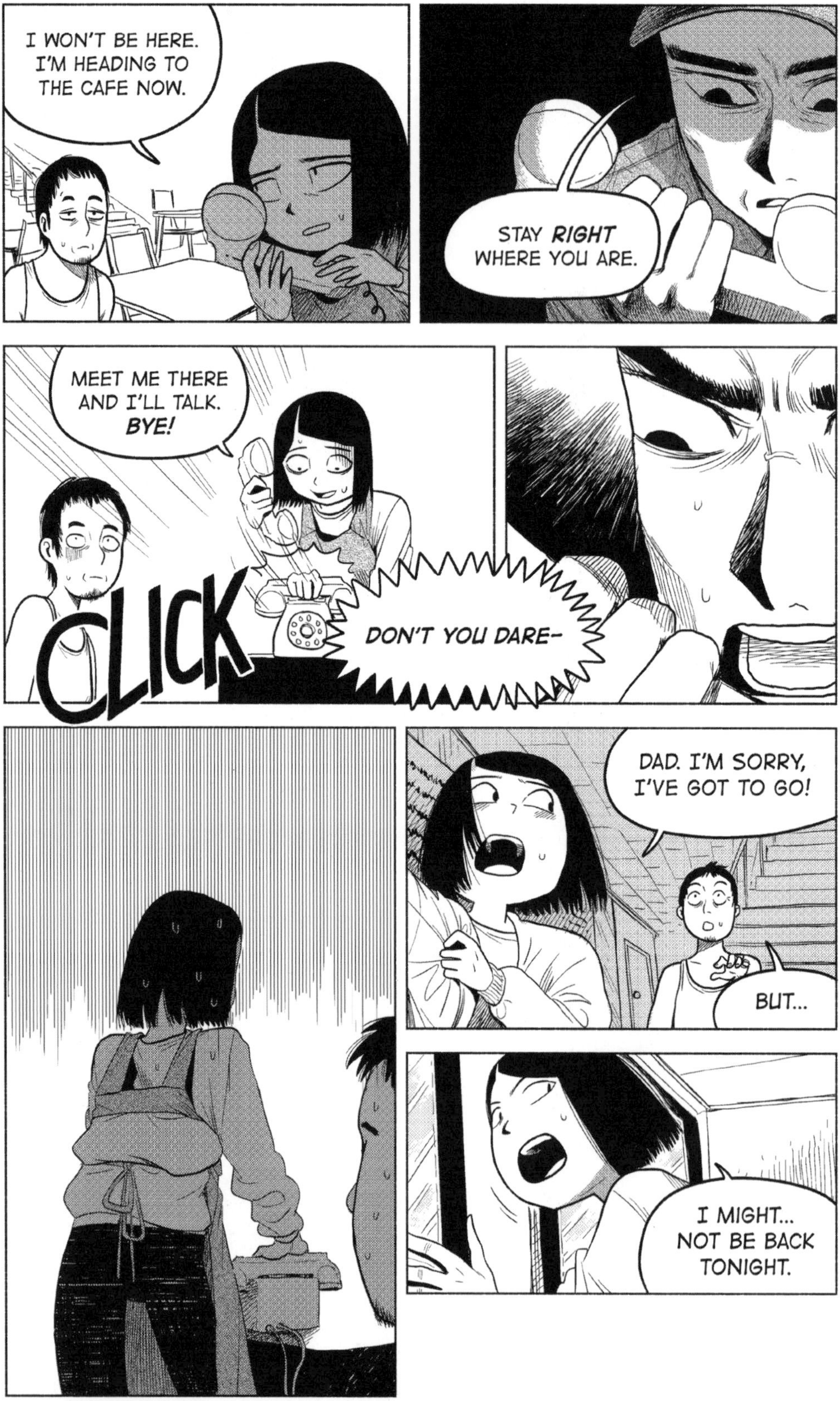
I WON'T BE HERE. I'M HEADING TO THE CAFE NOW.
STAY RIGHT WHERE YOU ARE.
MEET ME THERE AND I'LL TALK. BYE!
CLICK
DON'T YOU DARE-
DAD. I'M SORRY, I'VE GOT TO GO!
BUT...
I MIGHT... NOT BE BACK TONIGHT.

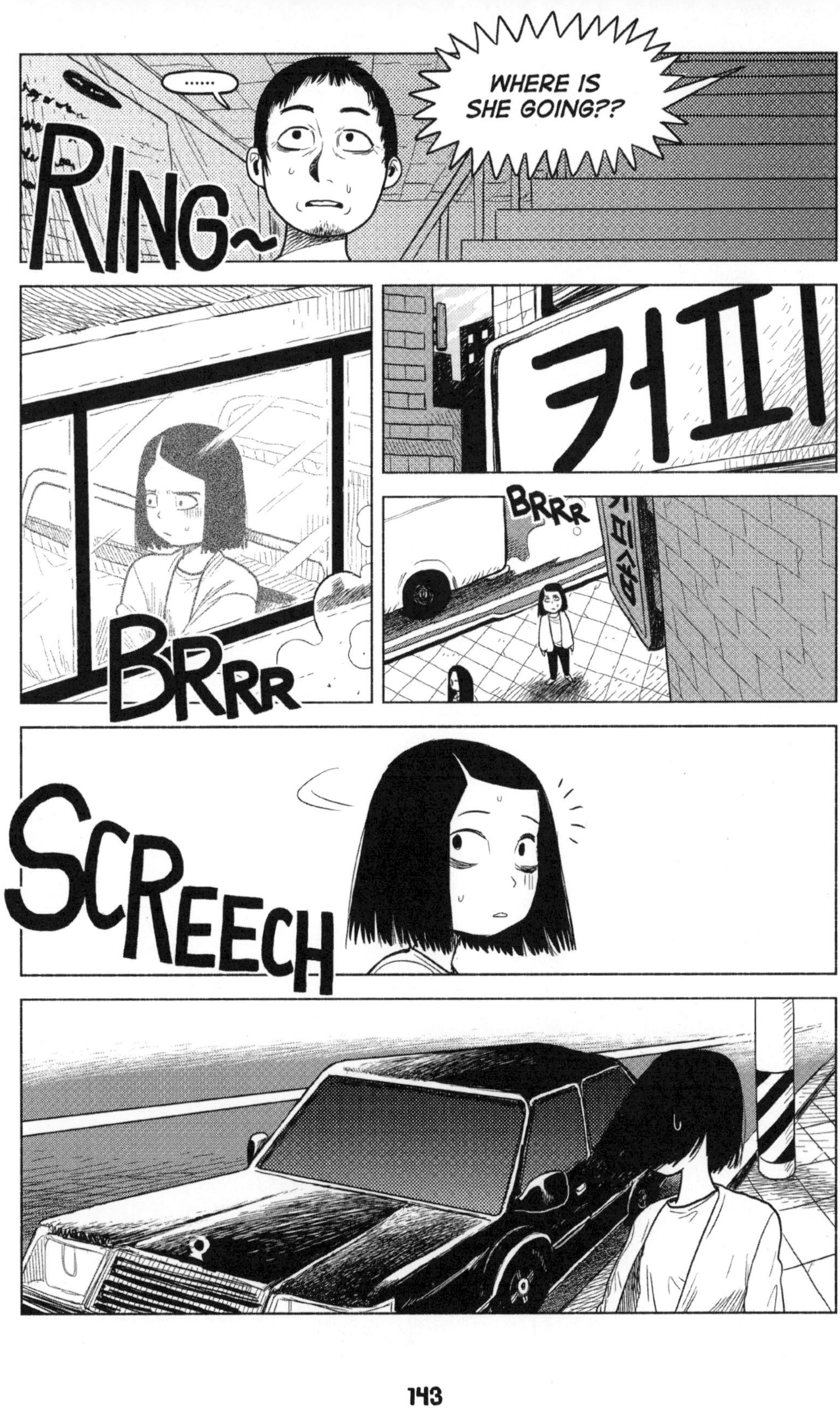
......
WHERE IS SHE GOING??
RING~
BRRR
커피
BRRR
SCREECH

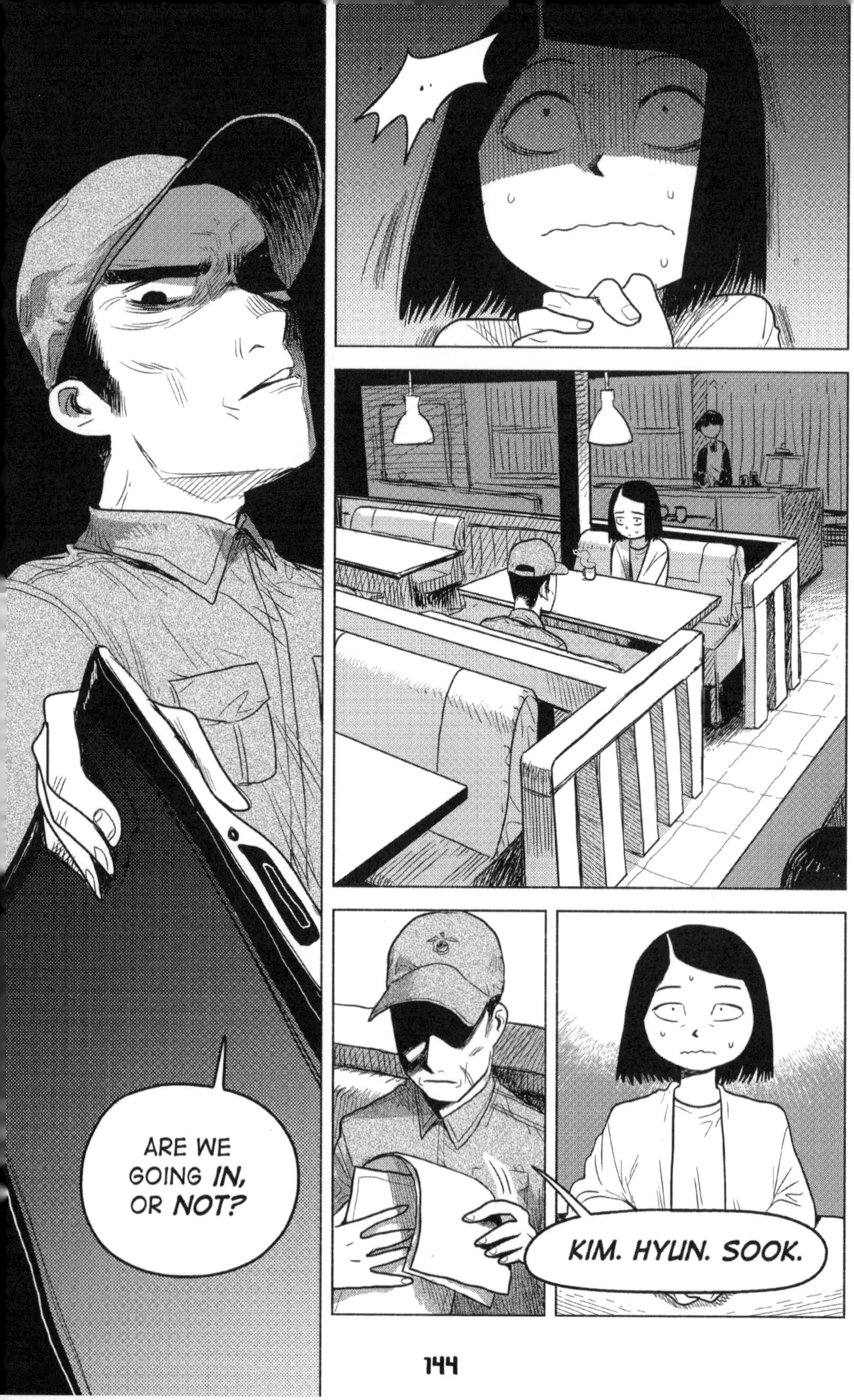
ARE WE GOING *IN*, OR *NOT?*
KIM. HYUN. SOOK.

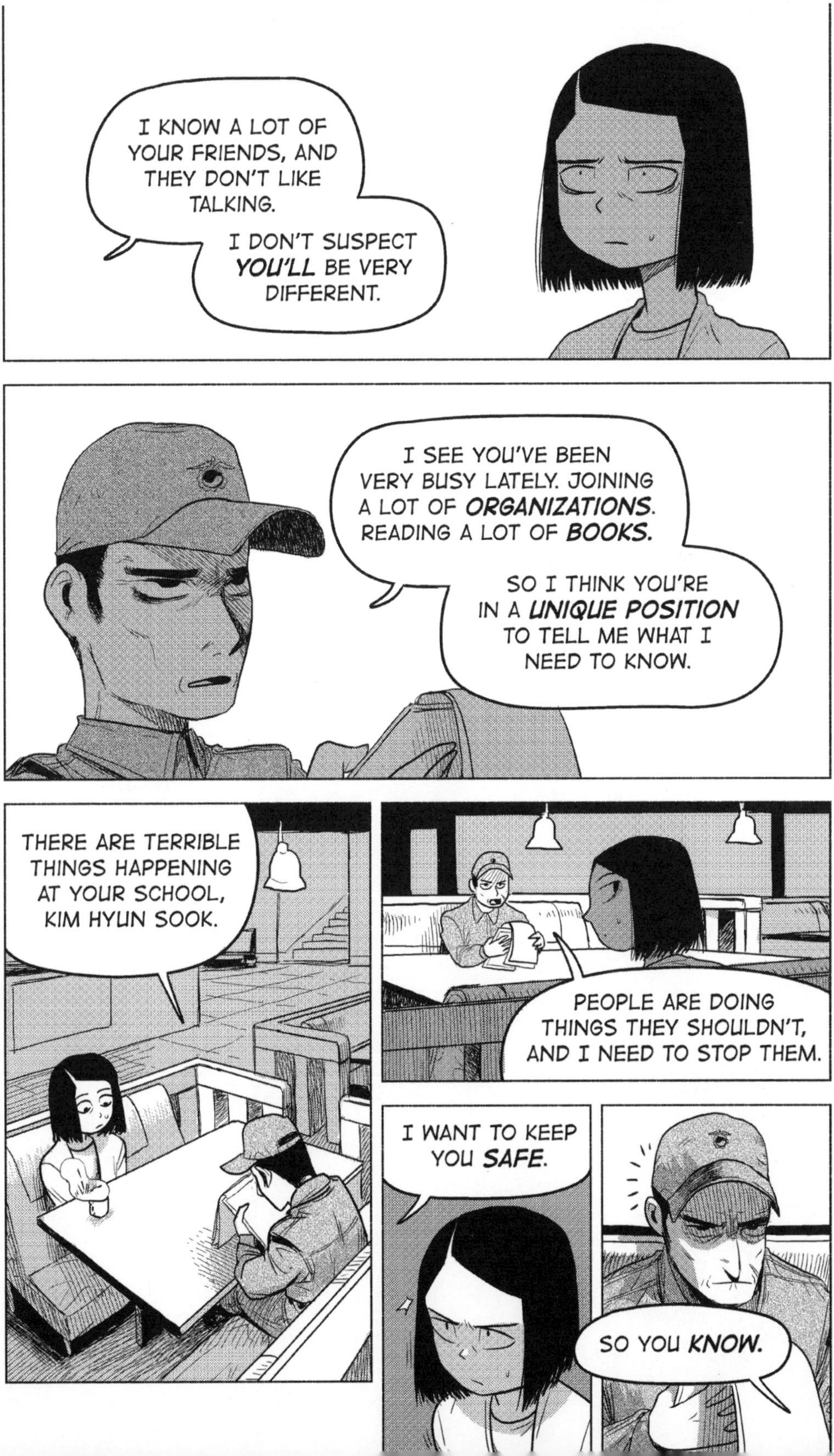
I KNOW A LOT OF YOUR FRIENDS, AND THEY DON'T LIKE TALKING.
I DON'T SUSPECT *YOU'LL* BE VERY DIFFERENT.
I SEE YOU'VE BEEN VERY BUSY LATELY. JOINING A LOT OF *ORGANIZATIONS*. READING A LOT OF *BOOKS*.
SO I THINK YOU'RE IN A *UNIQUE POSITION* TO TELL ME WHAT I NEED TO KNOW.
THERE ARE TERRIBLE THINGS HAPPENING AT YOUR SCHOOL, KIM HYUN SOOK.
PEOPLE ARE DOING THINGS THEY SHOULDN'T, AND I NEED TO STOP THEM.
I WANT TO KEEP YOU *SAFE*.
SO YOU *KNOW*.

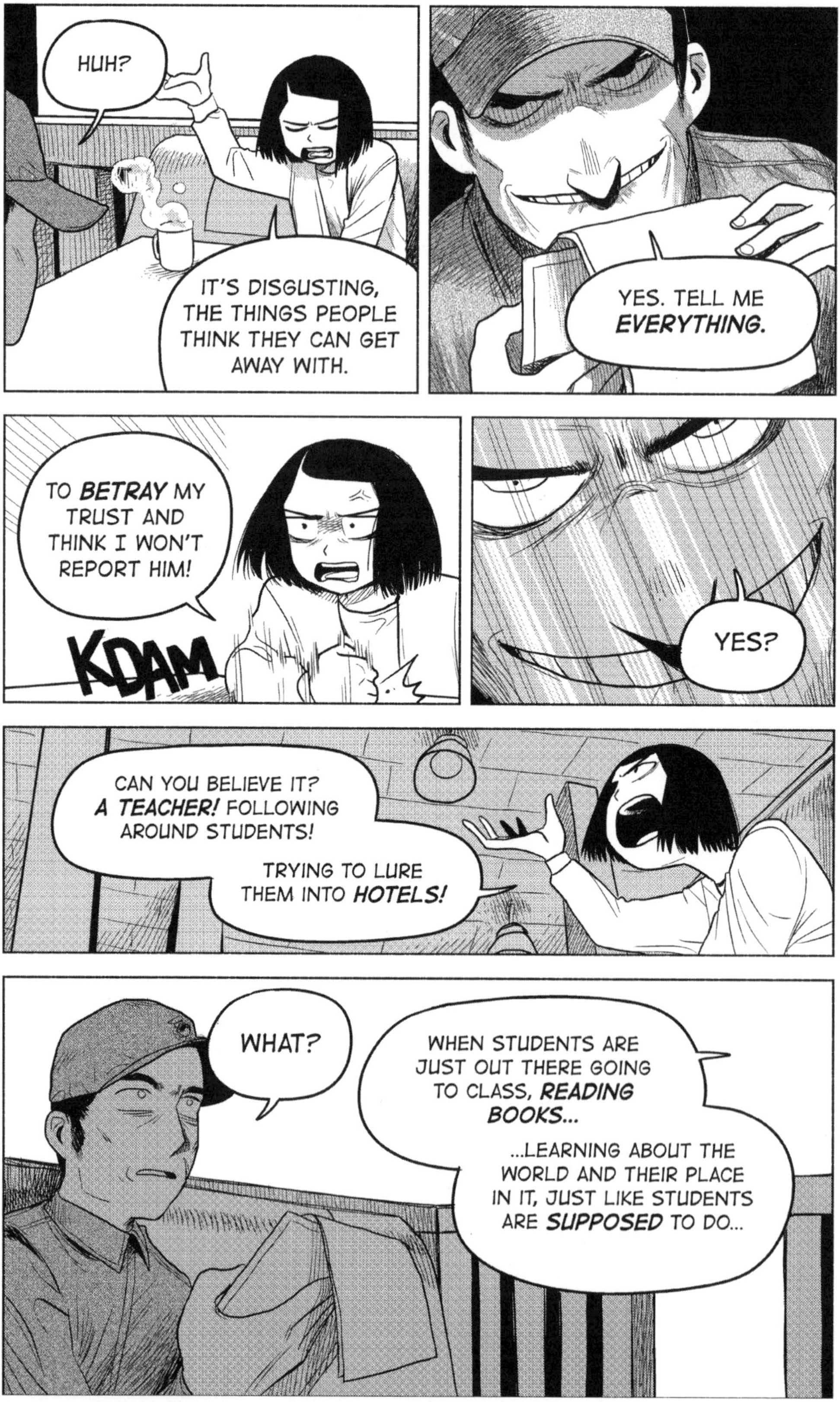
HUH?
IT'S DISGUSTING, THE THINGS PEOPLE THINK THEY CAN GET AWAY WITH.
YES. TELL ME EVERYTHING.
TO BETRAY MY TRUST AND THINK I WON'T REPORT HIM!
KDAM
YES?
CAN YOU BELIEVE IT? A TEACHER! FOLLOWING AROUND STUDENTS!
TRYING TO LURE THEM INTO HOTELS!
WHAT?
WHEN STUDENTS ARE JUST OUT THERE GOING TO CLASS, READING BOOKS...
...LEARNING ABOUT THE WORLD AND THEIR PLACE IN IT, JUST LIKE STUDENTS ARE SUPPOSED TO DO...

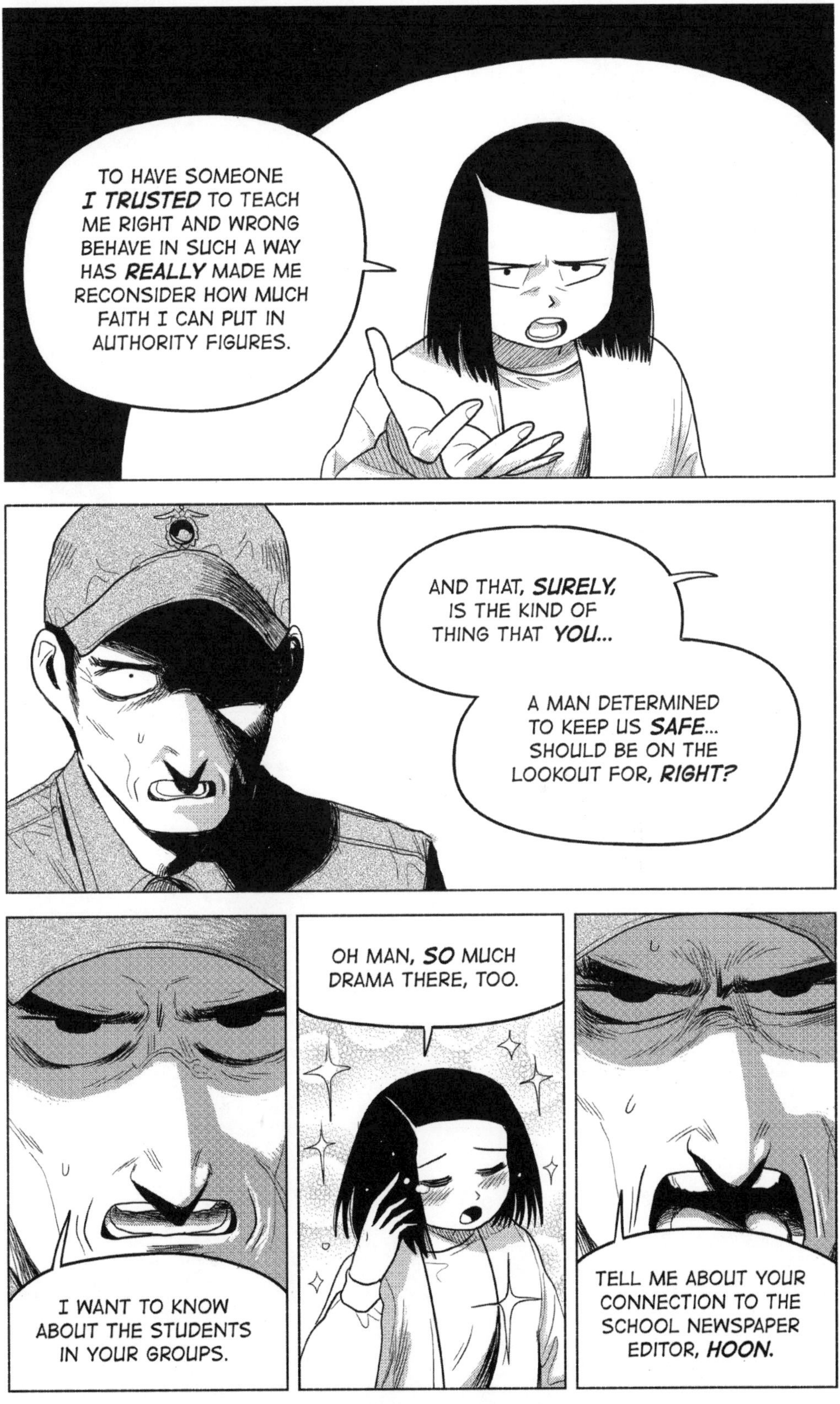
TO HAVE SOMEONE I TRUSTED TO TEACH ME RIGHT AND WRONG BEHAVE IN SUCH A WAY HAS REALLY MADE ME RECONSIDER HOW MUCH FAITH I CAN PUT IN AUTHORITY FIGURES.
AND THAT, SURELY, IS THE KIND OF THING THAT YOU...
A MAN DETERMINED TO KEEP US SAFE... SHOULD BE ON THE LOOKOUT FOR, RIGHT?
I WANT TO KNOW ABOUT THE STUDENTS IN YOUR GROUPS.
OH MAN, SO MUCH DRAMA THERE, TOO.
TELL ME ABOUT YOUR CONNECTION TO THE SCHOOL NEWSPAPER EDITOR, HOON.

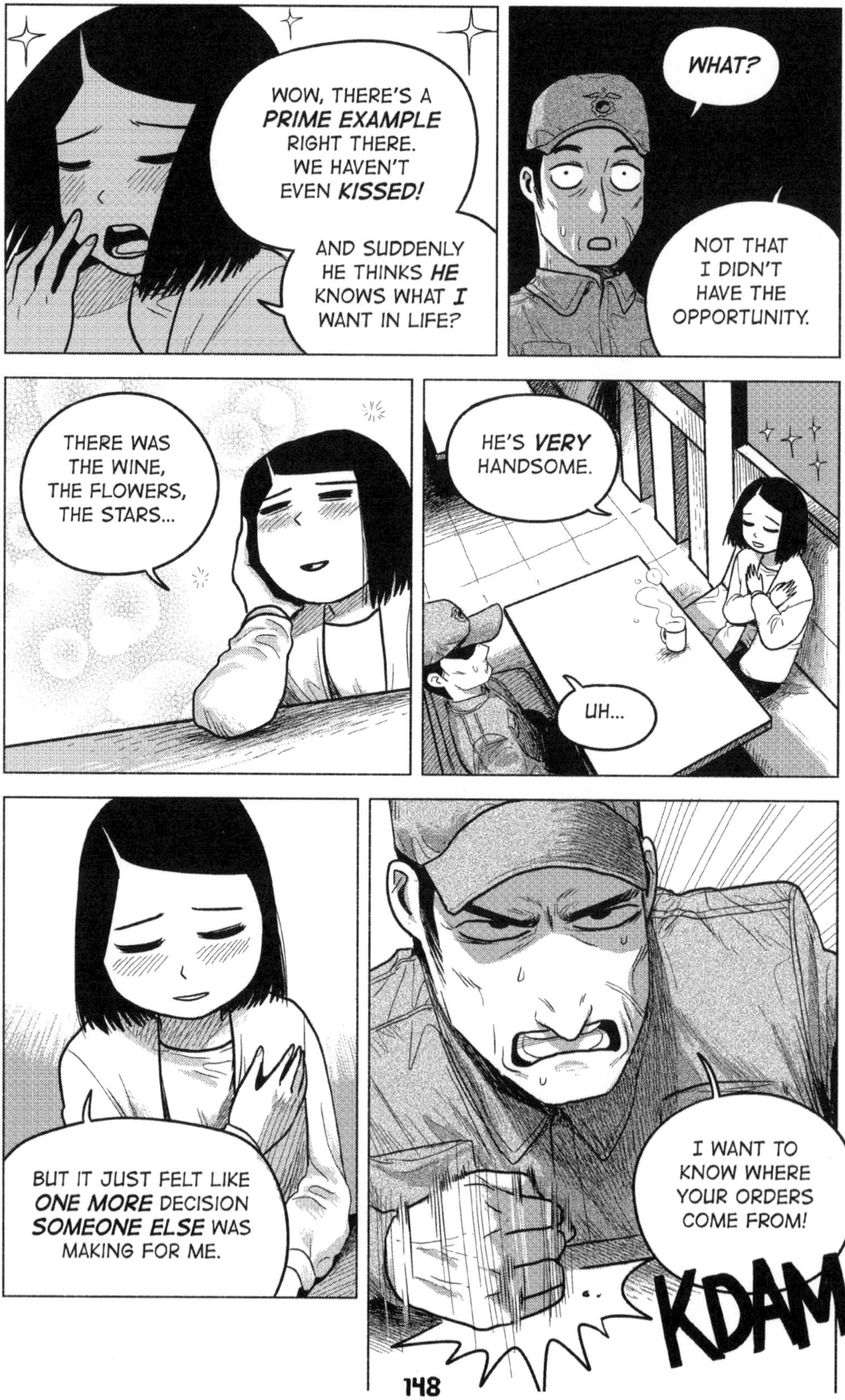
WOW, THERE'S A PRIME EXAMPLE RIGHT THERE. WE HAVEN'T EVEN KISSED!
AND SUDDENLY HE THINKS HE KNOWS WHAT I WANT IN LIFE?
WHAT?
NOT THAT I DIDN'T HAVE THE OPPORTUNITY.
THERE WAS THE WINE, THE FLOWERS, THE STARS...
HE'S VERY HANDSOME.
UH...
BUT IT JUST FELT LIKE ONE MORE DECISION SOMEONE ELSE WAS MAKING FOR ME.
I WANT TO KNOW WHERE YOUR ORDERS COME FROM!
KDAM

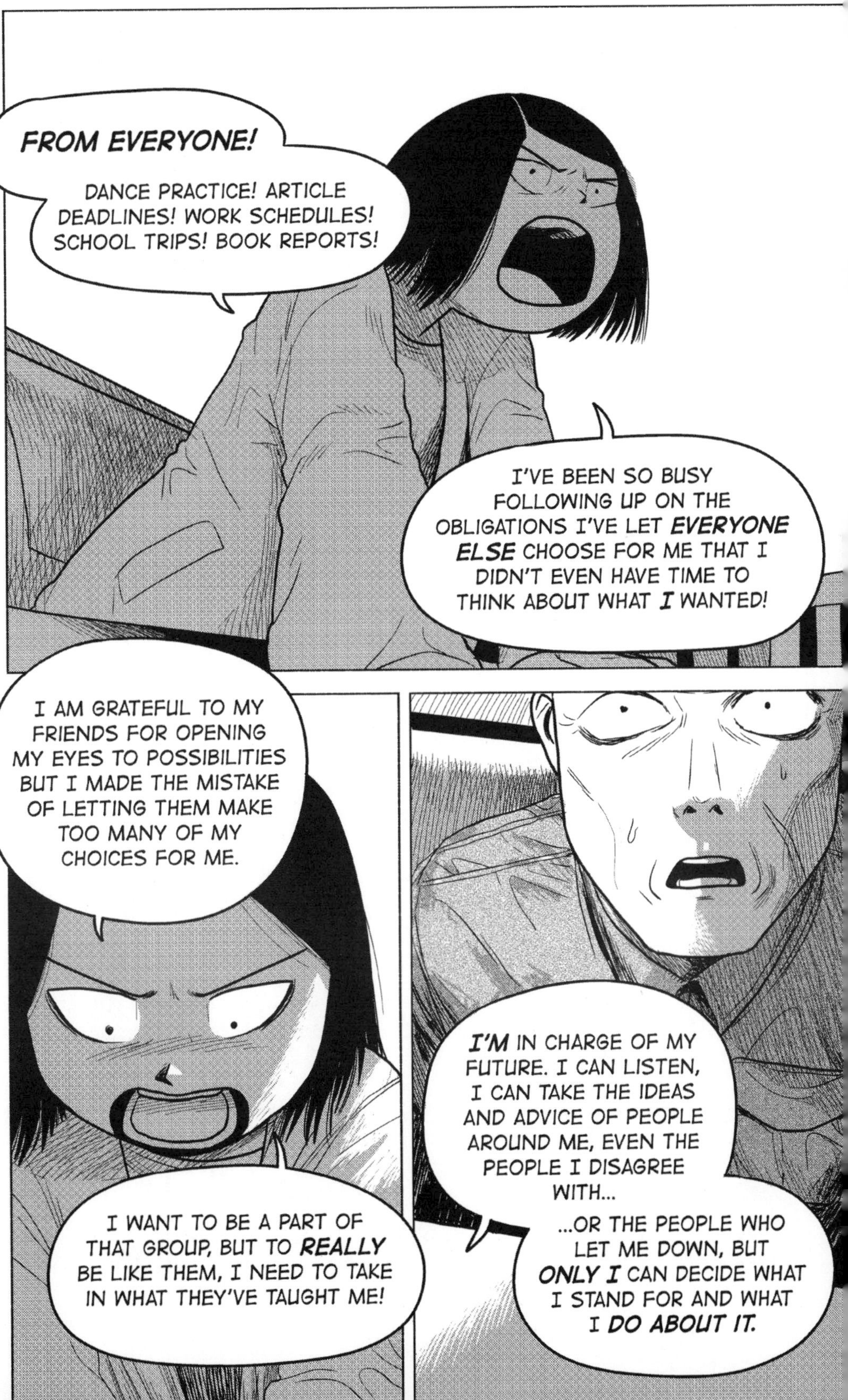
FROM EVERYONE!
DANCE PRACTICE! ARTICLE DEADLINES! WORK SCHEDULES! SCHOOL TRIPS! BOOK REPORTS!
I'VE BEEN SO BUSY FOLLOWING UP ON THE OBLIGATIONS I'VE LET EVERYONE ELSE CHOOSE FOR ME THAT I DIDN'T EVEN HAVE TIME TO THINK ABOUT WHAT I WANTED!
I AM GRATEFUL TO MY FRIENDS FOR OPENING MY EYES TO POSSIBILITIES BUT I MADE THE MISTAKE OF LETTING THEM MAKE TOO MANY OF MY CHOICES FOR ME.
I WANT TO BE A PART OF THAT GROUP, BUT TO REALLY BE LIKE THEM, I NEED TO TAKE IN WHAT THEY'VE TAUGHT ME!
I'M IN CHARGE OF MY FUTURE. I CAN LISTEN, I CAN TAKE THE IDEAS AND ADVICE OF PEOPLE AROUND ME, EVEN THE PEOPLE I DISAGREE WITH...
...OR THE PEOPLE WHO LET ME DOWN, BUT ONLY I CAN DECIDE WHAT I STAND FOR AND WHAT I DO ABOUT IT.

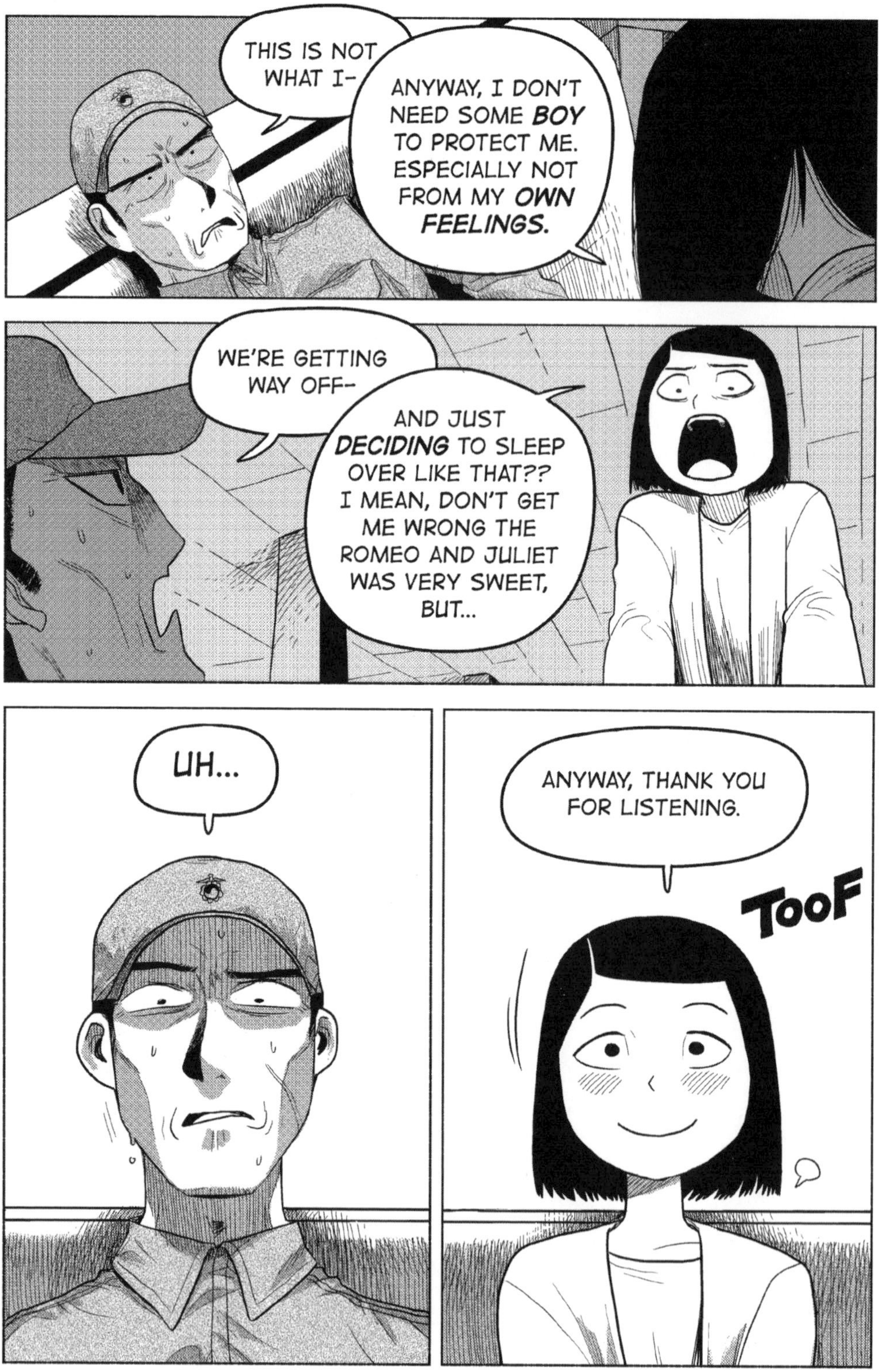
THIS IS NOT WHAT I-
ANYWAY, I DON'T NEED SOME **BOY** TO PROTECT ME. ESPECIALLY NOT FROM MY ***OWN FEELINGS.***
WE'RE GETTING WAY OFF-
AND JUST ***DECIDING*** TO SLEEP OVER LIKE THAT?? I MEAN, DON'T GET ME WRONG THE ROMEO AND JULIET WAS VERY SWEET, BUT...
UH...
ANYWAY, THANK YOU FOR LISTENING.
TOOF

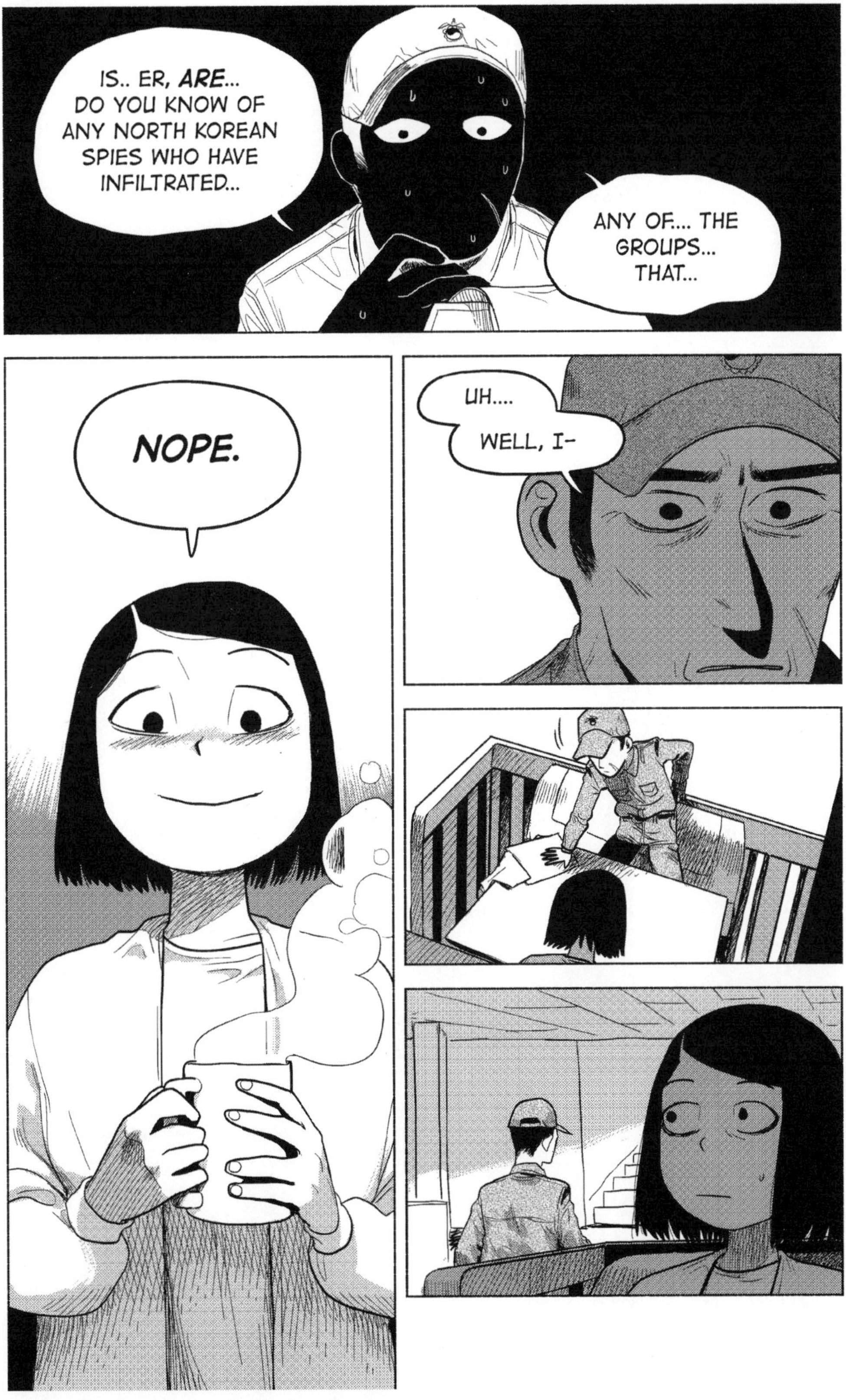
IS.. ER, ARE...
DO YOU KNOW OF
ANY NORTH KOREAN
SPIES WHO HAVE
INFILTRATED...
ANY OF.... THE
GROUPS...
THAT...
NOPE.
UH....
WELL, I-

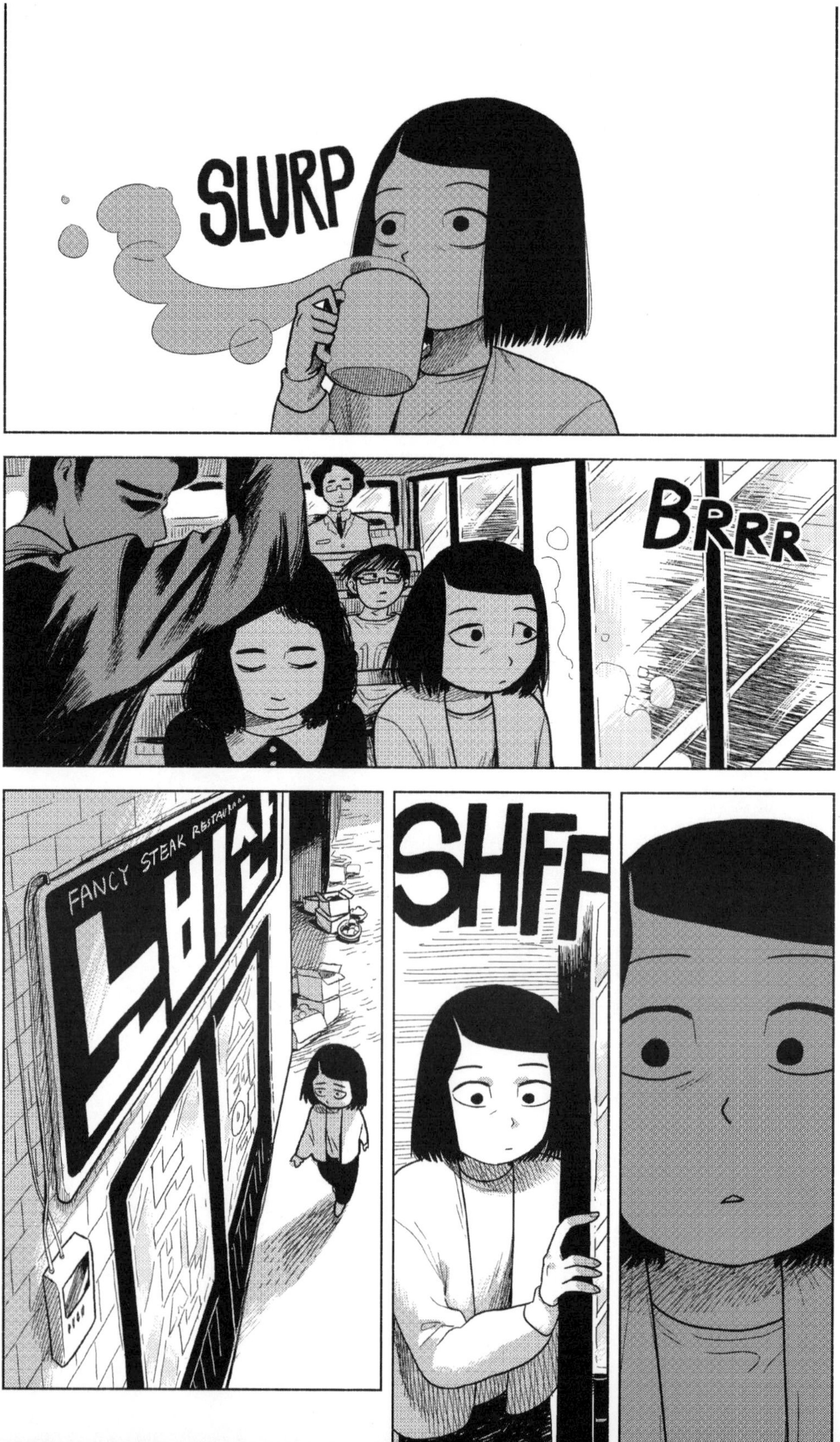
SLURP
BRRR
FANCY STEAK
SHFF

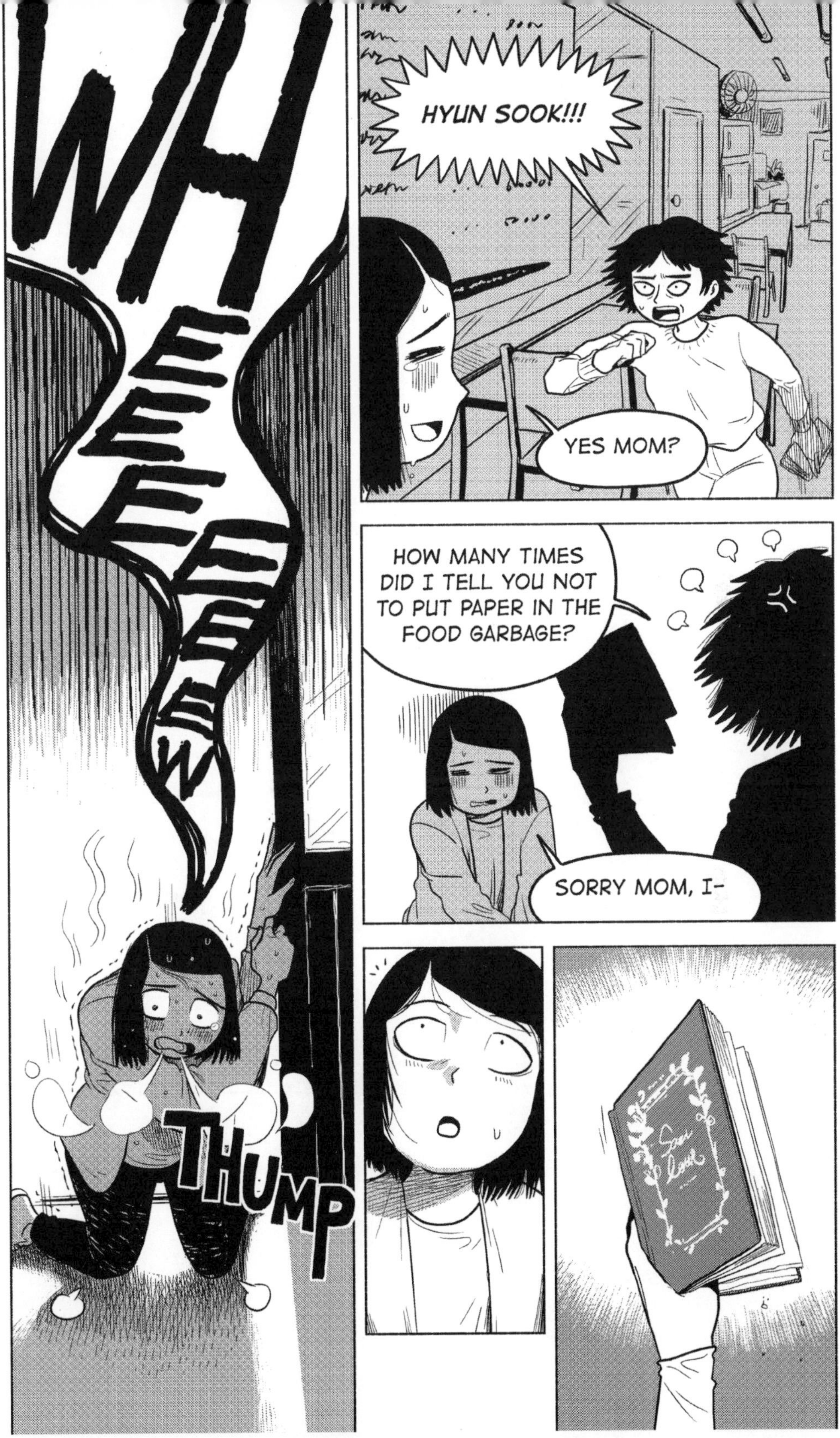
WHEEEEEEEW
HYUN SOOK!!!
YES MOM?
HOW MANY TIMES DID I TELL YOU NOT TO PUT PAPER IN THE FOOD GARBAGE?
SORRY MOM, I-
THUMP

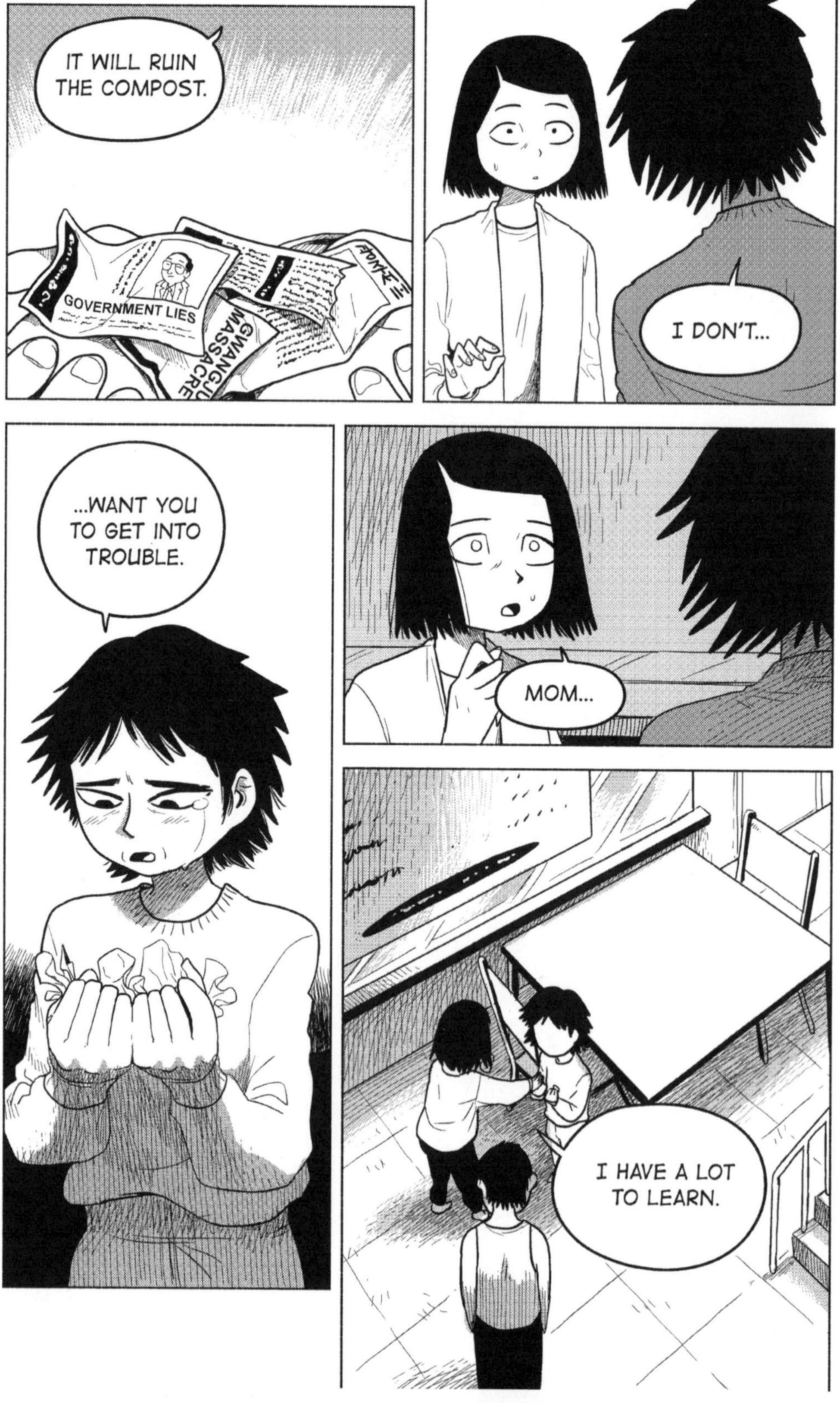
IT WILL RUIN THE COMPOST.
GOVERNMENT LIES
GWANGJU MASSACRE
I DON'T...
...WANT YOU TO GET INTO TROUBLE.
MOM...
I HAVE A LOT TO LEARN.

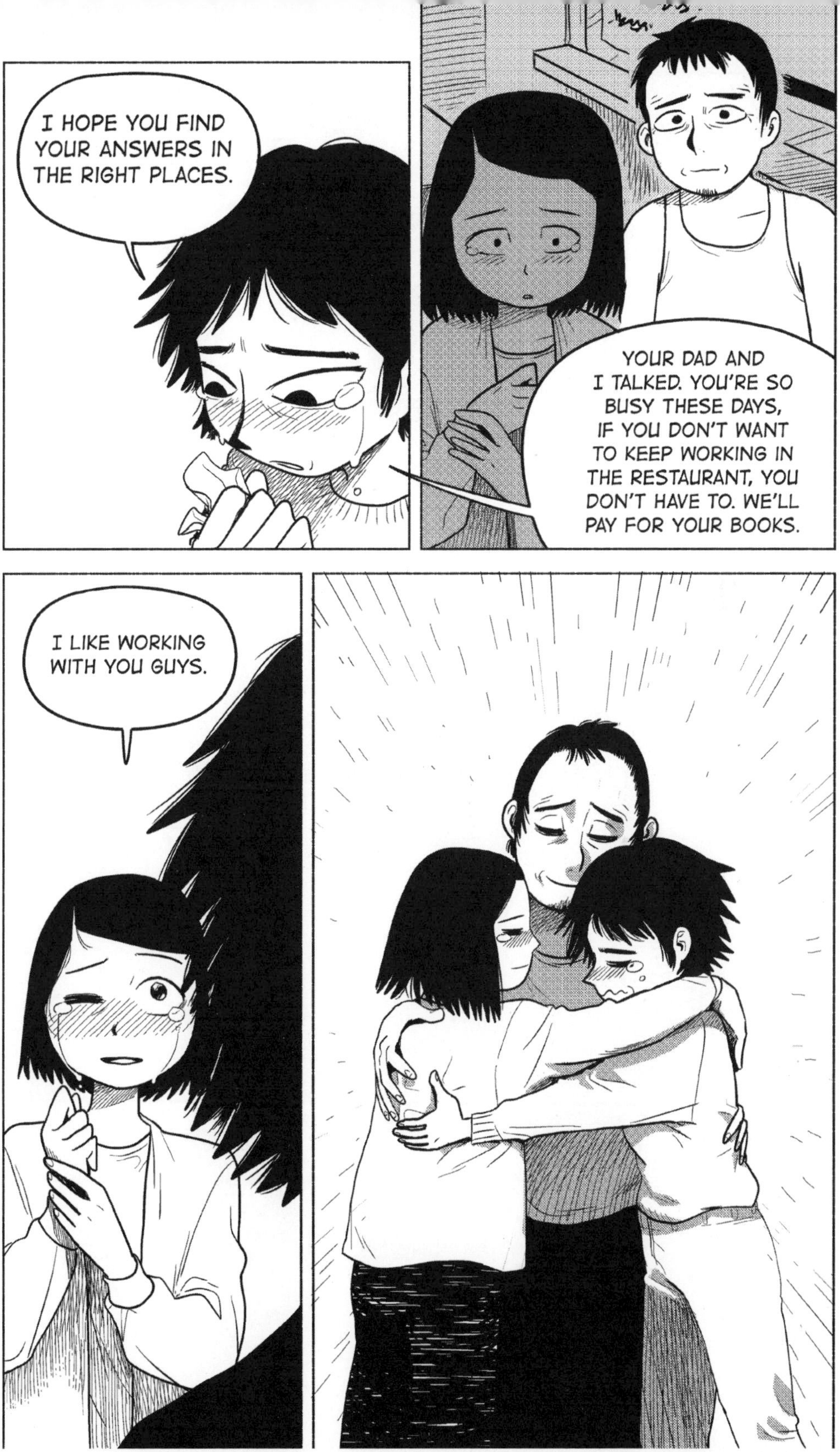
I HOPE YOU FIND YOUR ANSWERS IN THE RIGHT PLACES.
YOUR DAD AND I TALKED. YOU'RE SO BUSY THESE DAYS, IF YOU DON'T WANT TO KEEP WORKING IN THE RESTAURANT, YOU DON'T HAVE TO. WE'LL PAY FOR YOUR BOOKS.
I LIKE WORKING WITH YOU GUYS.

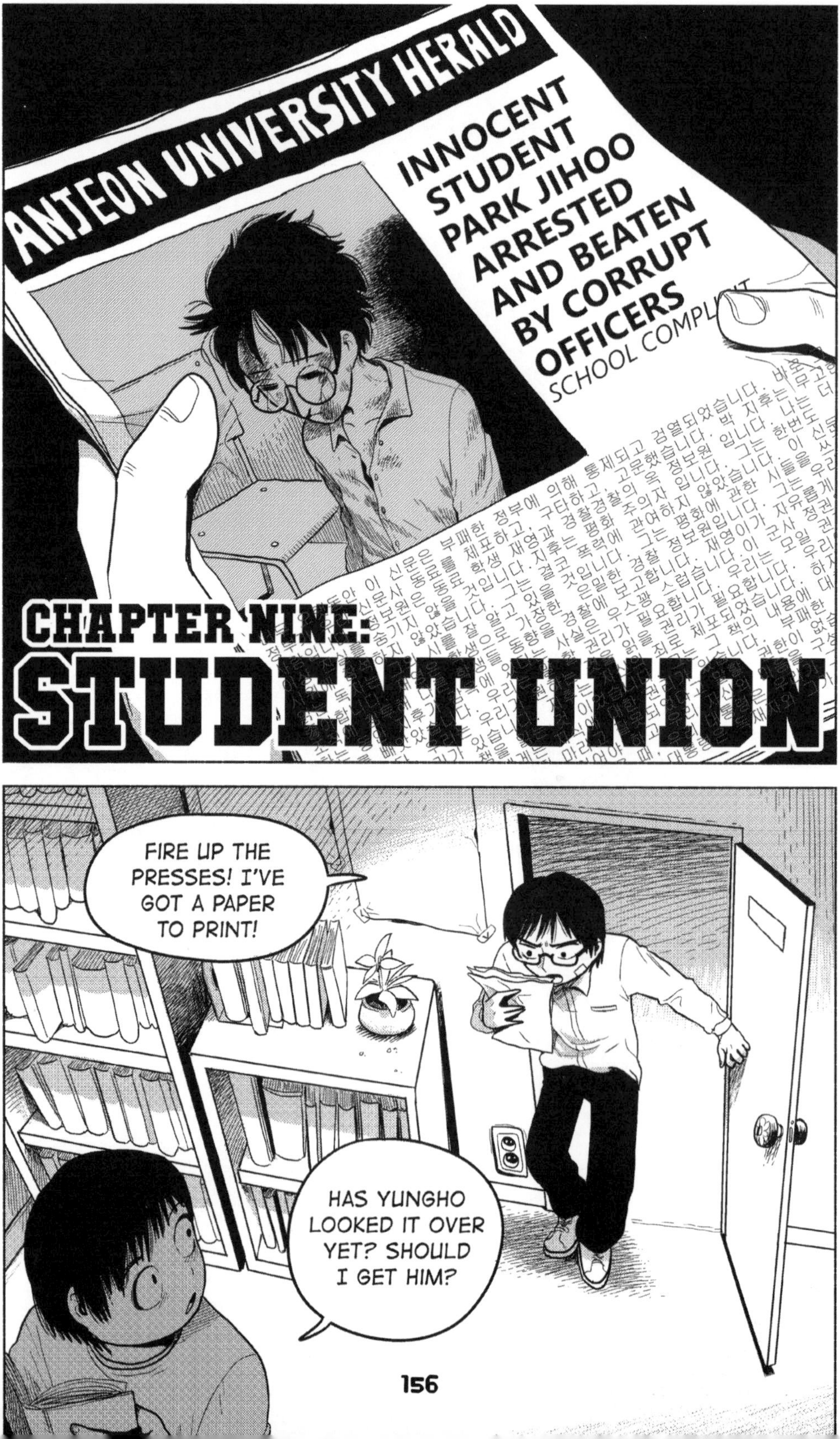
ANJEON UNIVERSITY HERALD
INNOCENT STUDENT PARK JIHOO ARRESTED AND BEATEN BY CORRUPT OFFICERS
CHAPTER NINE:
STUDENT UNION
FIRE UP THE PRESSES! I'VE GOT A PAPER TO PRINT!
HAS YUNGHO LOOKED IT OVER YET? SHOULD I GET HIM?

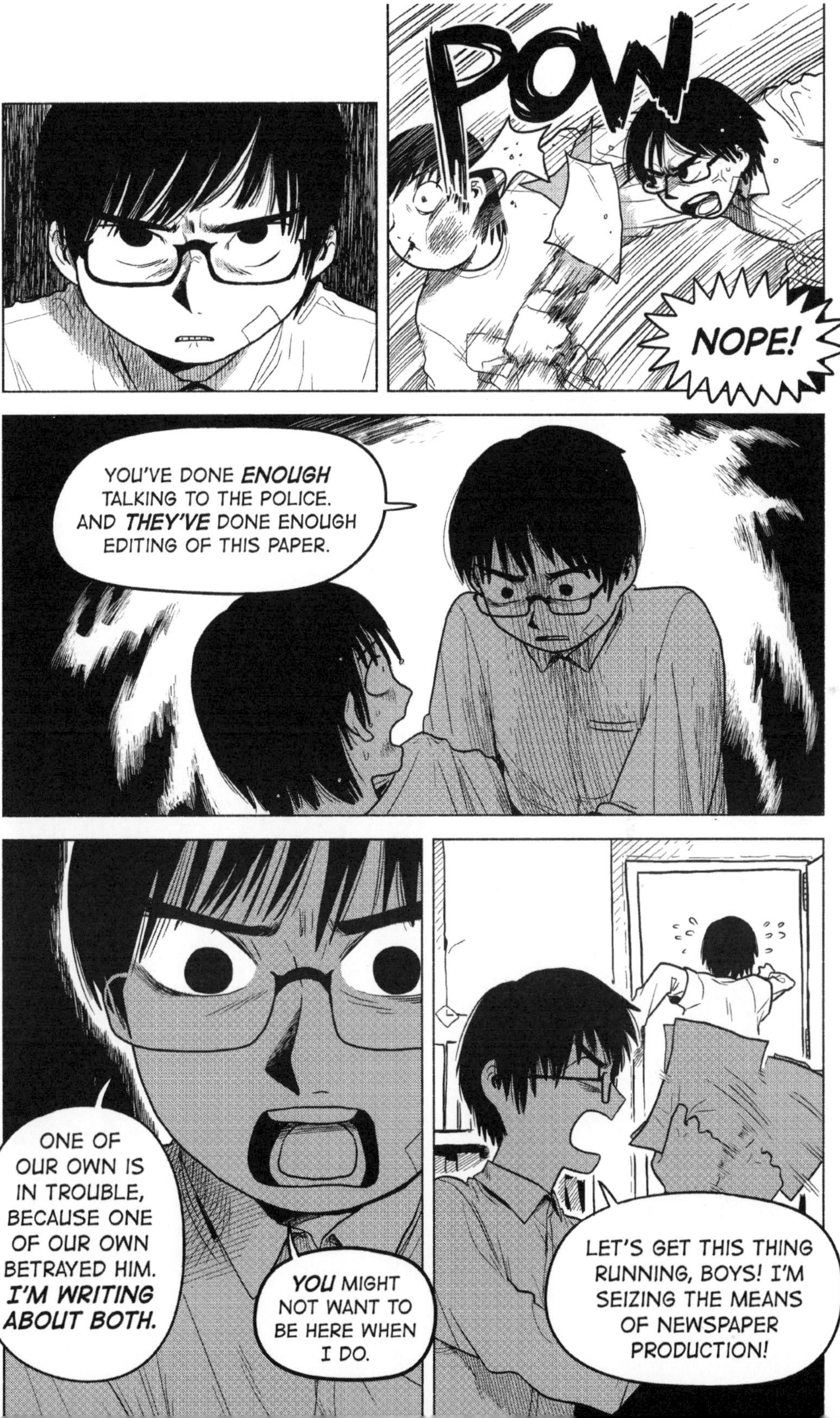
POW
NOPE!
YOU'VE DONE ENOUGH TALKING TO THE POLICE. AND THEY'VE DONE ENOUGH EDITING OF THIS PAPER.
ONE OF OUR OWN IS IN TROUBLE, BECAUSE ONE OF OUR OWN BETRAYED HIM. I'M WRITING ABOUT BOTH.
YOU MIGHT NOT WANT TO BE HERE WHEN I DO.
LET'S GET THIS THING RUNNING, BOYS! I'M SEIZING THE MEANS OF NEWSPAPER PRODUCTION!

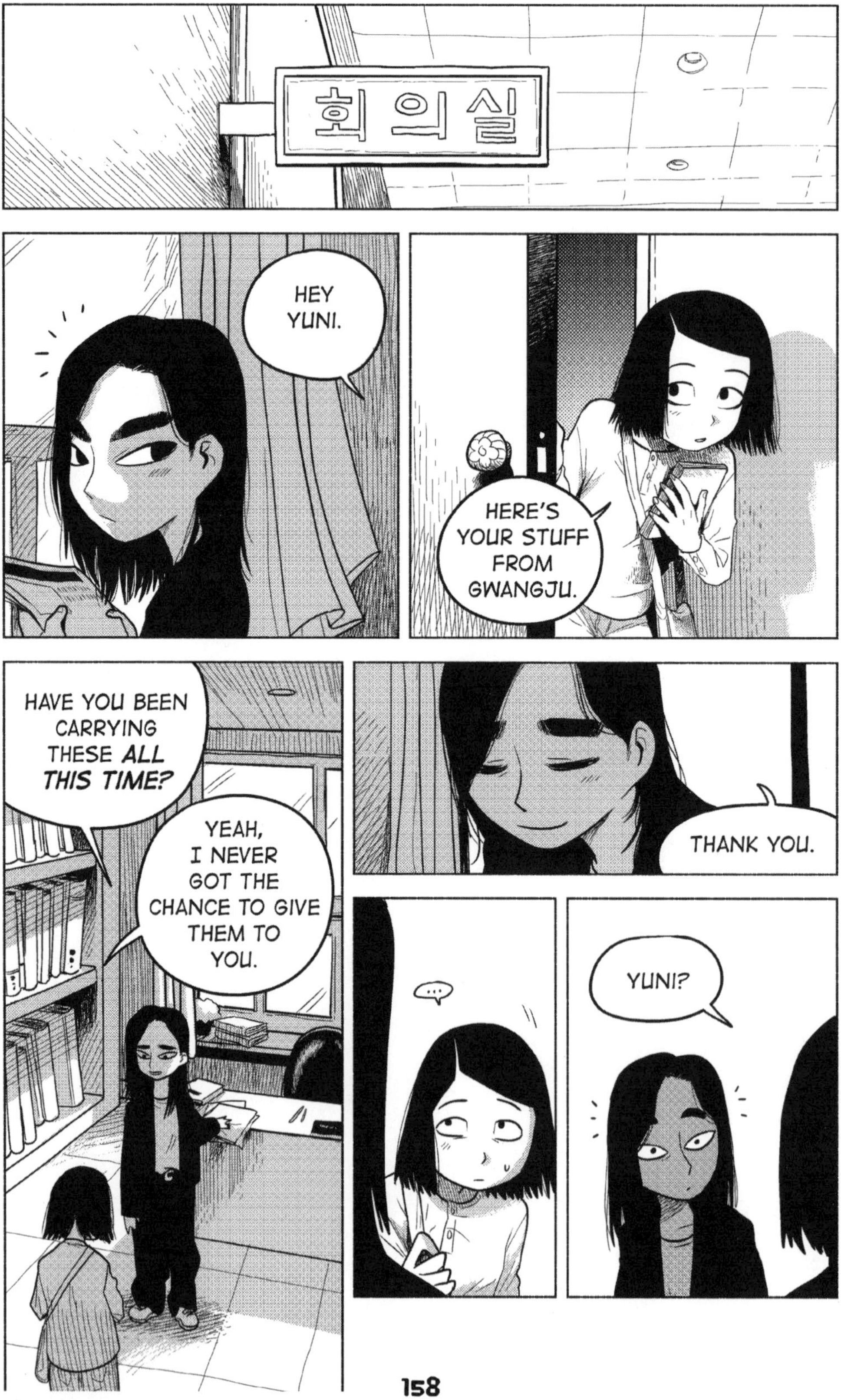
회의실
HEY YUNI.
HERE'S YOUR STUFF FROM GWANGJU.
HAVE YOU BEEN CARRYING THESE ALL THIS TIME?
YEAH, I NEVER GOT THE CHANCE TO GIVE THEM TO YOU.
THANK YOU.
...
YUNI?

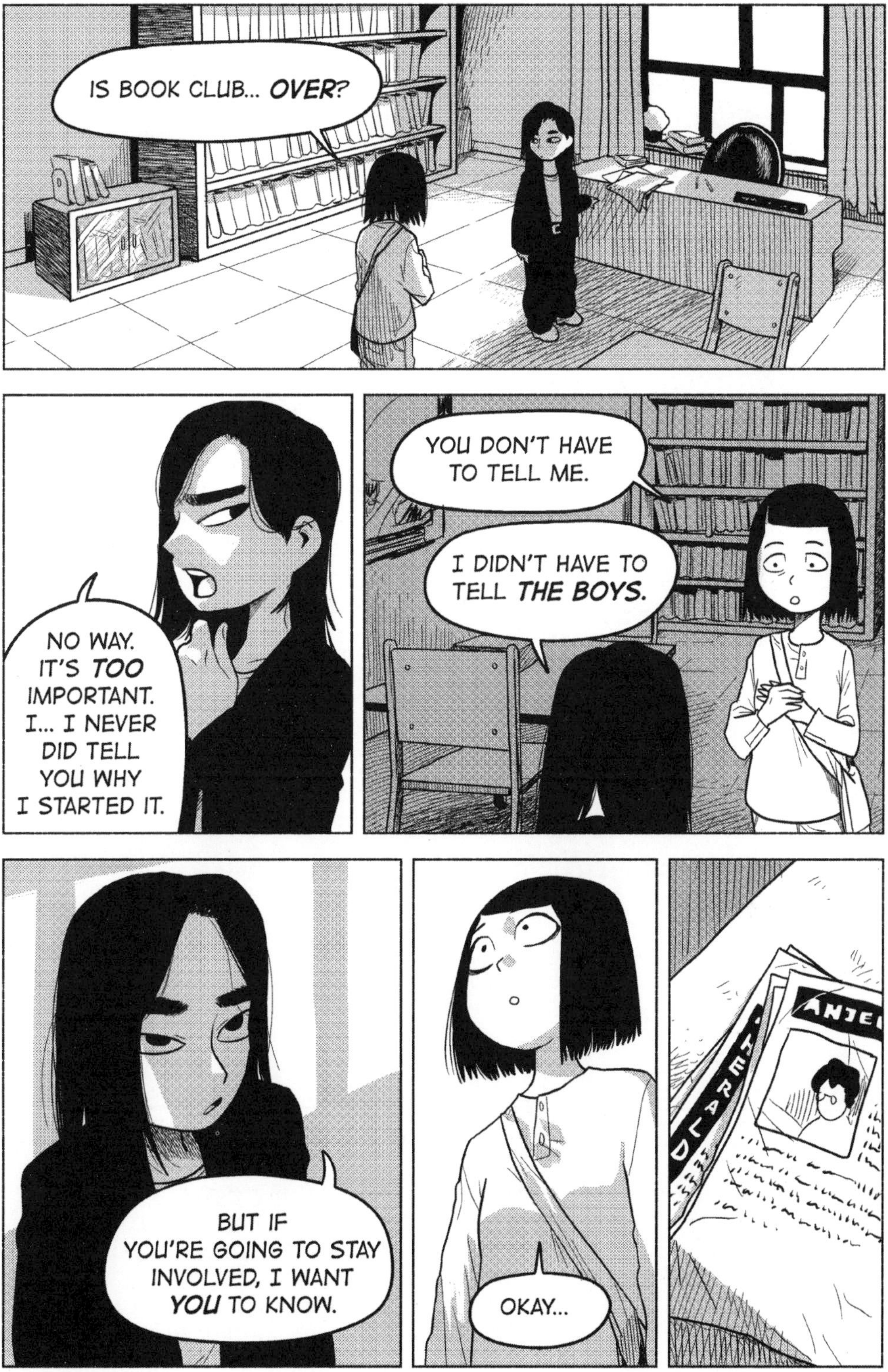
IS BOOK CLUB... OVER?
NO WAY. IT'S TOO IMPORTANT. I... I NEVER DID TELL YOU WHY I STARTED IT.
YOU DON'T HAVE TO TELL ME.
I DIDN'T HAVE TO TELL THE BOYS.
BUT IF YOU'RE GOING TO STAY INVOLVED, I WANT YOU TO KNOW.
OKAY...
HERALD
ANJEL

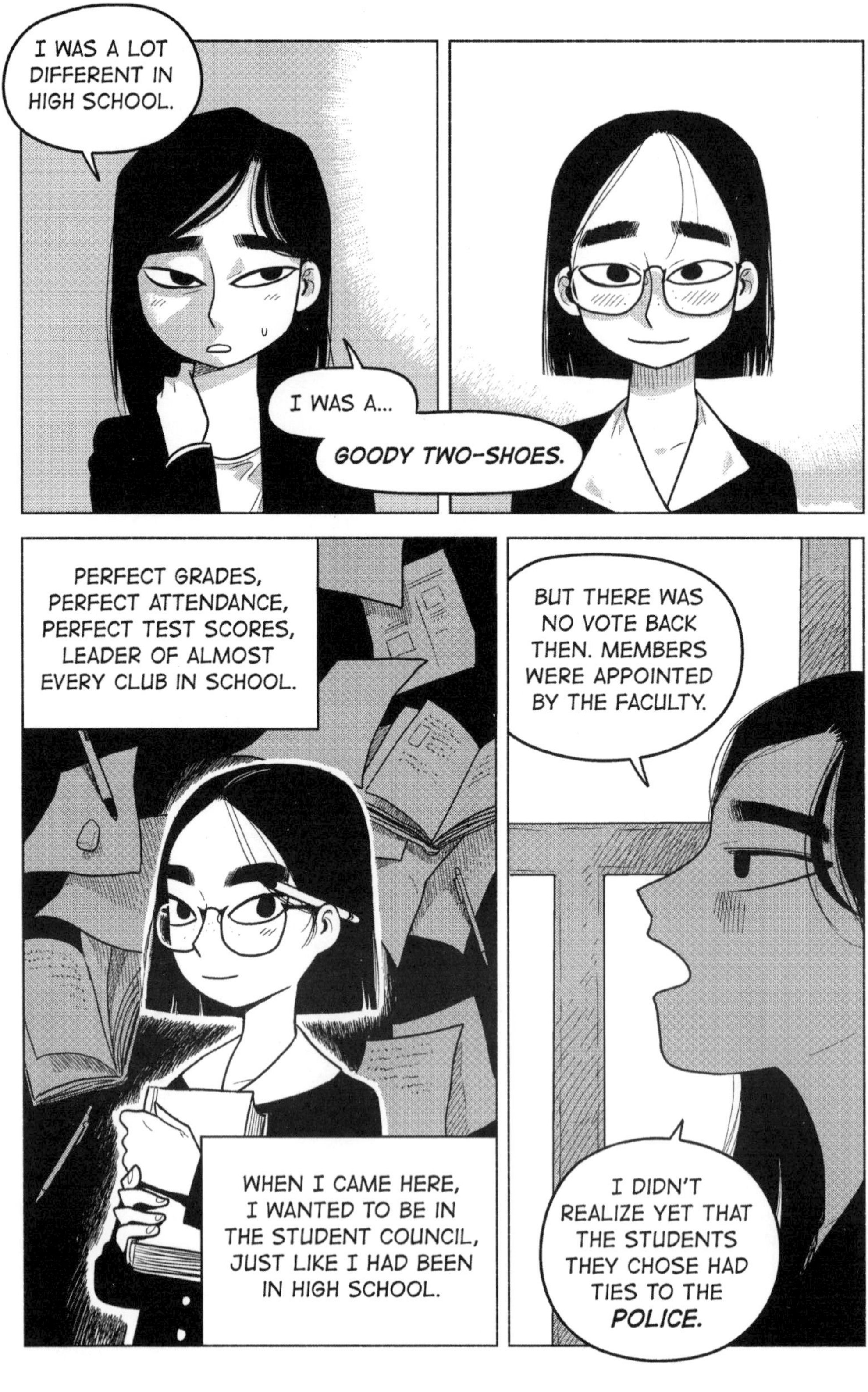
I WAS A LOT DIFFERENT IN HIGH SCHOOL.
I WAS A...
GOODY TWO-SHOES.
PERFECT GRADES, PERFECT ATTENDANCE, PERFECT TEST SCORES, LEADER OF ALMOST EVERY CLUB IN SCHOOL.
WHEN I CAME HERE, I WANTED TO BE IN THE STUDENT COUNCIL, JUST LIKE I HAD BEEN IN HIGH SCHOOL.
BUT THERE WAS NO VOTE BACK THEN. MEMBERS WERE APPOINTED BY THE FACULTY.
I DIDN'T REALIZE YET THAT THE STUDENTS THEY CHOSE HAD TIES TO THE POLICE.

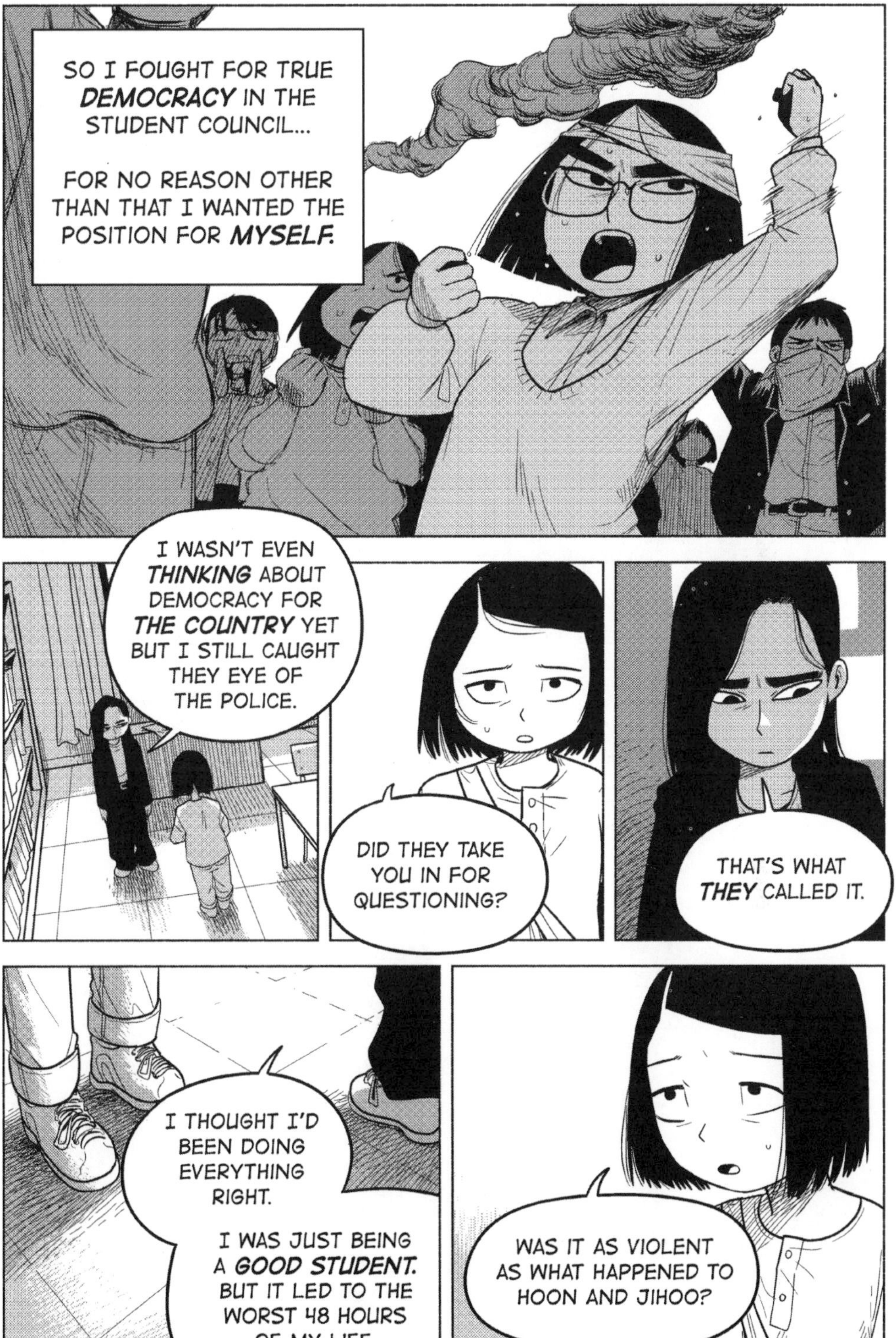
SO I FOUGHT FOR TRUE ***DEMOCRACY*** IN THE STUDENT COUNCIL...
FOR NO REASON OTHER THAN THAT I WANTED THE POSITION FOR ***MYSELF.***
I WASN'T EVEN ***THINKING*** ABOUT DEMOCRACY FOR ***THE COUNTRY*** YET BUT I STILL CAUGHT THEY EYE OF THE POLICE.
DID THEY TAKE YOU IN FOR QUESTIONING?
THAT'S WHAT ***THEY*** CALLED IT.
I THOUGHT I'D BEEN DOING EVERYTHING RIGHT.
I WAS JUST BEING A ***GOOD STUDENT.*** BUT IT LED TO THE WORST 48 HOURS OF MY LIFE.
WAS IT AS VIOLENT AS WHAT HAPPENED TO HOON AND JIHOO?

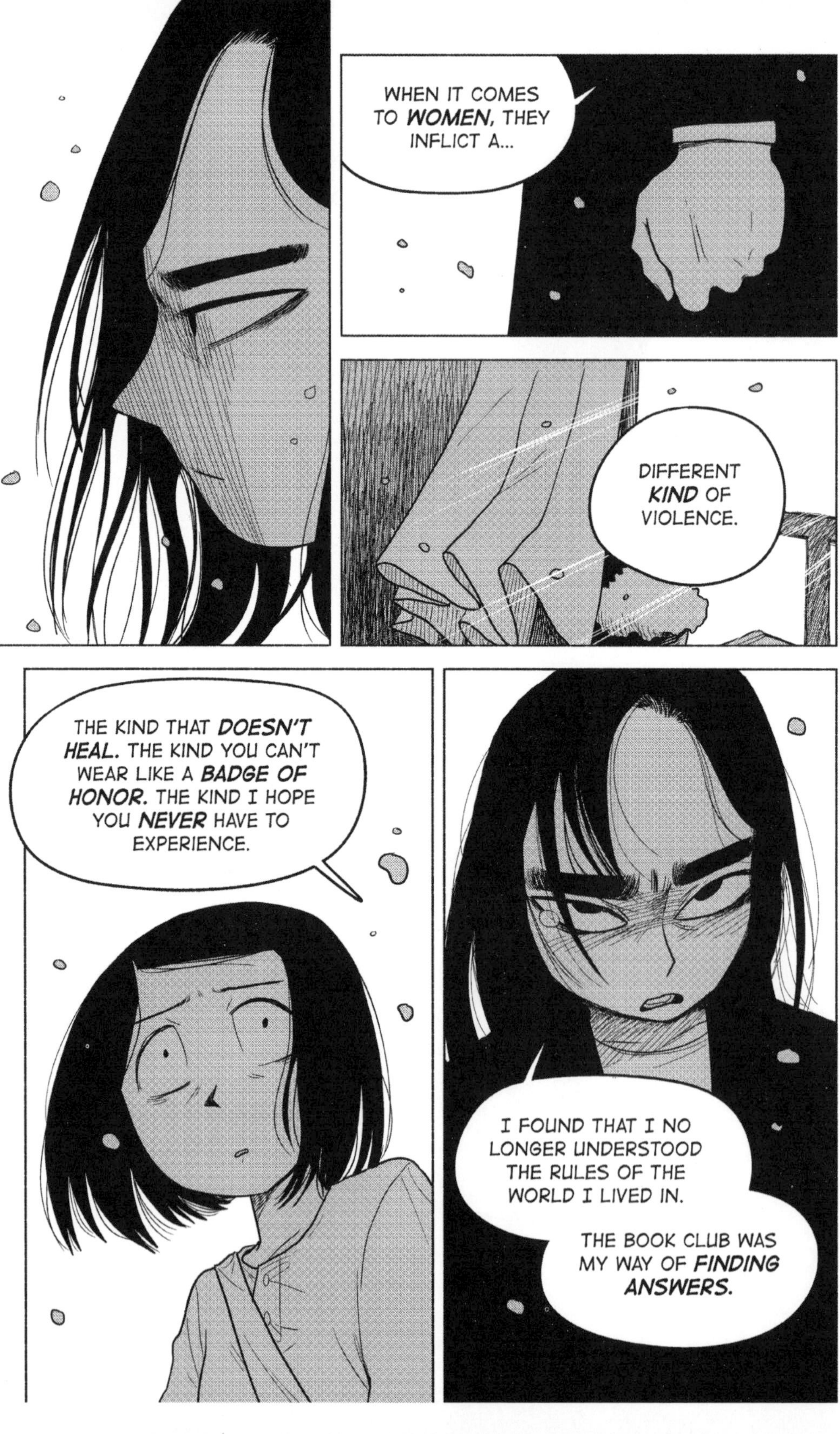
WHEN IT COMES TO ***WOMEN,*** THEY INFLICT A...
DIFFERENT ***KIND*** OF VIOLENCE.
THE KIND THAT ***DOESN'T HEAL.*** THE KIND YOU CAN'T WEAR LIKE A ***BADGE OF HONOR.*** THE KIND I HOPE YOU ***NEVER*** HAVE TO EXPERIENCE.
I FOUND THAT I NO LONGER UNDERSTOOD THE RULES OF THE WORLD I LIVED IN.
THE BOOK CLUB WAS MY WAY OF ***FINDING ANSWERS.***

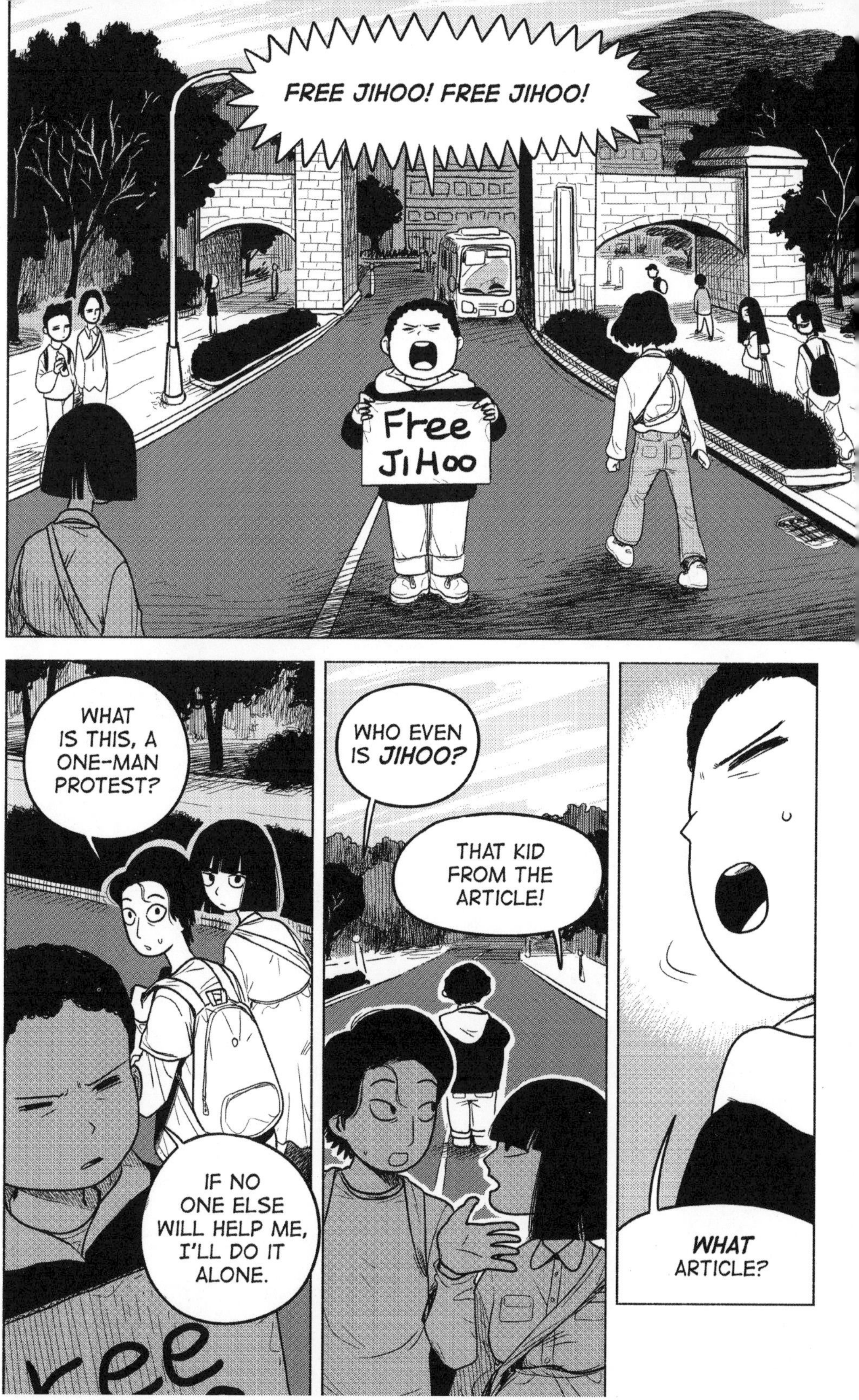
FREE JIHOO! FREE JIHOO!
Free JiHoo
WHAT IS THIS, A ONE-MAN PROTEST?
IF NO ONE ELSE WILL HELP ME, I'LL DO IT ALONE.
WHO EVEN IS *JIHOO?*
THAT KID FROM THE ARTICLE!
WHAT ARTICLE?

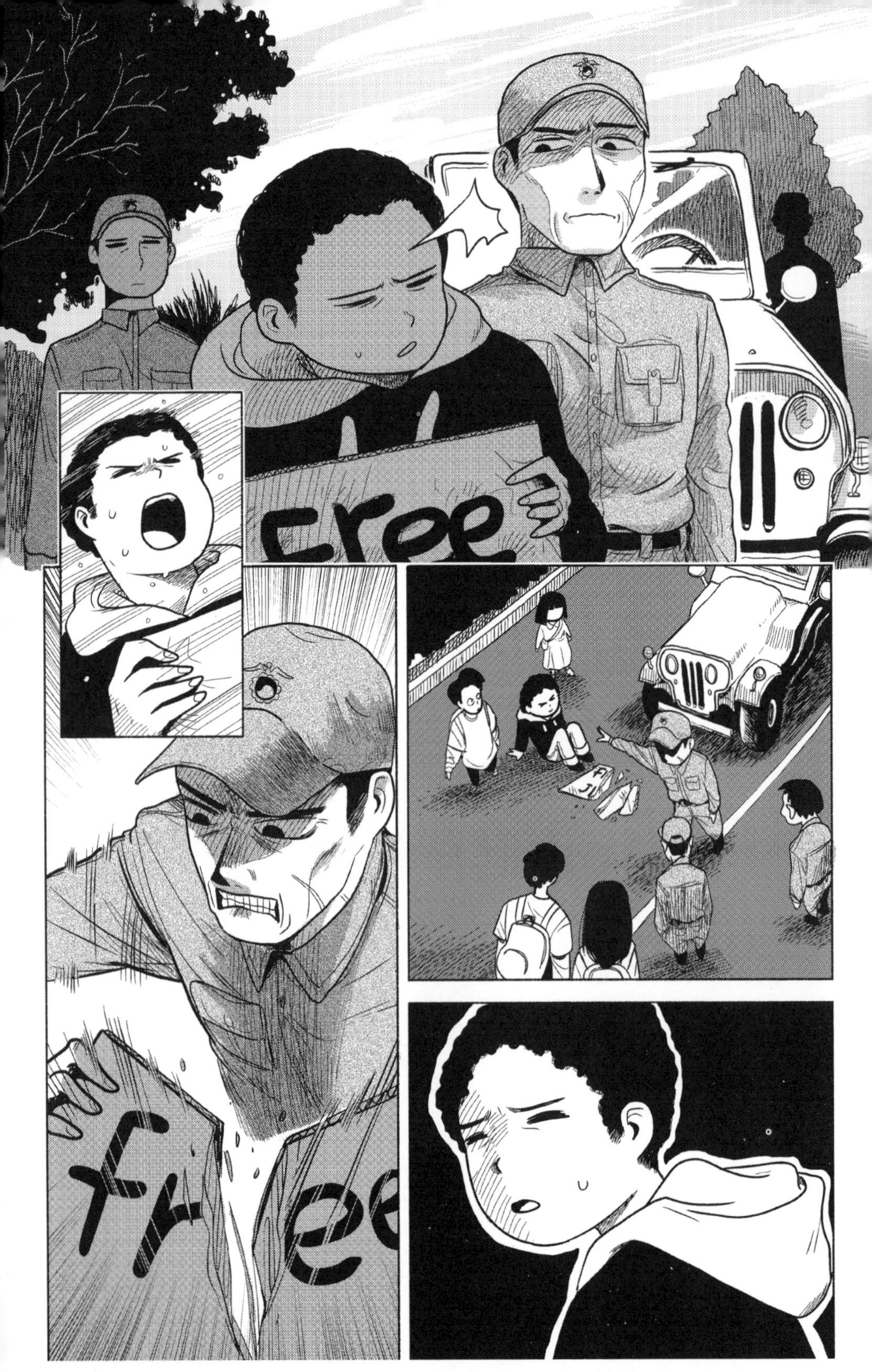
Free

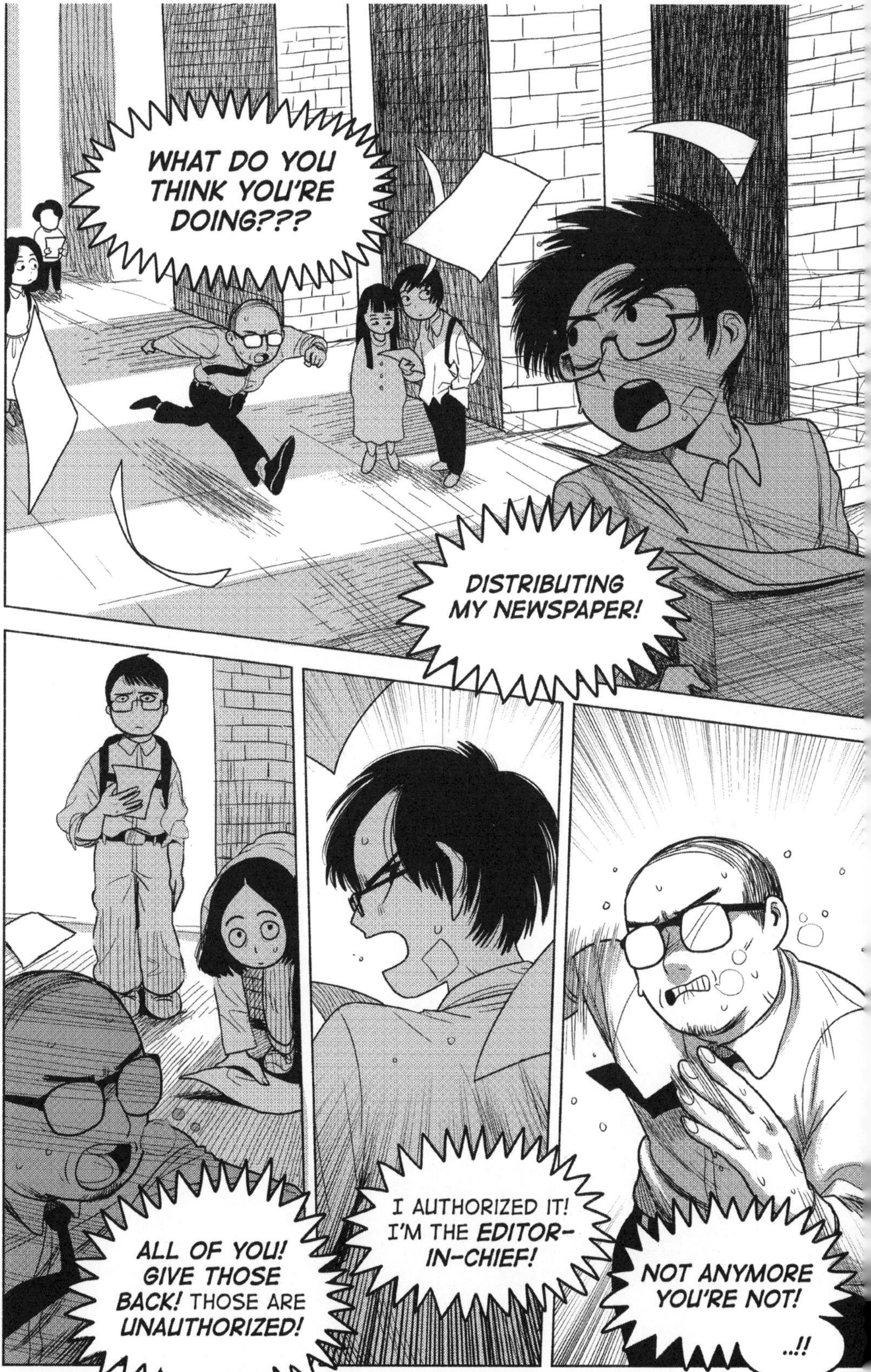
WHAT DO YOU THINK YOU'RE DOING???
DISTRIBUTING MY NEWSPAPER!
ALL OF YOU! GIVE THOSE BACK! THOSE ARE UNAUTHORIZED!
I AUTHORIZED IT! I'M THE EDITOR-IN-CHIEF!
NOT ANYMORE YOU'RE NOT!
..!!

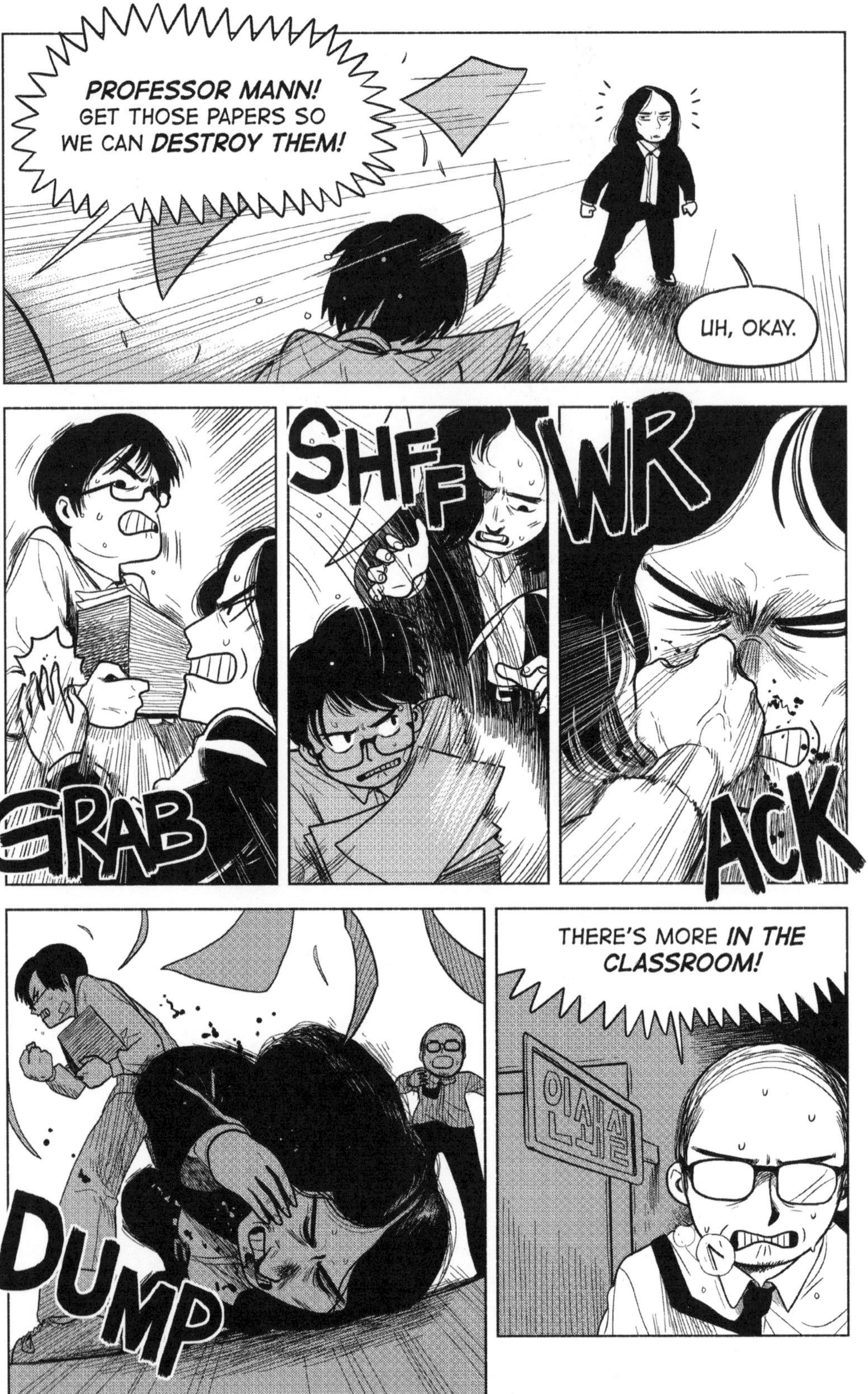
PROFESSOR MANN! GET THOSE PAPERS SO WE CAN DESTROY THEM!
UH, OKAY.
GRAB
SHFF
WR
ACK
DUMP
THERE'S MORE IN THE CLASSROOM!

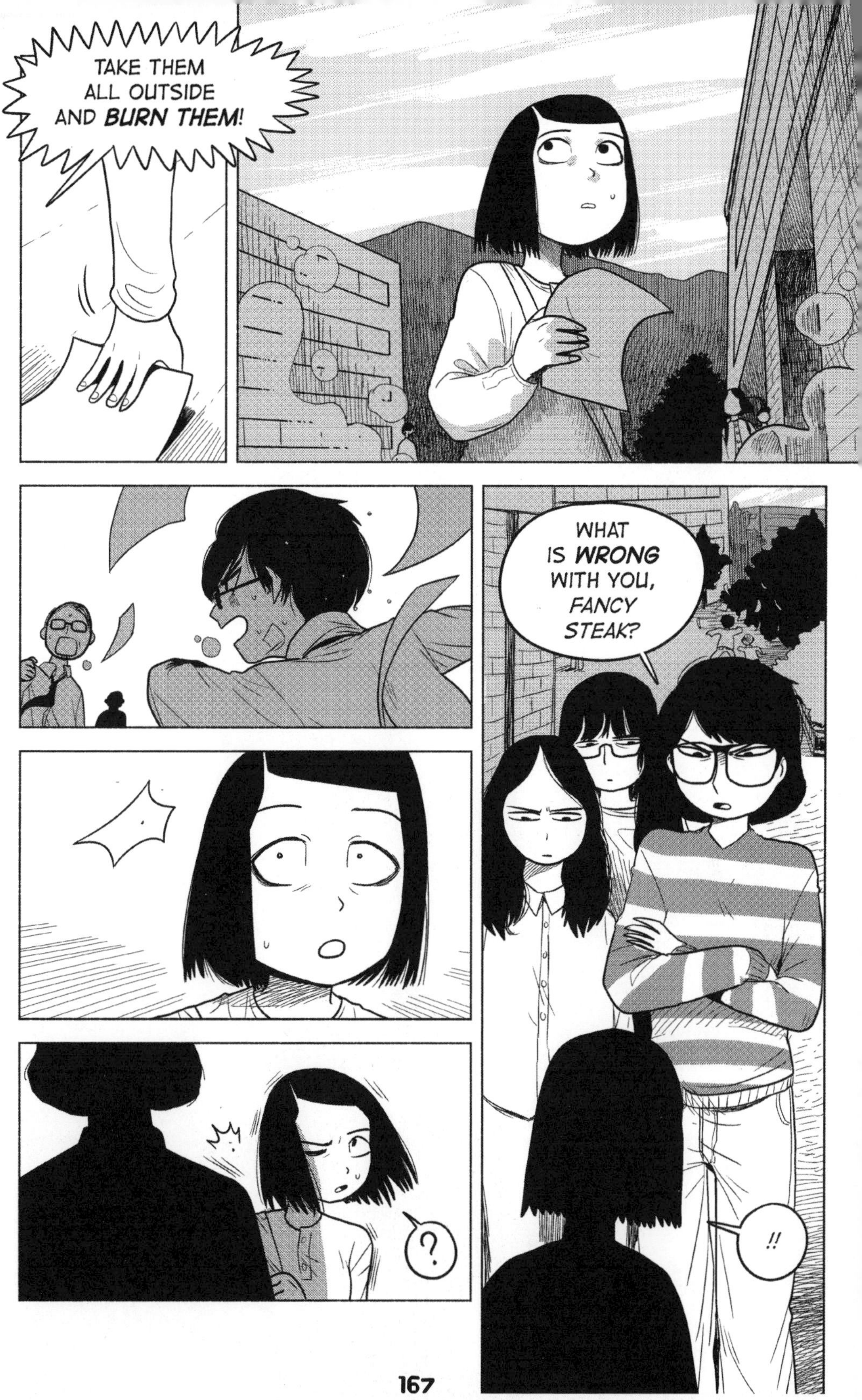

TAKE THEM ALL OUTSIDE AND **BURN THEM!**
WHAT IS **WRONG** WITH YOU, *FANCY STEAK?*
?
!!

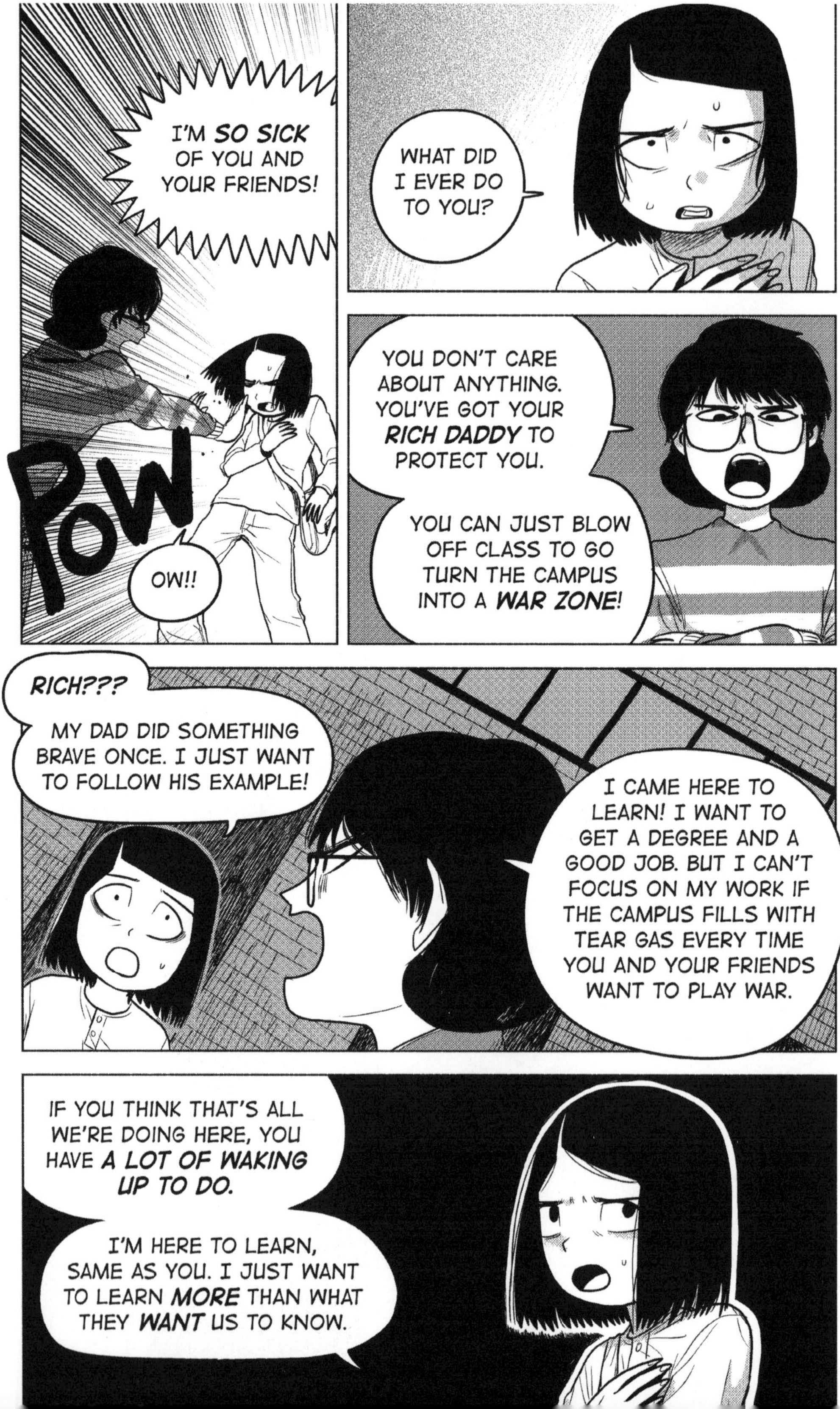
I'M SO SICK OF YOU AND YOUR FRIENDS!
POW
OW!!
WHAT DID I EVER DO TO YOU?
YOU DON'T CARE ABOUT ANYTHING. YOU'VE GOT YOUR RICH DADDY TO PROTECT YOU.
YOU CAN JUST BLOW OFF CLASS TO GO TURN THE CAMPUS INTO A WAR ZONE!
RICH???
MY DAD DID SOMETHING BRAVE ONCE. I JUST WANT TO FOLLOW HIS EXAMPLE!
I CAME HERE TO LEARN! I WANT TO GET A DEGREE AND A GOOD JOB. BUT I CAN'T FOCUS ON MY WORK IF THE CAMPUS FILLS WITH TEAR GAS EVERY TIME YOU AND YOUR FRIENDS WANT TO PLAY WAR.
IF YOU THINK THAT'S ALL WE'RE DOING HERE, YOU HAVE A LOT OF WAKING UP TO DO.
I'M HERE TO LEARN, SAME AS YOU. I JUST WANT TO LEARN MORE THAN WHAT THEY WANT US TO KNOW.

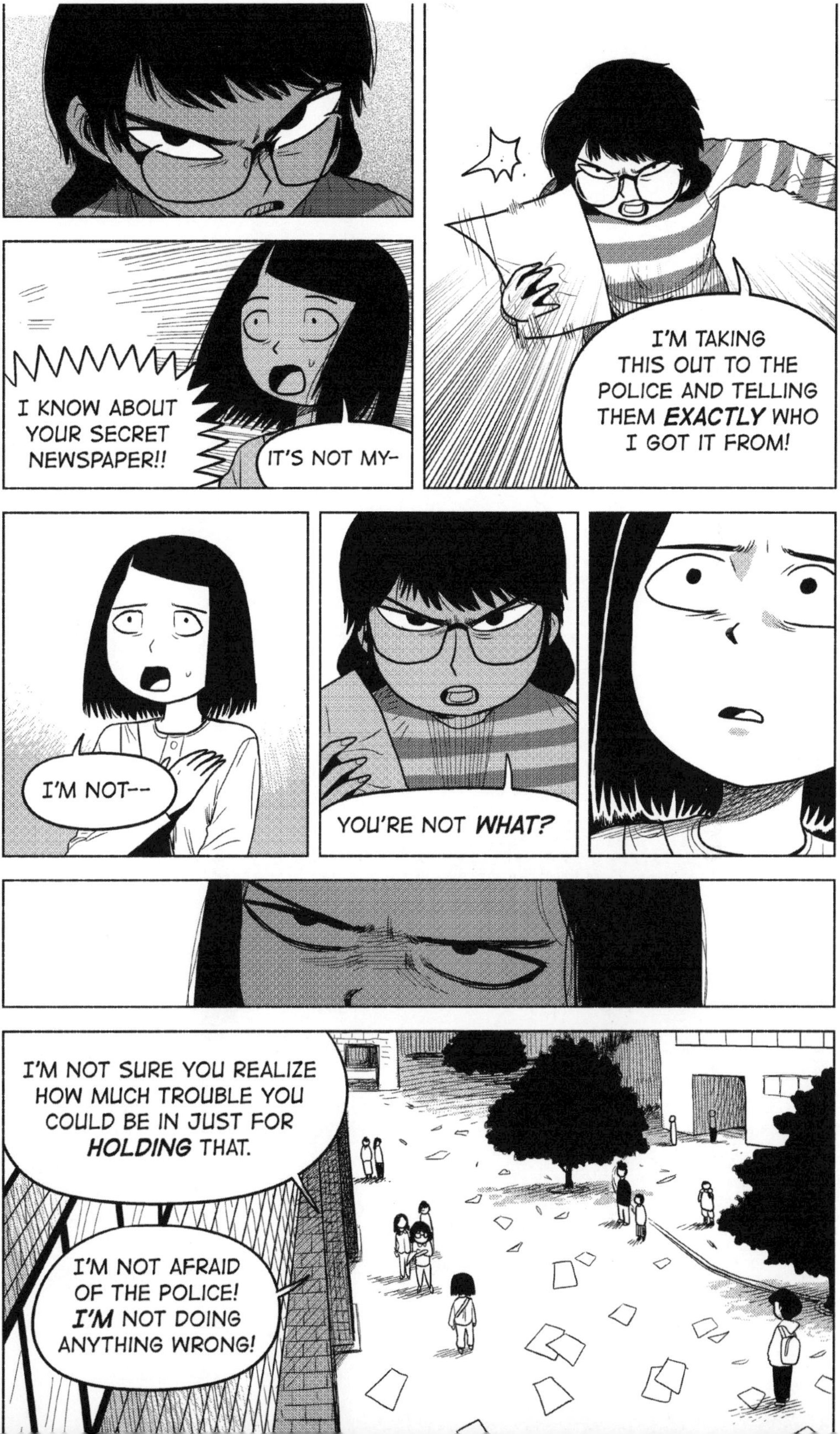
I KNOW ABOUT YOUR SECRET NEWSPAPER!!
IT'S NOT MY-
I'M TAKING THIS OUT TO THE POLICE AND TELLING THEM *EXACTLY* WHO I GOT IT FROM!
I'M NOT--
YOU'RE NOT *WHAT?*
I'M NOT SURE YOU REALIZE HOW MUCH TROUBLE YOU COULD BE IN JUST FOR *HOLDING* THAT.
I'M NOT AFRAID OF THE POLICE! *I'M* NOT DOING ANYTHING WRONG!

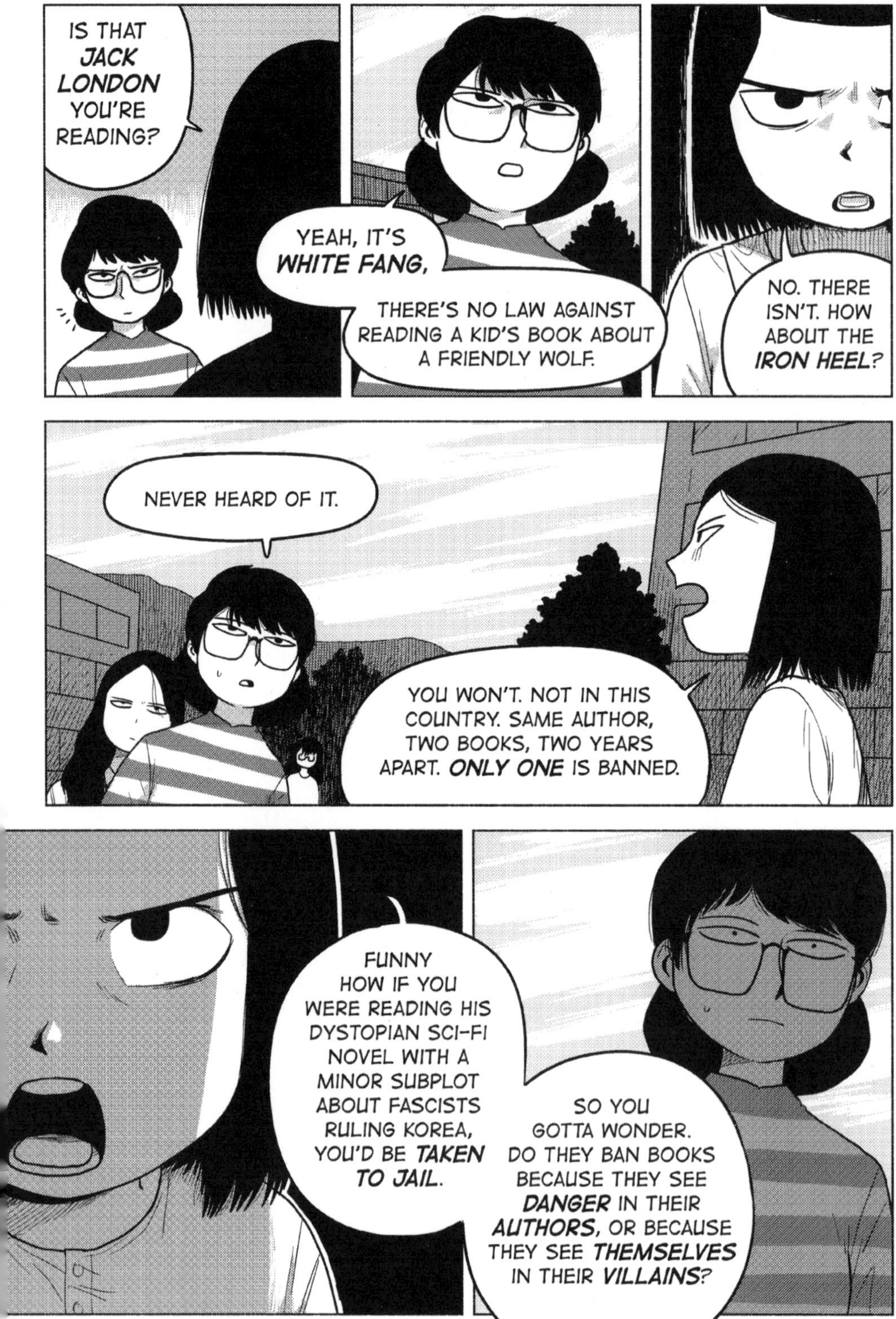
IS THAT *JACK LONDON* YOU'RE READING?
YEAH, IT'S *WHITE FANG*.
THERE'S NO LAW AGAINST READING A KID'S BOOK ABOUT A FRIENDLY WOLF.
NO. THERE ISN'T. HOW ABOUT THE *IRON HEEL*?
NEVER HEARD OF IT.
YOU WON'T. NOT IN THIS COUNTRY. SAME AUTHOR, TWO BOOKS, TWO YEARS APART. *ONLY ONE* IS BANNED.
FUNNY HOW IF YOU WERE READING HIS DYSTOPIAN SCI-FI NOVEL WITH A MINOR SUBPLOT ABOUT FASCISTS RULING KOREA, YOU'D BE *TAKEN TO JAIL*.
SO YOU GOTTA WONDER. DO THEY BAN BOOKS BECAUSE THEY SEE *DANGER* IN THEIR *AUTHORS*, OR BECAUSE THEY SEE *THEMSELVES* IN THEIR *VILLAINS*?

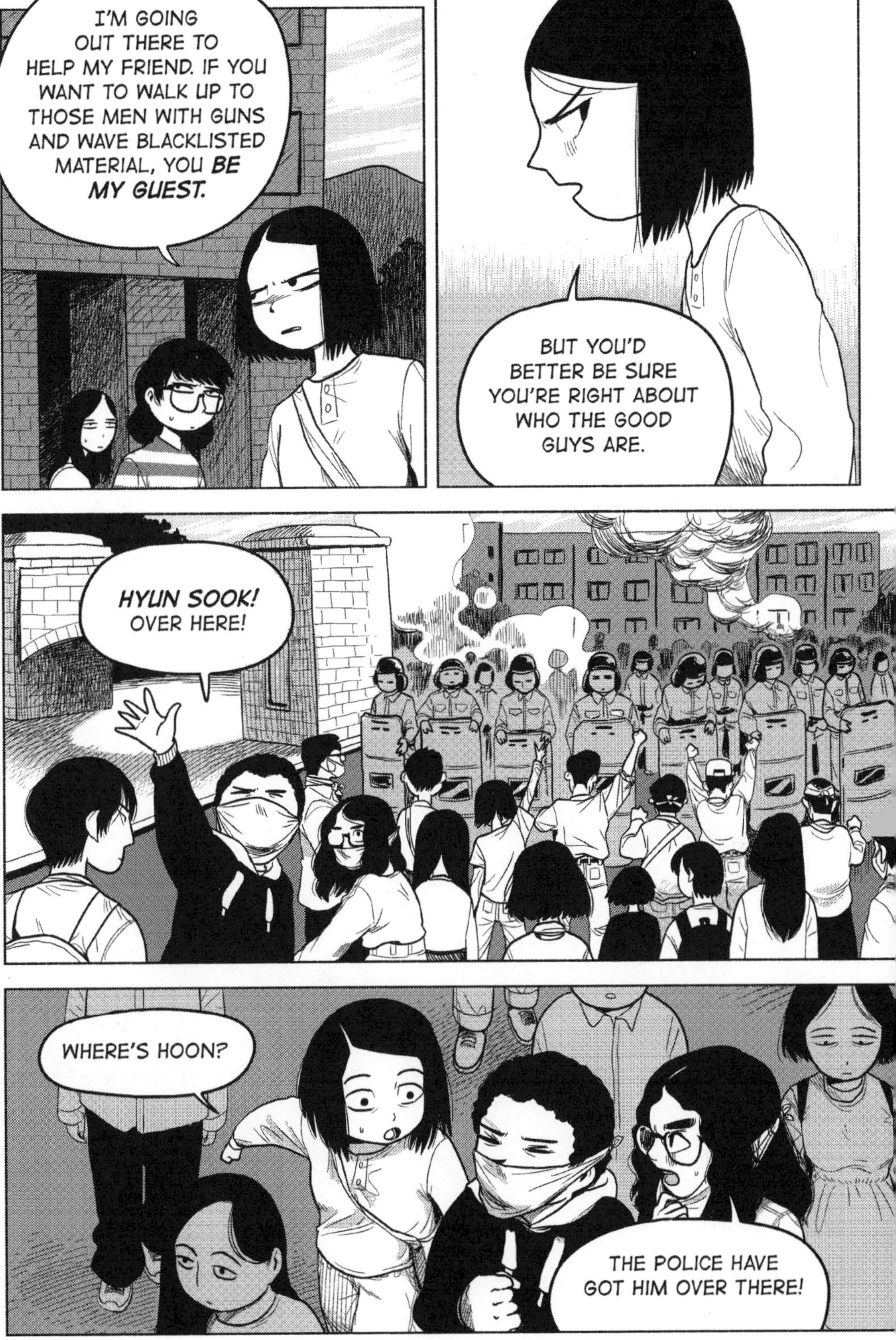
I'M GOING OUT THERE TO HELP MY FRIEND. IF YOU WANT TO WALK UP TO THOSE MEN WITH GUNS AND WAVE BLACKLISTED MATERIAL, YOU ***BE MY GUEST.***
BUT YOU'D BETTER BE SURE YOU'RE RIGHT ABOUT WHO THE GOOD GUYS ARE.
HYUN SOOK! OVER HERE!
WHERE'S HOON?
THE POLICE HAVE GOT HIM OVER THERE!

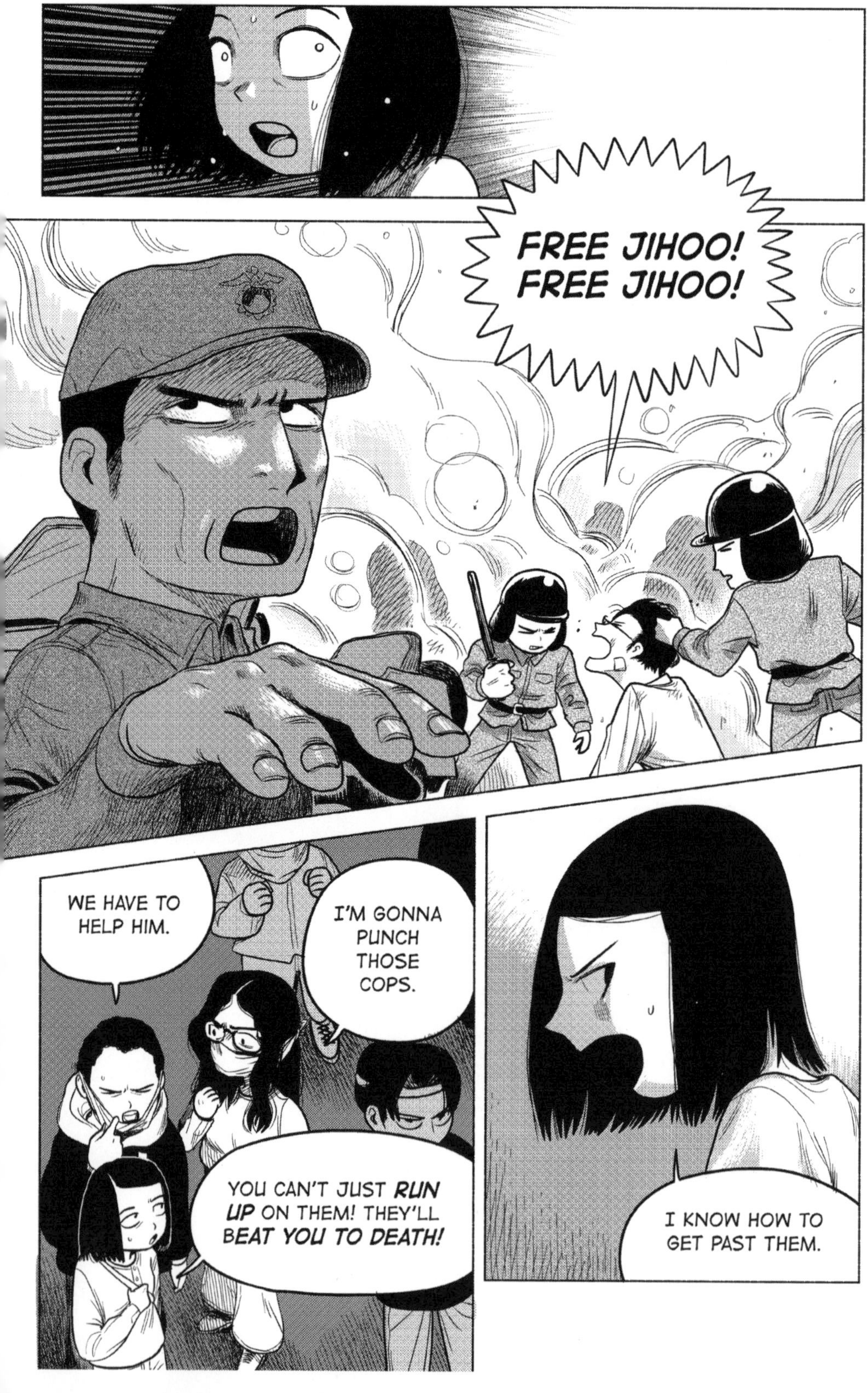
FREE JIHOO!
FREE JIHOO!
WE HAVE TO HELP HIM.
I'M GONNA PUNCH THOSE COPS.
YOU CAN'T JUST **RUN UP** ON THEM! THEY'LL **BEAT YOU TO DEATH!**
I KNOW HOW TO GET PAST THEM.

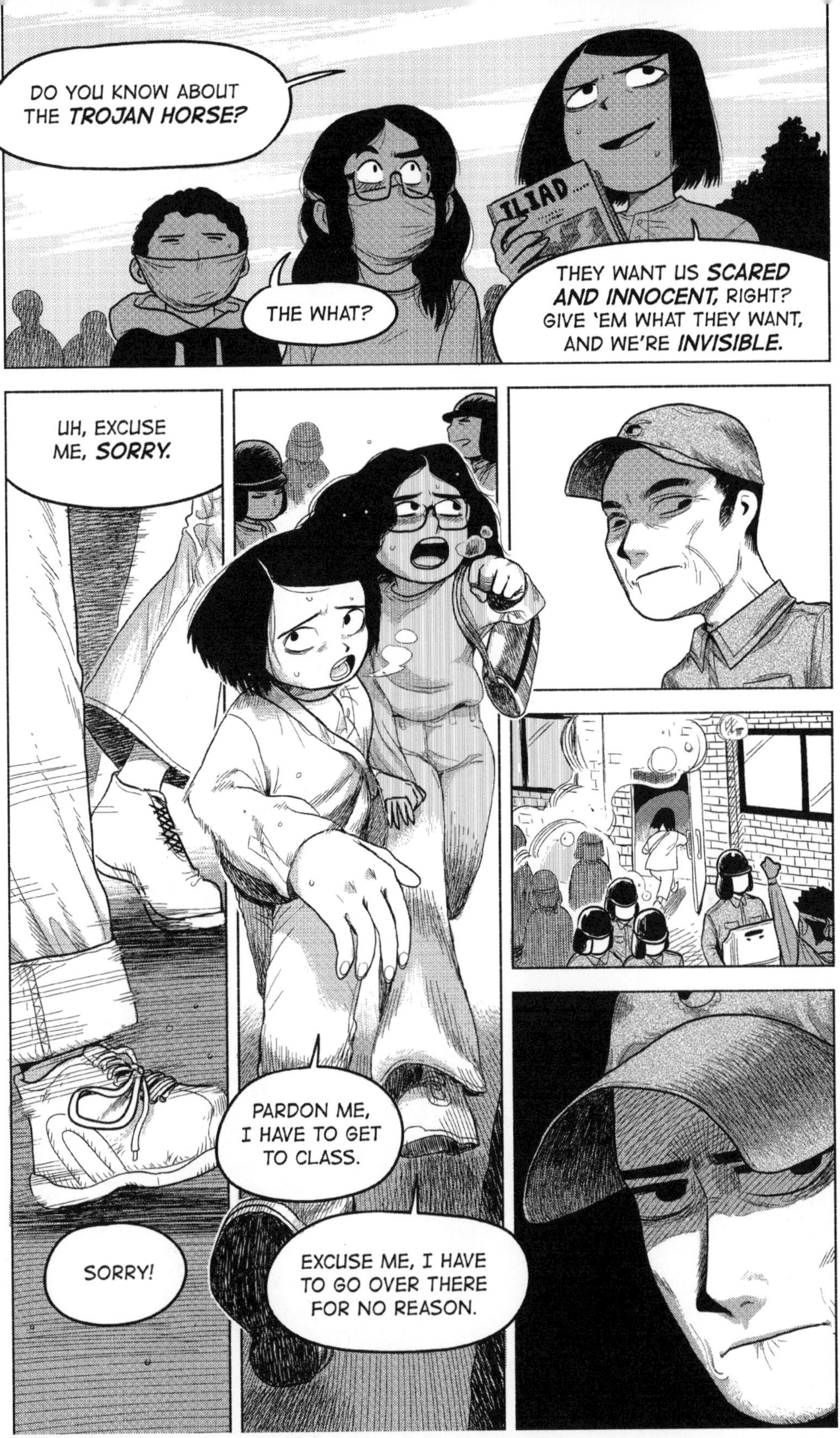
DO YOU KNOW ABOUT THE ***TROJAN HORSE?***
THE WHAT?
ILIAD
THEY WANT US ***SCARED AND INNOCENT,*** RIGHT? GIVE 'EM WHAT THEY WANT, AND WE'RE ***INVISIBLE.***
UH, EXCUSE ME, ***SORRY.***
PARDON ME, I HAVE TO GET TO CLASS.
SORRY!
EXCUSE ME, I HAVE TO GO OVER THERE FOR NO REASON.

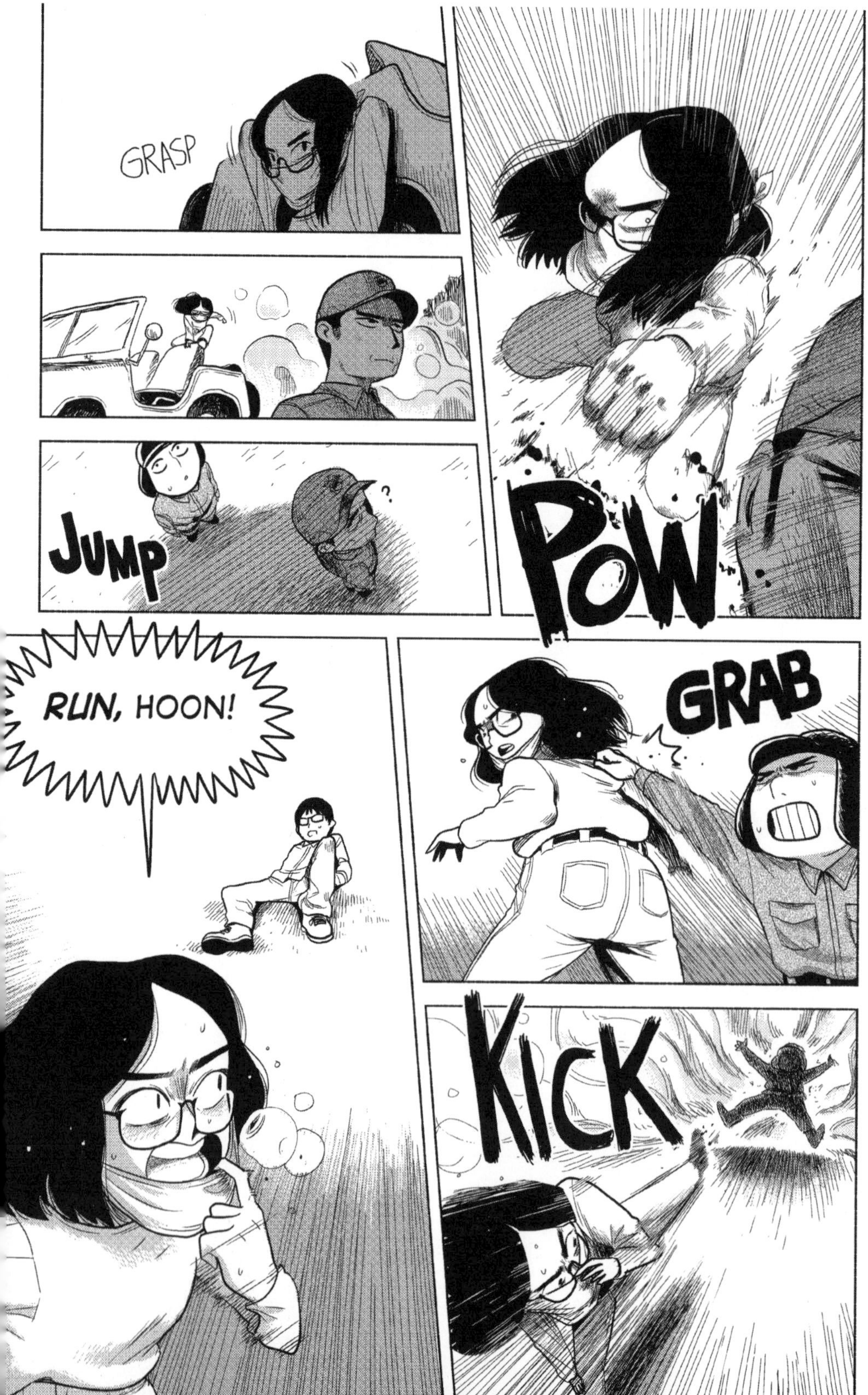
GRASP
JUMP
?
POW
RUN, HOON!
GRAB
KICK

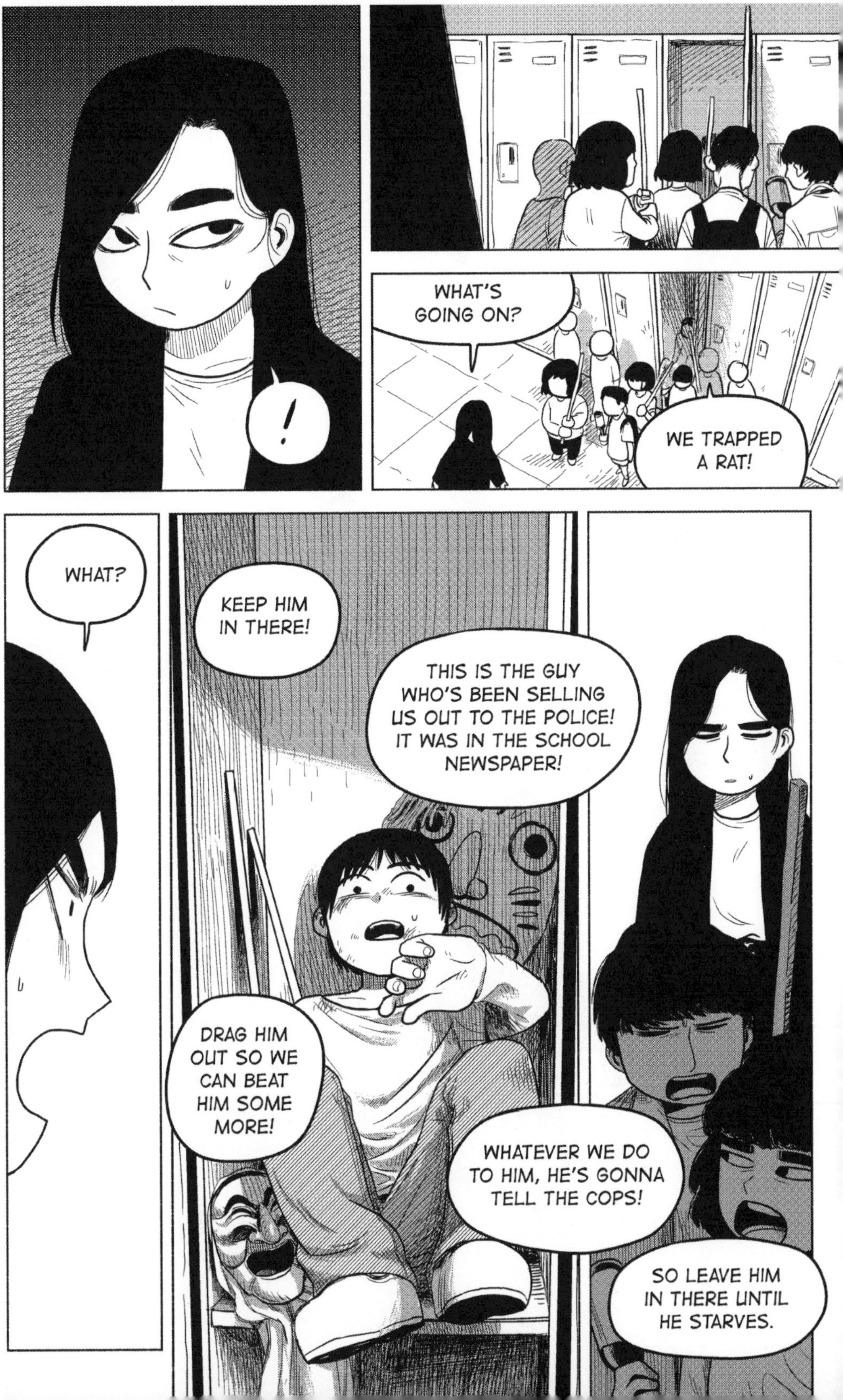
!
WHAT'S GOING ON?
WE TRAPPED A RAT!
WHAT?
KEEP HIM IN THERE!
THIS IS THE GUY WHO'S BEEN SELLING US OUT TO THE POLICE! IT WAS IN THE SCHOOL NEWSPAPER!
DRAG HIM OUT SO WE CAN BEAT HIM SOME MORE!
WHATEVER WE DO TO HIM, HE'S GONNA TELL THE COPS!
SO LEAVE HIM IN THERE UNTIL HE STARVES.

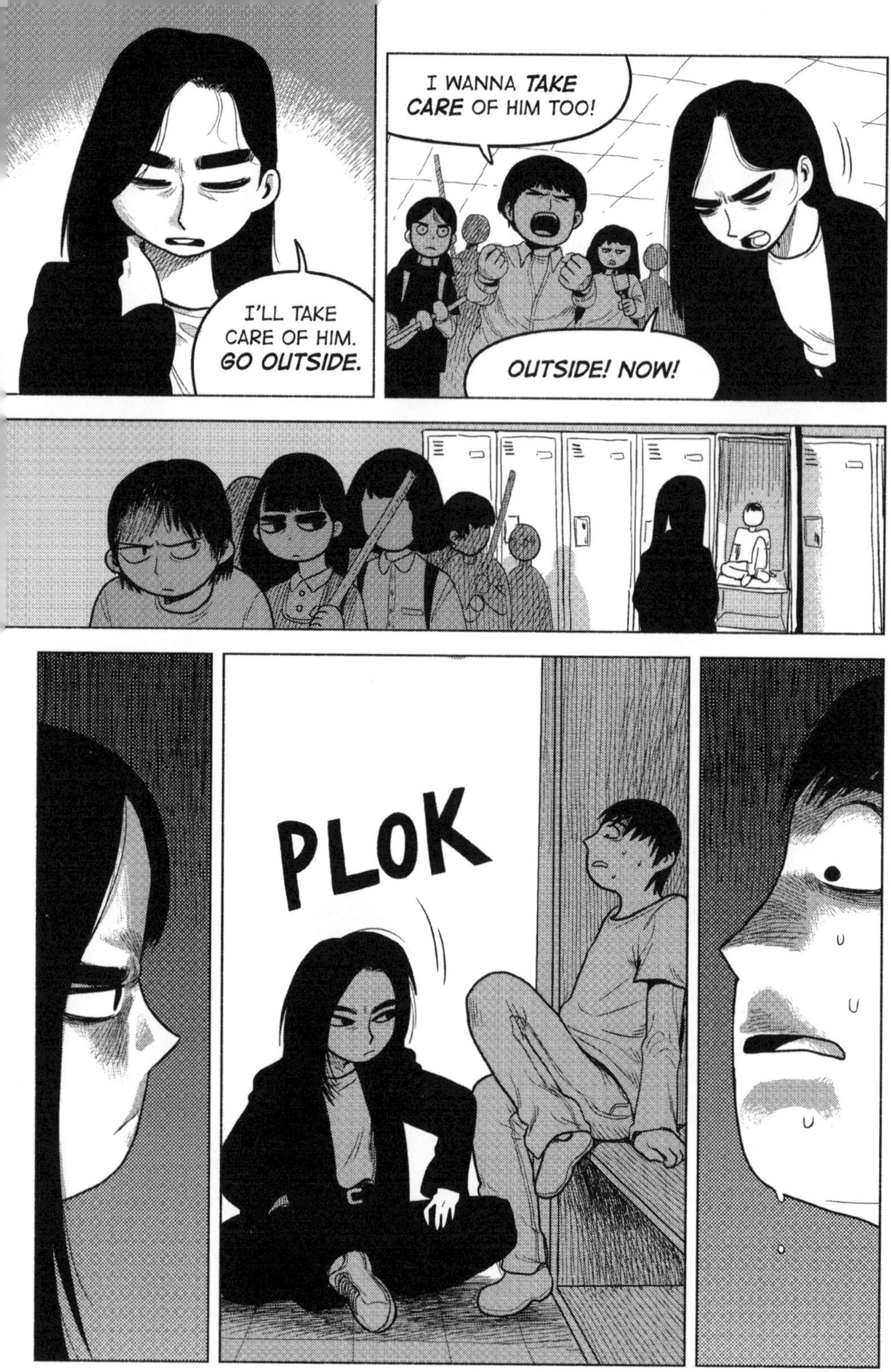
I'LL TAKE CARE OF HIM. GO OUTSIDE.
I WANNA TAKE CARE OF HIM TOO!
OUTSIDE! NOW!
PLOK

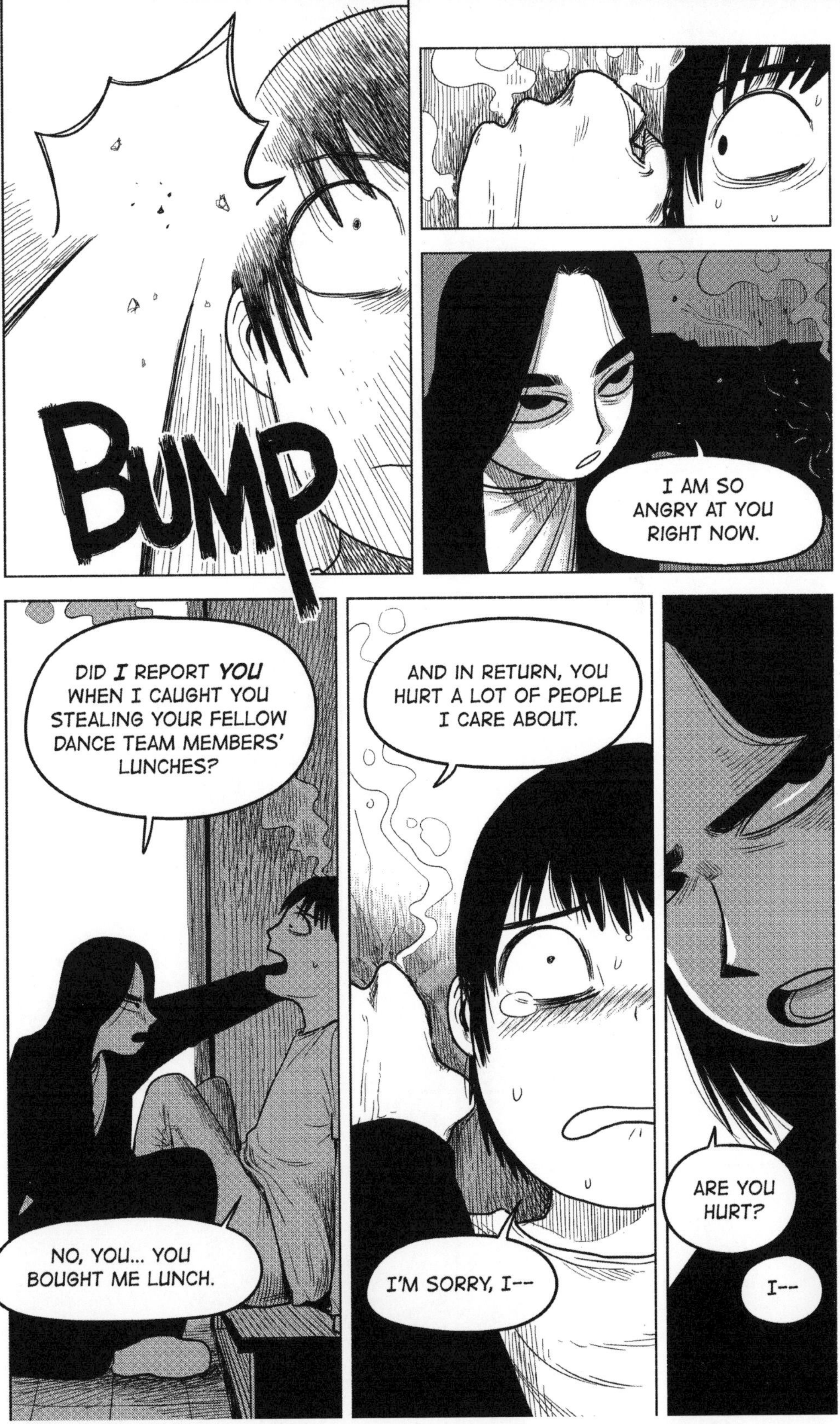
BUMP
I AM SO ANGRY AT YOU RIGHT NOW.
DID I REPORT YOU WHEN I CAUGHT YOU STEALING YOUR FELLOW DANCE TEAM MEMBERS' LUNCHES?
NO, YOU... YOU BOUGHT ME LUNCH.
AND IN RETURN, YOU HURT A LOT OF PEOPLE I CARE ABOUT.
I'M SORRY, I--
ARE YOU HURT?
I--

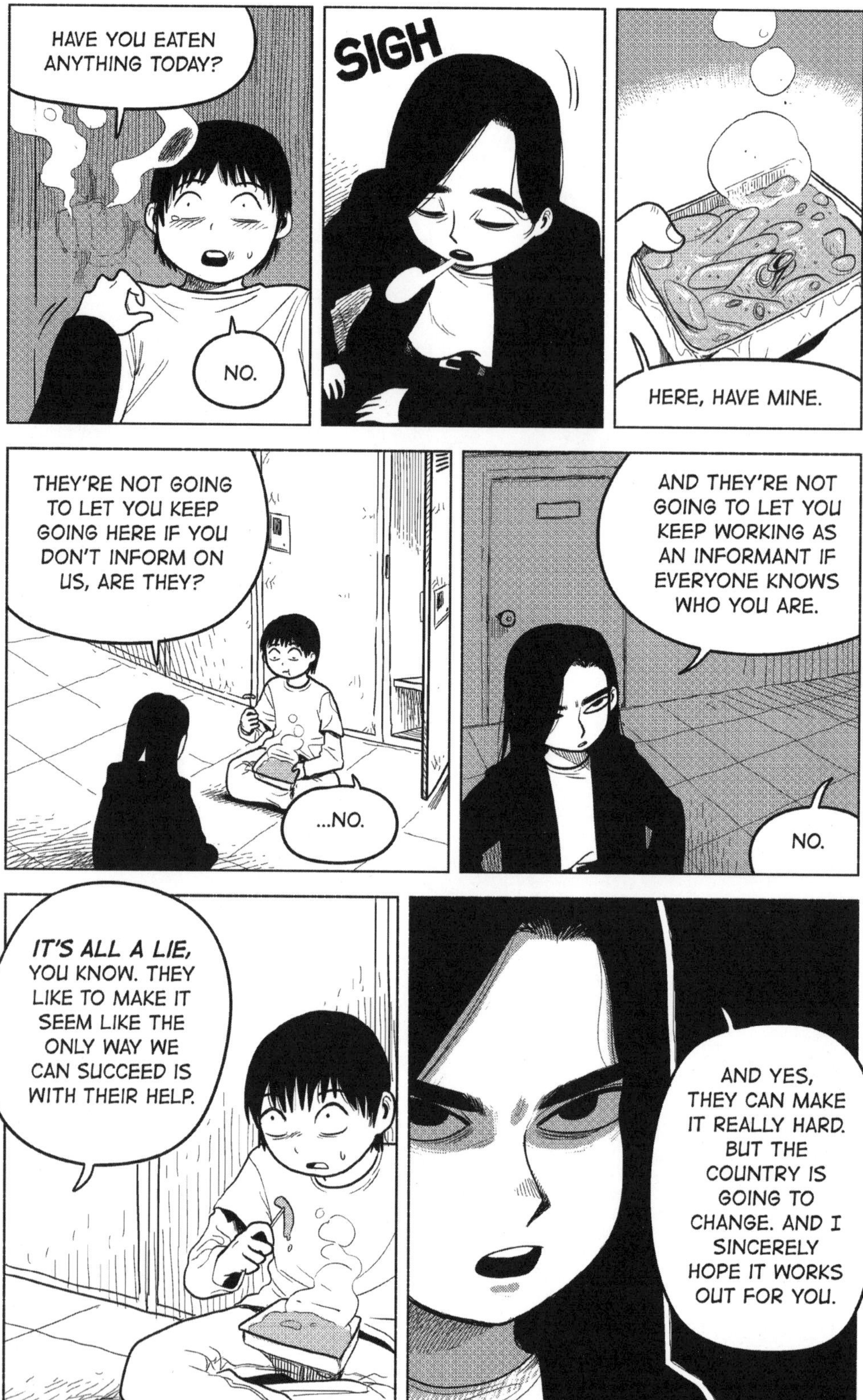
HAVE YOU EATEN ANYTHING TODAY?
NO.
SIGH
HERE, HAVE MINE.
THEY'RE NOT GOING TO LET YOU KEEP GOING HERE IF YOU DON'T INFORM ON US, ARE THEY?
...NO.
AND THEY'RE NOT GOING TO LET YOU KEEP WORKING AS AN INFORMANT IF EVERYONE KNOWS WHO YOU ARE.
NO.
IT'S ALL A LIE, YOU KNOW. THEY LIKE TO MAKE IT SEEM LIKE THE ONLY WAY WE CAN SUCCEED IS WITH THEIR HELP.
AND YES, THEY CAN MAKE IT REALLY HARD. BUT THE COUNTRY IS GOING TO CHANGE. AND I SINCERELY HOPE IT WORKS OUT FOR YOU.

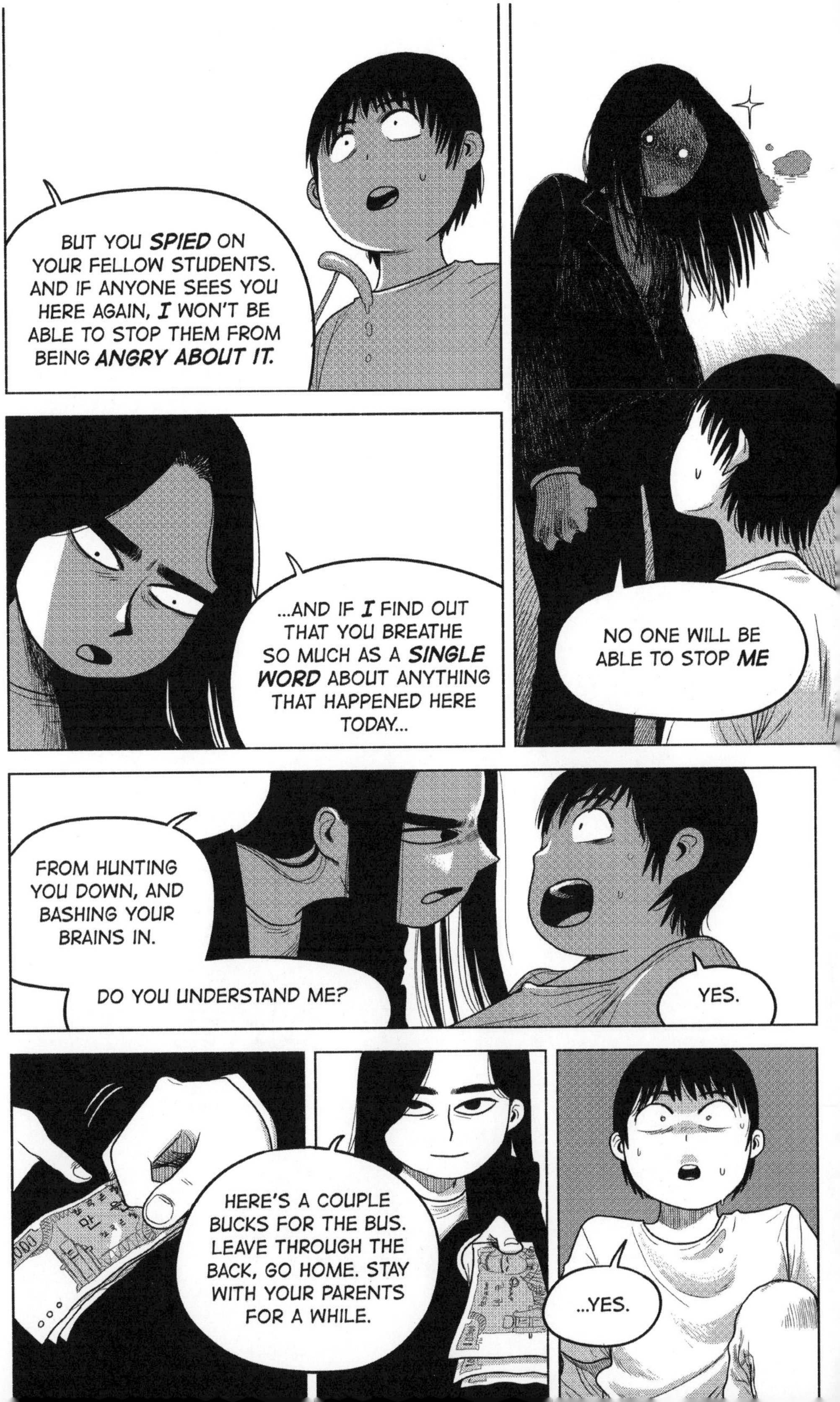
BUT YOU SPIED ON YOUR FELLOW STUDENTS. AND IF ANYONE SEES YOU HERE AGAIN, I WON'T BE ABLE TO STOP THEM FROM BEING ANGRY ABOUT IT.
...AND IF I FIND OUT THAT YOU BREATHE SO MUCH AS A SINGLE WORD ABOUT ANYTHING THAT HAPPENED HERE TODAY...
NO ONE WILL BE ABLE TO STOP ME
FROM HUNTING YOU DOWN, AND BASHING YOUR BRAINS IN.
DO YOU UNDERSTAND ME?
YES.
HERE'S A COUPLE BUCKS FOR THE BUS. LEAVE THROUGH THE BACK, GO HOME. STAY WITH YOUR PARENTS FOR A WHILE.
...YES.

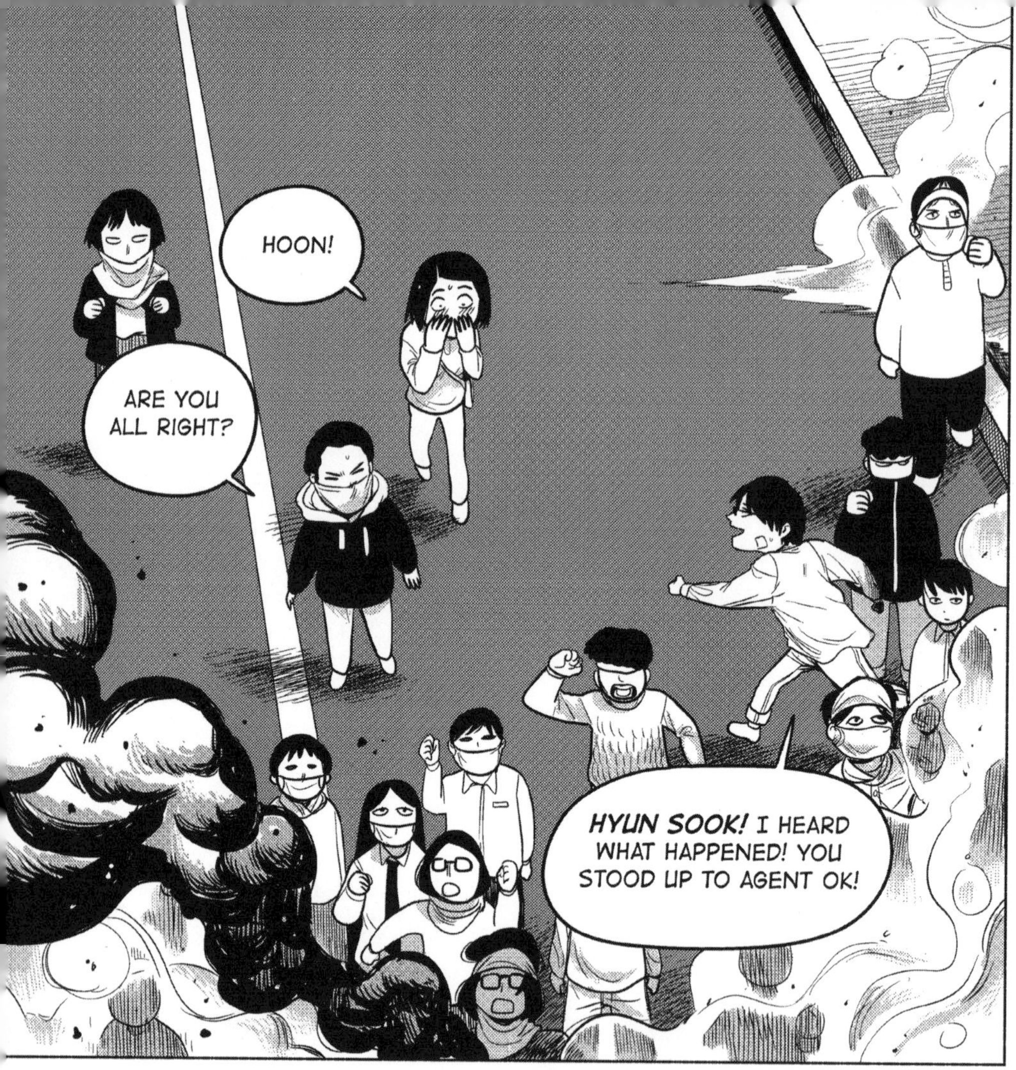
HOON!
ARE YOU ALL RIGHT?
HYUN SOOK! I HEARD WHAT HAPPENED! YOU STOOD UP TO AGENT OK!

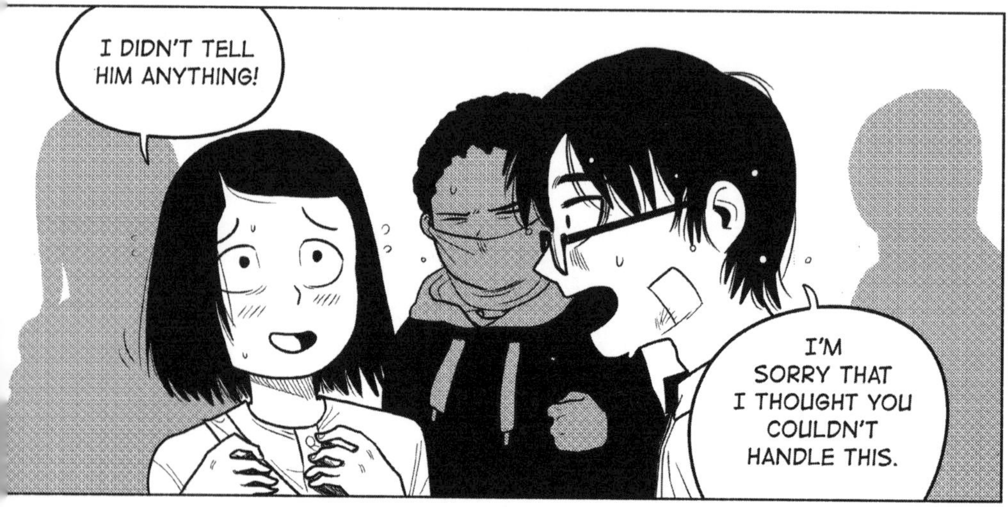
I DIDN'T TELL HIM ANYTHING!
I'M SORRY THAT I THOUGHT YOU COULDN'T HANDLE THIS.

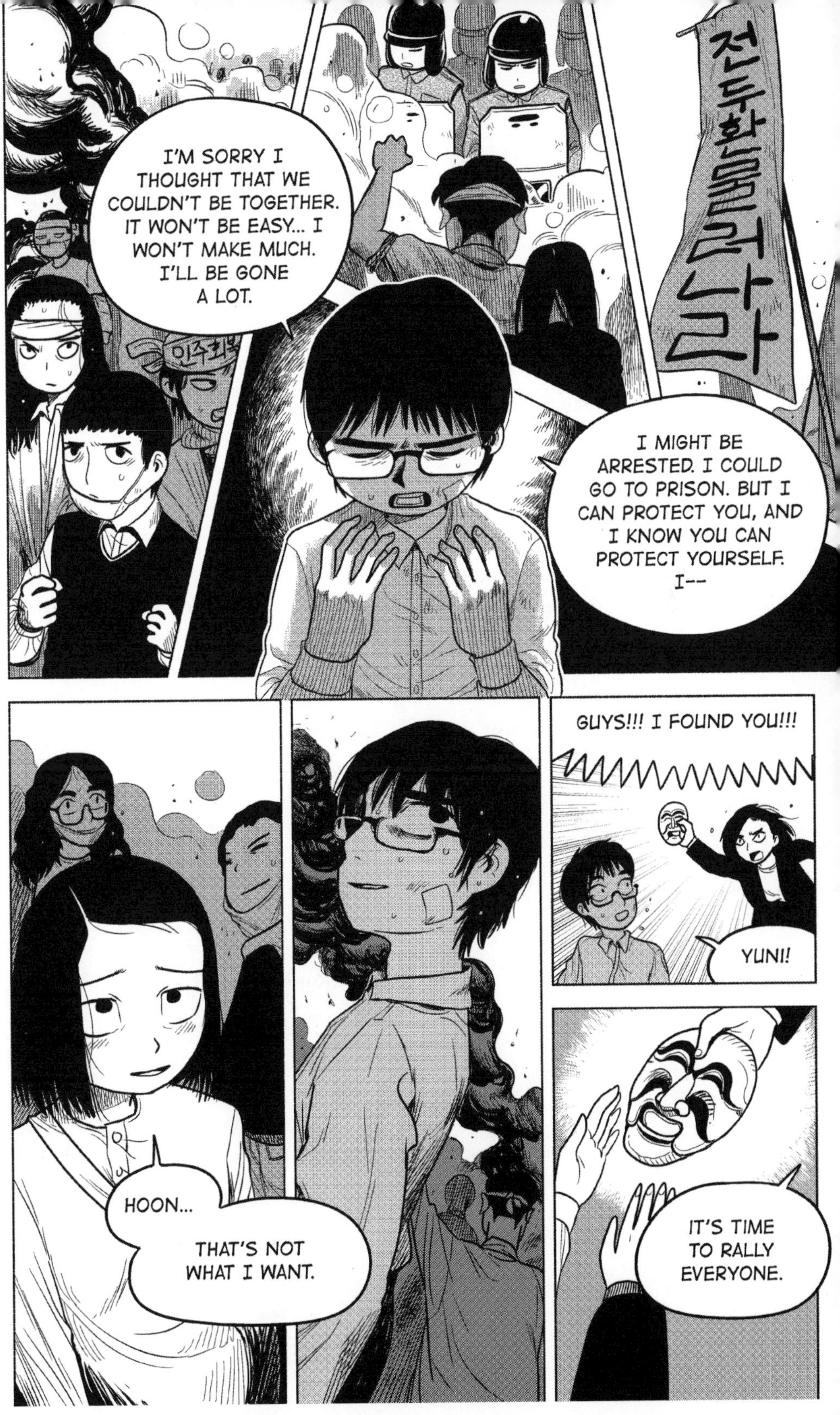

I'M SORRY I THOUGHT THAT WE COULDN'T BE TOGETHER. IT WON'T BE EASY... I WON'T MAKE MUCH. I'LL BE GONE A LOT.
전두환물러나라
I MIGHT BE ARRESTED. I COULD GO TO PRISON. BUT I CAN PROTECT YOU, AND I KNOW YOU CAN PROTECT YOURSELF. I--
HOON... THAT'S NOT WHAT I WANT.
GUYS!!! I FOUND YOU!!!
YUNI!
IT'S TIME TO RALLY EVERYONE.

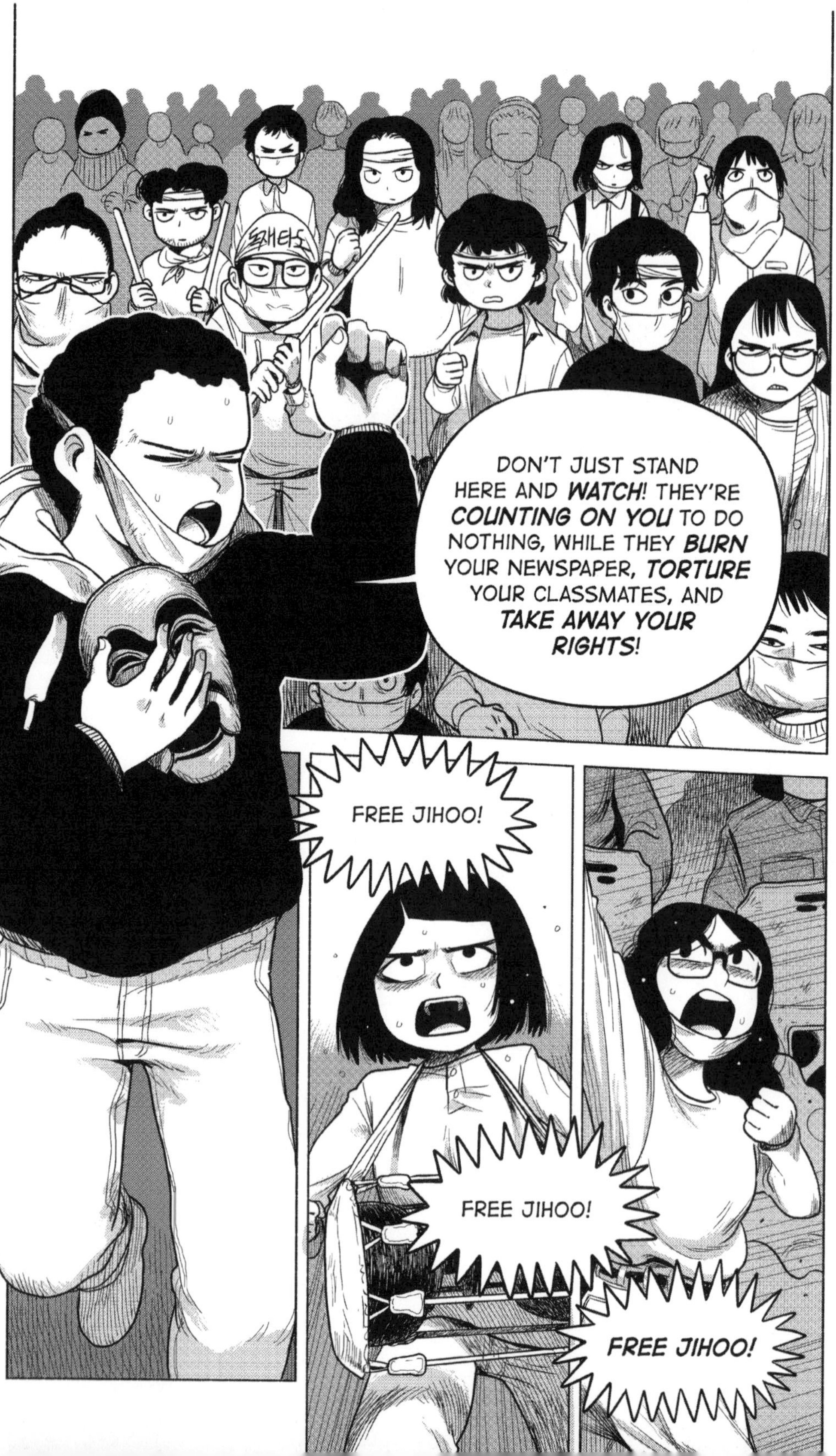
DON'T JUST STAND HERE AND WATCH! THEY'RE COUNTING ON YOU TO DO NOTHING, WHILE THEY BURN YOUR NEWSPAPER, TORTURE YOUR CLASSMATES, AND TAKE AWAY YOUR RIGHTS!
FREE JIHOO!
FREE JIHOO!
FREE JIHOO!

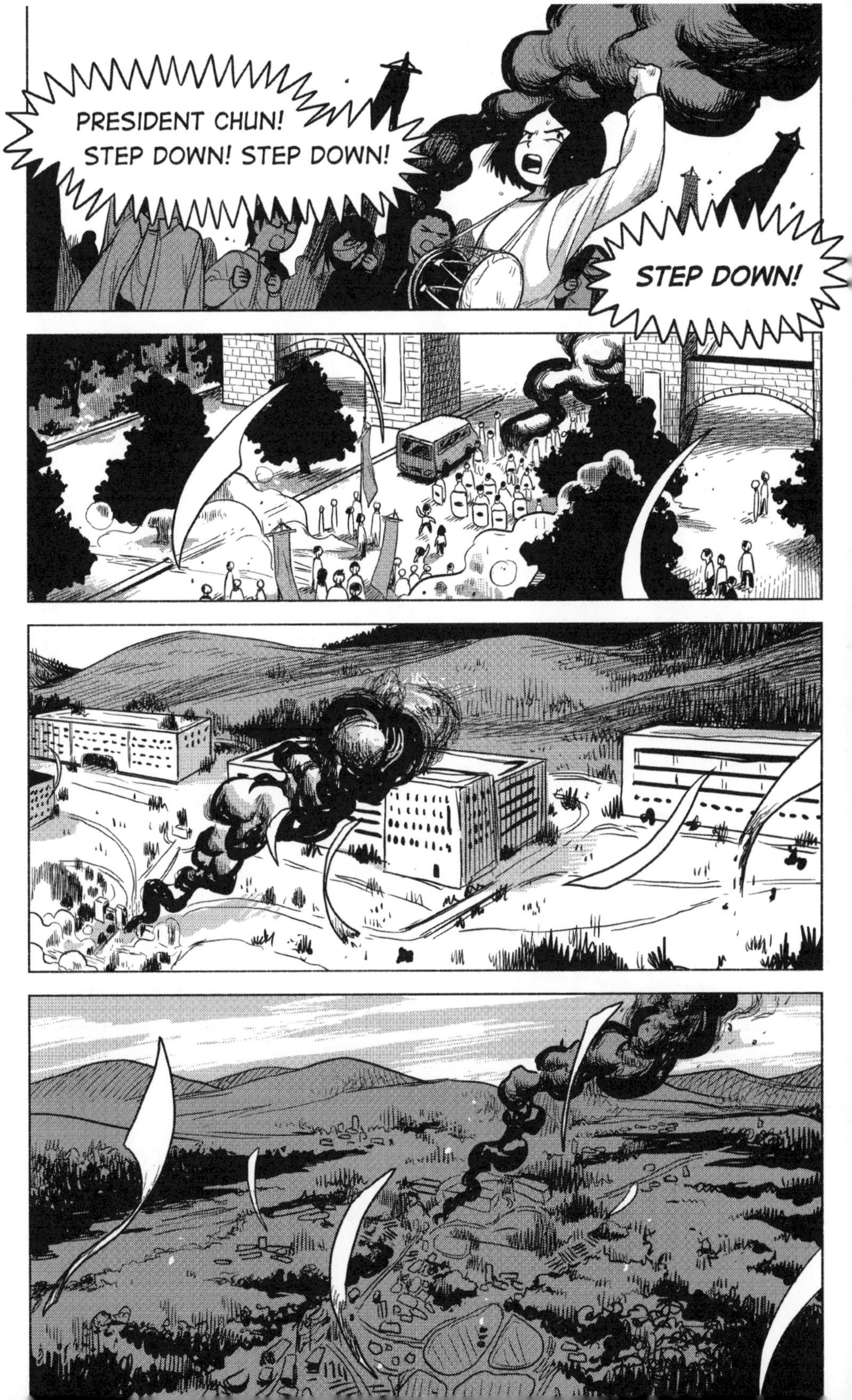
PRESIDENT CHUN! STEP DOWN! STEP DOWN!
STEP DOWN!

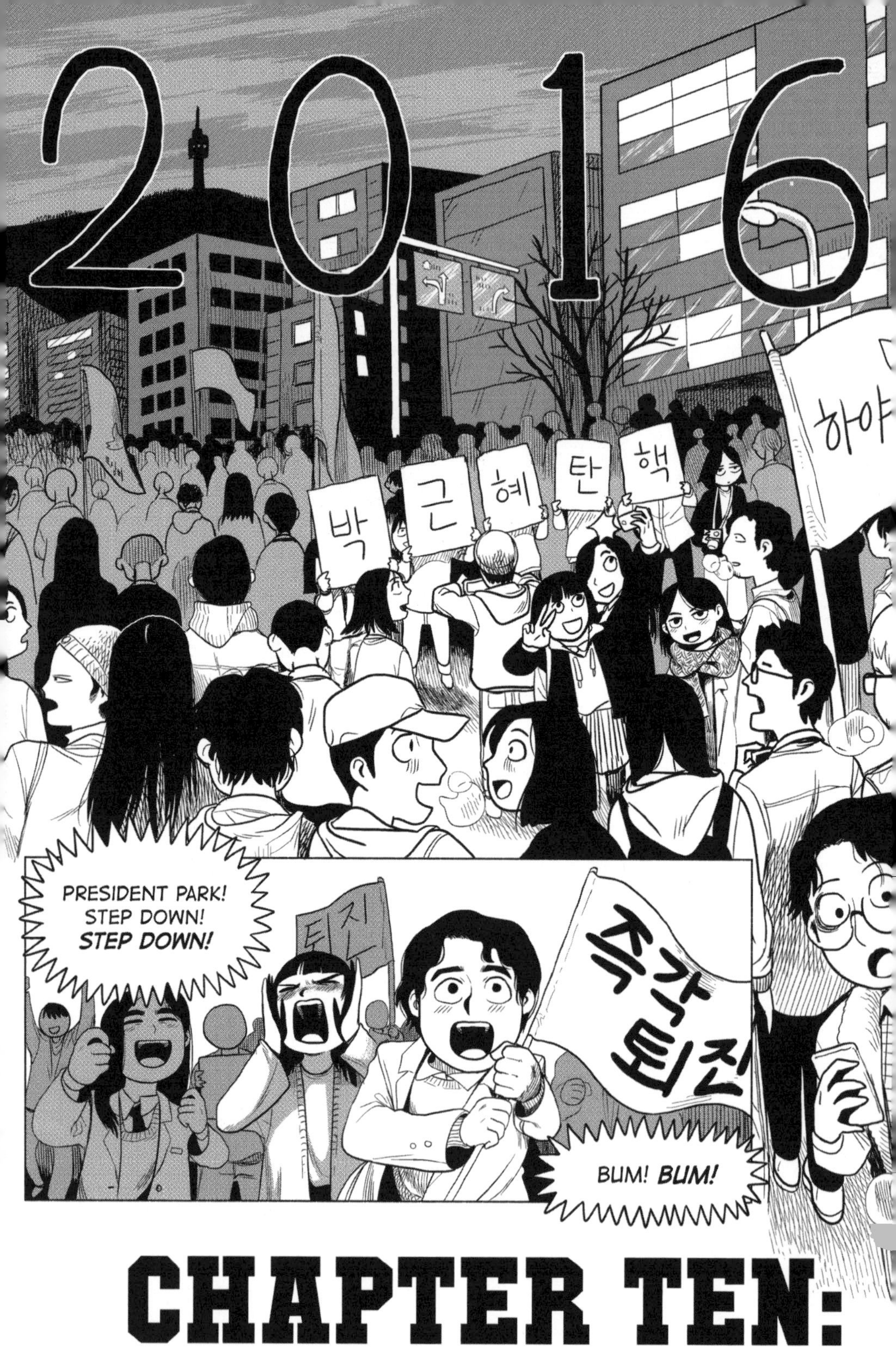
2016
박 근 혜 탄 핵
하야
PRESIDENT PARK! STEP DOWN! *STEP DOWN!*
퇴진
즉각퇴진
BUM! *BUM!*

CHAPTER TEN:

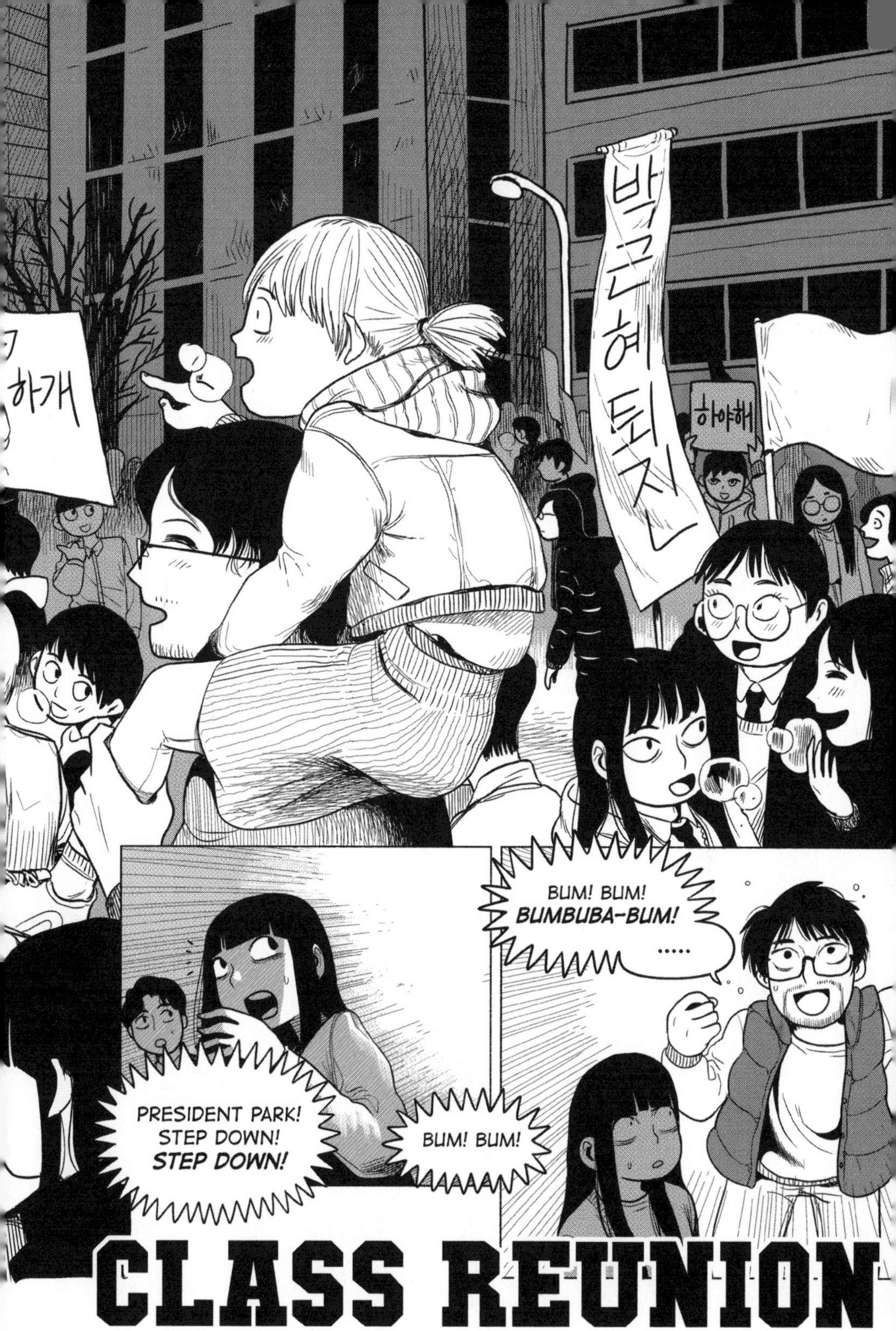
박근혜퇴진
하개
하야해
PRESIDENT PARK!
STEP DOWN!
STEP DOWN!
BUM! BUM!
BUM! BUM!
BUMBUBA-BUM!
.....

CLASS REUNION

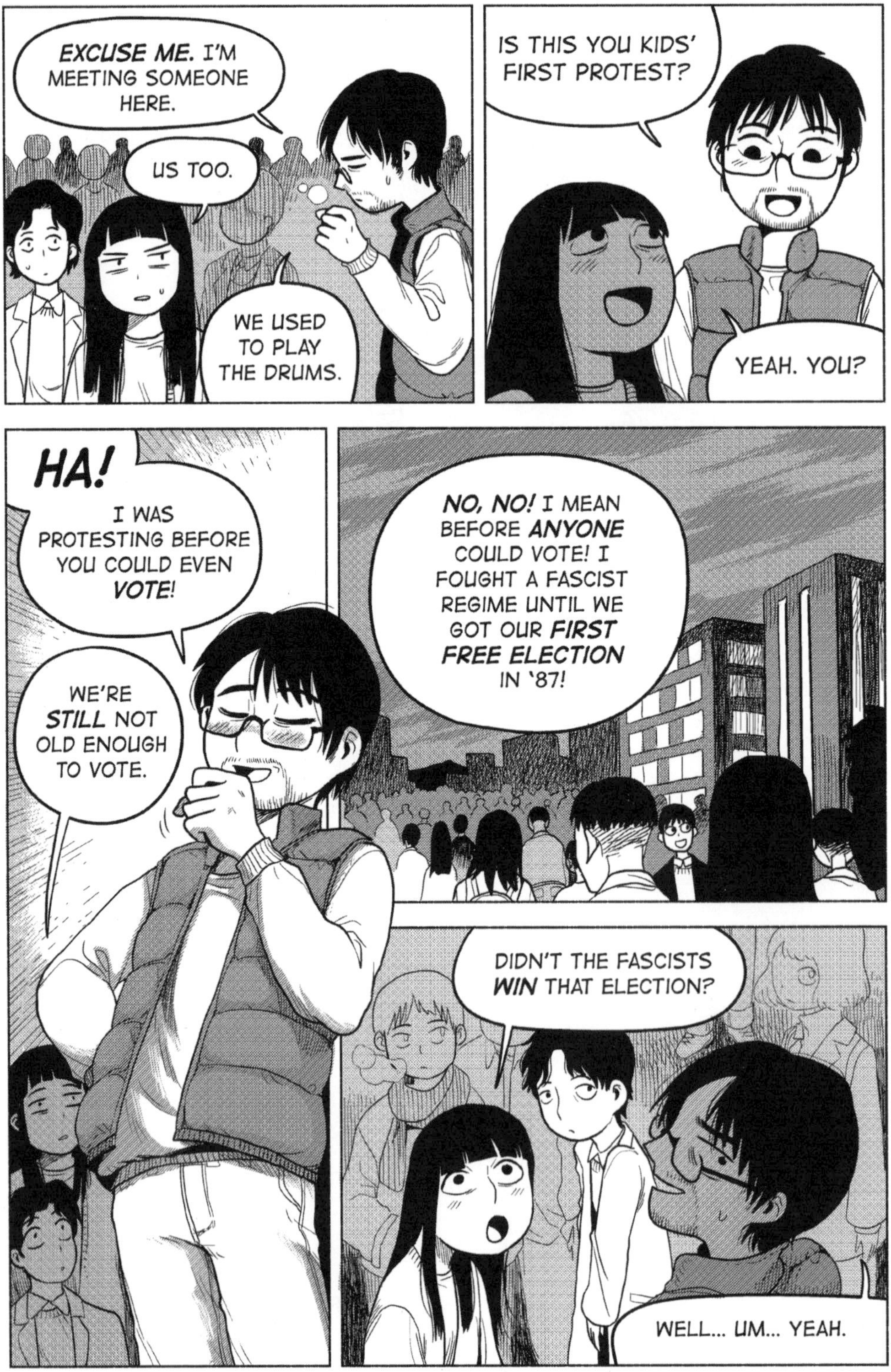
EXCUSE ME. I'M MEETING SOMEONE HERE.
US TOO.
WE USED TO PLAY THE DRUMS.
IS THIS YOU KIDS' FIRST PROTEST?
YEAH. YOU?
HA!
I WAS PROTESTING BEFORE YOU COULD EVEN VOTE!
WE'RE STILL NOT OLD ENOUGH TO VOTE.
NO, NO! I MEAN BEFORE ANYONE COULD VOTE! I FOUGHT A FASCIST REGIME UNTIL WE GOT OUR FIRST FREE ELECTION IN '87!
DIDN'T THE FASCISTS WIN THAT ELECTION?
WELL... UM... YEAH.

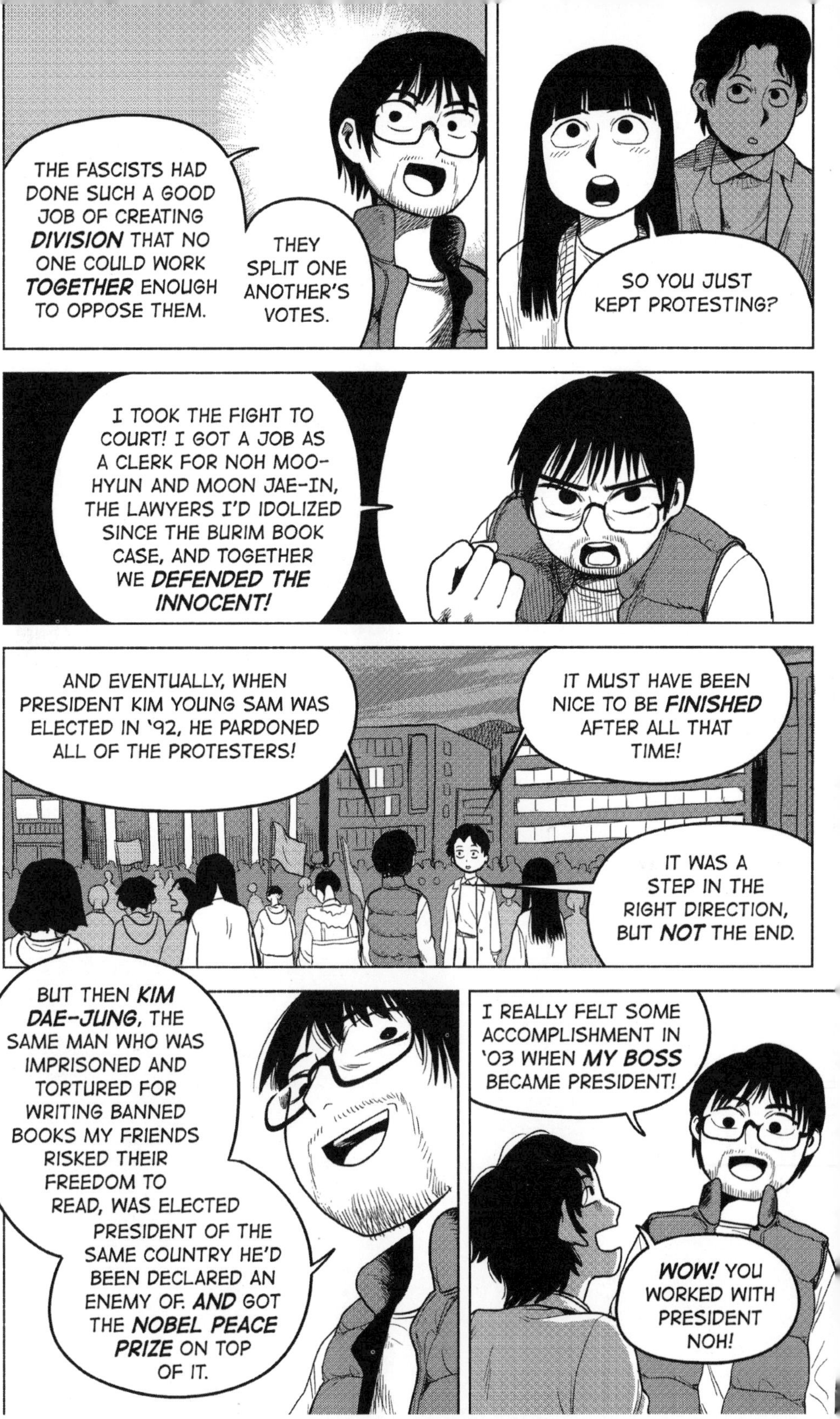
THE FASCISTS HAD DONE SUCH A GOOD JOB OF CREATING *DIVISION* THAT NO ONE COULD WORK *TOGETHER* ENOUGH TO OPPOSE THEM.
THEY SPLIT ONE ANOTHER'S VOTES.
SO YOU JUST KEPT PROTESTING?
I TOOK THE FIGHT TO COURT! I GOT A JOB AS A CLERK FOR NOH MOO-HYUN AND MOON JAE-IN, THE LAWYERS I'D IDOLIZED SINCE THE BURIM BOOK CASE, AND TOGETHER WE *DEFENDED THE INNOCENT!*
AND EVENTUALLY, WHEN PRESIDENT KIM YOUNG SAM WAS ELECTED IN '92, HE PARDONED ALL OF THE PROTESTERS!
IT MUST HAVE BEEN NICE TO BE *FINISHED* AFTER ALL THAT TIME!
IT WAS A STEP IN THE RIGHT DIRECTION, BUT *NOT* THE END.
BUT THEN *KIM DAE-JUNG*, THE SAME MAN WHO WAS IMPRISONED AND TORTURED FOR WRITING BANNED BOOKS MY FRIENDS RISKED THEIR FREEDOM TO READ, WAS ELECTED PRESIDENT OF THE SAME COUNTRY HE'D BEEN DECLARED AN ENEMY OF. *AND* GOT THE *NOBEL PEACE PRIZE* ON TOP OF IT.
I REALLY FELT SOME ACCOMPLISHMENT IN '03 WHEN *MY BOSS* BECAME PRESIDENT!
WOW! YOU WORKED WITH PRESIDENT NOH!

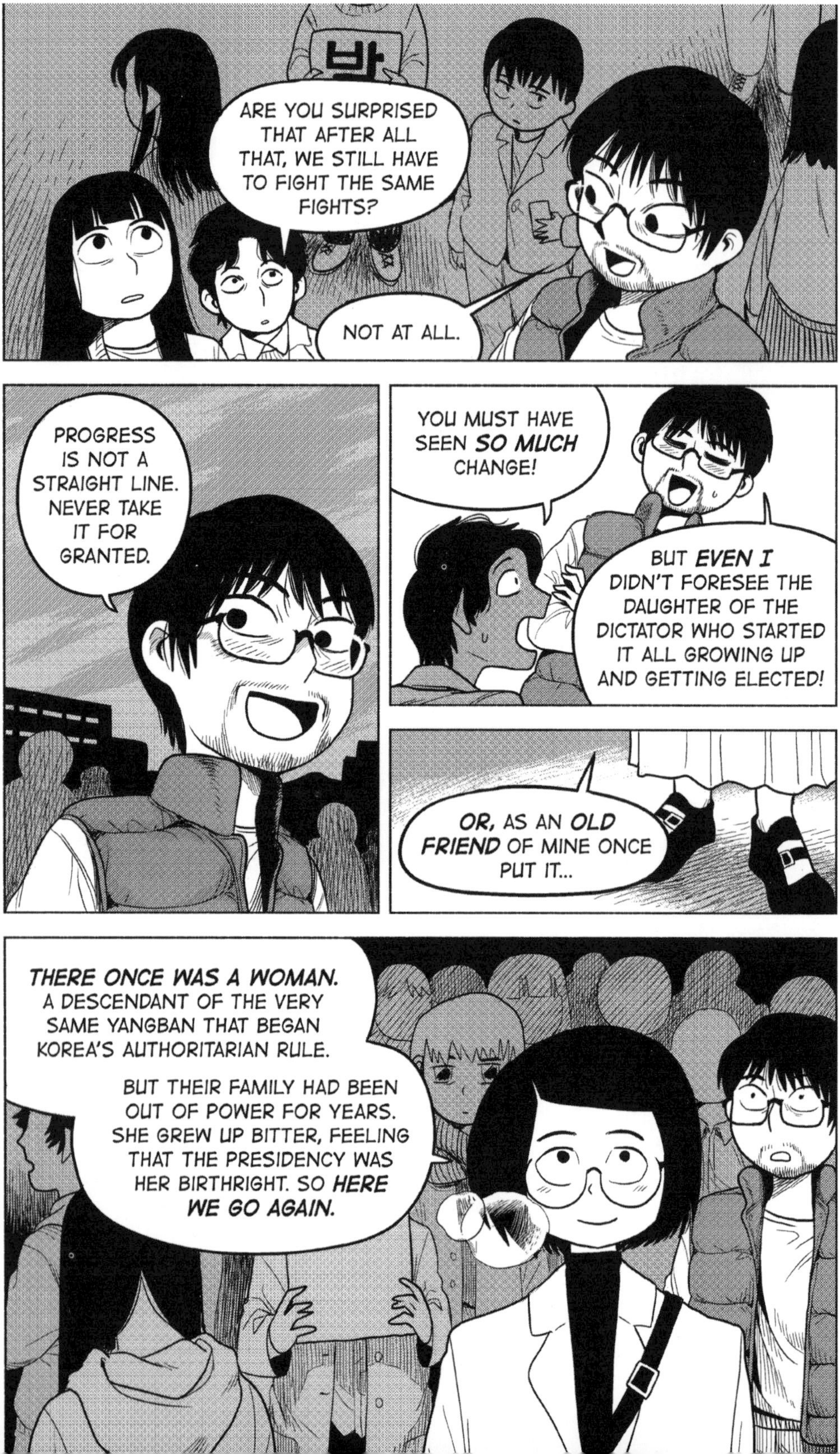
ARE YOU SURPRISED THAT AFTER ALL THAT, WE STILL HAVE TO FIGHT THE SAME FIGHTS?
NOT AT ALL.
PROGRESS IS NOT A STRAIGHT LINE. NEVER TAKE IT FOR GRANTED.
YOU MUST HAVE SEEN SO MUCH CHANGE!
BUT EVEN I DIDN'T FORESEE THE DAUGHTER OF THE DICTATOR WHO STARTED IT ALL GROWING UP AND GETTING ELECTED!
OR, AS AN OLD FRIEND OF MINE ONCE PUT IT...
THERE ONCE WAS A WOMAN. A DESCENDANT OF THE VERY SAME YANGBAN THAT BEGAN KOREA'S AUTHORITARIAN RULE.
BUT THEIR FAMILY HAD BEEN OUT OF POWER FOR YEARS. SHE GREW UP BITTER, FEELING THAT THE PRESIDENCY WAS HER BIRTHRIGHT. SO HERE WE GO AGAIN.

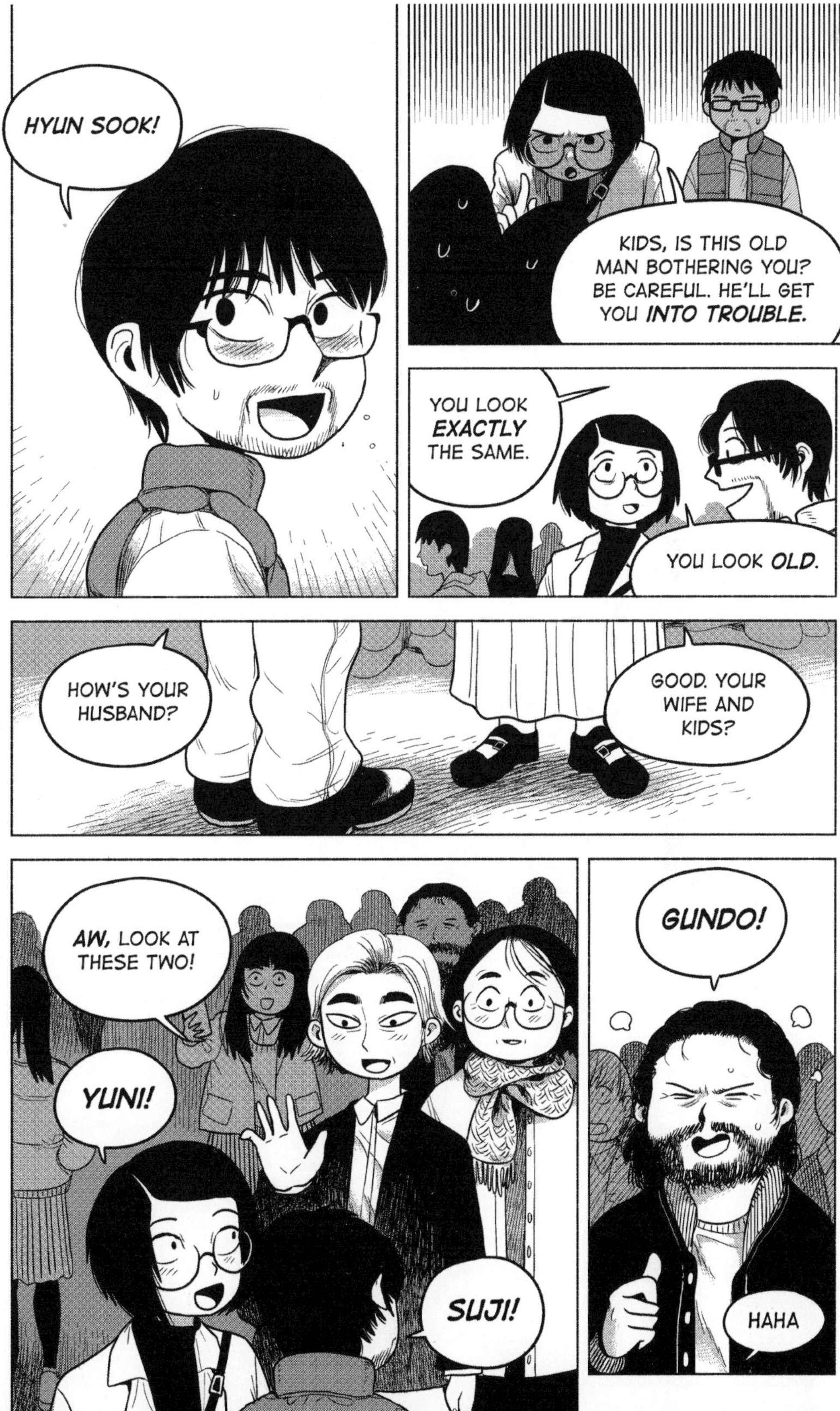
HYUN SOOK!
KIDS, IS THIS OLD MAN BOTHERING YOU? BE CAREFUL. HE'LL GET YOU INTO TROUBLE.
YOU LOOK EXACTLY THE SAME.
YOU LOOK OLD.
HOW'S YOUR HUSBAND?
GOOD. YOUR WIFE AND KIDS?
AW, LOOK AT THESE TWO!
YUNI!
SUJI!
GUNDO!
HAHA

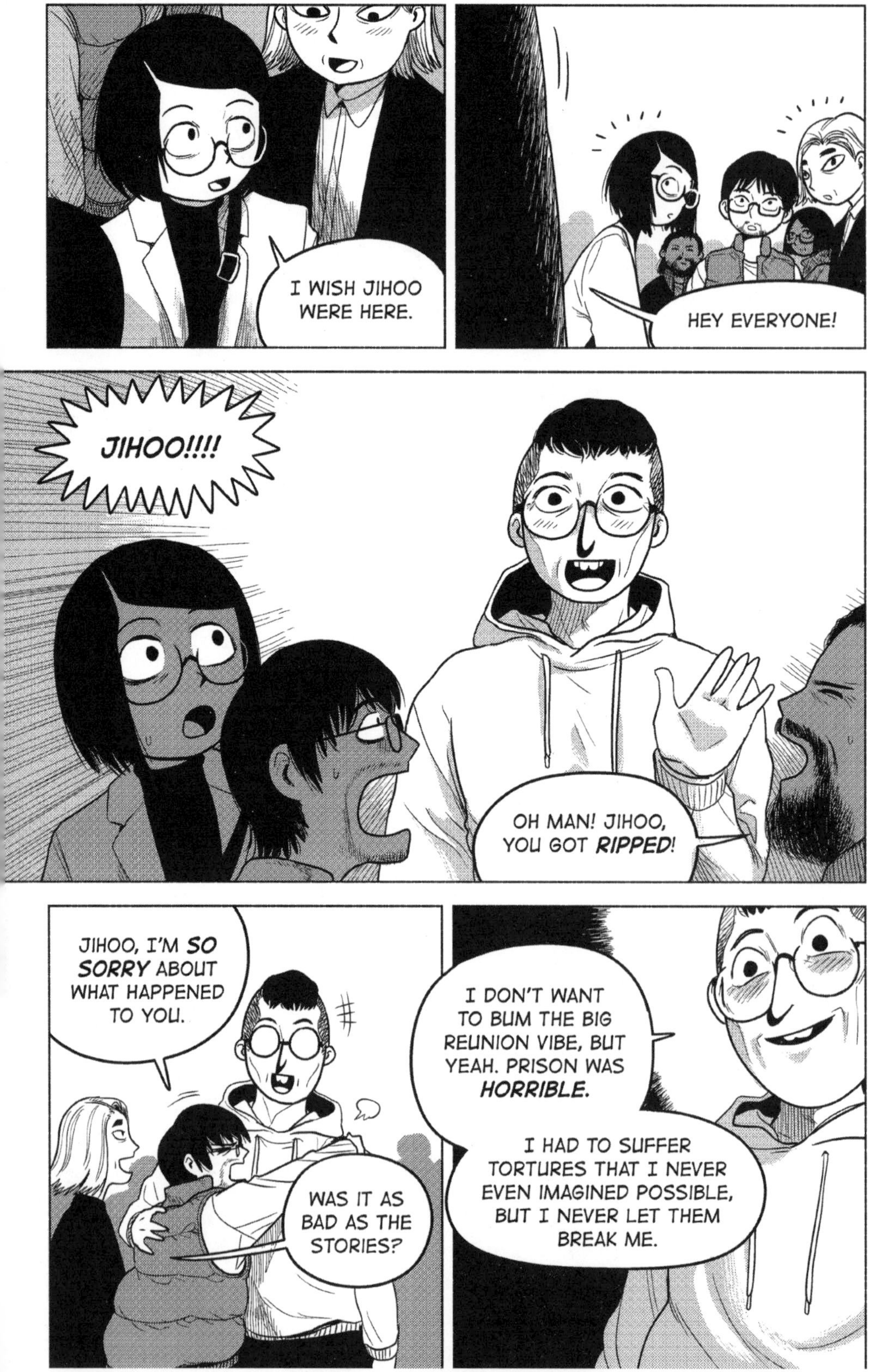
I WISH JIHOO WERE HERE.
HEY EVERYONE!
JIHOO!!!!
OH MAN! JIHOO, YOU GOT RIPPED!
JIHOO, I'M SO SORRY ABOUT WHAT HAPPENED TO YOU.
WAS IT AS BAD AS THE STORIES?
I DON'T WANT TO BUM THE BIG REUNION VIBE, BUT YEAH. PRISON WAS HORRIBLE.
I HAD TO SUFFER TORTURES THAT I NEVER EVEN IMAGINED POSSIBLE, BUT I NEVER LET THEM BREAK ME.

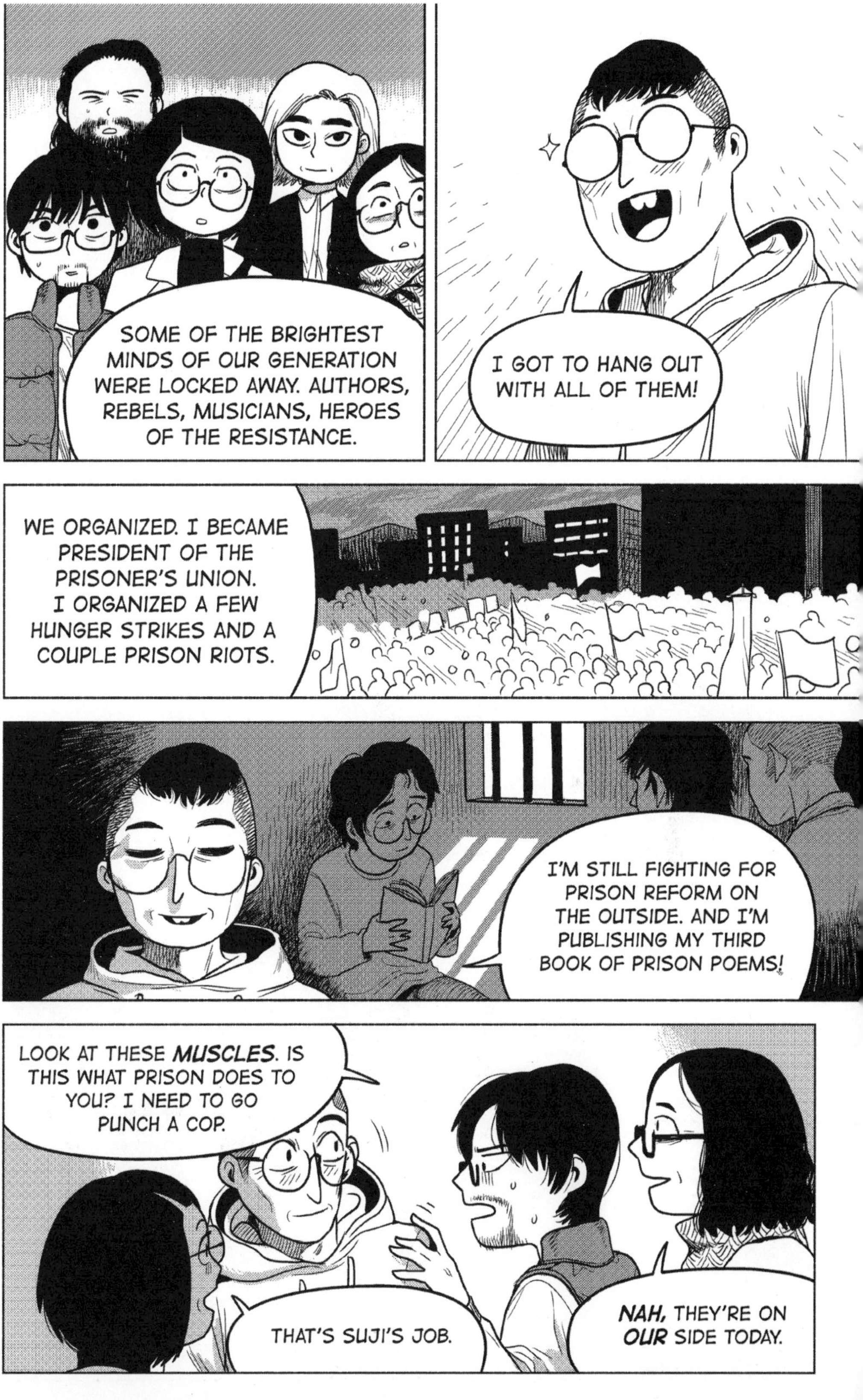
SOME OF THE BRIGHTEST MINDS OF OUR GENERATION WERE LOCKED AWAY. AUTHORS, REBELS, MUSICIANS, HEROES OF THE RESISTANCE.
I GOT TO HANG OUT WITH ALL OF THEM!
WE ORGANIZED. I BECAME PRESIDENT OF THE PRISONER'S UNION. I ORGANIZED A FEW HUNGER STRIKES AND A COUPLE PRISON RIOTS.
I'M STILL FIGHTING FOR PRISON REFORM ON THE OUTSIDE. AND I'M PUBLISHING MY THIRD BOOK OF PRISON POEMS!
LOOK AT THESE *MUSCLES*. IS THIS WHAT PRISON DOES TO YOU? I NEED TO GO PUNCH A COP.
THAT'S SUJI'S JOB.
NAH, THEY'RE ON ***OUR*** SIDE TODAY.

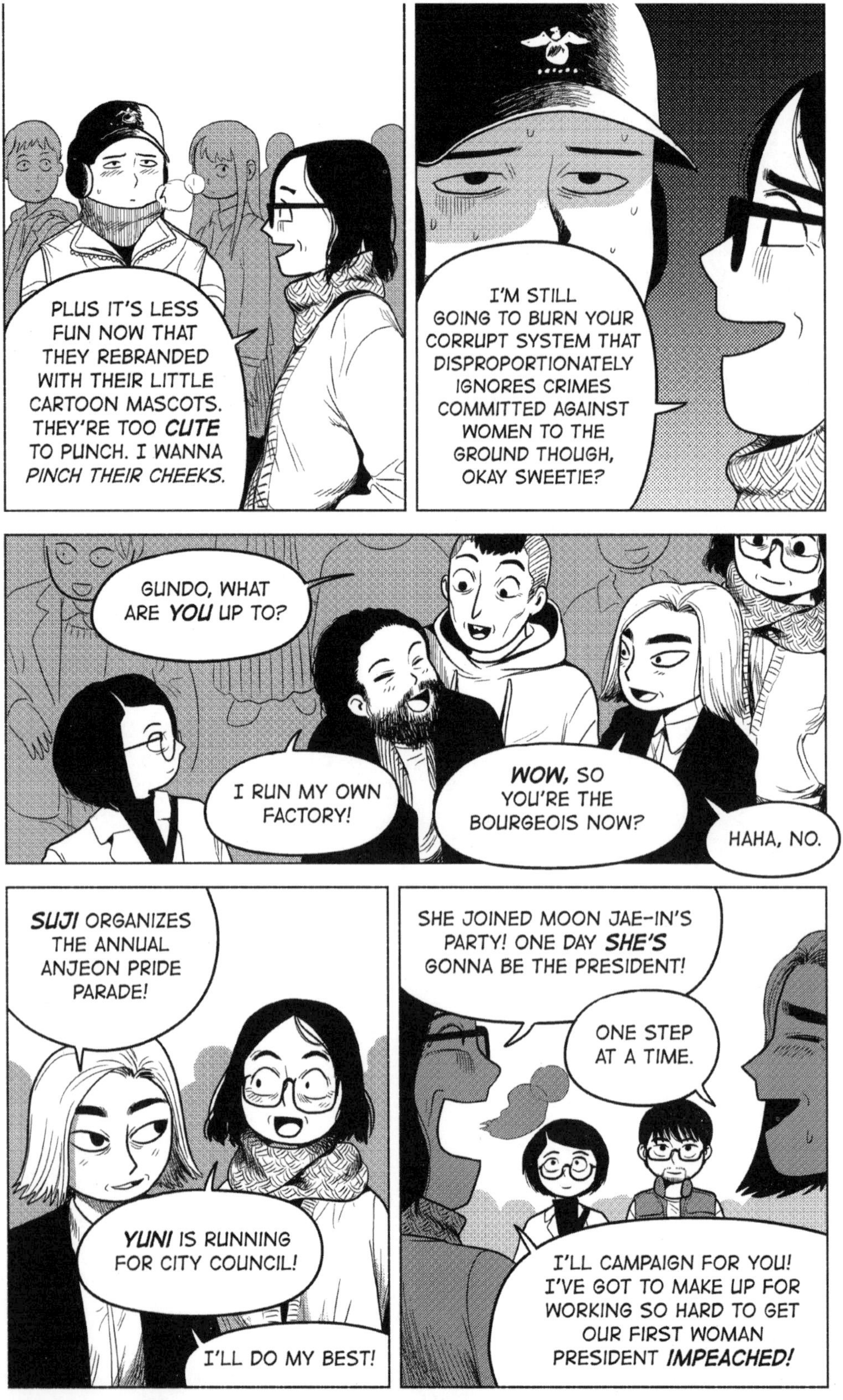

PLUS IT'S LESS FUN NOW THAT THEY REBRANDED WITH THEIR LITTLE CARTOON MASCOTS. THEY'RE TOO *CUTE* TO PUNCH. I WANNA *PINCH THEIR CHEEKS.*
I'M STILL GOING TO BURN YOUR CORRUPT SYSTEM THAT DISPROPORTIONATELY IGNORES CRIMES COMMITTED AGAINST WOMEN TO THE GROUND THOUGH, OKAY SWEETIE?
GUNDO, WHAT ARE *YOU* UP TO?
I RUN MY OWN FACTORY!
WOW, SO YOU'RE THE BOURGEOIS NOW?
HAHA, NO.
SUJI ORGANIZES THE ANNUAL ANJEON PRIDE PARADE!
YUNI IS RUNNING FOR CITY COUNCIL!
I'LL DO MY BEST!
SHE JOINED MOON JAE-IN'S PARTY! ONE DAY *SHE'S* GONNA BE THE PRESIDENT!
ONE STEP AT A TIME.
I'LL CAMPAIGN FOR YOU! I'VE GOT TO MAKE UP FOR WORKING SO HARD TO GET OUR FIRST WOMAN PRESIDENT *IMPEACHED!*

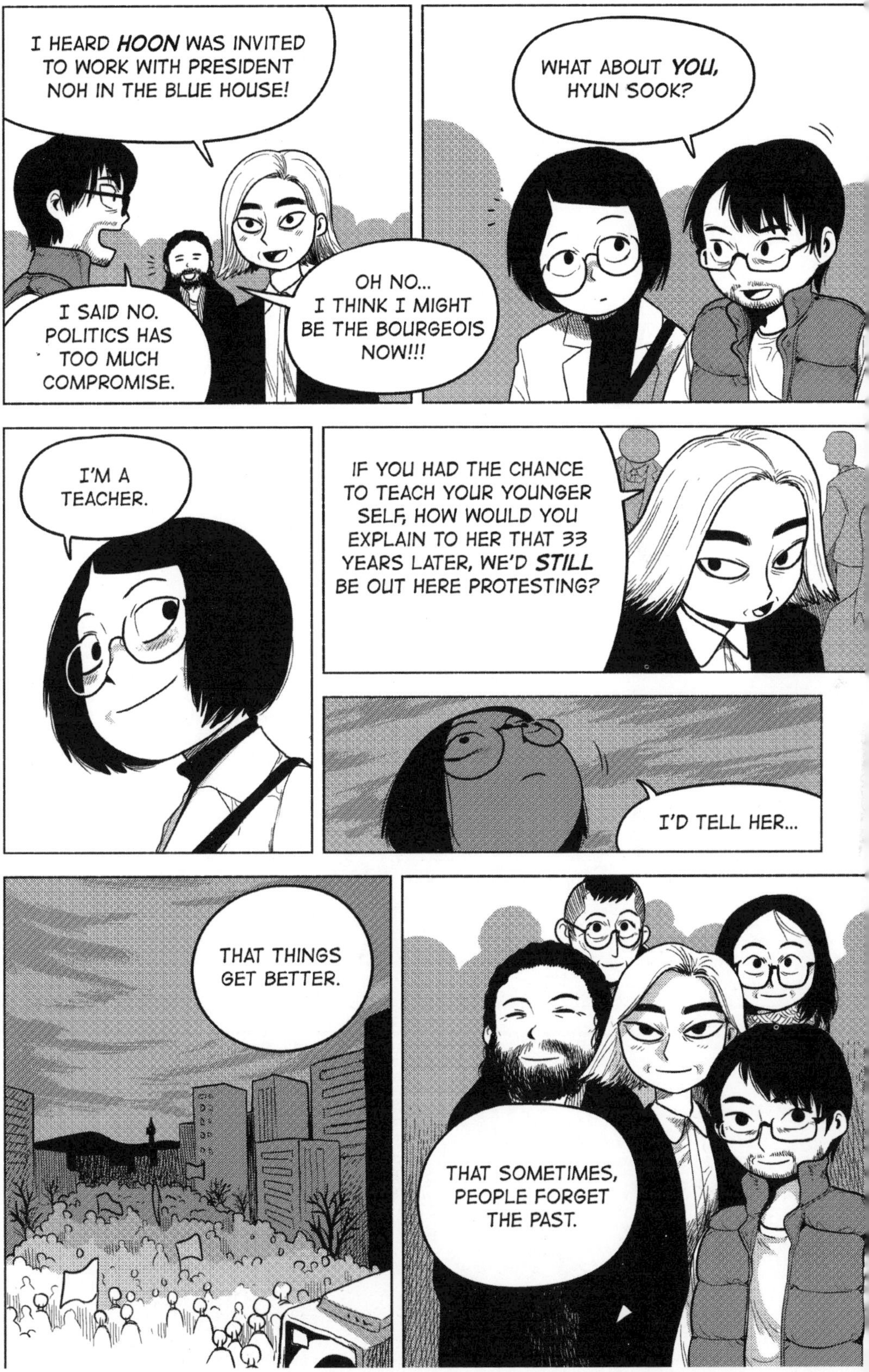
I HEARD HOON WAS INVITED TO WORK WITH PRESIDENT NOH IN THE BLUE HOUSE!
I SAID NO. POLITICS HAS TOO MUCH COMPROMISE.
OH NO... I THINK I MIGHT BE THE BOURGEOIS NOW!!!
WHAT ABOUT YOU, HYUN SOOK?
I'M A TEACHER.
IF YOU HAD THE CHANCE TO TEACH YOUR YOUNGER SELF, HOW WOULD YOU EXPLAIN TO HER THAT 33 YEARS LATER, WE'D STILL BE OUT HERE PROTESTING?
I'D TELL HER...
THAT THINGS GET BETTER.
THAT SOMETIMES, PEOPLE FORGET THE PAST.

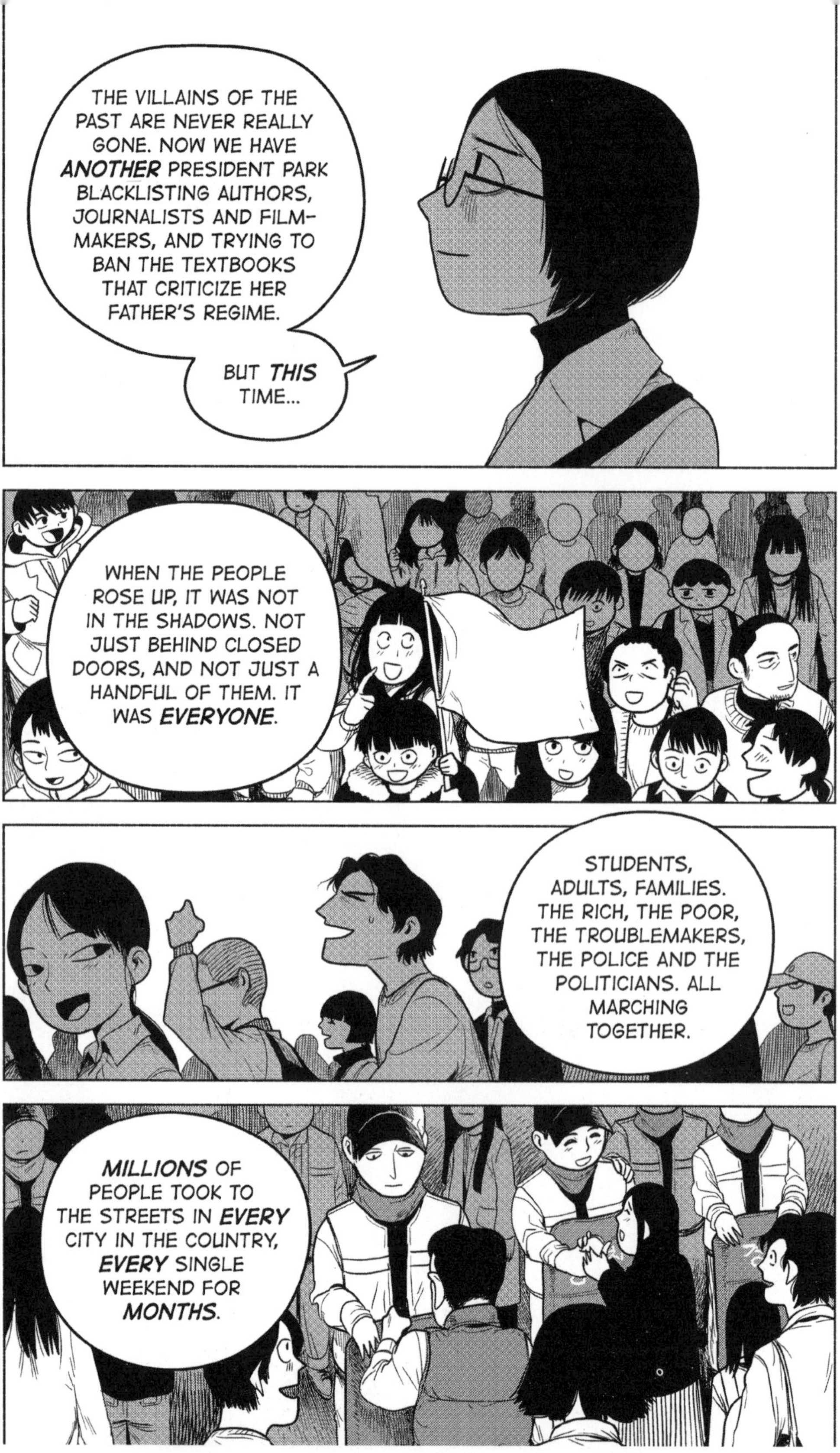
THE VILLAINS OF THE PAST ARE NEVER REALLY GONE. NOW WE HAVE ANOTHER PRESIDENT PARK BLACKLISTING AUTHORS, JOURNALISTS AND FILM-MAKERS, AND TRYING TO BAN THE TEXTBOOKS THAT CRITICIZE HER FATHER'S REGIME.
BUT THIS TIME...
WHEN THE PEOPLE ROSE UP, IT WAS NOT IN THE SHADOWS. NOT JUST BEHIND CLOSED DOORS, AND NOT JUST A HANDFUL OF THEM. IT WAS EVERYONE.
STUDENTS, ADULTS, FAMILIES. THE RICH, THE POOR, THE TROUBLEMAKERS, THE POLICE AND THE POLITICIANS. ALL MARCHING TOGETHER.
MILLIONS OF PEOPLE TOOK TO THE STREETS IN EVERY CITY IN THE COUNTRY, EVERY SINGLE WEEKEND FOR MONTHS.

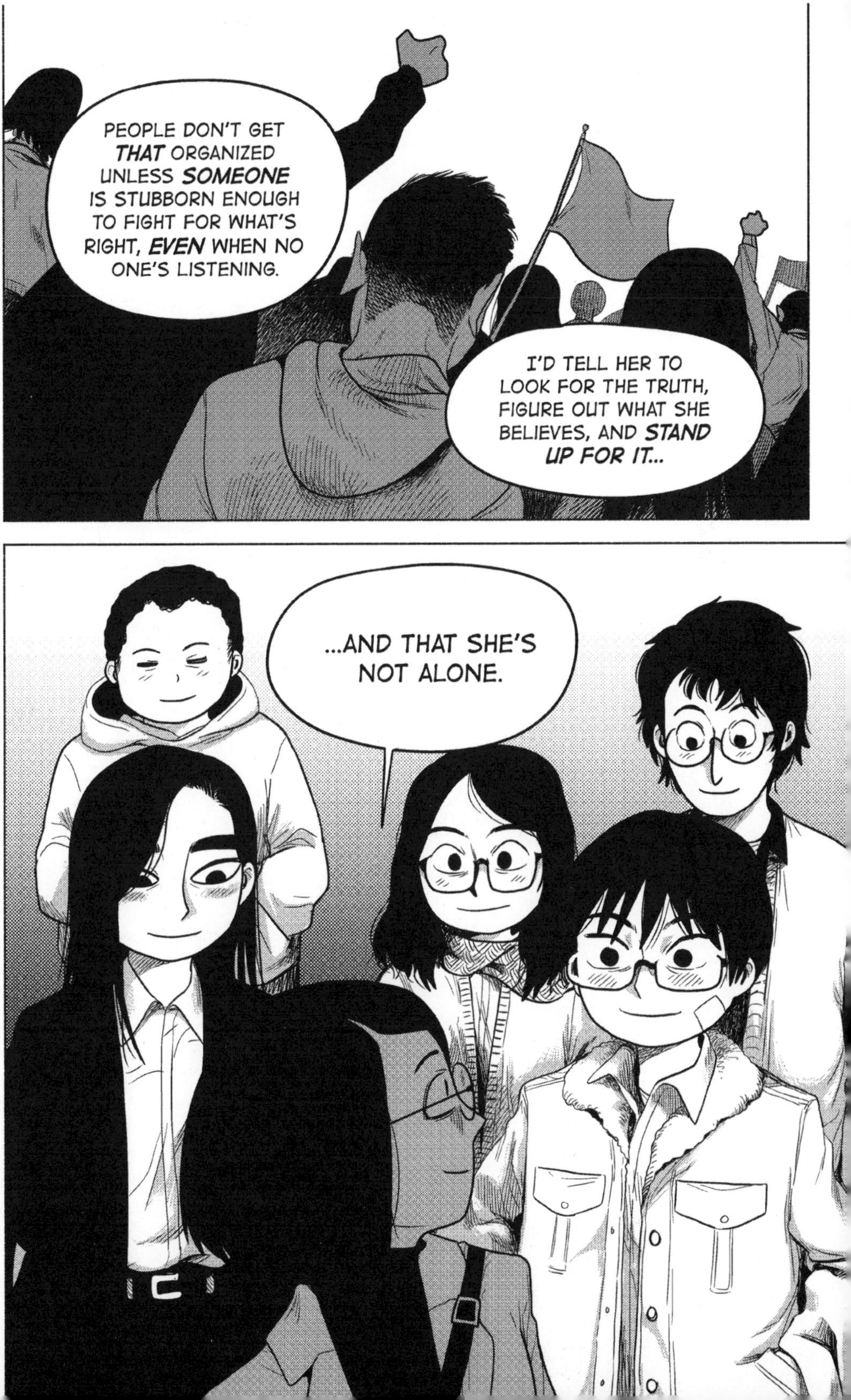
PEOPLE DON'T GET *THAT* ORGANIZED UNLESS *SOMEONE* IS STUBBORN ENOUGH TO FIGHT FOR WHAT'S RIGHT, *EVEN* WHEN NO ONE'S LISTENING.
I'D TELL HER TO LOOK FOR THE TRUTH, FIGURE OUT WHAT SHE BELIEVES, AND *STAND UP FOR IT...*
...AND THAT SHE'S NOT ALONE.

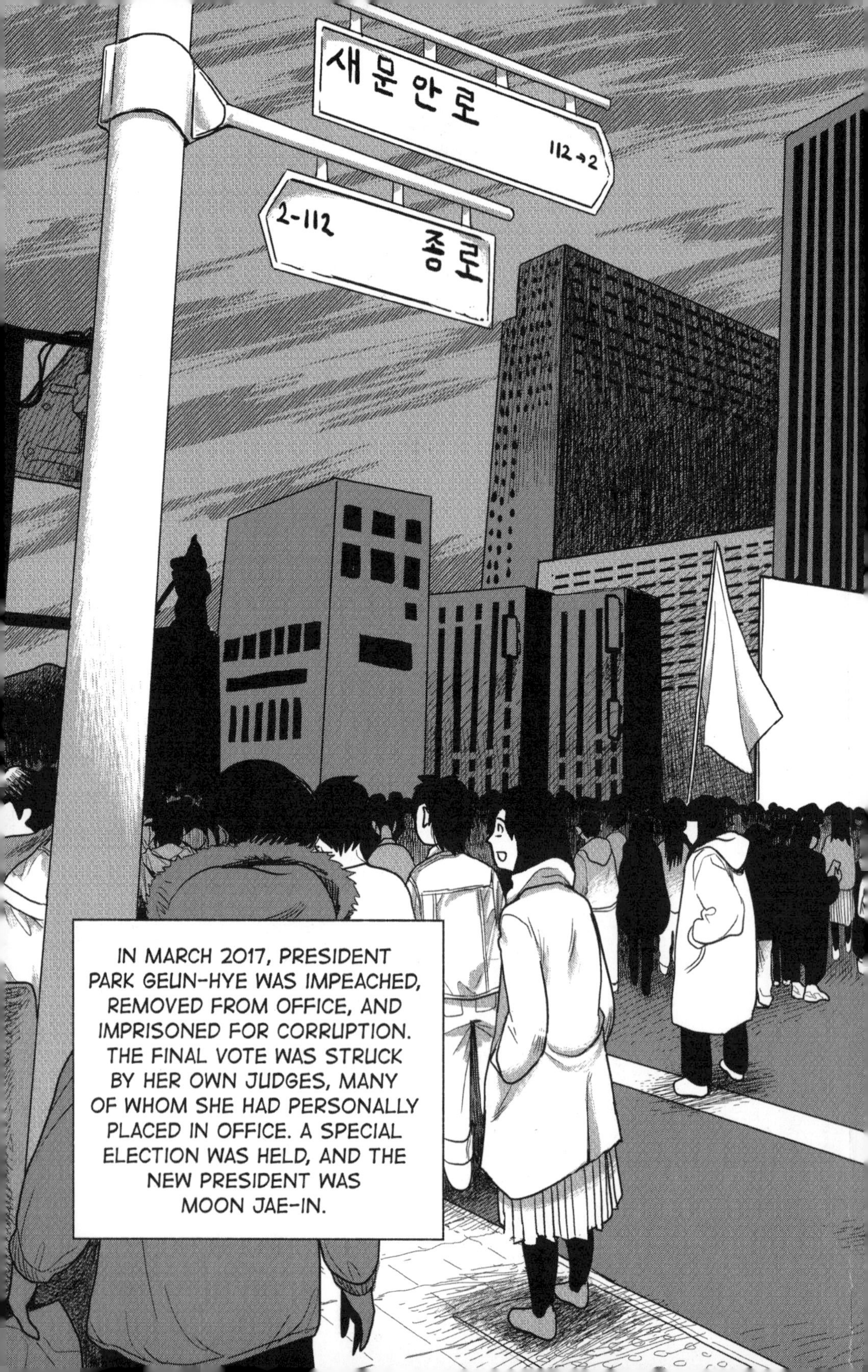
새문안로
112→2
2-112
종로
IN MARCH 2017, PRESIDENT PARK GEUN-HYE WAS IMPEACHED, REMOVED FROM OFFICE, AND IMPRISONED FOR CORRUPTION. THE FINAL VOTE WAS STRUCK BY HER OWN JUDGES, MANY OF WHOM SHE HAD PERSONALLY PLACED IN OFFICE. A SPECIAL ELECTION WAS HELD, AND THE NEW PRESIDENT WAS MOON JAE-IN.

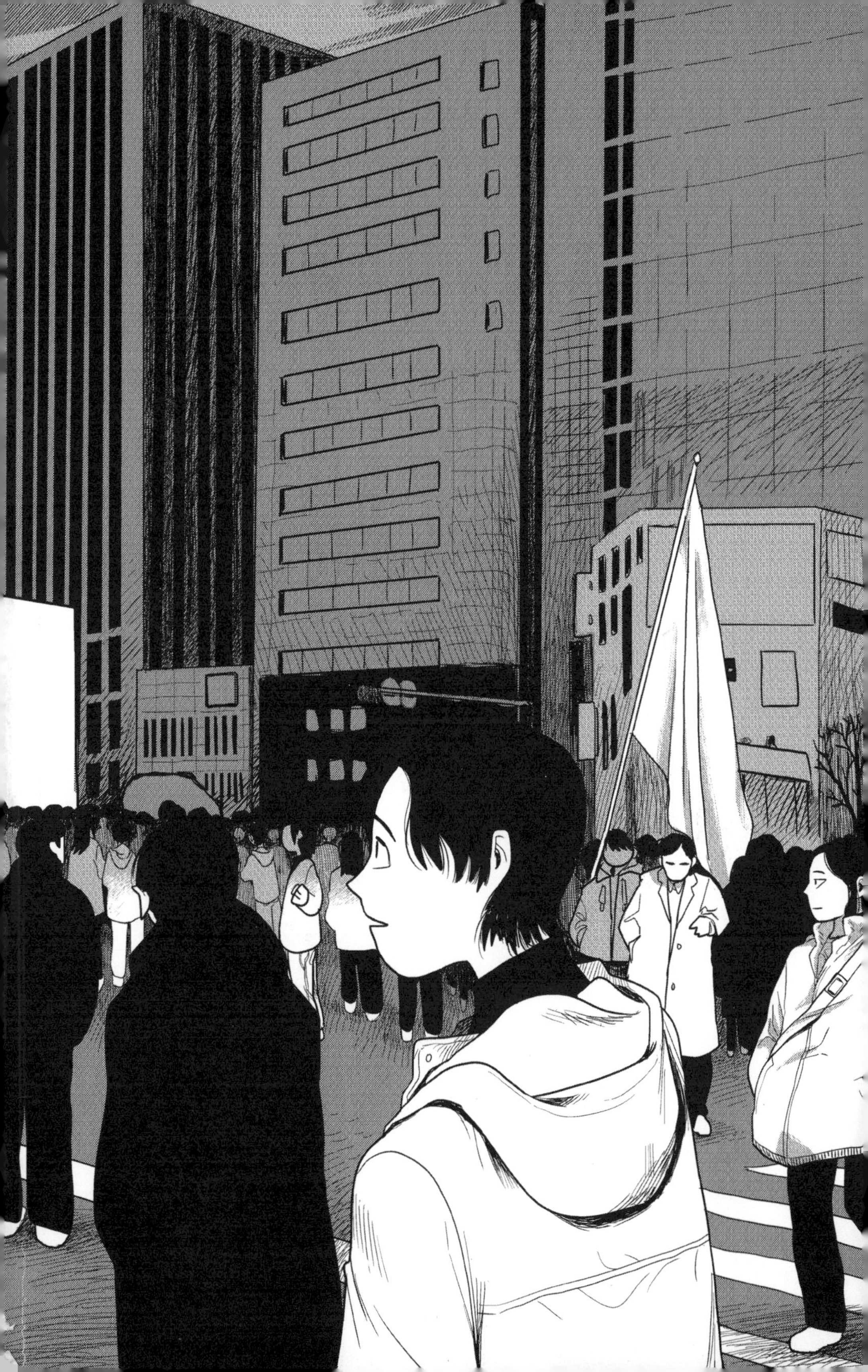

In the formerly banned book "What Is History," E.H. Carr says: *"History consists of a corpus of ascertained facts. The facts are available in documents, inscriptions and so on, like fish on the fish monger's slab. The historian collects them, takes them home, and cooks and serves them in whatever style appeals to him."*

The ingredients for *this* book were true stories from a network of friends over the course of four years. For the privacy and safety of our subjects, we sliced, diced, and blended them into one narrative starring a handful of amalgamated characters at a fictional university.

We would like to thank the following people for their interviews, stories, advice and assistance: Kim Jongha, Kim Gyeong Yeong, Kang Bo-Soon, Yoon Jeom-Bun, Jihoon Yi, Ju Myungja, Lee Mikyung, and Cho Sumin.

This book is dedicated to father, friend, and fancy-steak innovator Kim Donghae. (1937-2018)